The Art and Science of
Project Management

The Art and Science of
Project Management

Third Edition

by
Roger D. H. Warburton
Vijay Kanabar

RW-Press

Third Edition:

Current Version: 3.0a, August, 2018.

Second Edition: *Latest Version: 2.4, July 19, 2016.*
First Edition: *April, 2012.*

ISBN: 978-0-9993320-2-3

www.projectmanagementartandscience.com

Cover Design by Nye Warburton, nyetoon.net.

Cover Images by Sir John Tenniel: The White Rabbit and Queen of Hearts.[1]

> When suddenly a White Rabbit with pink eyes ran close by. There was nothing so very remarkable in that; nor did Alice think it so very much out of the way to hear the Rabbit say to itself,
> *Oh dear! Oh dear! I shall be late!*

> The Queen turned crimson with fury, and, after glaring at her for a moment like a wild beast, screamed
> *Off with her head! Off —*
> *Nonsense!* said Alice.[2]

Cover font Pero W01, (C) 2014, Ryoichi Tsunekawa, from oNlineWebFonts.com, licensed by CC By 3.0.

Published in the United States of America by *RW-Press, LLC.*
150 Eustis Avenue, Newport, RI 02840. USA.
www.rw-press.com

[1] Tenniel created the black and white illustrations for Lewis Carroll's *Alice's Adventures in Wonderland* (1865) and colored illustrations for *Nursery Alice* (1890). [1]

[2] These days, the Queen of Hearts feels all too real.

To Eileen and Dina
— for their continued patience.

CONTENTS

**The Art and Science of
Project Management**

LIST OF FIGURES

LIST OF TABLES

PREFACE

Is project management an art or a science? *Both!*

In reality, there is an element of science within art. You can't expect to be a good artist without understanding the scientific issues. You can't expect to be a good scientist without understanding the artistry.[3]

In spite of the longstanding false dichotomy between art and science, within project management and the world at large, we hope you will value both the artistry of scientific analysis and the science of artistic management.

A magician makes the trick look easy, but that takes thousands of hours of practice. Success in project management is not magic, it takes hard work, training, practice, and continuous education.

My customer is	unreasonable, demanding, crazy.
My sponsor is	unpredictable, volatile, capricious.
My boss is	relentless, unreasonable, meddling.
My staff is	untrained, inexperienced.
The project is	impossible.

For a project manager, there are no excuses. It is your problem, get on with it.

Why Project Management?

At this point, many books about PM claim that studying the book will allow you to: *Deliver your projects on time and on budget!*

Unfortunately, most projects fail to meet their objectives in either cost, schedule, or more importantly, customer satisfaction. It seems self-serving, perhaps even arrogant, therefore, to guarantee that reading a book can cure this problem.

[3]Is there anything more artistic than $E = mc^2$?

We prefer to say that there are excellent reasons for studying PM, and rather than make some outrageous claim about delivering on time, we prefer to tell you the truth, such as, "Earned Value can predict the amount of your cost overrun."

In our opinion, the excellent reasons for studying project management include:

- You are not alone, others have left breadcrumbs for you to follow.

- There are powerful tools and proven techniques that are powerful and useful.[4]

- There are jobs for project managers.[5]

- The stress of project management can be reduced by working smart.[6]

The number of projects in the world is increasing. This is due to selection factors, changing industries, and a superb job of marketing by the Project Management Institute. Many companies are only recently realizing that they are project-oriented. Even, small, non-profit organizations, such as theaters, charities, and arts groups are learning that many of their activities, such as fund-raising events, are projects.

Project Management is revolutionizing business

The study of traditional management is at a cross roads.[7] Paul McDonald suggests that *Management 1.0* was founded on the manufacturing paradigm, which has reached the limits of its relevance, and that it is time to consider a new *Management 2.0* based on the global, information age paradigm in which modern businesses compete. [2] McDonald argues that six powerful forces will redefine the future of management, forces that will require a new kind of management thinking: The virtualization of work, open source practices, the decline of organizational hierarchy, the rise of Generation-Y values, the tumult of global markets, and the imperative of business sustainability.

Companies such as Apple and Google, who now overshadow one-time giants such as General Motors, typify the transition from a manufacturing-driven economy to a knowledge-based economy. While some people view McDonald's theory as extreme and futuristic, we believe that the concepts underlying his six forces are woven throughout *current* project management thinking.[8]

We conclude that *project* management is at the forefront of modern management.

[4]In fact, there's no excuse not to use them.

[5]OK, we admit this is pandering to the reader.

[6]The critical path might only involve 25% of the activities, so worry about those, and then enjoy your weekend.

[7]General Management, as distinct from Project Management.

[8]For more on this topic, see [3].

Project Management is revolutionizing education

Many of the most innovative and interesting ideas are emerging from the business sector, rather than from academia. Traditionally, the teaching of project management has been buried in a course on Operations. Therefore, the explosive growth in PM in the past two decades has left an academic vacuum, which has been filled by non-traditional academic units.

Many people who seek project management education are working graduate professionals, and the best way to meet their needs is by offering online education. Project management is consequently at the forefront of an emerging trend: online education in non-traditional academic units.[9]

Acknowledgments

First, we thank all the students who have put up with our methods. "It's hard," they cry, but we don't apologize for relentlessly challenging our students. By challenging students, we are empowering them to succeed later—in real world projects where the stakes are higher.

We are fortunate to have worked for two brilliant and dedicated department chairs, Dr. Kip Becker and Dr. John Sullivan, both of whom constantly challenged us to innovate and grow. Our lives are made so much easier by the endless hard work of the superb Administrative Sciences department staff: Susan Sunde, Lucille Dicker, and Fiona Niven, Frank Cassidy and Bill McGue. Thanks!

Our warm thanks go to both our previous Dean, Jay Halfond, and our current Dean, Tanya Zlateva, for their whole-hearted support of the PM program. We have benefited enormously from the efforts of the first-class Boston University Distance Education department. To everyone there, a huge, grateful, *Thank You*.

Our students are our best critics and we listen carefully to all of their suggestions. Many students pointed out errors, ambiguities, and typos in the previous editions, and we sincerely thank them for taking the time to bring them to our attention.

Eileen Warburton copy-edited the entire book. Without her talents, there would be random commas and peculiar wording throughout. Any mistakes remain our responsibility.

Preface to the Third Edition

Several factors motivated us to write the 3rd Edition. Vijay has been teaching *Agile Project Management* for a while now and recently became a certified scrum

[9]We should explain, in the interest of honesty, that the authors both teach online courses in Boston University's Metropolitan College, a college whose mission has been redefined the past two decades to provide *Graduate Professional Education*.

master. We took advantage of his unique expertise to add the topic of *Agile Project Management,* which has become such a hot topic. We added a new chapter in Duration Estimation, which is based on the new research by Warburton & Cioffi, who showed how to accurately estimate the future duration. We added a major new section on Agile Project Management. We also added a new chapter in Portfolio Management, as we believe it is an important and neglected topic. We added a new chapter on Stakeholders, because there is a growing appreciation for their importance. Finally, we wished to be consistent with the 6th edition of the Project Management Body of Knowledge (the PMBOK). [4]

We also took the opportunity to revise the content of several chapters, especially The Project Manager and Stakeholders.

Preface to the Second Edition

The primary motivation for the second edition was the publication of the 5th edition of the PMBOK. [5]. We also added examples, templates and new chapters: The Graduation Picnic Party project and a tutorial in *Microsoft Project®*. We also took the opportunity to revise the order of the chapters, which, we felt, was now more logical. We moved all Technical Skills (Scope, Work Breakdown Structure, Network, Earned Value, etc.) to Part II because it is logical to study these chapters directly after completing Part I. We made minor updates to correct typos.[10] We added a new chapter, The Graduation Picnic Party, which illustrate the entire project management process and its deliverables using templates.

---

[10]Many heartfelt thanks go to Meera and Anish.

INTRODUCTION

The important thing is not to stop questioning.
Curiosity has its own reason for existence.

Albert Einstein

Project management and Boston significantly contributed to who we are. Despite our diverse backgrounds, Boston is where our project management grew to maturity. We love the Big Dig, baked beans, and the Red Sox.

This book introduces the student to the world of project management. We assume nothing and start from zero. Our goal is to produce a useful reference, so we devote a good deal of effort to defining concepts and establishing first principles.

Many of our students are already project managers, but without having studied project management. We call them *Accidental Project Managers*. Typically, you get called into your boss's office and are told, "Congratulations, you are now a project manager." Visions of pay raises and glory stream through your mind. You wake up the next morning and realize you know nothing about project management.

For the accidental project manager, our job is to define the concepts clearly and precisely. We hope that combining your valuable practical experience with the established, powerful theoretical concepts, all expressed in the correct vocabulary, will take your project skills to new heights.

This book's content has been tested in introductory and advanced courses, both undergraduate and graduate. Our students are typically non-traditional, are usually older with families and careers, are committed to their education, and are motivated. Therefore, we have the luxury of assuming an intelligent reader.

As a result, you will not find in sections entitled *What you will learn in this chapter* or *Overviews*.[11] Our mission is to provide a readable, easy to understand book that carefully defines the tools and techniques of project management, is up to date in

[11] We believe all that just clutters up a book.

accepted wisdom (i.e., research), and can serve long-term as a reference for the working professional.

To accomplish that mission, we cover all project management concepts, explain the technical tools and techniques, and provide practical worked examples.[12] Along the way, we cover the PMBOK in detail.

Structure of the Book

The book is divided into the following parts:

- *Part I: Projects, Project Managers, and The Project Environment:* We define a project and explore the environment in which it exists. We cover the role of the Project Manager in depth. We also cover Portfolio Management because, if the research is to be believed, companies are quite poor at it.

- *Part II: Technical Skills:* We cover the skills that a project manager must master to be effective and we generally follow the project life cycle.

- *Part III: Sample Projects:* Throughout the book, we use cases and sample projects to illustrate the concepts. Students can use these as models for their own projects:

    - *The New Kitchen Project:* This illustrates the entire project management process for the design and implementation of a new kitchen with examples of deliverables, tools, and techniques.[13]

    - *The Graduation Picnic Project:* Students of project management decided to hold a picnic at the end of the academic year and selected a classic American theme of hamburgers, hot dogs, and beer. The project, which is presented using templates, follows the PMBOK®.

    - *The PMA Project:* The Project Management Association (PMA) is a small, Boston-based (hypothetical) organization dedicated to educating its members about project management. PMA is considering implementing a new web site with the following features: manage and increase memberships; facilitate social networking; distribute marketing emails to members; and display useful research materials.

    Unlike the Kitchen and Picnic cases, the PMA case is used throughout the book to illustrate the topic under discussion. By using the same case throughout, details do not have to be repeated.

[12]We point the reader towards relevant research if they want more depth.

[13]Vijay was overheard to say that if he had to listen to Roger's obsessing over his new kitchen, at least he was going to make him put it to practical use in the book.

- *The SAMPL Agile Project:* This is covered in Part V, where we follow the development of the Student Academic Mobile Planning App (SAMPL), which is accomplished as an *agile development* using sprints.

- *Part IV: Agile Project Management:* Chapter 20, Agile, covers the terminology, fundamental principles, and processes of agile development focusing on the project management aspects rather than software development. Chapter 21 describes agile *Sprints.* Chapter 22 is devoted to the development of the SAMPL app, which follows an agile scrum process with sprints.

- *Part V: Microsoft Project 2013® Tutorial:* The graduation picnic project is implemented in *Project.* Assuming no previous knowledge of *Microsoft Project,* the tutorial gradually explains how to create the schedule and analyze the cost. Annotated screens explain the commands, data entry, and output reports.

Advice to the Beginner

Projects surround us, but only recently have people begun to define carefully the characteristics of a project. Many people throw around the term "project" without understanding that it is a precisely defined concept. Also, projects are often confused with programs, which are totally different. As a result, there is a lot of confusion surrounding the word *project.*

Advice to Instructors

The chapters stand alone so they can be taught in any order. Typically, we first cover the materials that define and characterize projects in Part I and then work sequentially through the Technical Skills in Part II, covering one or more chapter per week in a one-semester course. We have used the book in both undergraduate and graduate courses in Project Management for project management majors; for students in other disciplines, such as finance, supply chains, innovation, and e-commerce; and for Information Technology Project Management (ITPM) majors.

Whatever the course, all students are encouraged to develop their own project from their experience. Developing the deliverables and documentation for a specific project is considered an essential aspect of the project management curriculum.

The *Microsoft Project Tutorial* is a stand-alone chapter that can be covered in a few hours. We usually include it after Chapter 11, Schedule.

Conventions

One of the challenges students face is to master the large, intimidating project management terminology. Therefore, throughout the book, formal project management terms are italicized. This includes documents, e.g., *Scope*; and important terms, e.g., *Critical Path*.

Side notes provide immediate, contextual information. They are easy to find because they are numbered sequentially throughout each chapter and appear on the same page as the number.[14] Side notes are also where we put our personal observations and comments. When we express an opinion, we want it to be clear that it is *our opinion*. We do not do this lightly. We have strong views that are backed by years of experience in project management research, performing projects, and teaching. Hopefully, we have backed our opinions with research supported by references.[15]

Formal references to other works, i.e., citations, are collected in the *Bibliography* at the end of the book. Citations are provided as numbers in brackets, e.g., our previous book on project management: [6].

Definitions appear as follows:

This is not a definition, but it sure looks like one.

We firmly believe that precision is important and have added lots of index entries and references.[16] There is no separate glossary, as that duplicates information.

Challenge Everything

We tell our students to challenge everything. When reading a paragraph, ask yourself: Does this make sense to me? Do I have experience that either reinforces or contradicts the premise of what I am reading?[17] But challenges must be backed up from an intellectual perspective or from experience, i.e., using facts, data and, preferably, references.[18] When it comes to citing references, the gold standard is to quote from an academic journal. We are not being pedantic here but setting the standard. [19] Random quotations found in a quick Google search carry no weight.

[14] This is a side note. It falls towards the bottom of the same page as the number.

[15] But if you want to challenge our opinions, feel free to do so. Challenge everything.

[16] There is only one index, because we think that looking up authors separately is confusing. Everything and everyone are in the single index.

[17] To challenge everything is not to be a cynic. A cynical person is someone who denies the sincerity of people's motives and is often sarcastic or sneering. This is not a useful attitude.

[18] Otherwise, you are plagiarizing.

[19] Academic journals define the accepted state of the art and contain the accumulated wisdom.

Part I

Projects, Project Managers, and Their Environment

1

PROJECTS

**Don't undertake a project unless it is manifestly important
and nearly impossible.**

Edwin Land

Projects are everywhere.

Examples of projects include building a house or skyscraper, organizing and holding a birthday or anniversary party, developing a new drug, designing a new airplane or ship, filming a movie or producing a play, or developing a new web site.

The chief distinguishing characteristic of a project is that it is a new endeavor, it has not been attempted before. This is in contrast to routine activities, which are performed repetitively. Examples of routine activities include cutting grass, cooking daily meals, manufacturing drugs, maintaining an airplane or ship, showing a movie or performing a play, and maintaining a web site.

The concept of a project is very old. The Pyramids of Ancient Egypt and the Roman Colosseum were magnificent, sophisticated, and complicated projects. However, it is only recently that the precise definition of a project has emerged.

Projects are not necessarily large endeavors. Small, non-profit organizations also engage in projects, for example, when they conduct fund-raisers, or introduce new plays or dances. They resort to routine activities when they take tickets. We insist that the skills and techniques of project management are applicable and valuable to such small organizations and that project management need not be large and bureaucratic. Even a small organization needs to know if their project might be late and if the costs might overrun.

There is a tendency for students to look at the jargon, the vast quantity of information, and the diverse collection of tools and assume that project management only applies to large projects. Not so. The tools and techniques of project management can be easily adapted to small projects.

For example, a key project management lesson is that the scope document, which precisely describes the project content, is the most important document. Therefore, even for a small project, it is worth the effort to produce a clear and concise scope, which need not be a long, bureaucratic tome. Also, modern project management tools operate on personal computers and are relatively easy to learn. In particular, tools that manage costs and schedules are cost effective, even for small projects.[1]

You often hear people talking about their "projects," but not all of these activities satisfy the precise definition and, as a result, there is considerable confusion. All organizations have their own terminology and, once the word "project" is embedded in a company, it is likely to stick, even if the outside world does not regard what they are doing as projects.

For example, almost all of the activities in a manufacturing plant are routine, non-projects: parts are ordered, delivered into inventory, and then repetitively assembled into products. These operations are much the same from week to week. However, people who work in manufacturing often describe their activities as projects. For example, they may refer to the week's manufacturing target as their "project."

It is easy to develop standardized procedures for routine activities. Since projects typically have not been done before, it is much harder to develop a standardized approach and this presents one of the challenges of project management.

1.1 The Project Management Institute

I think it's wrong that only one company makes the game Monopoly.

Stephen Wright

The Project Management Institute (PMI) is the professional organization devoted to the furthering of project management. PMI is growing rapidly, which is an indicator of the growing importance of project management.[2] PMI has done an excellent job

[1] We occasionally hear a comment like, "My project is too small to need a network diagram." To which we reply, "It's so small that you don't need to know if it is behind schedule?"

[2] The PMI website *pmi.org* has a massive collection useful information on all aspects of project management.

of defining the characteristics of projects through global standards that are widely accepted. PMI's most important standard is, *A Guide to the Project Management Body of Knowledge* [4] known as the *PMBOK®*.[3] [4]

The PMBOK describes the knowledge within the project management profession and, while it mostly addresses project management, it also contains information about the project environment, such as programs and portfolios. It also refers to information from other management disciplines, such as communications theory, risk management, and quality control. The PMBOK also explicitly references other documents and standards, such as PMI's *Code of Ethics and Professional Conduct.* [7]

While the *PMBOK* is the definitive standard, we do not feel obligated to slavishly follow every word. We are quite comfortable challenging the *PMBOK* when we have experience or research that suggests a better approach. In fact, we encourage our students to examine critically all their readings, including the *PMBOK*.[5]

1.2 What is a Project?

We begin with the formal PMBOK definition of a project:

> *A project is a temporary endeavor undertaken to create a unique product, service, or result.*

A project is considered to be a unique endeavor, in that it has never been done before. This immediately distinguishes projects from routine activities, which are repetitive in nature.

This is a somewhat cryptic definition that obscures a lot of important information.[6] For example, the word "temporary" is expanded to mean that a project has definite beginning and end dates.[7] The word "temporary" is also a little unusual because it implies a short duration activity while projects often continue for long periods. A skyscraper may take many years to build, but, even so, the project to build the skyscraper is referred to as a *temporary endeavor.*

We use the word "unique" to mean that the project has not been done before. There are of course, repetitive aspects of a project, even if the overall result is unique. In our skyscraper example, the building may be highly original in design and, therefore, unique. Within the construction, however, many activities are repetitive and routine, e.g., installing the light fixtures in each floor.

The uniqueness of projects requires further clarification. Suppose one is building ten houses in a development and all of the houses have the same plan. One might

[3] *PMBOK* is usually pronounced as pim-bock.

[4] See Chapter 25, section 25.4 for a discussion of changes in the 6th edition.

[5] Challenge Everything!

[6] And, therefore, we have no problem challenging it.

[7] An activity without an end date is, technically, not a project. This is a favorite trick question on exams.

argue that the first house is a project, since it is unique. On the other hand, building the tenth house might be considered routine and not really a project. It is likely, though, that one would continue to treat all the houses as projects, even the tenth, and project manage their construction in a disciplined way.

A definition should stand alone and precisely define a concept. We believe the above definition does not work very well in this regard.[8] Therefore, we provide another definition that we believe is more helpful:

> *A project is a unique, non-routine effort, limited by time and budget, defined by a performance specification, and designed to meet stakeholder needs.*

Rather than defining a project as temporary, we used the phrase "unique, non-routine." This clarifies the idea that a project is different from anything that went before. Also, by avoiding the word "temporary," we eliminate the confusion about projects that take many years, or even decades, to complete. The definition also clarifies the important distinction between routine activities and projects.

The limitations on cost and schedule are also important additions. Often, the first questions asked about a project are: How much will it cost? When will it be completed? Since every project is limited by cost and schedule, it is appropriate to include these ideas in the definition.

Including the performance specification explains how the project is defined. The performance specification is part of the scope, which is the most important document in the project and highlighting it in the definition elevates its importance.

Finally, the project must meet stakeholder needs. We note the use of "stakeholder," who is anyone with a stake in the project. Sometimes, the word, "customer," is used, but the customer is only one of many stakeholders. Stakeholders are so important that they deserve to be included in the definition of a project.

Projects are characterized as follows:

- *Projects have an established objective.*

  In the early stages of a project's conceptual development the project is defined by its charter, which is a short overview of the goals and objectives and, perhaps, a desired schedule and budget. The first activity of the project is typically the development of the scope, which precisely defines the project.

- *Projects have a well-defined life span.*

[8] It needed several paragraphs just to clarify the idea of "temporary."

Projects have a beginning date and an end date. If activities continue indefinitely into the future, then, technically, it is not a project. In general, it is a good idea to break up long projects into several shorter projects, each with a well-defined objective, budget, and completion date.

- *Projects require staff participation from across the organization.*

Projects are inherently multi-disciplinary. For example, when building a house, the project manager must interact with the architect and the contractor, as well as assorted subcontractors such as roofers, plumbers, electricians, and carpenters. There are also technical requirements, which are documented in the voluminous fire codes, electrical codes, and environmental regulations. Project managers also frequently interact with professionals such as accountants, lawyers, structural engineers, and human resources personnel. Project managers quickly find themselves immersed in many disciplines.[9]

- *Projects have constrained schedules and budgets.*

No project has the luxury of an infinite cost or schedule. Customers always have an assigned budget and a preferred delivery schedule.

- *Projects have limited resources.*

Resources include staff and equipment, which must be managed, along with other factors such as the availability of funds.

- *Projects have multiple, often competing, stakeholders.*

The project manager and the team are obvious stakeholders, but there are many more, including the sponsor (who pays the bill), customers, users, and trainers. Upper management also has a stake in the project's success and, if things are not going well, they may cancel the project.

- *Projects create value.*

Projects should create both tangible and intangible value. Tangible value includes stockholder equity and market share, while intangible value includes brand recognition and reputation. Some projects are undertaken to satisfy legal, accounting, or regulatory requirements.

1.2.1 Project Time Scales

Projects have widely different time scales. Table 1.1 shows typical time scales for projects in different industries.

[9]There is a fascinating debate about whether a project manager can be successful if he or she does not possess technical expertise in the project's discipline. Does a project manager need to be a subject matter expert, or are project management skills universally applicable?

Table 1.1: Project time scales by industry.

Industry	Typical Project Time Scale
Military Jet	15-20 years
Mega Project Construction	10-15 years
Skyscraper Construction	3-5 years
House Construction	3-6 months
Software System	1-2 years
Web Site Construction	3-6 months
Insurance Product	1 month

1.3 Project Management

> **You want to study project management?**
> **Read more, sleep less.**
> _____
> *John Cable*

Project management is the term applied to the process of managing projects. The Project Management Institute (PMI) defines project management as:

> *Project Management is the application of knowledge, skills, tools, and techniques to project activities to meet the project requirements.*

Because projects are unique, it is difficult to develop a completely standardized approach. There is seldom a "right" way to proceed, one is always dealing with uncertainty. On the other hand, standardized methods have evolved that reduce the risks associated with dealing with the unknown.

As with other professions, such as law, medicine, and accounting, the body of knowledge rests with the practitioners and academics who apply and advance it. The PMBOK includes proven traditional practices that are widely applied, as well as innovative practices that are emerging.[10]

> *The PMBOK Guide® provides guidelines for managing individual projects. It defines project management and related concepts and describes the project management life cycle and the related processes.*

[10]As a result, the *PMBOK* is constantly evolving, which is often neglected. However, as a student of project management, your job is to question the standard and to improve it, wherever possible.

8

How should the *PMBOK* be used? The project team should consult the PMBOK to identify the processes that are relevant to their own individual project objectives. For example, it may be decided that a process called *Identify Risks* is necessary and should be integrated into the project life cycle. It is then useful to identify the relevant inputs and outputs and any forms or company templates that already exist that can be used as a guide.

The entire life cycle should be tailored to meet the project's and sponsor's requirements in the most efficient manner. The workload of including a process must be balanced against the elimination of the associated deliverables. Every project needs a well-constructed *scope* and, so, eliminating the *Define Scope* process is a bad idea. On the other hand, if there are no subcontractors, then one can safely eliminate *Procurement Management Planning*.[11]

As an illustration of tailoring the *PMBOK* for small projects, we frequently combine the risk processes: *Identify Risks, Perform Qualitative Risk Analysis, Perform Quantitative Risk Analysis*, and *Plan Risk Responses*. We define a customized process called, *Perform Risk Management*.[12]

Since every project is unique, no two life cycles will be the same and the rigor with which each process is executed varies. If the project is mission critical, or if the project team is not experienced, one should use more rigor, e.g., ensure that all processes are completed and conscientiously review all deliverables.

1.4 Benefits of Project Management

There are two main benefits to a disciplined approach to project management:[13]

- *You are not alone.* There is a mountain of information available, including research literature, templates, and advice. You can access it and learn from others. Someone has probably done something similar.

- *Powerful Tools.* The critical path tells you which activity is the most important one to work on now. Earned value tells you how much your project is over budget and behind schedule.[14]

1.4.1 Project Success

A significant challenge of project management is that every project must aim to be successful. In a routine manufacturing environment, the failure of a few products (out of a million) might not be regarded as catastrophic. However, the failure of a project critical to the mission of a company might lead to a crash of the entire

[11]We do not recommend eliminating this entirely from the Management Plan. It is better to briefly state, "No subcontractors are planned." That way, if you later decide you need subs, you have a place to put the information.

[12]Note that we actually use the *PMBOK* as a checklist to ensure that we include all the necessary pieces. It would do no good if we forgot to plan the risk responses.

[13]As explained in the introduction, we are resisting the urge to say that you will deliver your project on schedule and on budget.

[14]You may not like the answers, but at least you'll know the truth.

9

company. Projects are almost always produced to a tight deadline with constrained funds. This all adds pressure to the project manager to succeed.

When discussing "success," however, it is important to distinguish between: [8]

1. *Project management success.* This is defined in terms of the quality of the process, e.g., whether the project was delivered on schedule and within budget.

2. *Project success.* This is defined in terms of user satisfaction and measured by whether the project met its overall objectives.[15]

One should also distinguish between size and importance because a small, mission-critical project may be much more important than its larger, non-critical cousins. Neither is technical complexity related to size. Small, mission-critical, technically challenging projects will require the best from a project manager.

The subject of project failure garners a lot of attention. First, we point out that *failure* is a complex concept: Is a project a failure if it successfully meets stakeholder needs but comes in late and over budget? Is a project successful it is on time and on budget, but leaves many stakeholders unhappy?

One of the most quoted sources of project failure is the *CHAOS Report* by the Standish Group who studied 365 companies with a total of 8,380 Information System applications. [9] The report divided projects into three distinct outcomes, as shown in Table 1.2.

Table 1.2: The CHAOS data on project failure.

Project Outcome	1994	2009	Definition
Successful	16%	32%	Completed on time and budget, with all features as specified.
Challenged	53%	44%	Completed, but were over cost, over time, and/or lacking features
Impaired/Failed	31%	24%	Abandoned or canceled **Total losses!**

The first percentage is for the original data from 1994 and the second is for 2009. While these are Information Technology (IT) projects, similar data exists for other types of projects in other countries and industries. While things have improved somewhat in 15 years, the CHAOS data suggest that most projects fail. However,

[15]Despite being over budget and late, did the project deliver value to the stakeholders?

there are major criticisms of the Standish interpretation of "failure." [10] For example, a project 25% over budget that meets stakeholder needs and is on time is a failure according to the Standish criteria.

Another interesting factor is the forecast bias: the data ignores projects that underrun in cost and time. Since most people underestimate their forecast, the Standish data are highly suspect.[16] These are excellent examples of a technique that we wish to inculcate into our reader: Challenge Everything! [17]

1.5 Project Life Cycles

> **Life is what happens to you while you're busy making other plans.**
>
> *John Lennon*

All projects go through natural life cycle patterns or phases. While the details differ from one industry to another, all projects have an orderly sequence of activities. We describe a few project life cycles from various industries to illustrate the diversity of patterns.

A simple, informal way to remember the project life cycle is by what we call the A-B-C-D-E-F stages:[18]

Alignment:	of project goals with company strategy.
Business Case:	the need and reason for the project's existence.
Charter the project:	officially launch it and identify the project manager.
Develop the project:	plan it.
Execute the project:	do it!
Finish the project:	close it down and learn its lessons.

Projects may have sub-projects, which also follow the same life cycle. The life cycle should seamlessly integrate the project management functions and processes with the technical aspects of the project. Life cycle activities include:

- *Organizing:* Determining the quality and quantity of resources needed and using communication skills to obtain and manage them.

- *Motivating:* Creating an environment that provides satisfaction to the team members and encourages them to perform their best.

- *Directing:* Providing management and leadership to stakeholders and influencing them to achieve project goals

[16]Whether underestimation is by design or ignorance is another fascinating question.

[17]Just because you read it in a fancy report, you don't have to take it for granted. Ask questions. Examine assumptions. Find your own data.

[18]At this point, you can get carried away with, G: evaluate goals, etc.

11

1.5.1 Products and Services Life Cycles

We must carefully distinguish between the *product* and *project* life cycles. The Product Life Cycle begins when a product is conceived and put into development. It is then introduced to the market, followed by a growth in sales, a sales peak, and a gradual decline. See Figure 1.1.

Profits follow a different curve. There is an early investment when the product is in development and profits do not accrue until the product has been in the marketplace for a while. Eventually, if the product is successful, there is a period of profitability, called the mature stage, followed by a decline, and the product's withdrawal from the market.

Figure 1.1: The product life cycle

Many issues complicate the reality. Successful products rarely exist in isolation and often evolve through product lines, which enhances their life. Successful products engender competition and technological innovations may make products obsolete.

The services life cycle also generally follows that of Figure 1.1, although many services are not designed to be profitable, e.g., renewal of a driver's license and computer telephone support. Other services are designed to be profitable, such as legal and accounting, restaurants, and bars. Many services are performed by large, non-profit organizations, such as universities and theaters.[19]

[19]While most universities are 'non-profits,' they operate with all the same constraints as profit-making entities on sales, staff utilization, and overhead.

For new products and services, the development stage is typically a project. Once the product or service is introduced to the market, it is no longer a project, as the activities become routine: manufacturing, sales, distribution, etc. There may be additional projects later, such as a product improvement, a new advertising campaign, or the implementation of a new supply chain.

1.5.2 Project Phases

Projects may be divided into phases, which are logical divisions that allow for efficient development through an orderly sequence of integrated activities.[20] A phase is:

> *A project phase is a collection of logically related project activities that culminates in completion of one or more deliverables.*

The number of phases depends on the size and complexity of the project and they may occur in series or in parallel. Some phases may even be iterated or repeated. In the usual case, the phases are sequential and the outputs from one phase are evaluated and form the basis of the decision about whether to proceed to the next phase.

A *Decision Gate* is often held at the end of a phase where the performance and progress are reviewed.

Some phases can genuinely proceed in parallel. An example might be a system with software and hardware components. Once the formal specification is complete and the interfaces defined, the hardware and software development phases can proceed in parallel. Conducting the phases in parallel incurs risks, since mistakes can result in re-work of both hardware and software components. Therefore, when deciding whether to proceed with parallel phases, the project manager must spend time to precisely define the inputs to the phases.

Phases share the same characteristics:

- *A phase is formally initiated and closed.* Phases typically produce specific deliverables, which are the basis for the decision of whether to continue to the next phase.

- *A phase is coherent and distinct.* The work of a phase should be as independent as possible from other phases or projects.[21]

- *A phase's major deliverables are carefully controlled.* The output is a go/kill decision and, so, careful attention must be paid to the deliverables.

- *A phase typically follows the project management process.*[22]

[20]Note that project *phases* are not the same as *process groups*.

[21]If a phase is closely inter-related with another phase, the phase is badly specified and the phases probably should have been redesigned.

[22]The PMBOK says that phases follow the process groups.

13

1.5.3 PMA Case: Growth Project Phases

Suppose the PMA decides they want to increase their membership. This is not yet a project. First, they must study the problem and evaluate methods for increasing the membership (e.g., email blast, advertising, networking at conferences, etc.). Next, they evaluate the costs vs. potential growth from a particular strategy. Once they have analyzed the data, they can decide whether to proceed, and if so, with which method. This project, therefore, has two phases as shown in Table 1.3.

Table 1.3: PMA growth strategy phases.

Phase (Stage)	Deliverables	Gate
1. Select Growth Strategy	Growth Strategy Document Cost/Benefit Analysis	Growth Achievable?
2. Implement Strategy	Increased Membership	Target Growth Achieved

1.5.4 Project Life Cycle Phases

There are three phases in the project life cycle:

1. *Pre-Project Phase:* The primary job of the pre-project phase is to ensure that there is a viable project, before one invests money in it. This is referred to as requirements definition, although design work is required to validate major technical issues. Also required at this stage are preliminary cost and schedule estimates.

   Building a prototype is often an efficient way to determine feasibility, estimate the cost and schedule, and analyze major risks. Of course, a prototype can be considered to be a separate project.

2. *Implementation Phase*

   During the project implementation phase, a project goes through a structured development life cycle, where the product or service is defined, designed, built, tested, and accepted by the sponsor.

   The products of this phase are the project deliverables, including the product or service itself, as well as intermediate deliverables such as the design. Other deliverables in this phase are the outputs from project management processes, e.g., *The Charter* is an output of the *Create Charter* process.

   Each phase should have a clearly specified *Decision Gate*, which is a critical decision point where the deliverables are carefully reviewed, along with the cost and schedule. At a decision gate, the team, customer, and stakeholders review the products and select among three possible outcomes: move to next phase, fix the products by revisiting activities, or kill the project.

Activities in the pre-project phase include recognizing a business opportunity, creating a business case, and obtaining seed funding.

3. *Post-Project Phase*

The post-project phase begins as soon as the product or service is commissioned and operational. The activities in this phase are typically not part of the project, consisting of such things as manufacturing, routine services, and maintenance activities, e.g., painting bridges when they rust.

In some industries, the post-project phase is very expensive. For example, the decommissioning and retirement of a nuclear plant is extensive, rigorous, and can take several years.

They key idea is that each phase consists of activities that produce deliverables and is concluded with a *decision gate*. Table 1.4 gives some examples.

Table 1.4: Example of Activities, Deliverables, and Decision Gates.

Activities	Deliverables	Decision Gate Questions
Feasibility Study	Business Case Preliminary Plan Stakeholder Register	Customer support exists? Customers perceive value? Delivery dates acceptable? Cost & schedule acceptable?
Requirements Analysis	Specification Scope Risk Register	Is the project feasible? Performance metrics acceptable? Risks acceptable? Contingency funds available?

1.6 Industry Life Cycle Examples

Each industry has its own version of the project life cycle with their own terminology, approach, and deliverables.[23]

1.6.1 The Software Development Life Cycle

The software development life cycle consists of:[24]

[23] Despite the different vocabulary, the PM should still focus on scope, milestones and deliverables.

[24] The software life cycle is covered in more detail in Chapter, 20, Agile.

15

1. *Definition phase:* The customer's problems are defined and the requirements elicited. The team conducts systems analyses and develops the project plan. The deliverable is the specification, which contains the user requirements and a test plan to measure compliance.

2. *Design phase:* The software and business analysts design an acceptable solution for the customer. The deliverable is the design document and the project manager finalizes the baseline cost and schedule.

3. *Construction phase:* The software is coded and unit testing may occur here.

4. *Testing phase:* The product or service is tested against the specification.

5. *Acceptance phase:* The customer analyzes the acceptance test results and, if satisfactory, signs the acceptance agreement. Customer training may occur during this phase. The operation phase begins after customer acceptance.

1.6.2   The Pharmaceutical Industry Life Cycle

To contrast with the software development life cycle, we present a brief overview of a typical pharmaceutical life cycle, which consists of:[25]

- *Research and Development*: New potential drugs are identified.

- *Discovery and Screening*: Drugs are refined and tested.

- *Pre-clinical Development*: The effects on trial populations are determined.

- *Clinical Trial Phase*: The drug goes from laboratory sample to pilot production and, finally, to commercial production.

- *Registration Phase*: Government forms and compliance documentation are completed and, hopefully, the drug is approved.

- *Post Registration Phase*: Packaging and marketing occurs.

1.6.3   The Construction Industry Life Cycle

The key stages in the construction life cycle are:[26]

- *Apply for Permits.*

- *Site Work*: Clear ground, install temporary power and utilities. Inspection.

[25]More information on the pharmaceutical life cycle can be found in [11].

[26]This is based on a template for Microsoft Project [12].

16

- *Foundation*: Excavate, concrete, basement walls, waterproof and insulate. Inspection.

- *Framing*: Install joists, frame walls. Inspection.

- *Dry In*: Sheathing, roof decking, shingles, doors and windows. Inspection.

- *Utilities*: Plumbing, electrical, HVAC, phone, cable, computers, alarms. Inspection.

- *Interior Finishing*: Insulating, dry wall, paint and wallpaper, cabinets, tile and appliances. Inspection.

- *Landscaping and Groundwork*: Driveway, sod, plantings. Inspection.

- *Final Acceptance*: Walk-through, inspection and complete punch list. Conduct final acceptance for Certificate of Occupancy.

Notice that in the construction life cycle, each phase explicitly ends with an inspection, which is a useful lesson for other industries.

1.6.4 The Agile Life Cycle

The agile development framework is covered in detail in Part III, Agile Project Management.

2

THE PROJECT MANAGER

> **Managing is essentially a loser's job, and managers are about the most expendable pieces of furniture on the earth.**
>
> *Ted Williams, The Splendid Splinter.*

Let's begin with the definition:

> *The project manager is the person assigned to lead the team that is responsible for achieving the project objectives.*

In this book, we are always going to assume that you, dear reader, are the project manager. Whenever we ask a question, or expect you to analyze a problem, we always assume that you should answer it from the project manager's point of view.

The project manager must demonstrate three characteristics: Possess knowledge about project management; be able to perform as a project manager; and exhibit personal effectiveness, which encompasses both skills and personality traits. One of the most important skills is that a project manager must be a good communicator, with the team and with stakeholders.

2.1 Responsibility and Authority

The project manager often has responsibility without authority. That is, the project manager is responsible for the product. But usually, the project manager can only suggest and induce the team to perform. In this respect, the project manager is rather like the conductor of an orchestra.

The project manager does not perform the project activities, the team does. The project manager provides direction, leadership, planning, and coordination, roles that all require significant communication skills.[1]

Rarely does the project manager have the luxury of being able to order people around. The interdisciplinary nature of projects, and the diverse skills required, means that few of the staff work directly for the project manager. Therefore, one of the key skills required of a project manager is being able to *induce* the right people to do the right thing at the right time. This includes their staff, stakeholders, customers, and even upper management. This leads to one of our most cherished beliefs:

> Project managers *induce* people to perform.

The role of the PM is to:

1. Plan and organize the project from start to finish.

2. Manage relations with stakeholders and, in particular, customers.

3. Manage relations with the parent company.

4. Develop and manage the project team.

5. Monitor and control project progress, particularly the costs and schedule.

6. Deal with uncertainty and changes.

7. Deliver the product or service and get the customer's acceptance.

Project managers must exercise control and provide leadership to their team. Since they cannot do everything, they must learn to delegate, follow up, and provide training and encouragement as needed.

[1] These roles resemble those of the conductor of an orchestra.

Since projects have not been done before, project managers must deal with uncertainty. Almost everything in project management is a compromise, there are rarely

20

correct answers. Projects are inherently messy, and change is a fact of life. Project managers must deal with complexity and ambiguity, and be able to prioritize.

Project managers live in a permanent competition for resources. They compete for staff and with other projects for resources. They referee stakeholders, all of whom have different goals, objectives and priorities.[2]

2.2   Project Manager Skills

Table 2.1 summarizes the skills required by a project manager, which can seem daunting. Fortunately, coming to the aid of the project manager is a discipline and methodology that provides support and professionalism.

Table 2.1: A summary of the project manager's technical, behavioral, and business and strategic skills.

Technical Skills	Behavioral Skills	Strategic & Business Skills
PM Principles	Plan, Distribute, & Manage Communications	Strategic PM
Phases and Processes	Team Building and Motivating	Supply Chains
Planning and Integration	Leadership	Legal Aspects
Resource Management	Identifying & Engaging Stakeholders	Business & Commercial Aspects
Estimating Costs	Organization & Context	Governance
Risk Management	Managing Global Projects	Agile PM
Quality	Virtual PM	Portfolio & Program Management
Procurement and Contracts	Ethics & Professionalism	
Finance & Budgeting		
Scope		
Project Control		
Business Analysis & Requirements Management		
Handover, Closeout, Reviews		
PM Information Systems (PMIS)		

[2]Challenging enough for you?

21

2.2.1 The PM's Friend: The Technical Director

The role of the project manager (PM) is to manage the customer, the money, and the schedule. An interesting question is, who manages the project's content?[3]

For example: Do the deliverables meet customer requirements? Does the project actually work?[4]

In every project there is always a role for a person we call the *Technical Director* (TD) whose job it is to manage the technical aspects of the project.[5] There is a natural, and inherent, tension between the PM and the TD:

PM: Ship it on time on Friday!
TD: No! It's not ready!

Another word that describes the role of the TD is *architect*, in its most general sense. For example, on an IT project, there may be an architect, whose job it is to create the design, including the human interface, the database structures, etc.

In the movie industry, we suggest that the TD is the director, who controls the performance factors: directing, casting, camera angles, staging, lighting, etc. The producer controls the money, the schedule, and interfaces to the studio (the customer). The producer is fulfilling the role of the PM. What makes the movie case interesting is that, sometimes, the director (TD) has more power than the producer (PM).[6]

Conflicts often arise when major deliverables are due, and the situation typically evolves as follows: The project manager presses the team to meet the schedule for a major deliverable. The technical director resists, explaining:

- The performance is not up to the *specification*.

- To meet the required performance, extra time and money is required.

- Therefore, the deliverable is going to be late.

This is really bad project management.

It is not the team's fault, it is the fault of the project manager. A bad project manager will continue to insist that the team deliver on time, and more forcefully as the deadline approaches. Meanwhile, the PM assures the customer the project is on schedule and within budget.

When the delivery date rolls around, lo and behold, the product is not ready, is over budget, and behind schedule.[7]

---

[3] This entire topic is neglected in the *PMBOK* and most books. We happen to think it is an interesting topic of discussion.

[4] We are deliberately staying away from the word *quality* here. Many organizations have a Quality Control group, but they work after the design and construction to check everything. What we are referring to is the responsibility for the creative design aspects and the idea that the project satisfies the mission and objectives.

[5] For small projects the PM and TD may be the same person, which leads to schizophrenia.

[6] Think, Steven Spielberg.

[7] Meanwhile, the team are all whispering, "We told you so!"

Let's roll the clock back and suggest a better approach. First, as soon as the TD is assigned, the project manager sets about getting to know the TD. They discuss the project's content, the deliverables, the budget, and the schedule. They discuss all of the estimates and where problems might lie.[8]

The PM and TD jointly develop a workable project. The TD designs the approach, and the PM the cost and schedule, but they cooperate. The project manager sells the cost and schedule to the customer. The TD sells the product to the customer who agrees to the *spec.*

When technical issues arise, the TD meets with the PM and explains the problem. Together they work out the impacts and discuss options. When cost and schedule issues arise, the PM meets with the TD and explains the problem. Together they work out the impacts and discuss options.

In our view, if you are a project manager, it's your problem. Whatever it is.

Late?	Your problem.
Over budget?	Your problem.
TD whining?	Your problem.

As the project manager it is your job to *induce* the team to perform, to *induce* the stakeholders to approve the project, and to *induce* the customer to pay for it.[9]

2.2.2 PM Interactions

The project manager interacts with many different constituencies:

- *Stakeholders.* This is the most important group and failure to carefully manage them will jeopardize the project. Stakeholders are usually a diverse group with competing priorities.

- *Upper Management.* The project manager must understand the role of the project in the company's strategy, and be able to defend its budget.[10]

- *Sponsor.* The person who pays for the project will want regular cost and schedule updates.

- *Customers.* The people who set the expectations for the final product.

- *Project Team.* It is the project manager's job to *induce* the team to perform to the best of their ability.

- *Functional Areas.* These are typically the company departments that provide the staff to the project, and may include:

[8]Start now. Make sure the TD is your best friend.

[9]No exceptions. No excuses.

[10]We regard this a nothing less defending one's job security.

23

– System designers and architects.

– Subject matter experts.

– Business analysts, lawyers, and accountants.

– Contractors and subcontractors.

– Testers and quality control staff.

2.3 Project Manager Competencies

A project manager needs to acquire three types of skills:

1. *Technical Skills:* These are the analytical skills in specific domains, e.g., develop the scope and track the cost and the schedule.[11]

2. *Behavioral Skills:* These are the personal skills, the most important of which is communications. Other skills include the ability to identify and engage with stakeholders, exhibit leadership, manage virtual and global projects, and exhibit ethical behavior and professionalism.

3. *Strategic and Business Skills:* These skills require knowing what to accomplish and why and include program and portfolio management, governance, and emerging topics such as agile Project Management.

2.3.1 Technical Skills

The technical skills cover the theory and practice of Project Management and provide the knowledge perform a wide variety of activities, such as determining the value of the project, performing a cost estimate, constructing a work breakdown structure, building a network diagram, determining if the project is on schedule, and, during production, whether it is over or under budget. Technical skills also include risk and quality management, and contract procurement.

An overview of the technical skills follows:[12]

[11]We prefer to think of these as the *science* of project management.

[12]This is a summary of the Knowledge Modules developed for the PMI *Curriculum Framework.* [13]

- *Project Management Principles:* This skills area is generally considered to be one of the most important for effective project management. Key skills include understanding the business case and the benefits of the project; the role of the Project Manager; the project's environment; alignment of the project with organizational and business strategy; portfolios and project selection; and competencies in managing sponsors and stakeholders.

24

- *Project Phases and Processes:* Key skills include life cycles; process groups, processes, and knowledge areas; and international standards.

- *Project Planning and Integration:* Key skills include developing the project plan, charter, scope, specification, WBS, network diagram, and schedule.

- *Project Resource Management:* Key skills include identifying and acquiring the required personnel, equipment and materials.

- *Estimating Costs:* Key skills include the principles and concepts of cost estimation; managing, estimates; and understanding direct and indirect costs, overhead, expenses, contingency costs, and management reserves.

- *Project Scheduling:* Key skills include techniques for planning, managing, and controlling the schedule and managing the critical path.

- *Opportunity and Risk Management:* Key skills include risk and opportunity planning, identification, analysis, response, monitoring, and control.

- *Plan and Control Quality:* Key skills include understanding the definitions of quality; and using quality tools and techniques to measure project quality.

- *Procurement and Contract Management:* Key skills include planning procurements; determining contract types, risks, and incentives; selecting vendors; and awarding, monitoring, and managing contracts.

- *Finance and Cost Budgeting:* Key skills include constructing a budget, monitoring and controlling costs, and understanding the fundamentals of accounting, finance, capital expenditures, and historical cost data.

- *Project Scope Management:* Key skills include developing the scope and specification, collecting and defining requirements, and managing change.

- *Project Control:* Key skills include Earned Value Management (EVM), controlling changes, and communicating project status to stakeholders.

- *Business Analysis and Requirements Management:* Key skills include evaluating business needs, eliciting requirements, and managing change.

- *Project Handover, Closeout, and Reviews:* Key skills include project closeout; handling special cases of abrupt termination; conducting formal audits and final acceptance; managing contract closure and payments; and documenting lessons learned.

- *Project Management Information Systems (PMIS):* Key skills include their uses, benefits, and applications.

2.3.2 Behavioral Skills

Behavioral skills deal with the personal, professional, and organizational aspects of Project Management and include guiding, motivating, and directing the team.

- *Plan, Distribute, and Manage Project Communications:* Key skills include developing and distributing information; techniques for engaging and influencing stakeholders; and presenting performance reports.

- *Project Team Building and Motivating:* Key skills include leadership, motivation, and conflict resolution; and decision-making.

- *Project Leadership:* Key skills include recognizing the roles of manager and leader; understanding leadership styles and f power; developing trust and negotiating conflicts; and recognizing the roles of business and personal ethics.

- *Identifying and Engaging Stakeholders:* Key skills include identifying and engaging stakeholders, and prioritizing them by power, influence, and interest.

- *Project Organization and Context:* Key skills include techniques for managing organizational behavior, roles, and power relationships; managing strategic and organizational changes; and managing risk tolerance.

- *Managing Global Projects:* Key skills understanding large global projects and their complexity factors, logistics, distance, time zones, jurisdictional challenges, languages, and cultures; and communicating with global project teams in multicultural environment.

- *Virtual Project Management:* Key skills area include techniques for managing and leading geographically dispersed, cross-cultural, and cross-border teams.

- *Ethics and Professionalism:* Key skills include understanding how ethics and personal responsibility are critical to project success; navigating political and social issues, such as whistle blowing, compensation, and conflicts of interest; dealing with sustainability and green issues; and embracing greater accountability of both the project manager and the team.

2.3.3 Strategic and Business Skills

These skills require understanding of the strategic relation between projects and their sponsoring organizations.

- *Strategic Project Management:* Key skills include techniques for aligning projects with the business strategy; and strategic evaluation and selection of projects.

- *Supply Chains in Projects:* Key skills include knowledge of procurement and managing connected supply chains.

- *Legal Aspects in Project Management:* Key skills include techniques for contract and procurement management and understanding topics such as labor law, health, safety, employment law, data protection, and data privacy.

- *Business and Commercial Aspects of Projects:* Key skills include understanding innovation, strategic alignment, project benefits, finance and cost management for nonprofit organizations, government, and public services projects.

- *Governance in Projects:* Key skills include the understanding of governance structures; harmonizing processes to achieve project goals; reducing the risk of conflict; and understanding projects, programs, and portfolios.

- *Agile Approaches to Project Management:* Key skills include understanding frameworks, such as Scrum, agile processes and roles; when to use agile; and key metrics and resources.

- *Portfolio and Program Management Principles:* Key skills include identifying strategic objectives; understanding the critical success factors; and developing metrics for portfolio performance.

2.3.4 The PMI Talent Triangle

PMI has published their own view of the Project Manager's desired skill set, which they refer to as the *Talent Triangle*®. PMI research suggests that, while technical skills are essential, companies are seeking added skills in "leadership and business intelligence, competencies that can support longer-range strategic objectives and that contribute to the bottom line." [14]

The second side of the PMI Talent Triangle is referred to as "Leadership Skills," whereas we referred to the second side as "Behavioral Skills." We believe that 'behavioral' is a better description as it includes a much wider set of skills and, especially, as one of the behavioral skills is 'Leadership.'

3

THE PROJECT ENVIRONMENT

> **There are two ways of being creative. One can sing and dance.**
> **Or one can create an environment in which singers and dancers flourish.**
>
> *Warren G. Bennis*

A project manager must be aware of both the internal and the external environments surrounding the project.

3.1   The Internal Environment

The internal project environment influences the team members' attitudes and their desire to perform. The internal environment is influenced by policies and procedures and the available corporate assets. For a project to succeed, the project manager must create an environment where team members are committed to the project's goals and care about producing quality products.[1] A positive internal environment includes:

1. A corporate culture that acknowledges and appreciates team members.

2. Good working relationships among team members.

3. Clear and open communications.

[1] Again, we see the idea that you cannot order someone to succeed, you can only create an environment that induces them to perform.

29

4. An environment of trust.

5. A willingness to take risks.

6. Recognition of efforts and achievements.

Apart from the first item, which depends on the corporate climate, these qualities are the responsibility of the project manager who must ensure that everyone understands both the objectives and their own roles. As each project is unique, the team is venturing into uncharted territory and the project manager should encourage the team to take risks.

The available corporate assets are often referred to as *Organizational Process Assets (OPAs)* and include processes, policies and procedures, and knowledge databases.

3.2 The External Environment

There are two sets of external influences, those within the company and those external to the company. The internal company influences are referred to as *Enterprise Environmental Factors (EEFs)* and include:

- The parent company, including upper management.

- Organizational assets, including policies and procedures, lessons from previous projects, etc.

- The company's governance structure, its culture, staff, and resources.

- The company's information technology capabilities and its investment in tools and technologies.

EEFs external to the company include:

- The political environment, including government policies, tax incentives, legal agreements, and regulations.

- The business climate, including the company's financial health, business strategies, and access to funds.

- The geographical setting, including environmental issues.

- Social commitments, including benefits and working conditions.

- Academic research and available best practices.

3.2.1 The Project's Rationale

An important and critical aspect of the external environment is the business need for the project, i.e., its rationale for existence. This need is typically documented in the business case.[2] The project's objectives must be aligned with company's objectives because, if the need for the project disappears, the project will also disappear. A threat to all projects is an evolution of the business that eliminates the need for the project.[3]

3.3 The Company Environment

There's no crying in baseball!

Tom Hanks, A League of Their Own

The project manager is *responsible* for the project. This means that project managers must do whatever it takes to get the job done and satisfy the stakeholders. What happens when these ideas conflict with the goals or culture of the company?

This is an important issue for all project managers, because in most respects, companies and projects have completely different goals. However, both companies and projects must be successful: companies must flourish while project goals must be achieved. The trick is to balance the needs of a project with the needs of the company.

The competition between projects and companies is inherent in their structures and the stress created on project managers is a fundamental part of the job. If you wonder why organizations structure themselves in the complex ways discussed below, it is because they are trying the balance the goals of the company and the goals of their projects.[4]

3.3.1 Projects Goals vs. Company Goals

Projects violate most of the ideas that companies consider as good management.[5] To be specific, project goals are almost always in direct conflict with those of the company that sponsors it.

The goal of a company is to manage efficiently, which implies repetitive actions that can be continuously improved. The Japanese have a word for it: *kaizen*.[6] A simple example is travel expenses: It doesn't make any sense to allow each department to have their own travel forms and procedures. Companies therefore, insist on a standardized, company-wide, travel reimbursement process.

[2] This is further elaborated in Chapter 4, Portfolios.

[3] Project managers must be on the lookout for this. No project, no job.

[4] But, remember, as a project manager, you are responsible. Paraphrasing Tom Hanks, *There's no crying in project management*.

[5] This is a strong statement, but we firmly believe it to be true in most instances.

[6] When considered as a philosophy, *kaizen* becomes the process of continuous improvement.

31

On the other hand, by definition, projects are unique. How can you improve something if you only do it once?

Many of the key characteristics of projects are listed in Table 3.1, along with the opposite characteristic, which is what companies typically desire. We argue that for almost all project characteristics, the goals of the project (on the left) are completely opposite to the goals of the company (on the right).

Table 3.1: Project Goals vs. Company Goals.

Projects	Companies
Unique	Manage efficiently
Creative	Routine
Individualistic	Repetitive
Inter-Disciplinary	Departments with expertise
Integration skills	Technical expertise development
Project expertise	Creation of subject matter experts
Specific, narrow needs	Wide, general capabilities
PM in charge	Department managers in charge
Staff rewarded for	Staff rewarded for
project performance	company performance

Projects are inherently interdisciplinary, while companies are organized into departments, usually with a single expertise. Departments are good for companies because they acquire and develop expertise by investing in the skills of their employees, which generally enhances the capabilities of the company. Company departments stay current by investing in technology, staff training, etc.

On the other hand, projects are typically shortsighted because a project's technology may be static. Once the project team has learned enough about the technology to implement the current project, there is no incentive on the part of the project to invest in staff growth or in new technology. In fact, projects are defined by their scope document, to which changes are actively discouraged. Therefore, it is not unusual for the skills of people working on long-term projects to become obsolete.

Departments are silos of expertise, and they have little or no incentive to become interdisciplinary. In fact, this is often discouraged as it dilutes their capabilities. An accounting department needs expertise in accounting and doesn't really care about environmental regulations or web design. On the other hand, projects are inherently interdisciplinary, and a project manager may have to worry about accounting, environmental regulations, and web design.

3.4 Cultures

A nation's culture resides in the hearts and in the soul of its people.

Mahatma Gandhi

You need to make sure your project does not infringe on cultural norms, which are the values, beliefs, and expectations that permeate the company. The team can either adopt or reject the organization's values, beliefs, and expectations, and their attitude will directly affect the project's success.[7]

Cultures are defined by *cultural norms*, which include common knowledge regarding how to get the work done, what is acceptable, and who is influential. [15] Organizational norms typically include:

1. Shared visions and beliefs: What makes your company good?

2. Unspoken company expectations: Is quality work expected? Can you slip a deadline to get it right?

3. Explicit policies and procedures: Every company has such manuals.

4. Views of authority and power: Can you easily approach the President?

5. Work hours: Are you expected to work extra hours to get the job done?

6. Ethics. What is considered right?

Often, there is a whole collection of unwritten rules that one has to learn when you join a new organization. For example, is the CEO a gregarious person who chats with everyone, or is the CEO a tyrant that nobody dares speak to?

Think about the culture of your own organization. What are the myths and stories that get passed down between employees? What are the first things you tell a new employee?[8] When you showed up, what was the first thing you noticed about the organization?

A project manager needs to understand the culture of the organization because it is very difficult to go against. For example, if the company allows and encourages flexibility in its working hours, then a project manager cannot arbitrarily impose a regime of time clock punching. In a flexible working situation, the project manager must insist on deliverables, and let the team figure out how to best deliver them.[9]

[7] The aspect of culture that we considering here is *organizational culture*, and in particular, the aspects that apply to the project team.

[8] Especially the off-the-record stuff.

[9] You can measure the progress of deliverables without asking what time people showed up for work.

33

One of my favorite examples of a culture clash occurred when I was assigned to write a piece of a proposal teamed with another company. I had to work at their site and the assignment lasted several weeks. Near the end, we all had to work over a weekend. I was told that dress was informal for weekends and I could wear anything I wanted.

I showed up in jeans and a Red Sox T-shirt.[10] They all showed up identically dressed in khakis and polo shirts. I was not dressed correctly. Their khakis and polos were just another uniform, and I was definitely not regulation. This is a good example of an organizational norm: It was unwritten but very specific. Everyone eventually learns to comply with these unwritten expectations.

Research suggests that there are ten characteristics that capture the essence of an organization's culture and these are described in Table 3.4.[11]

Each of the characteristics in Table 3.4 has two extremes, which are defined in Table 3.3. Usually, the desires of projects and companies favor opposite extremes. For example, a project would probably prefer the team member to identify with the task at hand (i.e., the project), while the company might prefer identification with the organization.

The interesting question is: How do the above characteristics affect projects? Generally, projects tend to prefer the left hand extreme in Table 3.3.

3.4.1 The Abilene Paradox

It was a hot day in Coleman Texas, but Jerry Harvey was cool and enjoying lemonade on his back porch, playing dominoes with his wife and in-laws. Harvey's father-in-law was concerned that the others were bored, so he suggested that they all drive to Abilene for lunch. No one wanted to go, but nobody spoke up.

So, they all drove 106 miles, ate really bad food, and then drove back.

Nobody wanted to leave the back porch, the fan, the lemonade, or the dominoes. But, no one spoke up. Nobody wanted to go to Abilene, but they all went anyway.

Harvey describes this as an inability to manage agreement. [16] However, the Abilene Paradox also includes the implications of speaking up. Does your organization encourage speaking up? If a project manager does not encourage people to speak up, then everyone will drive to Abilene!

Upper management's power to hire and fire can squelch speaking up. Does the company discourage a frank and outspoken discussion when safety is being compromised for profit? The Abilene paradox explains the inability of the participants

[10]This was deliberate, because I was in Orioles country.

[11]For an excellent set of references on the topic of corporate culture, see Gray and Larsen, page 81. [15]

Table 3.2: Cultural Characteristics and Project vs. Company Goals.

Cultural Characteristic	Project vs. Company Goal
Member identity	Do you identify with the project or the company? In projectized organizations, the team tends to identify with the project, while in functional organizations they identify more with their department.
Group emphasis	Do you prefer to work in a group, or as an individual? Projects favor group work, although a project needs good technical skills to solve problems.
People focus	Do management decisions incorporate the views of the employees, or do they tend to strictly focus on projects, or even the bottom line?
Unit integration	Are departments structured to work independently, or are they encouraged to work together?
Control	Do rules, policies, and procedures tend to dominate employee behavior? Does the company encourage independent thinking? Can PMs bend the rules?
Risk tolerance	Are employees encouraged to take risks, and even allowed to fail occasionally? Projects require innovation, which means voyaging into uncharted territory.
Reward criteria	Are salary increases and promotions awarded according to project or department performance, or other secret criteria?
Conflict tolerance	Are employees encouraged to speak out and openly air their views? How does the company handle dissent?
Means-ends orientation	Does management focus on the outcomes and results or the processes to achieve them? Projects need to have discipline and procedures (means) but must deliver (ends).
Open focus	Does the organization encourage open discussion? Who is allowed to talk to customers?

to speak the truth when faced with policies they do not support. Discouraging dissent confuses telling the truth with disloyalty and, even, betrayal.[12]

[12]Someone experiencing this conflict may be left with ethical and emotional challenges related to self-betrayal, shame, guilt, and moral failure for not having acted upon his or her appraisal of the situation.

35

Table 3.3: Cultural Characteristics and their Extremes.

Project Dominance	Cultural Characteristic	Company Dominance
Task	Member Identity	Organization
Individual	Group Emphasis	Group
Task	People Focus	People
Independent	Unit Integration	Interdependent
Loose	Control	Tight
Low	Risk Tolerance	High
Project Performance	Reward Criteria	Department Performance
Low	Conflict Tolerance	High
End	Means-Ends Orientation	Means
Internal	Open Communications	External

3.4.2 A Cultural Clash

A colleague of ours experienced an interesting example of the clash of norms. He is an animator and was working on a movie that was close to its scheduled release date and everyone was forced to work 60 hours per week. That was acceptable. But, the producer sent around junior assistant producers to see what time the animators arrived at their desks.

Animators are bunch of independent arty types, who don't respond well to authority.[13] One morning, there was a huge pile-up on the freeway and everyone arrived late. Most of the animators had worked late the night before and didn't appreciate junior assistant producers[14] yelling that they should be at their desks by 9 am.

3.4.3 Rewards

A second example from the same project illustrates the problem of attempting to reward productivity. The producer tried to reward the team that completed the most shots,[15] but chose as the reward a free Sunday lunch at the animators' favorite watering hole.

My colleague's team connived to come in *second* every week. That way, they were seen as productive team players. But, as they were already working 6 days a week, the last thing they wanted was to give up a Sunday—their only day off.

[13] The 'creatives,' as they refer to themselves.

[14] The 'suits'

[15] A reasonable goal.

This shows how problematical the use of rewards can be. People will manipulate the system in creative ways to achieve goals you would never have thought of. If you insist on checking every detail, you cannot expect the team to take risks. If you curtail freedom, you cannot expect people to experiment. If you yell at people when they fail, they will never try anything new without checking with you first.

When the project manager does not understand the culture, the team will find ways around the system. We've seen many project failures from project managers trying to impose unreasonable discipline on creative types. The key is the deliverable. If they deliver, who cares how they do it?[16]

3.5 Project Structures

> **Peace is a daily, a weekly, a monthly process, gradually changing opinions, slowly eroding old barriers, quietly building new structures.**
>
> *John F. Kennedy*

Companies set up multiple types of structures in which to execute projects and each has different strengths and weaknesses. Rarely does the project manager get to choose the company structure, so it is important to understand the role of projects in the organization and the challenges that will arise.

3.5.1 Organic Structure

Organic projects are performed by people working informally, usually side-by-side. There is little formal project management and perhaps a part-time project manager who may function more as a coordinator.

3.5.2 Functional Structure

In functional organizations, strong departments with a specific mission tend to dominate. The managers of the departments are referred to as *functional managers.*

When a project arises, a team is assembled from the departments and the power of the project manager is weak. Once the project is over, the team members return to their home departments.

The functional approach is common in small organizations that do not want to create an expensive project structure. Management is handled through normal departmental channels and, so, the project management tends to be informal with

[16]Of course, we could just be explaining our personal philosophy here.

37

few resources. Table 3.4 describes the advantages and disadvantages of performing projects in functional organizations.

Projects may be performed in a single centralized department (e.g., marketing) or distributed among departments.

Table 3.4: The advantages and disadvantages of *Functional* Organizations.

Advantages	Disadvantages
No organizational changes required	Unclear motivation for a project
Easy to create teams	Hard to prioritize projects
Departments build expertise	Staff are loyal to their department
Staff have expertise	Hard to coordinate interdisciplinary activities
Team returns to department when project is complete	Lack of ownership for the project

An example of a functional organization is a university, which is organized into academic departments. Occasionally, a project arises that needs an interdisciplinary team, e.g., hiring staff, developing a marketing strategy, and rewriting the web site. Each of these requires expertise from many departments and, typically, a committee is formed to accomplish the project. The team members meet and work to accomplish the project, but do not leave their departments.

Suppose the Dean calls me up and asks me to chair a committee to hire a new Director for the student admissions department. I say 'OK.'[17] But I do not work directly for the Dean, I work for my department chair, who signs my pay raises.[18] In this example, the academic department manager is a *functional manager*.

But I still need to do a good job on the search committee. I can expect to get subject area expertise from the student admissions department. As chair, I am the project manager and responsible for the schedule (the person should start at the beginning of next semester), the budget (can I take the candidates to lunch at expensive restaurants?), and the resources (committee assignments). But I am a classic project manager in that I cannot order them around.[19]

While the project is important to the University, it is not my major priority. In a choice between answering emails from students and my committee assignment, which will I chose? Student emails.[20] In this example, we see many of the issues associated with performing projects in functional organizations.

[17]Because she is the Dean, and I have no real choice.

[18]So you can bet that I will want to keep him happy.

[19]I have to *induce* them to perform.

[20]Nothing makes a professor's life more miserable than a bunch of angry students.

3.5.3 Matrix Structure

The matrix structure is a hybrid in which the project team is assembled from departmental staff. There are two chains of command: A project chain and a department (or functional) chain and, as a result, team members report to two managers: The project manager on project matters, and their functional manager on technical matters. This is a source of pressure for the team members, who must keep two bosses happy.

While complex, the matrix organization gives companies the best of both worlds. Projects get the advantage of a dedicated project manager, and a Program Management Office that invests in projects. The company realizes the long-term benefits and efficiencies of departmental structures, which are better at nurturing technical expertise and can move staff between projects. The advantages and disadvantages of performing projects in Matrix Organizations are summarized in Table 3.5.

Table 3.5: The advantages and disadvantages of *Matrix* Organizations.

Advantages	Disadvantages
Clear project management Investment by PMO	Conflict between PM and TD
Easy to create teams	Team members have two bosses
Departments build expertise	Staff are loyal to their department and not to the project.
Departments provide resources to projects	Stressful, multiple bosses
Team members return to their department when project is complete	Department goals compete with project goals
Flexible assignment of staff to small and large projects	Can be slow and bureaucratic
Standard corporate policies and procedures for all projects	Corporate goals may conflict with project goals

Matrix organizations are classified as strong, balanced, or weak, where the adjective applies to the power of the project manager. A strong matrix behaves like a projectized organization (see below), while a weak matrix looks somewhat like a functional organization. The balanced matrix is the traditional form, where the project manager is responsible for the project and the functional managers have responsibility for its technical performance. Many large Defense Contractors are organized in a matrix structure.

The matrix structure is the most important one to understand:

1. It is a powerful way of accomplishing complex projects, while simultaneously balancing the needs of the organization and the needs of the project.

2. All of the managerial, staffing, and technical issues that occur in the matrix structure also occur in the other structures. The issues are much clearer in the matrix structure and easier to understand.[21]

3.5.4 Projectized Structure

In a projectized organization, most of a company's work is performed in projects. Each project has its own independent team under the leadership of a project manager, who is usually dedicated to the project. In such organizations, the project manager is powerful and has total control. The advantages and disadvantages of projectized organizations are summarized in Table 3.6.

Table 3.6: The advantages and disadvantages of *Projectized* Organizations.

Advantages	Disadvantages
Teams are easily assembled	No standard policies
Clear authority–the PM	Resources may be duplicated
Responsive	Rivalries between project teams
Cohesive and committed	Limited technical expertise
Efficient communication	No place for staff when project is complete
Explicit staff expertise	No long-term growth plan for staff

[21] If you understand the problems in matrix organizations, you will understand the issues wherever or whenever they occur.

[22] That is a polite way of saying that either there is another project for the team to work on or they are unemployed.

[23] Or, to unemployment.

An example of a projectized organization is a construction company. Each new building is a project and teams are assembled as needed: steel workers, plumbers, carpenters, etc. When the project is complete, the team members all move on to other projects.[22]

Another example of a projectized organization is a movie. The team is assembled from independent contractors: the director, scriptwriters, actors, lighting technicians, grips, etc. When the project is over, they all move on to the next movie.[23]

3.5.5 Virtual Structure

The virtual structure is usually described as a network of nodes, where the nodes are the distributed staff members. The virtual structure resembles a weak matrix with the added complication that the team members are not co-located.

3.5.6 PMO Structure

This is where the Program Management Office (PMO) controls the projects. The structure often resembles a strong matrix with powerful project managers.[24]

3.6 Programs

> **David Letterman: How did you know so much about computers?**
> **Grace Hopper: I didn't, I was the first one.**

Rear Admiral Hopper, U.S. Navy

A *program* is a collection of projects managed in a coordinated way.[25] However, there is more to a program than just managing the projects as there are important non-project activities. Therefore, there are two parts to the definition of a program:

> *A group of related* **projects** *managed in a coordinated manner to obtain benefits not available from managing them individually.*
>
> *Activities associated with the integration and development of business strategies and organizational goals and objectives.*

Suppose a company's marketing department creates a program to launch a new product. That program might include the following projects:

- Plan and implement the project's launch the product at a national trade show.

- Plan and implement a marketing campaign.

- Design and implement the supply chain for the product.

- Create new marketing channels for the product.

[24]The PMO is covered in section 3.6.4.

[25]This section summarizes the key ideas of *Program Management* and is based on the PMI *Program Management Standard.* [17]

41

Sometimes a program has routine activities as part of its mission. In the above example, routine activities might include updating the marketing materials and publication of a weekly sales brochure to selected clients.

An organization that uses the term "program" in the way we have defined it is National Aeronautics and Space Administration (NASA). For example, NASA's Mars exploration program consisted of many projects, including Spirit and Opportunity Launches, 2001 Mars Odyssey, Mars Express, and the Mars Reconnaissance Orbiter.

3.6.1 The Program Manager

The person who manages a program is called the *Program Manager* and the key skills are aligning projects with company strategy, defending projects, understanding and improving *project* management, and selling the benefits of both projects and programs. Therefore, a good *Program Manager* focuses on:

- Defining a clear business strategy and the role of projects in that strategy.

- Creating and managing the portfolio of projects

- Standardizing approaches to project to accumulate coordinated benefits.

- Defining and analyzing *program* metrics for accurate status reporting.

- Creating and consistently improving a centralized repository of expertise, tools, and techniques.

- Setting up and managing centralized processes for identifying and communicating risks, resolving issues, reviewing projects and deliverables.

- Defining roles and responsibilities of stakeholders.

While most of the above functions involve project management skills and knowledge, the *Program Manager* views projects from significantly different perspective. The Program Manager must think more of the big picture, as a program is not a big project, but an interconnection of many projects with links to business strategy and stakeholders. As a result, a Program Manager should take a longer view of costs, schedules, risks, and quality. Also, Program Managers deal with different types of information as their reports and metrics focus more on strategic, long-term benefits. [18]

Just as *Project Management* is the knowledge and skills base for projects, the definition of *Program Management* is:

Program Management is the application of knowledge, skills, tools and techniques to meet program requirements.

3.6.2 The Program ↔ Project Interface

The Program Manager's most important and complex relationship is with the Project Managers. Program Managers should actively build positive, collaborative relationships with their project managers. They should focus on providing value to the individual projects and should take care not to be perceived as an additional management layer or as oversight undermining the project manager's role. Other important aspects of the Program Manager's job are to *develop* skills and to establish credibility with project managers, management, and customers.

While Program Managers may be experienced in project management, their Project Managers need to feel that they are in control of their own projects. Their authority could be undermined if the Program Manager is too actively involved with stakeholders and with team members. Therefore, Program Managers should work to build trust with the Project Managers to create a common framework for assessing progress and employing tools and resources.

On the other hand, the Program Manager is accountable for the success of the program. Therefore, Program Managers should ensure that the Project Managers understand the program role and should be clear about the benefits that projects receive by being part of a program.

Therefore, a successful program manager:

- Respects the role of the project manager and provides them with the freedom to manage their projects.

- Minimizes active involvement in project issues.

- When issues arise, works with the project manager, rather than stakeholders, to reduce public undermining of the project manager's authority.

- Ensures that project managers have the tools and information to manage their projects.

- Establishes a clear, compelling vision for the PMO and helps project managers to understand strategic goals.

- Helps project managers to understand how different projects work together and manages cooperative assets, e.g., risk, finances, tools, and processes.

- Establishes open communications by scheduling regular reviews with project managers, and their staffs, to provide up-to-date program status.

3.6.3 Program Management Performance Domains

Program Management has five performance domains:

1. Strategy Alignment: Programs must be aligned with company strategy to generate long-term benefits. Program managers should identify opportunities and benefits that achieve strategic objectives.

2. Benefits Management: Program managers define and sustain the benefits of the program. Benefits should be measurable improvements as perceived by the stakeholders.[26]

3. Stakeholder Engagement: This includes capturing and understanding stakeholder needs and expectations; gaining and maintaining stakeholder support; and mitigating and channeling stakeholder opposition.[27]

4. Governance: This involves establishing processes and procedures for maintaining program management oversight and for decision-making.

5. Life Cycle: This includes program definition, benefits delivery, and closure, and includes elaborating strategic objectives; seeking approvals and securing funding; determining budgets and schedules; managing risk funds; and developing charters and roadmaps.

3.6.4 The Program Management Office

Program management is often accomplished in a Program Management Office (PMO).[28] The definition of a PMO is:

> *The PMO is an organizational structure that standardizes the project-related governance processes and facilitates the sharing of resources, methodologies, tools, and techniques.*

The functions of a PMO are to manage:

- Business Alignment: Ensuring that the program and individual projects align with corporate strategy, which involves managing the portfolio and interfacing with stakeholders, customers, and vendors.

[26]There may be negative benefits, sometimes called 'disbenefits,' which are outcomes perceived as negative by one or more stakeholders.

[27]The tools and techniques of stakeholder engagement for Programs are essentially the same as for projects and are covered in Chapter 7.

[28]Note: The PMBOK defines the PMO organization as the *Project* Management Office. A program is a collection of projects and managing them collectively is the job of the PMO. Therefore, we believe it is more correct to call it the *Program* Management Office. Besides, almost all companies call it that.

- Practice Management: Determining and enhancing the PMO's benefits and creating a Center of Excellence for lessons, methodology and tools.

- Infrastructure Support: Standardizing project methodology and governance, and participating in reviews, planning, auditing, and recovery.

- Resources and Skills: Acquiring and developing staff and physical resources.

- Technical Support: Developing and sharing metrics and tools for managing scope, cost, schedule, risks, quality, and stakeholders.

The PMO has its own set of stakeholders, who include the company's Board of Directors, the CEO, sponsors and funders of the PMO, clients, business units and departments, vendors and partners, line managers, and support functions, such as Information Technology, Quality Control, Legal, and Accounting.

The projects are the most important stakeholders and consist of the project managers and their development teams. Therefore, a PMO is responsible for the coordinated management of projects and its role is to:

- Coordinate and communicate across projects.

- Coach, train, monitor and develop the project managers.

- Develop and manage the company standards, and policies and procedures.

- Monitor the performance of projects and project managers.

- Invest in project management technology, best practices, tools and techniques, and implement them across projects.

- Manage the Project Management Information System (PMIS).

- Supervise functions that are managed centrally, such as the portfolio management and risk pools.

- Collect and manage lessons learned.

3.6.5 PMO Challenges

Some large organizations, such as the military and NASA, have long-established PMOs that work well. However, as companies realize they are performing more project-based work, many companies are investigating and setting up PMOs to coordinate projects to realize the benefits of common approaches. However, organizations with new PMOs often experience major challenges:

- The closure and restructuring of PMOs happens frequently and, as a result, most have only a short time to demonstrate their value. Experience suggests that it takes six months to two years to implement a successful PMO.[29]

- The cost of setting up a PMO is significant and, initially, PMOs have a very small staff. Only 50% of PMOs are seen as relevant and adding value.

- PMOs have widely differing roles and functions and there is great variability in the number of projects within new PMOs. Decision making authority also varies significantly. The key seems to be that high-performing PMOs are seen to be meeting strategic needs of the company.

3.6.6 The PMI Program Management Standard

According to PMI, the standard for Program Management aims to be a "clear, concise, comprehensive, and contemporary description of program management practice." [17] Its goal is to accurately reflect the higher-level business functions that are essential aspects of the program manager's job.

The Program Management Standard covers the five domains (Strategic, Benefits, Stakeholder Engagement, Governance, and Life Cycle). The model is somewhat intimidating as it lists 72 tasks and 126 knowledge areas applicable to the domains.[30]

---

[29] Most PMOs have been in existence for less than two years.

[30] The details can be found in [17].

4

PORTFOLIOS

There are two ways of being creative. One can sing and dance. Or, one can create an environment in which singers and dancers flourish.

Warren G. Bennis

A portfolio is an entity that is managed from a *business* perspective and is defined as follows:

> *A portfolio is a collection of programs, projects, products, and routine activities managed together for mutual benefit.*

That is, a portfolio consists of all the activities necessary to make a product (or project) a business success. Portfolios, therefore, may include projects, programs, as well as routine activities.

A comparison of portfolios, programs and projects is shown in Table 4.1, which is based on a similar table in the PMBOK.

Developing a new product satisfies the definition of a project, but the activities to make the product successful include many routine activities such as marketing, product maintenance, inventory control, and customer service. A new product cannot be successful without all of these non-project activities, so it makes sense for a company to manage it all as a coherent whole, i.e., as a portfolio.

Table 4.1: A comparison of portfolios, programs, and projects.

	Projects	Programs	Portfolios
Definition	Unique, temporary endeavor.	Group of related project managed for *cooperative* benefits.	Projects, programs and operations managed to achieve *strategic* objectives.
Scope	Clearly defined objectives	Wider scope producing coordinated benefits	Business objectives aligned with corporate strategy
Planning	Progressive elaboration of project objectives	Program plan	Business Plan
Management	The project	The program	The portfolio
Success	Meets stakeholder objectives, within quality, cost & schedule	Meets business objectives	Meets corporate objectives

4.1 Mission, Goals, Objectives, and Strategy

A project manager must be able to define and articulate clearly the link between their project and the company's mission, goals, and objectives. Projects compete for company funds and resources, and projects without a clear link to the mission are at risk of cancellation.[1] Every project manager should have an "elevator speech" about why the company cannot possibly survive without their particular project.[2]

Therefore, it is important to understand the mission, goals, objectives, and strategy, as well as their relation to portfolios, programs, and projects.

4.1.1 Mission

The mission is the company's reason for existing. The mission statement is often aspirational, providing the vision and values for the company. It defines who you are, what you do, and why. Every project must have a clear link to the mission and strategy. Otherwise, why do it?

For example, Google's mission is to "organize the world's information and make it universally accessible and useful." Notice that this does not say anything about search engines.[3]

[1] Again, it is simply job security to be able to defend your project.

[2] The notion of an elevator speech is that if you find yourself in the elevator with the President of the corporation, you have about 60 seconds to justify your existence. Practice it.

[3] If I had asked you what Google is known for, you'd probably say something about web searching.

48

4.1.2 Goals

The goals are what you wish to accomplish. For example, a company goal might be to: *Diversify our products to get into new markets.*

4.1.3 Objectives

Objectives are detailed, specific statements about what the company wishes to achieve. An example of a specific objective, related to the above goal of diversifying into new markets, is *Increase market share by 15% in 3 years.*

When listing objectives, the acronym SMARTO is often used—see Table 4.2[4] The above objective of increasing market share by 15% in 3 years satisfies all of the SMARTO criteria.

Table 4.2: SMARTO objectives.

S	Specific	in the target objective
M	Measurable	indicators of progress
A	Assignable	to a specific person
R	Realistic	in what can be done
T	Timed	with schedules and deliverables
O	Open	for everyone to see

4.1.4 Strategy

The strategy defines precisely how the company will accomplish the objectives. For example, the strategy to accomplish the above objective of increasing market share by 15% in 3 years might be:

- Invest $50,000 in new product development.

- Set up a new portfolio evaluation method.

- Develop three new innovative products and dramatically enhance two existing lines.

- Diversify the portfolio into two totally new market areas.

4.2 Portfolio Management

Which new products should a company invest in?[5]

[4]Actually, most textbooks use the acronym SMART (without the 'O' at the end). We believe that a vital part of successful project selection and evaluation is openness. Everyone in the company should see what is being funded and what rejected.

[5]This section describes *Product Selection* and borrows heavily from the research on *New Product Development*. However, because developing a new product is a project, the research also applies to *selecting projects*.

New products often account for over 50% of a company's growth and 40% of their profits. [19] Therefore, it is not much of an exaggeration to say that a company's future depends on the success rate of its new products. Selecting the products to invest in requires predicting which of them will be successful.[6]

Therefore, while difficult, businesses are obliged to attempt to predict the future. That is, which of their new products will return the best investment?[7] This field is called *New Product Development.*

Many companies struggle with this question and, if the research is to be believed, most are not very good at answering it. In fact, only one out of four product development projects succeed commercially, one-third of all new product launches flop, and over 45% of development resources are wasted on ventures that fail. [19]

The lack of a formal process for evaluating products results in companies missing positive opportunities for significant product improvements. They fail to take advantage of evolving marketing information and evaluations of early test versions by customers. The overall result is that companies tend to release too many mediocre products and too few genuinely successful winners.

4.2.1 Product Portfolio Management (PPM)

[6]Niels Bohr, the Nobel Prize winning physicist, famously said that "prediction is very difficult, especially about the future."

[7]And equally importantly, which of their new *projects* will return the best investment?

[8]Cooper's *Winning at New Products* presents these issues in a clear and readable way.

[9]Cooper suggests that the processes "fit management's way of working," which is a polite way of saying they are simple enough for even management to understand.

On the other hand, a few companies do actually excel at introducing new products and *Fortune's* list of the most admired companies contains some of the most innovative firms: 3M, Intel, Guinness, General Electric, Johnson & Johnson, Procter & Gamble, and others. For such companies, effective portfolio management is a competitive weapon.

What can be learned from these successful companies? One of the most important observations is that successful products provide customers with *unique and valuable* benefits and the success rate for such products can exceed 80%.

If greater success in new product development can, in fact, be achieved, it should be possible to educate companies in the successful methods that lead to improvements. The process of selecting the right portfolio of products is called *Product Portfolio Management* (PPM). And, indeed, PPM methods and techniques are validated, successful, and surprisingly straightforward.[8] Once the critical success factors are understood, business processes can be implemented that are both easy-to-understand and effective.[9]

4.2.2 Dynamic Portfolio Management (DPM)

Recent research has shown that company portfolios are dynamic, and that the traditional, static methods of PPM need to be upgraded to accommodate evolution and change in the portfolio from both internal and external factors. [20] Internally, the portfolio must react to evolving customer demands, differing rates of project progress, and revised marketing priorities. The external business environment is also dynamic, and the portfolio must react to strategic company initiatives, market changes, and technological and social forces.

As product development proceeds, a prototype may be delivered, marketing data becomes available, and an evolved picture of the product emerges.[10] This new information requires re-assessment of the technical and marketing position of the product as well as its strategic contribution to the portfolio. Dynamic processes are required to support changes in technical content, to adapt to evolving markets, and generally to evolve the portfolio consistent with corporate strategy.

Historically, Product Portfolio Management focused on selecting new products based on their projected financial rewards. The situation changed dramatically during the 1990s, when PPM research identified the factors critical to the success of new products.[11] The research, which was validated in companies in many business sectors and all over the world, laid the foundation for techniques that are both easy-to-understand and effective. [19]

More recently, there is a growing acceptance that portfolios are dynamic and that processes are required to adapt the portfolio continuously to product evolution and external business uncertainties. *Dynamic Portfolio Management* (DPM) enhances PPM by adding techniques that focus product selection towards achieving a company's *strategic* goals and objectives. [20]

4.2.3 Compliance Projects

Projects may spring up in unexpected areas. For example, when tax and environmental regulations change, systems and processes must be upgraded. These so-called *compliance projects* are not glamorous, they cost money, and do not improve the bottom line. However, the project selection mechanism must enforce the selection of these types of projects.

4.3 Portfolio Selection

What makes for a successful project? Research shows that a good portfolio is characterized by:

[10]This product dynamism operates in addition to the classic project management issues of changing scope, costs, and schedules.

[11]Interestingly, financial rewards turned out to be one of the poorest methods for selecting successful products.

51

- *The right number of projects.* Many companies take on too many projects with the result that their projects do not have enough resources, either money or staff, and it should come as no surprise that their portfolio performs poorly. Therefore, an essential aspect of good portfolio management is the killing of under-performing projects.

- *Good balance.* Portfolios need to have a mix of highly innovative projects, moderate extensions to successful, existing lines, and compliance projects.

- *Clear ties to the company's mission and strategy.* The company's investment in the portfolio should reflect corporate goals.

There are many ways of prioritizing and selecting projects. Until recently, financial methods were popular and dominated the selection process. However, research has shown that selecting a project based on its return on investment is now considered to be the *worst* way to select projects. Early in the life of a project it is very difficult to estimate quantities such sales, profitability, and return on investment.

4.3.1   Critical Success Factors

> **Success is the result of perfection, hard work, learning from failure, loyalty, and persistence.**
>
> *Colin Powell*

[12]For an excellent practical book on new product development, see the book by Cooper. [19]

Research has established that there are specific factors that are essential to the commercial success of projects and they are known as *critical success factors.* (CSFs).[12]

[13]We are actually quoting research on what makes successful new *products*, not projects, because there is a significant, body of evidence for what makes a successful product. Since each new product development is a project, we feel comfortable presenting this as "project selection."

Many studies have been conducted on what makes a successful commercial product[13] and the most important *critical success factors* are:

1. *A unique, differentiated product that provides significant benefits and superior value to the customer.* This is the most important CSF and is much more important than any other factor in the eventual success of a product.

[14]If there is not lots of money, why bother?

2. *A strong market-driven, customer-focused orientation aimed at an "attractive market."* An attractive market is one in which there is lots of money[14] and, preferably, no competitors. Also, an attractive market is defined from the customer's perspective, which makes it vital to build in the voice of the customer. That is, to determine the project's value, solicit opinions from

potential customers, not the project manager. Also, carefully assesses the competition and their potential responses to your project.

3. *Solid up-front project definition.* The project's most important document is the scope, so investment of time up front is critical. Don't rush in. Clearly define the project.

4. *Don't stray from core competencies.* What are you good at? You can branch out into new areas, but if you do be sure you know that it is risky.

5. *Execute a disciplined process.* Practice good project management and garner upper management support. Implement a portfolio management system with tough Go/Kill decisions. Continually check the customers' views of the products, costs, margins, and revenues.

4.3.2 The Scoring Matrix

If it doesn't matter who wins or loses, then why do they keep score?

Vince Lombardi

Products are evaluated using a *scoring matrix*, which has been shown to achieves a balanced portfolio. An example of a scoring matrix is shown in Table 4.3. The top row lists the evaluation criteria, which are the factors against which projects will be scored. The CSFs established above are the foundation of the evaluation criteria in the scoring matrix. For example, knowing that a unique, differentiated project is the #1 CSF, we need a way to evaluate projects against this criterion. Other company goals may be added as less highly weighted criteria.

Each evaluation criterion is assigned a weight, which is shown in the second row of Table 4.3. These weights represent how important the criterion is to the company. Weights are typically scored from 1 — 5, where 5 represents a criterion vital to the company. For example, a company with an aging portfolio may add "Innovative" as a criterion and give it a weight of 4. Projects that score high in *Innovative* will then tend rise to the top of the list.

The projects to be evaluated are listed down the left-hand side. Each project is given a score out of 10 for each of the criteria. For example, Project #1 is assigned a score of 9/10 for the *Unique* criterion, and a 4 for Return on Investment (ROI).

The total project score is obtained by multiplying the weights by the scores. For example, the Project #1 score is:

$$9 \times 5 + 8 \times 4 + 4 \times 2 = 45 + 32 + 8 = 85. \tag{4.1}$$

53

Table 4.3: A sample scoring model.

Criteria	Unique	Innovative	ROI	
Weight	**5**	**4**	**2**	**Score**
Project #1	9	8	4	85
Project #2	6	2	3	44
Project #3	9	9	9	99
Project #4	6	4	5	56

Once all projects have been scored, they can be ranked and dollars assigned to the top performers.

Scoring models are efficient: They fit management's style in that they are simple to understand, do not take a lot of time, and do not require a tedious bureaucracy. Scoring models also yield portfolios with high value projects, support go/kill decisions, assign funds to strategic priorities, and result in well-balanced portfolios.

4.4 Selecting Projects for PMA

We now give an example of how the portfolio selection process might be accomplished for the Project Management Association (PMA), who is considering implementing several new projects. Several proposed new projects emerged from strategy sessions, from internal solicitations throughout the company, and from the marketing department.

Each project has a project manager[15] and a *Charter*, which briefly describes the project, its budget, and the primary objectives. PMA's list of proposed projects is:

1. A new web site to communicate with members.

2. A fundraiser solicitation by email to members.

3. A course in project management for members.

4. A membership drive to increase the membership.

[15]At this stage, the project manager is the person who will champion the project.

54

4.4.1 The Scoring Criteria

The mission of PMA is that they are dedicated to project management research and to the education of its members. Therefore, PMA has established the following criteria to evaluate their proposed projects:

- **Research.** Projects will be scored higher if they increase the research knowledge of members. Since this is the primary mission, the weight is 5.

- **Education.** Projects will be scored higher if they increase the education of members. This is important, but not quite as important as the research goal, and so it is assigned a weight of 4.

- **Growth.** Projects will be scored higher if they grow the membership of the organization. This is not so important as research and education, and so it is assigned a weight of 2.

The definition of each criterion was carefully elaborated during discussions. For example, the scoring for the *Research* criterion was defined in Table 4.4.

Table 4.4: Definition of scores for PMA's *research* criterion.

Score	Definitions for Scores
9-10	Valuable research information for most members.
7-8	Valuable research information for many members, or useful research capabilities for majority of members.
4-7	Research information useable by a few members.
0-3	No useful research information.

4.4.2 The Scoring Matrix

Once the CSF scoring criteria were defined, each project was given a score for each CSF, see Table 4.5. The projects were then ordered by their score (high scores at the top) to rank the projects. This is shown in Table 4.6.

4.4.3 The Budgets

So far, PMA has evaluated the projects solely on their match to the selection criteria and without any consideration of their budgets. When the projects were initially

Table 4.5: The scoring matrix for PMA's new projects.

Criteria	Research	Education	Growth	Total
Weight	**5**	**4**	**2**	**Total**
#1. Web Site	9	8	4	85
#2. Fundraiser	2	2	9	36
#3. PM Course	0	10	7	54
#4. Membership	0	0	8	16

Table 4.6: PMA projects winners and losers.

Criteria	Research	Education	Growth	Score	Budget	Allocated
Weights	**5**	**4**	**2**			
Funded Projects						
#1. Web Site	9	8	4	85	5,000	5,000
#3. PM Course	0	10	7	54	5,000	10,000
Losers						
#2. Fundraiser	2	2	9	44	1,000	0
#4. Membership	0	0	8	16	1,000	0

proposed, a rough budget was included, and the next step uses those data. The costs of the projects were entered in the *Budget* column in Table 4.6.

The final data required are the total funds allocated to be spent on the selected projects and PMA allocated $10,000. The top project was funded, so at this point PMA has allocated $5,000. Then, the next highest score was funded and the total allocated at this point was $10,000. Projects were funded until they reached the allocated amount, which was $10,000. The Fundraiser and Membership projects were not selected and were not funded. In the *Allocated* column in Table 4.6, PMA calculated the running total of the funded amount.

4.4.4 PMA's Strategy

The final step in the process was to decide if the funded projects make sense to PMA from a strategic perspective *as a group*. To do that, PMA studied the overall match to their mission and also examined the synergy between their selected projects. As a result, the PMA evaluation committee made some changes to the portfolio:

- *Cut the budgets.* Budgets are not sacred. Project managers may have padded their bids, assuming they would get cut. Very expensive projects were looked at carefully, even if they had high scores. The committee examined whether it was possible to do several small projects instead of a single expensive one. If the scores were close, the decision became one of strategy.

- *Combine similar projects.* The fund-raiser and the membership drive looked similar and the committee could ask the project managers to rebid them together taking advantage of synergy.

- *Beware of false precision.* Projects with similar scores were considered to be equally valuable because there is a lot of uncertainty in the scoring process. Also, a high score in one highly weighted category can dramatically affect the ranking of a project.

- *Conduct a sensitivity analysis.* After the projects were ranked, the committee examined the scores to see if small changes affected the order. The debate about the scores ensured that they were reasonable.

4.5   Setting Up a Selection Process

A company can set up a project selection process as follows:

- *Calibration of the criteria and weights:* This is performed first as described in section 4.5.1. A dozen projects that the company performed in the past are chosen for the calibration step. These historical projects should be selected so as to provide a representative sample of company projects, including spectacular successes and failures, as well as a wide range of ordinary projects. The scoring matrix is developed using the historical projects.

  The objective is to determine a set of selection criteria and associated weights that allow the best projects to float to the top, while the poor projects congregate at the bottom. Once everyone agrees that the results are reasonable, the criteria and weights are fixed and should not be changed. The matrix is then ready for use in the selection of future projects.

The calibration process is also an effective way to train people in the portfolio management process. Once calibration is complete, the process can be put in place for the evaluation of future projects.

- *Selecting new projects:* The calibrated selection criteria and weights are fixed and used to select new projects. Over time, as more data become available, the process becomes more reliable.[16] The criteria and weights should be reviewed periodically and adjusted to gradually improve the process.

Project selection should be performed by an independent committee.[17] The project selection process typically begins with a widely distributed solicitation for new project ideas. All ongoing projects should be included in the selection process, as they compete for funds with new projects. Existing projects are included to assess their progress, and to ensure that they still match the company mission and objectives. That is, funding is allocated on a year-to-year basis, and ongoing projects are not automatically funded. All project managers should be called in to defend their projects in front of the committee, which then assigns the project scores.

In practice, once the matrix with winners and losers is produced, a great deal of negotiation takes place. Good projects naturally rise to the top, while poor ones sink to the bottom and, so, most of the discussion takes place in the middle, where projects with similar scores compete for funds. At this point, a number of factors can be considered:

- The scoring model is based on opinions and future projections, so it is not an exact science. The scores must not be taken too literally. Projects whose scores do not differ by much should be considered as equal.

- Budgets are not sacred. The committee will often take funds from projects and reallocate the money to projects considered more worthwhile from a strategic perspective.

- The evaluation committee often uncovers synergies between the projects that the individual project managers are not aware of. The committee may combine projects and reassign budgets to get two for the price of one.[18]

- Occasionally, a poorly scoring project is seen as a valuable, strategic necessity. Funding a low-scoring project sends a message to everyone in the company about priorities.[19]

[16] Since you are forecasting the future, nothing is certain.

[17] Research data suggest that the president's pet project fails more often than most.

[18] Dear PM:
We have good news and bad news. The bad news is that your project was not funded. The good news is that if you talk to the project manager for the fund-raiser project and combine your efforts, we believe that together you have an excellent chance of being funded.

[19] Next year, there will be a bunch of proposals in that area.

The rankings are not as important as the overall strategy. After the scores have been analyzed, the budgets massaged, and the synergies exploited, there should be coherence to the list of projects to be funded. When asked, you should have a simple, justifiable answer the following question: *What was funded this year?*

A decent answer might be: *We funded growth projects this year, as membership has declined.*[20]

4.5.1 Calibration of the Weights

Projects are funded based on their ranking in the scoring matrix and the major factors that affects the ranking are the selection criteria and their weights. While the process is somewhat subjective, everything is defined in a way that is meaningful to the company.

The criteria and weights are somewhat arbitrary.[21] They are assigned based on what the company *thinks* is important. For a company starting out on the project selection process, this is about the best that can be done. Over time, however, the criteria and weights can be calibrated, making the selection process more reliable.

Calibration is accomplished by having the organization go through the scoring process using historical projects. Typically, several small teams are assigned to score a dozen or so projects, including several successes, failures, and other projects of interest that will help calibrate the matrix. The teams suggest evaluation criteria and their weights and compare their choices.

Next, the teams use the agreed upon criteria and weights to score the selected historical projects. This must be done by returning to opinions about the projects when they were first proposed.[22] The teams then rank the projects so that the highest scores are at the top.

If the criteria, weights, and scores are reasonable, the company's most successful projects will be at the top of the list.[23] In practice, the process usually works surprisingly well in that successful projects do tend to float to the top and the failures to the bottom. The selection criteria, the weights, the project scores, and the relative rankings should all be analyzed and discussed and, if appropriate, some of the data might be further tuned.

When the team feels that the matrix provides a reasonable representation of the successes and failures, the selection criteria and weights can be considered to be *calibrated*. These can then be used in the evaluation of future projects.

[20] Note the explicit link to the strategy. A poor answer is: Umm ... Joe's and Betsy's projects.

[21] Remember, we are predicting the future, so nothing is guaranteed.

[22] Otherwise, hindsight on successes and failures will corrupt the process.

[23] Or, as is often the case, the projects that people thought were going to be successful.

59

4.6 Financial Evaluation Criteria

Project managers must be able to calculate, evaluate, and most importantly, defend the financial implications of their projects, which is referred to as *Return on Investment* (ROI). The two main methods are *Payback* and *Net Present Value* (NPV).

4.6.1 Payback

Payback is a simple calculation of the time it will take to recover the up-front investment in the project. We propose a project that will cost $30,000, and estimate it will improve cash flow by $10,000 per year. The payback is:

$$Payback = \frac{Investment}{Cash\ Flow\ Improvement} = \frac{\$30,000}{\$10,000} = 3\ years. \tag{4.2}$$

Shorter paybacks are obviously more desirable. Payback emphasizes cash flow, but ignores interest rates and profitability. Payback also depends on estimates of future cash flows, which are uncertain. Payback is often used to determine if a project is viable or not and, sometimes, the answer is so clear that further analysis is unnecessary.

4.6.2 Net Present Value

Would you rather have $1 now, or wait a year for it?

If I give you $1 now, you can invest it and a year from now you will have more. Therefore, the *value* of cash is a function of time. When evaluating a project's potential income, money received sooner is better. To allow for this, we use the net present value (NPV) formula:

$$NPV = -I + \sum_{n=0}^{n=N} \frac{CF_n}{(1+i)^n}, \tag{4.3}$$

where I is the amount invested in the project; N is the total number of years for which we will carry out the calculation; n is a quantity that indexes the years; CF_n is the net cash flow in year n; and i is the discount rate.

If the NPV is positive, then the project meets the minimum desired rate of return and the project is eligible for consideration, at least from a financial perspective. A project with a negative NPV is rejected.

The following examples illustrate the use of the NPV formula. First, we give a simple example that shows how to perform the mechanics of the calculation.

NPV Example #1

We invest $2 in a project. As a result, we expect that at the end of year 1, we will receive an **additional** $1. In years 2 and 3, we will receive an additional $2 and $3 respectively. We will use a discount rate of 10%.

$$NPV = -2 + \frac{1}{(1+0.1)} + \frac{2}{(1+0.1)^2} + \frac{3}{(1+0.1)^3} \tag{4.4}$$

$$NPV = -2 + 0.909 + 1.653 + 2.254 = 2.81. \tag{4.5}$$

The project is financially viable, since the NPV is positive. Note that if we just added the cash flows we would have: $-2 + 1 + 2 + 3 = 4$. The fact that the NPV is less than 4 is because the future value of cash is considered less valuable.

NPV Example #2

A company is planning to purchase a machine that will improve productivity by 10%, resulting in a cost savings of $15,000 per year. The machine costs $30,000 and has a potential life of 3 years. The company demands that any investment should pay off significantly better than stock market returns, insisting on a discount rate of 20%. Should the company invest in the machine?

The NPV calculation is presented in Table 4.7, where we see that the project has a positive NPV, and so is financially viable (but only just).

Table 4.7: NPV Example #2.

Year	Cash Flow	Rate	NPV	Net NPV
0	-30,000	1.0	-30,000	-30,000
1	15,000	$1/(1+0.2)$	$\frac{15,000}{1.2} = 12,500$	-17,500
2	15,000	$1/(1+0.2)^2$	$\frac{15,000}{1.44} = 10,417$	-7,084
3	15,000	$1/(1+0.2)^3$	$\frac{15,000}{1.728} = 8,681$	**1,598**

In any NPV calculation, one should examine the validity of all parameters: Are the cash flows realistic and sustainable? Is the discount rate reasonable? Has the calculation been carried out for an unreasonably long term?

In the above example, we should ask a number of questions. Is a 3-year life a reasonable assumption? Should we consider maintenance costs, which could negatively affect the cash flow?

Even a small extra cost will significantly reduce the attractiveness of the investment. For example, if the cash flow is reduced to $14,000 per year, the NPV turns negative ($NPV = -509$). The above calculation is very sensitive to the cash flow estimate and this does not look like a very promising investment.[24]

4.6.3 NPV in PM

The standard interpretation of NPV in the finance world is that one should only invest in a project with a positive NPV. In the world of project management, this is an overly rigid interpretation:

- *Future uncertainty*: Since a project has not been done before, the projections of cash flow into the future are likely to be uncertain.

- *Compliance projects*: Changes to government or environmental regulations may require upgrades to a company's information system. These projects are mandatory, but are unlikely to have a positive impact on cash flow.

- *Bias*: A project manager estimating future cash flows for their own project introduces bias and optimism. Their job is at stake.[25]

4.6.4 But, I work at a Non-Profit

Students who work for a non-profit agency often comment that their mission has little to do with cash flows and profits. NPV can still be applied; one just has to be creative about the quantity to measure.

One student worked for an agency whose mission was to help the homeless. Rather than measuring the financial return, she established the specific objective of helping more people (see SMARTO, section 4.1.3).

Just as it is preferable to have a dollar now rather than a dollar later, the student realized that it was also better to help someone now rather than to help them later. Therefore, the student applied the NPV formula to the *number of people helped*. Her revised NPV gave priority to projects that helped more people sooner. It was a brilliant adaptation of NPV.[26]

[24] Especially as we are attempting to predict the future.

[25] If management demands a 20% return for a project, guess what the PM will calculate?

[26] We like this example because it breaks the obsession of measuring everything in dollars. Often, there are more natural units to measure the value of a project. Look at your projects and ask yourself, "What really measures the value of my project?" Then think about using that to report the true measure of progress.

Part II

The Technical Skills

5

DELIVERABLES AND MILESTONES

Life isn't a matter of milestones but of moments.

Rose Fitzgerald Kennedy

Deliverables and milestones are so important they deserve their own chapter. All of the technical skills that are discussed in Part II have the goal of producing quality deliverables in a timely fashion. Therefore, we need to understand the definition of a deliverable and the associated milestone, i.e., when it will be delivered.

Projects begin with an end deliverable. That is, you'll know your project when you see it.[1] But how do you tell? More importantly, how will other people know it when they see it? The answer is *Deliverables*. Also, the *date* on which the product is delivered is an important *Milestone*.

As well as the end-deliverable, which is the project, there are also intermediate deliverables, such as the design and delivery of components. As well as the product, the project management process also results in deliverables, such as documentation and managerial reports. Examples of intermediary deliverables include:

- *The Scope.* This might actually consist of several, separate deliverables as the project proceeds: Preliminary Requirements, Conceptual Design, and Detailed Design.

[1] Just like love.

65

- *Cost and Schedule Estimates.* These are required at major milestones to report on the status of the project.

- *Intermediate project components.* These might include early prototypes and partial project deliveries.

- *Project Management Reports.* These include monthly reports, containing cost and schedule data, project status, risk updates, stakeholder issues, etc.

When a project is complete, it is because the end result is delivered. No deliverable, no project. A project is assessed and measured by its final deliverable and when that occurs is the final *milestone.* It naturally follows that the ongoing status and progress of the project is measured by intermediate deliverables and milestones. One assesses both the quality of the deliverables and the timing of the milestones.

Therefore, deliverables and milestones are the key to everything when it comes to assessing the project.[2]

5.1 Deliverables

The focus of most processes and tools is the development, completion, and assessment of the deliverables. e.g., the *Work Breakdown Structure* is a "deliverable-oriented hierarchy." Further, the entire theory of earned value depends on measuring the status of the project through the assessment of deliverables.

But what, exactly, are deliverables?

Deliverables are the tangible outputs of the project.

Deliverables are *tangible,* meaning you can see them and touch them.[3] It is important to recognize that deliverables are *outputs* of the project.

Sometimes, items are delivered *to* the project, but these are not considered to be deliverables. For example, in a construction project, the delivery of 2x4s, paint, and cabinets are not examples of deliverables; they are *deliveries.*

5.1.1 Measuring Deliverables

A project manager spends a lot of time and effort assessing deliverables. Every deliverable must be checked for compliance with the scope, whether it is on-time or not, and if it is within its budget. All of these questions hinge on some kind

[2]If you think about this for a moment, you will realize that it is hard to measure anything else.

[3]Even if the deliverables are electronic documents, we are still going to use the word *tangible.*

of assessment or measurement of the quality and acceptability of the deliverable. Therefore, when the deliverables are proposed, the project manager must consider how they are to be assessed and measured.

Some deliverables are actually quite easy to measure. Examples of easily measured deliverables are:

- Miles of roadway completed.[4]

- Linear meters of steel girders erected.

- Square meters of wall painted.

- Pages of documentation written.

Let's examine the last item a little more closely. When you propose a document as a deliverable, someone knowledgeable about the project should be able to provide an outline, a decent estimate of the number of chapters, and maybe even a rough page count. This is essential because it provides a foundation for cost and schedule estimation because most organizations have a good idea of how many pages per week a typical employee can produce.

When the activity of writing the document is assigned, you can communicate what is expected. After two weeks, you can reasonably measure the progress against expectations. If you expect 10 pages and you receive 5, you immediately know you have a problem and should investigate.

5.1.2 The Quality of a Deliverable

The quality of a deliverable is important. For example, a poorly written, or incomplete, scope document may not be accepted by the customer and cannot be considered complete. Therefore, it is important for the project manager to recognize the distinction between 'delivered' and 'approved.' Once the customer approves the delivered document, it is then complete.

This suggests that the completion of a deliverable involves several milestones, e.g., document written, document sent to customer for review, and customer review complete. If the customer rejects the document as unacceptable, there will more milestones associated with the rework.

5.1.3 Small Deliverables

Suppose you assign Tom to write a 100-page document. From experience with similar documents, the company estimates the typical production rate is about

[4]Drive by any road construction project and you can measure for yourself the miles completed.

5 pages per day. Therefore, the document should take Tom (whom we assume is about average) about 20 days (4 weeks) to produce.

After 4 weeks, Tom delivers only 50 pages, half of what you expected, with several major sections missing. You ask, "What happened?" Tom replies,

"The document was much more difficult than I anticipated"

This is not Tom's fault. This is bad project management.

Deliverables should be divided into small, discrete, manageable pieces. The above document should have been divided into chapters (or sections) of 10-15 pages each. Then after the first week, you should ask Tom, *"How ya doin'?"*

If the document is more difficult than anticipated, you know immediately, not after four weeks. You still have the problem of a difficult-to-write document, but you know about it much earlier. You now have options: You can assign more people. You can assign different people. You can revise the table of contents. You can even ask the customer if any sections can be deleted.

The key is to divide all deliverables into small, discrete, manageable pieces. In fact, a good rule for the size of deliverables is:

> *A deliverable should be able to be produced by one-to-two people in one-to-two weeks.*

Break all the deliverables into pieces with the above rule. That way, you can manage them. If someone gets into trouble, you will know immediately.

When dividing up a deliverable, there are several things to consider:

- *Small.* The earlier you can tell if the deliverable is in trouble, the more options you have to fix it. Small deliverables give the project manager options.

- *Discrete.* The more separable the deliverable is into independent units, the less interaction there is among both the content and the staff. When building a house, one naturally divides deliverables between the plumbers, electricians, carpenters, etc. The pieces are more manageable when divided into discrete technical sections that have little interaction.

- *Manageable.* Dividing the document into pieces also makes them manageable. It is easier to determine their cost and schedule, and to track their progress during production.

- *Parallel Development.* When it comes planning, dividing the deliverables into many smaller pieces often gives the project manager the ability to work on the activities in parallel, which shortens the schedule. Also, smaller deliverables can often be assembled in different ways, which increases flexibility, e.g., in staff assignments.

5.1.4 Progressive Elaboration

Since a project has not been done before, you learn as you go and the project manager must expect changes, which must be managed with care. The gradual evolution of the project plan is called *progressive elaboration.*[5]

> *Progressive Elaboration is the continuous improvement and detailing of the plan as more specific information, and more accurate estimates, become available.*

The progressive detailing of the project management plan is also called *rolling wave planning.*[6]

Developing a prototype is an excellent way of obtaining early data. A prototype will often solve technical problems, highlight risks, and lead to better estimates of the cost and schedule.

5.2 Milestones

> **It's a funny kind of month, October. For the really keen cricket fan it's when you discover that your wife left you in May.**
>
> *Denis Norden*

Milestones allow you to track the status of the project. For example, the completion of the scope is a major milestone for all projects. Every milestone should have a date associated with it. During project planning the date is the planned milestone and, after successful execution, it becomes the actual completion date.

> *A milestone is a significant point or event in the project.*

For example, the completion of project planning is a major milestone for a project. The milestone is marked by the completion of the *Project Management Plan* and

[5] Note that, technically, progressive elaboration applies to the project management plan.

[6] Both progressive elaboration and rolling wave planning apply to the plan, as distinct from *continuous improvement,* which is a part of quality improvement.

69

its acceptance by the customer. It is appropriate, therefore, to create a milestone called *Planning Complete* when the plan is accepted by the customer.

A milestone is also considered to be:[7]

A milestone is an activity with zero duration.

For example, in the PMA project, we could schedule an activity called *Design Complete*, and give it zero duration (which makes it a milestone). We can then link the milestone to end of the *Design* activity. That way, if the design is delayed, the completion milestone will automatically be delayed as well. The difference between the planned completion date for the scope and the actual completion date is useful information.

These milestone examples come from the New Kitchen project: As of June 1st:

- *Demolition Complete.* Planned: March 31st. Actually completed March 31st.

- *Gas line installed.* Planned: April 15th. Delayed by the gas company; completed May 15th.

- *Cabinet Delivery.* Planned: June 22nd. Not complete, on schedule.

Notice how the milestones accurately communicated the status of the project. In fact, project status meetings are usually all about milestones: Were the deliverables completed on time?

Major milestones are associated with major deliverables. Since the *scope* is an important document, it is vital to track its status, and this would be reported through a major milestone called *Scope Complete*.

Consider the PMA web site development project, the major milestones are: delivery and acceptance of the scope; completion of prototype user interface; completion of design; installation of web server; delivery of the major functional modules (there are several of these); delivery of documentation; integration complete; testing complete; user training conducted; and formal acceptance of the final project.

The status of a project at any point in time is clearly indicated by the completed milestones. Therefore, a project manager is expected to regularly report on the status of all deliverables during the execution of the project. If a milestone is late, the customer will immediately ask, "How late?" We leave the task of precisely determining the exact status of the cost and schedule of the deliverables to Chapter 12–Earned Value.

[7]This definition is also a technical convenience, which makes milestones equivalent to activities, which is useful, e.g., if the completion of an activity has a linked milestone, and the activity is delayed, then the milestone is also delayed.

More milestones mean better project management. Since completed deliverables are milestones, customers and stakeholders will be better able to judge what has been completed. But the milestones must make sense: They must be distributed appropriately throughout the project and, at least, indicate the completion of major deliverables.

An excellent example of a well-planned milestone comes from the New Kitchen project. In the contract, Mark listed several partial payments and one was *Upon delivery of blue board*. Note that this payment was tied to a delivery, not a date.

Mark billed for the blue board as soon as it was delivered. Since this was a major cash outlay, he received the money to pay for it. No matter how the schedule changed, by linking the payment to the delivery and not a specific date, Mark knew he would receive the money to pay for the blue board.

5.2.1 Milestone List for the PMA Case

Milestones play a key role in assessing the actual schedule against the plan as the project progresses. The accomplishment of major deliverables, at specific milestones, shows whether the schedule agrees with the stakeholders' planned expectations. It is useful to provide additional attributes for milestones, such as clarifying if the milestone date is Internal or External, and if it is Mandatory or Flexible.

Table 5.1 gives an example of a *Milestone List* for the PMA project.

Table 5.1: *Milestone List* for the PMA case.

Milestone	Date	Type
Initiation Phase Complete	1/15	Internal, Flexible
Project Planning Complete	2/1	Internal, Flexible
Initial Design Phase Complete	2/15	Internal, Flexible
Prototype Implementation Complete	2/28	External, Flexible
Full Website Complete	3/10	External, Mandatory
Closing Processes Complete	3/15	Internal, Mandatory

6

INTEGRATION

I'm not for integration and I'm not against it.

Richard Pryor

The *Integration Management* knowledge area is one of the least well understood aspects of project management. Partly, this is because PMI keeps changing its mind about what is in it and, partly, because it is hard to figure out what is actually meant by *Integration*.[1]

One way to understand this knowledge area is to view it as consisting of the activities that a project manager must perform in order to coordinate the project and keep an eye on the interactions between the various pieces. Integration, therefore, demands a global view of the project and strong communication skills.

For example, a change to the scope may impact the technical performance, introduce new risks, and require new team skills. It may also affect the project management, i.e., it may require a new estimate of the cost and schedule; a modified communications plan if the change introduced new stakeholders; and a sub-contract if the new work needs to be out-sourced. It is the project manager's responsibility to make sure that all technical aspects of the scope change are thoroughly analyzed and all impacts on the cost and schedule are considered.

[1] After you've said, "this is where you put all the parts together," it quickly gets fuzzy.

There are two major deliverables from the *Integration* knowledge area, the *Charter* and the *Project Management Plan*.

During execution of the project, there are several functions of the *Integration* knowledge area: manage the *changes*, which are handled through a process called *Integrated Change Control (ICC)*; directing the project work; closing projects and phases, and managing the project knowledge,[2] which involves using existing assets to improve project outcomes.

6.1   The Charter

The *charter* is defined as:

> The *Charter* is the document that is issued by the sponsor that formally authorizes the existence of a project.

The key point is that the charter grants to the project manager the authority to spend money and acquire staff for project activities. Therefore, without a charter the project does not exist.[3] No charter, no project.

A project does not exist until its charter is created, so someone outside the project usually develops it.[4] It is often developed as a partnership between the sponsor (who pays), the customer (who specifies performance), major stakeholders (users), and the performing organization.

The charter usually specifies, at a high level, what the project will accomplish, the funding required, and an overall schedule. A good use for the charter is to focus agreement on the key features of the preliminary specification.

Usually, the project manager is specified very early in this process and the charter identifies the project manager and the project champion. It also describes the project's purpose, description and goals, and they key requirements established by the stakeholders. Next comes a preliminary budget and primary milestones. Finally, the major stakeholders sign the charter to acknowledge their commitment to the project.

Some of the preliminary work on customer requirements may have been contracted out. This often happens on large projects where specific technical expertise is required to specify the performance. The data from such contracts are an input to the charter, and the Statement of Work (SOW) will be particularly useful, as it contains a concise summary of the project deliverables, the business need for

[2]This is a new process.

[3]We often suggest that when your boss calls you in and congratulates you as the new project manager for project X, you should immediately request a copy of the charter. "I can't be the project manager for a project that does not exist."

[4]The 6th edition of the PM-BOK explicitly states that the sponsor issues the Charter.

the project, a preliminary scope, and the value of the project from a strategic perspective.

Many organizations require a *Business Case* to be completed before the charter is created. The Business Case identifies the needs or problems that the project will address, and any related projects undertaken in the past that address the same, or similar, business problem.

The charter is often a short document that kicks off the project.[5] The key is to make sure that the charter accurately represents the goals of the stakeholders.

6.1.1 Inputs to the Charter

The inputs required in the development of the *Charter* are summarized in Figure 6.1. It is not unusual for the person creating the charter to have to troll through many existing company documents to assemble the required information.

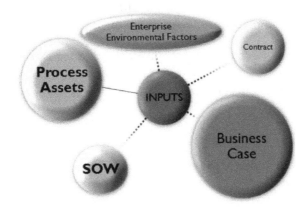

Figure 6.1: The inputs required to develop the *Charter*.

The following items can be used as a checklist to begin the search for the required *Charter* information.

1. **The Business Case**

   Why should the project be done?[6]

   The *Business Case* provides the data to justify, from a business perspective, that the project is worth its investment. There are many business reasons to perform a project:

[5]We once saw a one-page charter that authorized a $120 million dollar project.

[6]Every project manager should have an elevator speech that answers this question. You never know when you will run into your boss, who might ask, "Tell me again why are we doing that project?" Job survival depends on a really good answer.

75

- *Core Mission:* The development of a new product may be viewed as essential to maintain the company's position in the market space.

- *Market:* There is an untapped market the company believes it can satisfy.

- *Exclude Competition:* The company believes the project may prevent others from gaining entry into their market.

- *Core Technology:* The company wants to invest in a technology they believe will soon become important, and that will create a platform for future projects.

- *Image and Citizenship:* The project presents the company in a good light. Modern projects also consider their ecological impact.

- *Unreliable Suppliers:* The project will diversify its suppliers and make deliveries more dependable.

- *Changing Regulations:* Upgrades to the information system are necessary to comply with changes to tax, environmental, or legal regulations.

It is important for the project manager to periodically review the business case, particularly after major milestones. For example, when the scope is complete, it should be checked to ensure that it implements requirements in the business case.[7]

2. **Enterprise Environmental Factors**

Two important inputs to the charter are *Enterprise Environmental Factors* and *Organizational Process Assets.* These are not so much individual documents as collections of information.

These arise from answering the following questions:

- How does the organization conduct the business?

- What are the various departments and how do they operate?

- What is the market place condition for the project?

- What is the organizational environment in which the project exists?

- What infrastructure exists?

Examples of *Environmental Factors* can also include:

- Industry and government standards, such as ISO 9000, which specifies the fundamentals of quality management systems.

[7]It is easy to get carried away in scope development and end up with a great project that does not satisfy the business case. Also, changing market conditions can invalidate the need for the project, so checking the business case is project management job security.

- Marketplace data and business intelligence.

3. **Organizational Process Assets**

   Examples of *Organizational Assets* include:

   - Company assets useful to the project, such as standards, policies and procedures, tools, templates, and information systems.
   - Historical information, lessons learned, knowledge bases relevant to project management, and any templates from previous projects. Data from previous projects is particularly valuable if available in a searchable knowledge base.
   - Past project data, metrics, and measurement guidelines in a project management information system (PMIS), particularly if supported by cost and schedule management tools.

4. **Statement of Work (SOW)**

   The SOW defines who is to do which tasks, and when. Often, there is no formal SOW when the *Charter* is created. However, much of the information usually exists elsewhere. e.g., the completion date for the project may be in the business case, products must be available before the holidays, etc.

5. **Contracts.**

   The sponsor may delegate aspects of the project to an external entity, in which case the contract is an input to the *Charter*.

6.1.2 PMA Business Case

As an example, we present the business case for the PMA project in Table 6.1. It specifies the key benefits of the project and makes a strong case for management to fund the project. It could also discuss the following topics: Problem the project addresses; a cost/benefit analysis; risks, including the impact of not doing the project; and an implementation strategy.

6.1.3 PMA Charter

An example of a charter for the PMA website project is given in Table 6.2.

6.1.4 Charter vs. Scope

The PMBOK provides some clarity on the differences between the Project Charter and the Project Scope Statement, see Table 6.3.

Table 6.1: The *Business Case* for the PMA web site.

Key Project Benefits
Provide a comprehensive site for project management activity and collaboration, which will include the latest news, tools to assist the project managers, PMI resources, introductions to research, evaluations of new practical tools, and employment postings from both employees and employers.
To become an online resource for the project management community.
Increase awareness of graduate programs in Project Management and increase exposure to new companies.
Attract potential students to the graduate program in Project Management by showing our leadership position in the project management community.
Further the *state of the art* of project management by providing access to research, tools, templates, hints and tips to visitors to the site.
Provide a resource for students and alumni to receive and post available jobs from companies looking for highly skilled project managers.
Increase visibility for the Project Management Institute to foster a better working relationship with students.

6.1.5 Another Charter Example

Figure 6.2 presents a charter developed by one of our students for a party project.[8]

What we like about this charter is that while all of the information is there, it is also fun. As *fun* is an important theme of the party, it is perfectly appropriate to feature it in the charter.

Don't be fooled by the presentation, there is a lot of important information here. The stylish format matches the stakeholder goals: "a vivid, imaginative ideology." There are cost and schedule details (a budget of $250,000 and completed for March 10th) and even technical constraints match the party's philosophy: reduced paperwork, environmentally friendly products. (We present a more traditional charter for the PMA case in Table 6.2.)

The entire ethos of the party is clearly communicated throughout this innovative charter.[9] The bright colors and graphics all communicate the ambiance and style of the party to the stakeholders.

[8] This Charter was developed as a homework assignment by Vicky Morrissey in an undergraduate PM class. We are grateful to Vicky for allowing us to use her excellent example of a charter.

[9] If you do not know how to proceed on this project, you are not paying attention. Read the charter again.

Table 6.2: The charter for the PMA web site.

Project Title	**PMA Web Site**
Organization	**Project Management Association**
Start Date	**June 14, 2011**
End Date	**June 14, 2012**
Project Champion	**Dr. Vijay Kanabar**
Purpose	The Project Management Association (PMA) is a networking group for current students and alumni of Boston University employed or interested in the Project Management profession. The PMA web site project will create an environment for members of the community to share information, to be informed of current research, to obtain continuing education credits required to maintain certification, to learn about new employment opportunities and to get hints and tips on latest developments in the area of project management.
Description	The current Project Management website was implemented many years ago, and is not serving the needs of the PMA. The current website needs to be redesigned to keep up with new demands of the PMA, including access to research, changes in the project management profession, and improvements in tools and templates. This website project will create an environment that is both appealing and helpful to the project management professional, providing an equal balance of information sharing, tools and templates, and opportunities for networking.
Goals:	After installation, PMA should be able to: Increase the number of visits to the website by 50% over 2010 levels; decrease support costs of the website by 25%; and provide user friendly mechanisms to post, manage, update and remove content.
Success Criteria	1) Build a community of PMs. 2) Membership > 500 in the first year. 3) Analytics reveal popularity of site.
Project Budget:	$15,000
Milestones:	Initial Prototype to Stakeholders: 6/28/2011 Project Complete: 8/2/2011
Signatures:	Champion: PM: Stakeholders:

Table 6.3: The key differences between the *Charter* and the *Scope*.

Charter	Scope
Overview of project goals and objectives.	Detailed specification, SOW, Assumptions, etc.
Short, concise and unchanging.	Progressively elaborated.
High-level risks.	Preliminary risk assessment.
Desired schedule.	Target schedule and deliverables.
Cost target.	Planned budget.
Named Project Manager and Sponsor	Important stakeholders.

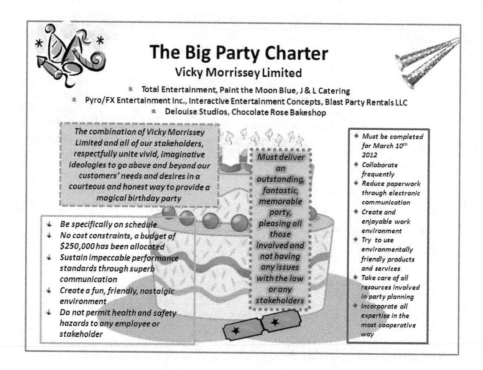

Figure 6.2: Vicky's Party Charter.

6.2 Integrated Change Control

Change is inevitable ... except from vending machines.

Steven Wright

A thread that re-occurs throughout the life of a project is the management of change. *Integrated Change Control* describes how changes are documented, approved, and managed. This is accomplished through a *Change Control System*, CCS, which is summarized in Figure 6.3.

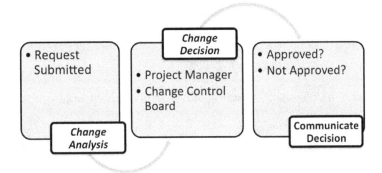

Figure 6.3: The Change Control System (CCS).

The definition of the *Integrated Change Control* is:

> *The activities of reviewing all change requests, approving and managing changes to the deliverables, organizational process assets, project documents, and the project management plan, and communicating the decisions.*

The word "integrated" reminds us that any changes have to be considered from a global project perspective, since even a small change can affect many different areas. Therefore, a *Change Control System (CCS)* is employed to ensure that changes do not result in chaos.

The first requirement for any proposed change is to determine if it is a refinement or an addition. Refinements are desirable and a natural part of progressive elaboration.

Additions, however, require a totally different attitude. Any proposed change that will add to the scope should be immediately halted and thoroughly evaluated.

Formally, the group responsible for approving or rejecting a change is the *Change Control Board* (CCB). The stakeholders should be informed of the potential cost and schedule impacts and, in particular, the customer and sponsor, who will have responsibility for the cost and schedule. These constituencies are represented on the CCB.

When the need for a change is detected, there are three possible actions:

- *Corrective action:* The project manager needs to bring the performance of the project into line with established objectives.

- *Preventive action:* The project manager can take action to reduce the probability of negative consequences arising from risks.

- *Defect repair:* The project manager needs to fix the problem.[10]

Each proposed change is reviewed for its cost and schedule impact and then either rejected or approved. Only *approved changes* are incorporated into the revised baseline.

As an example, consider the above PMA case, where a key programmer left the project. The project manager created a *change request*, which was reviewed and analyzed by the stakeholders. The project team came up with the following proposed solutions:

1. Hire and train a new team member.

2. Move team members to different activities.

3. Change the scope slightly to reduce the effort.

[10]There will inevitably be a lot of debate about whether it is really a defect or the customer's mistake in specifying the requirement. In other words, who is going to pay for it?

For the PMA project, keeping to the schedule is most important. The first two proposed solutions will result in a delay and, therefore, only the third option will maintain the schedule. After everyone agreed to the reduction in scope associated with the third option, the change was approved. The project manager documented all of the potential impacts of the proposed change in all relevant plans and also requested that the team members update the baseline configuration of the system.

6.2.1 Reasons and Causes for Changes

Real change, enduring change, happens one step at a time.

Ruth Bader Ginsburg

Changes occur for many reasons and, typically, by stakeholders requesting additional functionality. This results in scope creep, which is the uncontrolled growth of the project.

Even the project team can be responsible for scope creep as they implement improvements to the project by providing features that the sponsor did not request.[11] Sometimes, changes occur due to some unknown risks materializing and these may result in changes to the project cost or schedule.

An example of change management in the PMA case is given in Figure 6.4.

Change Requests

During the PMA project, changes will be requested through a formal system. A standard *Change Request* document will be prepared, which contains the proposed change; its rationale; and the potential cost and schedule impacts. The process for reviewing potential changes is outlined below.

- Change Request submitted formally using a form.

- Project Manager performs initial triage and studies impact.

- Stakeholders review the proposed change and assessed impacts.

- Change is either accepted, rejected or deferred by CCB.

- All stakeholders are notified.

Figure 6.4: The *Change Management Plan* for the PMA web site

6.3 The Project Management Plan

**Give me six hours to chop down a tree and
I will spend the first four sharpening the axe.**

Abraham Lincoln

Planning begins by carefully defining the scope of the project in concert with the stakeholders and then developing the cost and schedule estimates. Planning also

[11]This is often called gold plating.

involves: analyzing the risks to the project; defining how to assess the quality of the deliverables; establishing the communications between all parties; acquiring and training the team; and finally, deciding on the approach to sub-contractors.

The technical aspects of the planning processes are extensive and include: collecting the requirements and writing the project scope; evaluating constraints and creating the work breakdown structure; estimating costs, identifying resources and developing the network diagram; and determining the project schedule.

It is important to realize that planning is inherently iterative in nature. As stakeholder needs are refined, changes to the plan will be proposed, and not just technical or content requests, but also the real-world demands of cost and schedule. The progressive evolution of planning is referred to as *rolling wave planning*.

The writing of the *Project Management Plan* is a massive undertaking, as it contains dozens of sections. The plan documents the actions necessary to define, prepare, integrate, and coordinate all subsidiary plans. In the *Integration Management* knowledge area, the focus is on making sure that all of the plans are coordinated and consistent.

The Project Management Plan has many sub-components:[12]

- **Management:**

    - *Processes to be followed:* How much detail is required.
    - *The Life Cycle:* The various phases.
    - *Tools and Techniques:* Company assets and references to existing documentation is appropriate.
    - *Change Control:* This is an important aspect of project management, and so it is important to explicitly lay out the rules and tools.

- **Cost and Schedule:**

    - *Earned Value Management:* This is a vital component of project management and, so, it is important to explicitly lay out the approach to be followed and the tools to be used.
    - *Reviews:* Who and when? What information is distributed?

- **Sub-Plans:**

    - These include management plans for: Scope and requirements; schedule and cost; quality; human resources; communications; risks; and procurements.

[12]For small projects, a check-off of the issues might be all that is required.

84

Unlike many project documents, the *Project Management Plan* is actually a compendium of documents and should be really considered as a high-level reference to all of the sub-plans. We present a brief overview of the major sections:

- *The Project Management Plan*: This defines the entire plan, both technically and managerially.

- *Scope Plan*: The *scope* contains the user requirements and is the most important document in the project. For large projects, there may be a separate *Requirements Management Plan*.

- *Schedule Plan*: Here the project schedule is developed, and the *critical path* emerges, the most important concept in project management.

- *Cost Plan*: These are the steps required to develop the project cost estimate, and the budget.

- *Risk Plan*: The risks are identified, their impacts assessed, and how to mitigate them.

- *Stakeholder Engagement Plan*: The strategic approach to identifying and managing stakeholders.

- *The Sub-Plans*:

    - *Quality Plan*: This defines the quality standards for the project, both the process and the content.

    - *Resources Plan*: This defines how the project team is to be acquired and developed.

    - *Communications Plan*: This defines the distribution of information to stakeholders.

    - *Procurement Plan*: This defines the role of sub-contractors.

6.3.1 The PMA Project Management Plan

For the PMA membership growth project, Table 6.4 provides a template for the *Project Management Plan*. The template illustrates that the PM Plan does not repeat other documents, but provide links to the other plans.[13]

---

[13]In the modern world, the references can be hyperlinks.

85

Table 6.4: A template for the *Project Management Plan*.

Project Management Plan
PMA Membership Growth Project

1. Executive summary of Project Charter
   a. Abstract from the charter.
   b. Document any updates to the charter including assumptions and constraints.
   c. Scope Management plan.

2. Scope Statement.

3. WBS and Schedule.

4. Milestones and Estimated Completion Timeframe.
   a. Major milestones.
   b. Major deliverables.

5. Subsidiary Plans.
   a. Schedule Management Plan
   b. Cost Management Plan
   c. Quality Management Plan
   d. Human Resource Management Plan
   e. Communications Management Plan
   f. Risk Management Plan
   g. Procurement Management Plan
   h. Stakeholder Management Plan

6. Deployment Plan
   a. Describe the rolling out the application to the sponsors.
   b. Describe how the end users will be provided training.

CHAPTER 7

STAKEHOLDERS

Every single stakeholder has the potential to ruin your day.

Roger Warburton

Managing the interests of stakeholders is a vital activity. A major risk to project success comes from not realizing who all the stakeholders are or neglecting an influential contributor. In fact, mismanagement of any single stakeholder can lead to a disaster because an angry or disillusioned stakeholder can hold up deliverables, make trouble through an interest group, and generally cause havoc.

It is important to realize that not everyone will have a positive attitude to the project. Some individuals, or advocacy groups, might prefer that the project not be done at all. Such people are stakeholders because they have an *interest* in the project, but their negative attitude can be challenging. Also, some stakeholders may be in favor of the project once it is completed, but they may react negatively to its performance.

The formal definition of a stakeholder is:

> *A stakeholder is anyone actively involved in the project whose interests may be positively or negatively affected by the performance or the completion of the project.*

7.1 Identifying Stakeholders

**We must, indeed, all hang together,
or most assuredly we shall all hang separately.**

Benjamin Franklin

Since stakeholders are involved, the first step is to identify who can influence the project. Stakeholders exist both within the organization (e.g., the team, upper management) and external to it (e.g., users, trainers, sponsors).

Identifying stakeholders is a critical activity and it is quite easy to overlook some. Let's consider a project to repave the street in front of a classroom. One begins by asking, "Who will be impacted by this project?" Table 7.1 is a preliminary list of the stakeholders and their potential interests in the repaving project.

7.1.1 Inputs to Identifying Stakeholders

To identify stakeholders, it is useful to browse the existing documentation. Many of the inputs to *Stakeholder Identification* are the same as for the *Develop Charter* process and are illustrated in Figure 7.1.[1]

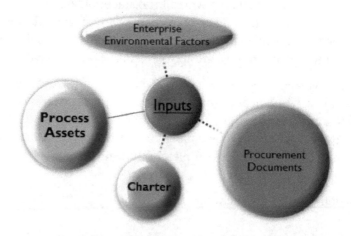

[1]Quite frequently, an output from a previous process is an input to the next process. That is true here: The *Charter* is a key input to the identification of stakeholders.

Figure 7.1: The inputs to the *Identify Stakeholder* process.

7.1.2 The Stakeholder Register

Table 7.1 is an example of a preliminary *Stakeholder Register*. It is a list of stakeholders and their potential interests and illustrates that repaving the street will be viewed quite differently by different stakeholders. Digging up the street will make a mess in front of stores and houses, angering the people who live and work there. This latter group can create challenges for the project manager. It is vital that the project manager actively manages *all* stakeholder expectations and reduces conflict over competing requirements.

Table 7.1: Stakeholders for the repaving project outside the classroom.

Stakeholder	Interest
Sponsor	Who pays for the project
Customer	The end user of the project. The customer (the city) may be different from the users of the project (the residents).
Project Manager	Wants to get the project done on time, on budget. Wants to keep the stakeholders happy.
Technical Director	Wants to get the project done right.
Project Team	Their jobs depend on the project. Even a simple construction project consists of many different subcontractors.
Trainers	Will train users when the project is over.
Students	During the project, are affected negatively by the disruption. Once completed, they will like the result.
Faculty	Hate the noise outside their window.
Police	Make extra money during construction.
Deans	Feel obligated to explain that construction will result in a better looking university.
The Mayor	Is happy the university will stop complaining about the poor street condition.
Shopkeepers	Complain business is down during construction
Residents	Complain there is less parking during construction.
Red Sox Fans	Miss the first inning because of the mess.

7.1.3 Stakeholder Analysis: Power and Interest

The next step is to begin a *stakeholder analysis* by adding to the *stakeholder register*, each stakeholder's potential influence, see Table 7.2.

Table 7.2: *Stakeholder Register* for the PMA web site.

Role	Expectations	Influence (IL = 1-5, 5 = high influence)
Executive Sponsor	**Key Stakeholder.** Provide direction, ground rules, and guidance by request.	IL = 4. Defines project success and adjudicates rewards for accomplishments.
Project Sponsor	**Key Stakeholder.** Provides guidance in weekly review and develops recommendations.	IL = 4. Defines project success and adjudicates rewards for accomplishments.
Steering & Guidance	**Key Stakeholder.** Provides guidance in weekly review and develops recommendations.	IL = 4. Provides direction for the team.
Project Manager	**Key Stakeholder.** Oversight of all activities.	IL = 5. Handles all status reporting to upper management.
Designer & Architect	**Key Stakeholder.** Design website.	IL = 5. Website design experience.
Lead Developer	**Key Stakeholder.** Implement website.	IL = 5. Website development experience.
Business Analyst	**Key Stakeholder.** Provide direction to maximize the effectiveness of the website.	IL = 3. Knowledge of markets and customers.
PMA Members	**Key Stakeholders.** End Users. Consumers expected to be the most active users of the website.	IL = 3. Will dictate the success of the project by frequency of visitation.
IT Dept.	**Medium Stakeholders.** Website maintainer upon completion of project.	IL = 3. Timeliness of maintenance will influence users' perception of quality.
Prospective Employers	**Medium Stakeholders.** End Users. Prospective employers will use the website to locate PMs.	IL = 2. Use by employers could contribute to success.
Alumni	**Minor Stakeholders.** Alumni may visit website.	IL = 1.
Prospective Students	**Minor Stakeholders.** Users. Students who use site for networking. May add content.	IL = 1.

Table 7.2 gives an example of a more detailed *stakeholder analysis* for the PMA website. It defines stakeholder roles, expectations, and influence. Stakeholder influence is scored from $1 \rightarrow 5$, where 5 represents the highest level of influence.

Stakeholder analysis continues throughout the planning process and is an example of *progressive elaboration*.[2]

Another useful tools in the stakeholder assessment strategy id to characterize them according to their power and influence. Stakeholders have varying levels of power and influence and, early in the project, the project manager must identify their ability to impact the project, which involves identifying their needs and understanding their perceived threats. Stakeholder analysis takes place continually and the *Stakeholder Register* is updated frequently.

Not all stakeholders have the same vested interest in the outcome of the project and not all have the ability to influence its outcome or override the interests of powerful groups. Therefore, the goal is to create a strategy for managing the various stakeholders, and a tool that helps accomplish this is the *Stakeholder Strategy*, which is illustrated in Figure 7.2.

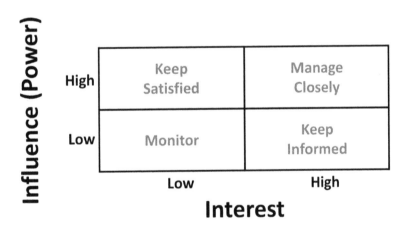

Figure 7.2: The tool to create the stakeholder management *strategy*.

In Figure 7.2, stakeholders are classified in two dimensions: The vertical axis indicates their power to influence the project and the horizontal axis indicates their interest, e.g., desire to take part in meetings, evaluate outputs, etc. Stakeholders are ranked as either "Low" or "High" in both categories and the recommended actions of the project manager towards the stakeholder groups are also shown in each of the four boxes and define the *Stakeholder Management Strategy*.

[2]This is characteristic of project management: Processes are seldom completed in one pass, but are continually refined as more knowledge about the project is accumulated.

For example, stakeholders with high power and high interest are assigned: *manage closely*. They should be frequently consulted and their views acknowledged, particularly with respect to deliverables. On the other hand, stakeholders with low power and low interest should be assigned: *monitor*.

It is necessary to consider stakeholders who are both internal and external to the project. External stakeholders include the project sponsor,[3] upper management, government agencies, customers, and users of the product. Internal stakeholders include functional managers and the project team. Stakeholders also include people impacted by the project. For example, a construction project might be disruptive to businesses in the neighborhood.

Figure 7.3 shows examples of stakeholders classified according to their power (influence) and interest.

Figure 7.3: An example of the stakeholder management *strategy*.

Some stakeholders may have specific requirements that they want included and the team must strive to meet those needs. While not all stakeholder requirements can be fulfilled, the failure to meet a particular stakeholder's expectations is a major risk factor, e.g., you run the risk of a stakeholder saying that you have failed an acceptance test. The key concept is *stakeholder expectations*, and managing them is a key role for the project manager.

When conflicts arise, the project manager must take the long-term view and treat stakeholders more as partners than adversaries. Short-term wins only make losers try harder in the future and they become better adversaries.[4]

---

[3]Remember, the sponsor is paying.

[4]For an excellent book on the softer skills of project management, see Meredith and Mantel [21].

7.2 Stakeholder Engagement

Stakeholder Engagement involves communicating with both internal and external stakeholders, especially about project progress and any issues that have arisen. This engagement often results in change requests, which are processed through integrated change control. *Stakeholder engagement* is defined as follows:[5]

> *Stakeholder engagement is the process of communicating and working with stakeholders to meet their needs and expectations, address issues, and foster appropriate stakeholder involvement.*

These activities increase support from and minimize resistance by stakeholders. As the project evolves and changes, new stakeholders might appear and the project manager must be constantly on the lookout, both for new stakeholders as well as for stakeholders with evolving roles and responsibilities. As new stakeholder roles are identified, they should be immediately classified as to their engagement level and their potential to disrupt the project.

A *Stakeholders Issues Log* can be used to document communications with stakeholders, and an example of for the PMA case is given in Table 7.3.

Table 7.3: The PMA *Stakeholders' Issues Log.*

Issue #	103
Date Reported:	02/10/2012
Reported By:	Bruce Lee, Programmer.
Issue Description:	Web site assets (videos and images) not provided to team in a timely manner.
Ranking & Classification:	High: Impacts critical path. Programming concludes in one week and we urgently need the media.
Impact to Project:	Delay of project schedule.
Resource Assigned To: Assignment:	Systems Analyst, Mary Contrary. Investigation & Resolution
Current Status:	Team plans placeholders for graphics and media as intermediate step. May require website redesign if media quality is poor.
Date Resolved:	Open. We hope to have this issue resolved by 02/17/2012
Resolution, Comments	Systems analyst Mary Contrary has been assigned to work with sponsor to get the media urgently. If sponsor does not respond within 3 days, the PM will escalate this issue.

[5]Stakeholder Engagement is a significant new focus of the later editions of the PMBOK.

7.2.1 The DISC Model

This section presents an overview of the DISC Model, which may, or may not,[6] be useful in explaining stakeholder communication styles. A version of the DISC model was proposed in William Moulton Marston's 1928 book, *Emotions of Normal People*. Marston was a psychologist with a Ph.D. from Harvard who theorized that emotions could be categorized into four primary types: Dominance (D), Inducement (I), Submission (S), and Compliance (C).[7] Walter V. Clarke, an industrial psychologist, was the first person to use it to build an assessment instrument in 1956.[8]

The characteristics of the four DISC types are:

- D – Dominance:

  The 'D' overcomes opposition and accomplishes results. They quickly solve problems, but challenge the status quo. They prefer direct communication and to be left alone. Their value is their willingness to take on difficult tasks and get results. Their issue is their need for control.

- I – Influence:

  The 'I' influences and persuades others. They are optimistic, tend to make a favorable impression, generate enthusiasm, and motivate others. They desire popularity and public recognition. Their value is that they get results from others. Their issue is they tend to talk too much.

- S – Steadiness:

  The 'S' cooperates within existing, standard procedures. They are loyal, good listeners, and patient, but they desire to maintain the status quo unless given good reasons to change. Their value is that they will implement the plan. Their issue is that they are easily persuaded.

- C – Conscientious:

  The 'C' works to ensure quality and accuracy. They are diplomatic, concentrate on details, think analytically, and clearly define expectations. Their value is that they help fine tune the plan by evaluating, investigating, and critiquing. Their issue is that they tend to question too much.

A key DISC claim is that the characteristics are behavioral and, since they are not personality types, are changeable. Therefore, a project manager can learn to adapt their communications to accommodate different stakeholder styles.

[6]Criticisms of assessments include that you get different answers each time, that it is not clear what it measures, and that it is of questionable accuracy. Caveat emptor.

[7]Marston's fascinating and unusual life is depicted in the film, *Professor Marston and the Wonder Women*.

[8]The assessment field has since become a multibillion-dollar industry and there are many different models, from dozens of commercial companies, with different levels of quality.

7.2.2 On the Other Hand

Many great thinkers have attempted to describe (usually) four psychological types. For example, 2,400 years ago Hippocrates used the Popular Sanguine (born entertainer who likes people and fun), the Perfect Melancholy (born thinker who likes solitude), the Powerful Choleric (born leader who likes action, loves work, and wants to direct others), and the Peaceful Phlegmatic (born follower who loves to relax and who thrives on harmony).[9]

In 2007, six respected university professors analyzed the research on the use of personality testing. [23] They concluded that faking on personality tests cannot be avoided and that the validity was low for a personality test to predict job performance. Professor Neal Schmitt said: "The validities haven't changed in the past twenty years and are still close to zero?"[10]

7.2.3 PM and DISC

Quoting Dr. Wendell Williams, [24]

> If you need some help understanding broad differences between people, and you are willing to take a test never intended for serious business use, then the DISC is a fun tool. When you want to facilitate a quickie workshop in communication styles, the DISC is for you.

Since we are not opposed to fun, we present some practical advice from the DISC model.[11] Our motive is to stress that project managers must engage with many different types stakeholder behavior and that no single method of presentation of status, no matter how accurate and well-thought-out, will be effective.

Project managers should listen carefully to stakeholder questions, not only to answer them, but to try to match the style of their answer to that of the questioner.

- From Dominance: What are we doing?

  Since the 'D' is driven by results, they are often skeptical, direct, and challenging. They expect you to be fast-paced and efficient.

- From Influence: Who is doing this?

  Since the 'I' is enthusiastic, they should be actively encouraged, but they may spend a long time talking and require follow up.

- From Steadiness: Why are we doing this?

[9] And before that, Empedocles 450 BC (air, earth, fire, water); Hippocrates 370 BC (blood, black bile, yellow bile, phlegm); and Plato 340 BC (artistic, sensible, intuitive, reasoning). For more on this, see [22].

[10] On a related note, in 1991, the National Academy of Sciences analyzed more than 20 studies of the Myers-Briggs Type Indicator (MBTI) and concluded that it had not demonstrated adequate validity and that "there is not sufficient, well-designed research to justify the use of the MBTI in career counseling programs."

[11] As always, we let the readers decide.

95

Since the 'S' fears unplanned change and prefers standard processes, they should be given explicit instructions and justification for their assignments.

- From Conscientious: How are we going to do this?

Since the 'C' values accuracy, they analyze concepts and rely on logic. Allow them to criticize because their diligence increases quality.

Since communication is such an important aspect of project management, in Table 7.4 we present some guidance in the form of dos and don'ts:

Table 7.4: Communication Dos and Don'ts for DISC types.

DISC	Do	Don't
D	Focus on results Exhibit confidence Expect bluntness, don't overreact	Don't ramble Don't challenge them, you'll lose Don't promise what you can't deliver
I	Expect talkative & straying off subject Keep them on track Make them center of attention	Don't be curt, cold, businesslike Don't talk down Avoid details & fine print
S	Break the ice first Expect them to be methodological & calm Give them time to think	Don't force quick response Don't interrupt Don't mistake willingness for agreement
C	Give lots of information Respond logically, not emotionally	Avoid being personal & informal Don't get too close. No touching.

Project managers must appreciate that they have to deal with multiple stakeholder behaviors and communication styles. Just because you prefer technical data presented at a fast pace with a boisterous discussion, be prepared to deal with stakeholders who may react negatively. You might have to schedule a separate meeting in which the same information is presented slowly and quietly, with many roundabout diversions and discussions.

8

THE SCOPE

**If you can't explain it simply,
you don't understand it well enough.**

Albert Einstein

The scope document describes both the project, as well as how it is to be accomplished. As such, it is by far the most important document in the entire project.

> *The scope document is a complete description of all the products and services in the project.*

The scope has two functions. First, it describes the features and functions that define and characterize the project. We will reserve the word *specification* for the document that precisely defines what the project is supposed to do.

A good example of a *specification* is an architect's conceptual design drawing, e.g., see Figure 23.2. Stakeholders can evaluate the proposed design to determine if it satisfies their needs (The "What"). At this stage, it is quite normal for the discussion to include all sorts of non-construction issues, such as: Is there enough space for the way we live? Does its style match its surroundings? Is it energy efficient?

Once the conceptual requirements are agreed to, the architect creates the specification (the detailed design–the "How").[1] The specification is usually developed by eliciting requirements from stakeholders.[2]

The second function of the scope is to list organizational and managerial information, such as milestones and deliverables, limits and constraints, and the requirements for communicating with customers and stakeholders. The scope also describes *who* will perform which activity, which is in the *Statement of Work* (SOW). The SOW is usually written based on information from the customer and defines the cost and schedule, the deliverables and milestones, and the reporting criteria on the status of the project. SOW

The scope is the foundation document—it describes everything about the project, both the precise definition of what it is or will do, and how it will be executed. It therefore functions as the primary communication tool between the project team and the stakeholders.[3]

For completeness, we provide the PMBOK definition of the scope:

> *The project scope describes the deliverables and work required to create those deliverables.*

Note that the scope includes *work* to create the deliverables. For example, the scope needs to define things like meetings with the customer, with deliverables (e.g., minutes) as well as the frequency, attendees, etc.

8.1 Beginning the Scope

> **By looking at the questions the kids are asking, we learn the scope of what needs to be done.**
>
> *Buffy Sainte-Marie*

[1] Notice there is still no project management information here, e.g., no cost or schedule.

[2] Unfortunately, as the old saying goes, a user will tell you anything you ask about, but nothing more.

[3] If you mess up the scope, the project is doomed.

It is important to begin with an excellent understanding of the project's high-level goals and objectives. This section develops those ideas by asking some useful questions that help to determine what goes into the scope. For example, suppose our project is to build a web site that registers students for courses.

- *What?*

    These are the requirements. For example, a web site that registers students would include details such as the response time, the number of students that can be handled simultaneously, the general look and feel of the site, testing criteria, etc. There may also be technical and legal requirements, e.g., fire codes for parties and data privacy issues for web sites.

- *How?*

  This is the design for the project. For example, for a web site, one could expect to see a mockup of the user interface, a preliminary database design, and details about networking and communications.

- *When?*

  This is the schedule for the project. For example, the web site should be up and running by the beginning of the next Fall semester.

- *Who?*

  Who will do what? For example, for the web site project, it could consist of a list of tasks to be performed and the person responsible for each task. This information will eventually become the Statement of Work (SOW).

8.1.1 The Theme

If you are planning a party, what is its theme? Suppose you specified the purpose (Mom's birthday), the time and place, as well as the guest list, budget, milestones, and deliverables. You are still missing an important piece: The Theme.

What kind of party is it going to be? Establish the theme early on because it will tell you the important characteristics of the party and explain how to measure success.[4]

8.1.2 Complete and Precise

The scope must be both complete and precise. If you are building a new web page, the scope document defines exactly what the web page is supposed to do. If the scope does not include how to log in, the scope document is incomplete—there is something missing. If the scope specifies that a user name is required, but not the number of allowed characters, then the scope is imprecise.

The scope should have only enough material to be complete and precise. Clear and precise writing is essential.[5] Tables, charts and diagrams accomplish this effectively. Resist the urge to describe a diagram, it duplicates information.

The scope must be complete. Forgetting to define the number of bathrooms will lead to a big problem later. The scope must also be precise. Specifying a bathroom is not precise enough. Does it include a bath or only a shower?

[4] For my Mom's party, there had better be dancing to 1940's Big Band music.

[5] We make no excuse for demanding excellent writing of project managers. Clear communication is an essential skill and good writing is essential.

99

One of the most useful phrases a project manager can use in meetings is, "What does the scope say?" This immediately focuses energy on what is *required*, not what someone would like to implement. Also, there is no arguing with the scope, it is what the customer wants.[6]

8.2 Scope Contents

There are many topics that should be included in a scope document, but we emphasize that the contents of this section should be considered as a checklist, not an outline. The scope for each project is different and the information should be laid out in the format most appropriate to the particular project.

On small projects it is efficient to combine several sections. On the other hand, for large projects, many of the scope sections will be separated out into independently controlled documents. The *Specification* and the *Statement of Work* are the scope sections most often separated out into controlled documents.

8.2.1 The Specification

> **Sometimes I can't figure designers out.**
> **It's as if they flunked human anatomy.**
>
> *Erma Bombeck*

The specification, which is often referred to as the "spec," is the most important piece of the scope. The spec defines what the project is all about.

For a party project, the spec is where one defines all of the features of the party, such as invitations, food, drinks, and venue. However, you must also pay attention to the party's *theme*, which explains what type of party it is supposed to be.[7]

The formal definition of the specification is:

> *The specification completely and precisely defines the required features and functions that characterize the project.*

The spec defines the content for project and it is so important that it is often made into a separate document. This is a good idea, even if the spec document is only a few pages long, because stakeholders constantly refer to it. Also, changes to a separate document are easier to control.

Let's examine some issues in the construction of the specification.

---

[6] Maybe it's not what they want, but at least it's what they agreed to.

[7] It is easy to get caught up in specifying the venue, contracts, and food deliveries and forget that the guests are supposed to have fun.

Design vs. Requirements

The first thing to emphasize in the definition is the word *required*. The specification explains *what is required* and not *how to do it*. Unfortunately, it is sometimes hard to distinguish the "what" from the "how."

In fact, it is naive to think that one can completely specify *what* is to be done without some notion of *how* it is to be accomplished. Suppose you ask a contractor to build a house. You can specify the requirements for the house: a kitchen, three bedrooms, two bathrooms, etc. However, the cost will certainly depend on how it is built, e.g., Is it on one floor or three?

Requirements cannot be specified without a context. That is, there needs to be a justification for each requirement. If you are going to specify eight bedrooms, you also have a responsibility to explain why you need them, that you have sufficient land for the house, and can afford the cost.

Therefore, most projects have a requirements definition phase and part of that work is preliminary design. This design work is not to define how to do the job, but to demonstrate the project's feasibility.[8] This is where you explain why you need eight bedrooms, estimate its cost, and acknowledge that you have the funds for an eight-bedroom house.

When writing the specification, you have the responsibility to demonstrate that the project is *feasible*. This includes cope performance requirements, cost, and schedule. For example, the preliminary design might demonstrate: that performance requirements are achievable (a web site's response time, the span of a bridge); that the cost is appropriate (the design allowed you to conduct a parametric cost analysis); and that the schedule is achievable (a preliminary network diagram resulted in a reasonable schedule).

The primary responsibility of the requirements definition phase is to produce a *feasible* specification.[9]

As you try to refine the requirements, it becomes harder and harder without including design details. For example, suppose you require 25% more kitchen cabinet space in a new kitchen. This is a well-defined requirement with a sound justification, e.g., the current cabinets are overflowing. But, it becomes difficult to specify it more precisely without explaining what the new kitchen will look like (i.e., you are specifying the design). For example, are the new cabinets in the kitchen or in another room, say a pantry? Is a separate pantry acceptable to the owner?

You have the responsibility to demonstrate that "25% more kitchen cabinet space" is feasible both technically (in a suggested plan) and practically (via preliminary cost

[8]The PMBOK defines this as *Collect Requirements*.

[9]It's easy to specify an unrealistic and impossible system with everything in it that you could possibly want. You just won't get it.

101

and schedule estimates). If the only way to get the 25% more space is to knock down walls, then a preliminary cost estimate for that (very expensive) activity should be developed. You can then compare the cost of knocking down walls to the budget and determine if the cost is prohibitive.

A requirements specification activity is also useful in that it helps to clarify the roles of the stakeholders. Discussing requirements will demonstrate the stakeholders' understanding of the project content, their technical competence, their desired level of engagement, and their commitment to the project.[10]

The specification may also include:[11]

- *Traceability information.* The name of a stakeholder is associated with each key functional requirement.

- *Acceptance criteria.* These are the specific, measurable properties of the delivered project. They form the basis of the tests to ensure that the stakeholder requirements have been met. One has to be able to answer questions such as: What are the criteria for satisfying the stakeholder? How are the requirements to be tested?

- *Priority of the Requirements.* Different stakeholders have different priorities that can be classified as "must have" or "nice-to-have," which is a useful way to indicate priorities.

- *Non-Functional Requirements.* These include such items as security, performance, and supportability issues. Specific examples of non-functional requirements are:

    - *Usability*, e.g., the system should be compliant with U.S. Department of Justice Americans with Disabilities Act (ADA).

    - *Availability*, e.g., the website should be hosted with a reliable provider that ensures access 99.9% of the time.

As an example, we present the requirements document for the PMA web site in Table 8.1.

8.2.2 The Project's Justification

Why are you doing the project?[12] The project might be justified as a new business opportunity, a fix to a problem, or a new business process. Often, a new project is motivated by changing regulations (tax, privacy, environmental, etc.) and, in this

[10] This is further elaborated in Chapter 7, Stakeholders.

[11] For small projects, these should be considered as a checklist. That is, a simple one-line statement may be all that is necessary to explain the role of these issues in a small project.

[12] The project manager needs to be able to articulate the case for the project.

Table 8.1: *Requirements document* for the PMA case study.

Category	Requirement	Stakeholder	Acceptance Criteria
Functional Requirements	A form to register new members	PMA Director	Should be user friendly form
	Email Newsletter to members	Marketing Director	Ability to send up to 3,000 emails to members
Maintainability Requirements	Edit Registration form	IT Staff	Easy to add and edit fields in registration form
	Update web site	IT Staff	System easily updated by IT staff
Security	Membership data will be encrypted in the database	Information Assurance Staff	Membership data secure against hacking tests

case, the motive is not profit, but compliance. Whatever the project's justification, it is important to demonstrate that the project is *essential* to the company.[13]

8.2.3 Deliverables and Milestones

For a complete discussion of deliverables and milestones, see Chapter 5. Examples of deliverables for a party are listed in Table 8.2. Note that we have divided them into the major milestones and intermediate milestones. We have also added dates, which might be considered information that goes in the schedule section. However, this is an example of combining information from different sections of the scope into one place. If a change occurs, you will only have to change the information once, eliminating a potential for errors.

Table 8.2: *Deliverables and Milestones* for a party.

Major Milestones	Date
Birthday Party	Aug 15, 2012
Planning Complete	June 30, 2012
Intermediate Milestones	**Date**
Select Venue	February 1, 2012
Contract with Venue	February 15, 2012
Invitations Designed	May 15, 2012
Invitations Sent	June 1, 2012

[13]The project's justification is often documented in the *Business Case* and summarized in the *Charter*.

103

8.2.4 Budget

Customers almost always have a budget, or a target cost, for the project and it should be included in the scope.

If possible, the cost drivers should be established so that a range of costs can be considered. For example, when planning a party, you determine that the major factor driving the cost is the food and drink, estimated at $20 per person. You are planning to invite 50 people, so you might establish a preliminary food and drink budget of $1,000 and an overall party budget of $1,500.

8.2.5 Acceptance Criteria

What will satisfy the stakeholders? How will you know when you are done?

Some thought about the acceptance criteria helps to clarify the scope. For example, for the PMA website, specifying response times will help to define ease of use.

8.2.6 Risks

While developing the scope, it is useful to list any major risks that are recognized at this stage.[14] For example, for a student party project that includes the serving of alcohol, one of the major risks is alcohol consumption by under-age students. Some thought needs to be given to the mitigation of this risk because, if the risk materializes, the consequences could be disastrous. Mitigation might involve hiring security guards to check IDs, but this will increase the cost.

8.2.7 Constraints

It is important to identify the constraints, so they can be analyzed and negotiated.

A constraint is any factor that limits the options for the project.

Some examples of constraints are:

- *Personnel Constraints:* The unavailability of a key technical person will hold things up. For example, in the kitchen project, the architect was the only one who had the skills to use the software program that analyzed beam loading. All changes to the structural design had to be checked by the architect. When he wasn't around, the project suffered a delay.

[14]Risks are discussed in detail in Chapter 17, Risks.

- *Equipment Constraints:* On construction projects, the availability of bulldozers and earth moving equipment is often a constraint, because they cannot be moved quickly from job to job.

- *Contractual Constraints:* The contract often contains staff restrictions, such as the specification of a particular project manager by name. It is not unusual for the customer to demand a "right of approval" for key personnel.

- *Financial Constraints:* Cash flow and borrowing can impose financial constraints.

- *Schedule Constraints:* Significant milestones are schedule constraints and the most important is the delivery date.[15]

Every constraint involves an associated risk because it limits one's options. Therefore, project managers should proactively manage constraints. For example, suppose the scope document for web site project must be available by a specific date. This is a schedule constraint and, if it proves problematic, the project manager may conduct a trade-off to analyze options.

The project manager may elect to accelerate the schedule by hiring an outside consultant, which will increase the cost. Adding a consultant may also introduce new risks because an outsider may not be familiar with critical content details. On the other hand, if the deliverable is a low priority, the project manager may propose to the customer that it be delayed or, perhaps even, deleted altogether.

These examples show how constraints affect projects and how trade-offs require the project manager to examine carefully the different aspects of the issues and propose appropriate solutions.

8.2.8 Limits and Exclusions

It is useful to define what the project will *not* do. This often provokes interesting discussions with the customer.[16]

8.2.9 Assumptions

We begin with the definition:

> *An assumption is any factor considered to be true.*

This a bit cryptic and, by itself, not much help. So, here's an example:

---

[15] Another example of a schedule constraint: In the City of Boston, construction of roads cannot continue after October 31st.

[16] Particularly when they discover that their favorite requirement is excluded.

105

The customer will provide the new computer for the web site.

First, the project manager has to recognize this as an *assumption*, which means it is assumed to be true. The project manager would then explicitly define the assumption in the scope document. Also, the project manager should assess the implications of the assumption and, in this case, might add:

The selected model shall process all transactions in the specified time.

We see immediately how important it is to document explicitly both the assumption and its implications. The above addition to the scope's assumptions clearly assigns responsibility for the hardware to the customer.

If the customer-provided hardware turns out not to perform the transactions satisfactorily, the project manager may seek schedule relief or additional funds from the customer to fix the problem. If the assumption were not explicitly documented, it is not clear who would pay to fix the problem.

If the hardware provided by the customer turns out not to meet the throughput requirement, the project manager may offer the following options to the customer:

1. If the current transaction throughput is close to the specified performance, it might be acceptable to the users. If so, the throughput requirement may be relaxed, i.e., the scope would be changed. Some minor modifications to the user manual and training may be also required. This is very low risk and will incur no additional cost or schedule delay.

2. Upgrade the server at a cost of $5,000. This is considered a low risk solution that has a high likelihood of solving the problem. There may also be a schedule delay associated with purchasing the new hardware.

3. Redesign the database to speed up the transactions at a cost of $8,000. This is considered high risk and still may not meet the throughput goals.

The project manager is offering the stakeholders options and they get to select the one that they are most comfortable with. Without the defined assumption (the assignment of the responsibility for the hardware), the customer may just say, "It's in the scope, make it work."

Assumptions and are sometimes hidden, or not obvious, and can arise from diverse issues: The customer's desire to review documents may introduce delays; interactions with company management may affect the acquisition of funds; specialist subcontractors may not understand the technical content.

Other examples of assumptions are:

- *Schedule Assumptions:* The approval date of permits by city or state governments; the availability of plans from an architect; the availability of hardware or software by certain dates.

- *Personnel Assumptions:* When redecorating, we all know how frustrating it can be to wait on plumbers, electricians, carpenters, and painters, who are frequently not available when you are, or when they were scheduled.

- *Financial Assumptions:* This may involve the availability of funds to purchase equipment or cash for the payroll.

8.2.10 Technical Requirements

Projects are subject to laws, regulations, and external standards, which are called *Technical Requirements*. Many technical requirements are found in industry standards, such as plumbing and electrical codes, environmental regulations, laws, and tax regulations. Other technical requirements are found in security controls, privacy standards, and human resources regulations.

For example, if you decide to include fireworks in your party, you must satisfy all fire department regulations and, even, pay for an on-duty fireman at the event. Other examples of technical requirements are the privacy regulations associated with collecting user data, some of which are legal requirements, some are good industry standards, and some depend on the country in which the data is held.

The details associated with Technical Requirements are not included in the scope, but are incorporated "by reference." That is, all applicable documents are formally referenced in the scope and all of their conditions must be upheld.

8.3 Statement of Work (SOW)

The SOW is the basis of the *contract* between the customer and the organization performing the project because it specifies who is to deliver what and when.

> *The statement of work (SOW) is a description of the products and services to be supplied during the project.*

The length and complexity of the SOW depends on the size of the project and it is usually a separate document from the scope. The SOW and the scope are closely linked, as the scope specifies what is to be done and the SOW specifies who will perform the task. There may be several versions of the SOW as the project evolves: A short SOW for a request for proposal; the winning bidder may then develop a detailed SOW. Whatever the stage of the project, and whatever its size, the SOW contains the following information:

- Tasks to be performed, and by whom.

- Deliverables and Milestones (with dates).

- Schedule of reviews with customers and stakeholders.

- Cost and schedule reporting criteria.

- Payment terms and the payment schedule.

- Legalities, such as cancellation clauses, Force Majeure,[17] etc.

An important part of the SOW is the *Customer Interface*, which specifies how often the project manager will meet with customers, and other stakeholders, and what information will be reported. As a minimum, the project manager reports progress on the status of the deliverables, the accumulating costs, and the predicted schedule.

The project manager must be careful not to introduce overlap and repetition between the sections of the scope. The SOW, in particular, is liable to contain duplicate information, such as deliverable dates. We emphasize therefore, that the sections described in this chapter should be regarded as a checklist, not a document outline. Where you put what will be different for each project.

The job of the project manager is to find creative ways to include all the information without repetition. Tables are an excellent way to combine sections of the scope without repeating information. For example, Table 8.2 combines milestones and deliverables. One could also add a column for the staff member responsible, which will avoid duplication in the SOW, as well as making important information clear.

[17]All contracts have one of these clauses, but few of us actually understand them.

8.4 The Triple Constraints

Projects change and, therefore, so does the scope. A key to managing the scope is to realize that any change will induce ripples throughout the project, which is indicated in Figure 8.1, as the "Jell-O® Triangle."[18]

[18]This is sometimes referred to as the *Iron Triangle*, but we prefer to think of it as the *Jell-O* triangle. Frankly, we can't think of anything less like iron.

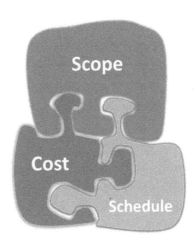

Figure 8.1: The Jell-O® Triangle: The triple constraints of scope, cost and schedule.

This is a visual device used to communicate the idea that changing any one of the three aspects of the project (scope, time, cost) will result in changes to the other two. For example, if the customer suggests adding content to the project, the cost will probably increase and the schedule will lengthen. Similarly, a reduction in cost can usually only be accommodated by a reduction in scope.

Sometimes, *quality* is inserted in the center of the triangle to indicate that quality is affected by the balancing the scope, cost, and schedule. Actually, everything is affected by such changes, including risks, contracts, etc.[19]

8.5 The Priority Matrix

Figure 8.1 illustrates that when a change is proposed, it is likely to affect the scope, cost and schedule. But which one has priority? Is holding the budget more important than keeping to the schedule? Complicating the decision is that different stakeholders will have conflicting views of priorities, making it difficult to propose a uniformly acceptable approach.

The tool to help manage this issue is called the *priority matrix* and an example is shown in Table 8.3. The *priority matrix* is created during scope development, but its real purpose is to manage changes during implementation. The idea is to establish the relative priorities between scope, cost, or schedule.

To do that, we first pick either the scope or the cost or the schedule and assign it to one of three categories:

[19]So why put just quality in the middle? Personally, we think this is dumb.

109

Table 8.3: The *Priority Matrix* for a fighter jet.

	Scope	Schedule	Cost
Constrain	■		
Enhance		■	
Accept			■

- *Constrain:* If we constrain the scope, we are saying that maintaining the scope is more important than keeping to the cost and schedule. In practice, this means that we refuse to compromise on the performance characteristics.

  An example of this situation occurs when developing a military system, such as a fighter jet. The scope specifies the requirements for the jet (speed, range, payload, etc.), which are not negotiable. For example, the maximum speed may be defined by the requirement that the jet be faster than all potential adversaries. During the development of the jet, changes might be proposed, but they will be rejected if they compromise the speed requirement.

- *Enhance:* Once we accept that the scope is constrained, we next chose between cost and schedule to enhance it as best we can, given that we cannot compromise the scope.

  Continuing the example of the jet, we might choose to enhance the schedule because we want the jet in place as soon as possible to replace its obsolete predecessor. That is, we take all opportunities to deliver early without compromising the scope.

- *Accept:* Once we accept that the scope is constrained and that the schedule is enhanced, we must accept the cost implications.

  Continuing the example of the jet, when a change is proposed, we only accept it if it does not compromise the performance characteristics in the scope and, after taking all opportunities to enhance the schedule, we must *accept* the cost implication, which is almost always a cost overrun.

This is all documented in Table 8.3, where the bullet in the *constrain* row is in the scope column. The scope is constrained, so we will accept no compromises on the performance. The bullet in the *enhance* row is in the schedule column, denoting that we will take all opportunities to enhance the schedule, but not compromise the performance. The bullet in the *accept* row is in the cost column, denoting that we will accept the cost implications that do not compromise the performance or the schedule.

The *priority matrix* is filled out with exactly three bullets, with only one bullet in each row and only one bullet in each column.

As another example, consider the project of organizing a party for my Dad's birthday. The *priority matrix* is shown in Table 8.4 and we have stated that the schedule is constrained because once we have fixed the date, it cannot change.[20] We decide that we are on a very tight budget, so we take all opportunities to save money. If that results in a slightly less fancy party, we will accept that.[21]

Table 8.4: The *Priority Matrix* for my Dad's birthday party.

	Scope	Schedule	Cost
Constrain		■	
Enhance			■
Accept	■		

The project manager should develop the priority matrix during scope development and put it on the wall for everyone to see.[22] When changes are proposed, the project manager uses the *priority matrix* to referee between stakeholders.

8.6 Scope Issues

8.6.1 Scope Creep

The customer is always right! Keep the customer happy!

Simply following these admonitions leads to a serious problem: *scope creep.*

Scope creep is the tendency of the requirements to grow over time.

Gold Plating is the phrase used to describe the process of adding things into the scope that are merely nice to have. The key is for the project manager to focus on *refining* the scope, not *embellishing* it.

Stakeholders and customers often try to add functionality and the project manager must guard against this by carefully managing changes.[23] Before implementing a proposed change, the project manager should review all proposed content changes, evaluate the risks, and estimate the impact on cost and schedule. Then the customer can decide whether or not to approve the change, balancing the improvement in performance against the cost and schedule implications.

[20] My Dad's birthday is August 21st. We can save money by having the party in September. Ain't gonna happen.

[21] Dad will be so happy we are having a party that he won't care where it is held.

[22] We suggest that there are at least two things that every project manager needs on the wall: The priority matrix and the network with the critical path.

[23] This is formally known as *Change Control.*

111

Most projects are under tight cost and schedule constraints and presenting the impact of changes will immediately force the customer to assess the true value of the changes and to prioritize them. Scope creep almost always results in cost overruns and delays, but, despite this, it is a common project affliction because of the relentless pressure to satisfy the customer.

While changes are inevitable, it is important to realize that scope creep is not. Clarifications and refinements are acceptable and, in fact, necessary. It is enhancements that must be ruthlessly assessed. Each proposed change should be analyzed to determine its impact on scope, cost, and schedule.[24]

A clear, well-defined specification immediately allows the project team to determine when extra work is being proposed. Therefore, a clear, detailed specification is an insurance policy against scope creep, while a specification that is broad and imprecise is an invitation for scope creep.

The tension between satisfying the customer and staying within cost and schedule is nicely illustrated by the practices of builders of super yachts.[25] A super yacht is a boat over 40 meters in length and they are typically built under a fixed cost contract. A 40 meter power boat costs around $60 million.

When the customer asks for an upgrade to the latest electronic gizmo, it is hard to justify asking for an extra few thousand dollars when the bill is already in the millions. Therefore, doing "small favors" for the customer is good business. However, when a major change is requested, the builder will attempt to renegotiate the contract to accommodate the major add-on.[26]

8.6.2 Avoiding Repeated Information

It is important that scope information not be repeated. If a data item occurs in multiple places in the scope, then, when a change is approved,[27] it is easy to miss the changes to the repeated data items.

For example, suppose the scope specified that transactions shall be processed at 100 per second and that this is duplicated in several places. After a timing analysis, it is decided that the data rate should be 120 transactions per second, but this is only updated in one place. The contractor will select the easiest one to implement (100 transactions per second).

When you conduct the acceptance test, you will determine that the system is only processing 100 per second and complain the developer. They will innocently point to the scope page where is says 100 transactions per second. Not only that, they will charge for the update to 120 transactions per second.[28]

[24]This is the subject of *Integrated Change Control*, see Chapter 6.

[25]As described by our colleague *Steve Leybourne* in [25]. People unfamiliar with the complexity and magnitude of super yacht projects may learn more by visiting www.feadship.nl and www.lurssen.com.

[26]And attempts to make up for previous favors.

[27]Which is inevitable.

[28]This is not far-fetched, I have seen it happen on numerous occasions.

One way to deal with this issue is to use a phrase such as, "the data transaction rate," throughout the scope. Then, in a clearly labeled section, you can define the numerical value for the data transaction rate. Usually, there are several of these parameters and they can be collected in a table, where they are clearly visible.

Dates are also candidates for repetition because they naturally occur in several scope sections, such as Milestones, Deliverables, Staff Assignments, and Schedule. One way to deal with this is to place all dates in a single table. Then, when any date changes, only one place needs to be edited.

Duplicate dates can arise is as follows. A team is working on a party project and decides to survey the guests to see if they had a good time. The team proposes to send out the survey two days after the party, which is planned for May 11th. They can write this requirement as:

1. The survey will be sent out on May 13th.

2. The survey will be sent two days after the party.

If the date of the party is changed, either during planning or if there is postponement due to rain, the date to send out the survey will also change and #1 will now be incorrect. However, #2 will still be correct, and is the preferred approach.

8.6.3 Plan, Scope & Specification

The plan covers the *management* of the project and describes the *process*. The plan also covers *how (and when)* the project is to be developed (e.g., first the charter, then the scope, etc.) and whether the process is to be agile or traditional.

The scope is a description of all the products and services and includes the specification, justification, business case, risks, constraints, assumptions, etc.

The critical piece of the scope is the specification, which details *what* is to be built (as distinct from the plan, which covers *how* it is to be built).

While separate entities, the plan, scope and specification are all closely related. For example, the plan contains cost and schedule estimates of deliverables, which are described in the specification. As the project proceeds, the actual cost of the deliverables is measured against the plan. Proposed changes also illustrate how these entities are related. Changes can be proposed to the plan (accept the late delivery), the scope (change the management process), or the specification (change the content to be delivered).

8.6.4 Writing the Scope

> **The most essential gift for a good writer is a built-in, shockproof sh**t-detector.**
>
> *Ernest Hemingway*

Good writing is essential in project management and nowhere is that more important than in the scope.[29]

One might be tempted to think that the scope is always a long and complicated document, which would be wrong.[30] While the scope must be complete and precise, one should ruthlessly cut it.[31] Clarity is the objective, not length.

The scope sections should be regarded as a checklist, not an outline. If you include a table of deliverables, you can satisfy the milestone requirement by simply adding a date column.[32] If a separate milestone table were included, information would have to be changed in two places, which is a source of errors and to be avoided at all costs.[33]

Many scope sections are interrelated. For example, a construction permit may involve an assumption (customer will obtain permit), a schedule constraint (permit in 30 days), and an exclusion (does not include environmental permit). All permit information should be one place, so that if anything about the permit changes, only one part of the scope need change.

Finally, early on it is vital to establish the key ideas—the *theme*. It is easy to get caught up in the technical details and forget to provide the essential feel of the project: Spanish dancing.[34]

To become a good project manager, practice writing.[35]

> *Do not put statements in the negative form.*
> *And don't start sentences with a conjunction.*
> *If you reread your work, you will find on rereading that a*
> *great deal of repetition can be avoided by rereading and editing.*
> *Never use a long word when a diminutive one will do.*
> *Unqualified superlatives are the worst of all.*
> *De-accession euphemisms.*
> *If any word is improper at the end of a sentence, a linking verb is.*
> *Avoid trendy locutions that sound flaky.*
> *Last, but not least, avoid clichès like the plague.*

[29] The difference between the right word and the almost right word is the difference between lightning and the lightning bug—Mark Twain

[30] I have only made this letter rather long because I have not had time to make it shorter—Blaise Pascal.

[31] There is but one art, to omit—Robert Louis Stevenson.

An elegant commandment that I have disobeyed to get you to obey it. How ironic.

[32] An example of specifying information in exactly one place.

[33] A friend of mine has a sign over his desk that says, **OHIO**—only handle it once.

[34] While leaving out the cost and schedule may be disastrous, failing to specify the Spanish costumes and dances will be much worse: A boring party.

[35] *Great Rules of Writing* — William Safire.

8.7 Sample Scope Statement

In Figure 8.2, we provide a sample scope statement for the kitchen project. Note that the scope references external documents such as building codes and the specification, which is described in Chapter 23—The New Kitchen.

Scope Statement

Objective:
To renovate a kitchen within 6 months at cost not to exceed $63,000.
Justification:
Old cabinets and small workspace. Unused spaces of little value.
Deliverables:
Conceptual Design and Detailed Design.
Sheet rock (Partial payment required).
Cabinets, Appliances, Flooring.

	Demolition Complete	Estimated March 31st.
Milestones:	Gas line installed	Estimated April 15th.
	Cabinet Delivery	Estimated July 1st.

Specification:
See Figure 23.2 and associated documents.
Cost Estimate:
See spreadsheet of the estimated costs. Cost estimate $63,000.
Risks:
Cabinet delivery is schedule risk. **Limits and Exclusions:**
Contractor responsible for all construction permits.
Constraints:
Schedule: Work substantially complete before guests arriving September 1st.
Assumptions:
Contractor responsible for all subcontractors and their costs.
Painting not included in the bid.
Technical Requirements:
Architect responsible for all safety and loading requirements.
All construction to be consistent with local regulations and codes:
carpentry, safety, plumbing, electrical, environmental, etc.
Customer Reviews:
Monthly meetings with Joan Smith (PM) and John Smith (Sponsor).

Figure 8.2: Sample *Scope Statement* for the New Kitchen project.

CHAPTER

9

THE WBS

**The secret of getting ahead is getting started.
The secret of getting started is breaking your complex
overwhelming tasks into small manageable tasks,
and then starting on the first one.**

Unknown

Once the scope is complete and approved, the next step is to create the Work Break-down Structure (WBS), which it is the foundation for all steps to follow, particularly the development of the cost and schedule.

The definition of the WBS is:

> *The WBS is a deliverable-oriented hierarchical decomposition of the work to be accomplished, with each descending level representing an increasingly detailed definition of the work.*

There are several important aspects to this definition.

- The WBS is a reorganization of the information in the scope, which means that no new information is being added.

117

- The WBS is hierarchical, which means that the project work is continually divided into smaller and smaller activities.

- The WBS is *deliverable-oriented*, which means the focus is on the deliverables that are produced in each piece.

The best way to understand a WBS is through an example. Suppose the project is to make the invitations for a party, a portion of its WBS is shown in Figure 9.1.

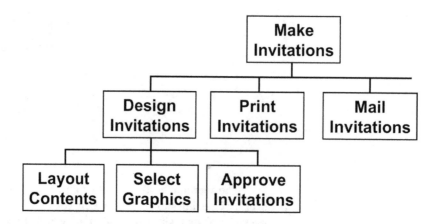

Figure 9.1: A portion of the WBS for a *Make Invitations* project.

The first thing to observe is that the WBS is hierarchical, which means that it is tree structured and decomposed into in layers. At the top, we have a box or, more correctly, an activity, that represents the entire project (*Make Invitations*). As one proceeds downwards, the layers contain more detail.

However, it is important that when decomposing a parent node, no new information is added in the child layers. For example, the *Design Invitations* activity only contains *design* activities, it does not include printing or mailing activities.

The second level of the tree contains three activities (*Design Invitations*, *Print Invitations*, and *Mail Invitations*). The *Design Invitations* activity is decomposed further into *Layout Contents*, *Select Graphics*, and *Approve Invitations*.

The meaning of the phrase, *deliverable-oriented*, is twofold: First, each activity in the WBS produces a deliverable and, second, its production is described by a verb. For example, the top-level activity produces of a deliverable (Invitations) and that production is described by a verb (Make). When constructing a WBS, the project manager must ensure that every activity produces a deliverable and that it is correctly described by its verb.

Care must be taken to select the appropriate verb. The top-level activity in Figure 9.1 could read either *Design Invitations* or *Buy Invitations*. Both are acceptable options with the same deliverable (Invitations), but with completely different verbs (Design vs. Buy) with different skills, costs, and schedules.

Buy Invitations is an easy activity, one simply goes to the store and purchases them, whereas *Design Invitations* requires a lot more work. Also, the activities produce subtly different deliverables. *Design Invitations* results in a paper design, while *Buy Invitations* results in actual invitations.

One also has to be careful not to unintentionally add information. The *Mail Invitations* activity may, or may, not be considered as a legitimate part of its parent, *Make Invitations* if the skills required for mailing are completely different from the skills required for designing and printing. On the other hand, the design group may have special skills for printing mailing labels, in which case, *Mail Invitations* correctly belongs as part of the Make Invitations box.

Notice that the decision as to whether *Mail Invitations* is part of *Design Invitations* is a decision specific to the project and illustrates an important aspect of the WBS: It is a *creative* process and there is no automated way to generate a good WBS.

Organizations often have WBS templates oriented to their specific business, which saves work and gets the process started. But a template is not the answer, as all projects are different, and the team should *design* a unique WBS for their project.

9.1 WBS Construction Rules

We have used the word, *activity* to describe the boxes in the WBS, but we have not yet defined it. Each piece of the WBS will become an *activity*, which is defined as:

> *An activity is anything that consumes time.*

We again see the importance of the verb: The activity consumes time while producing the deliverable. We can now describe the rules to follow in the construction of a WBS:

WBS Rule #1
Each WBS activity is derived explicitly from, and traceable back to, the scope.[1]

The traceability from Scope → WBS ensures that nothing is left out of the project.

[1] Technically, the chunks of the WBS are components of the system and/or deliverables. They do not become activities until later in the project development cycle. However, since they will almost always turn into activities, we occasionally cheat and use the word here. It is clearer to talk about "activities" than components.

119

WBS activities can come from many sources. Obviously, work is necessary to create the project deliverables. However, there are also project activities that have to do with the *process*, and these need to be in the WBS to ensure that all activities are in the Statement of Work.

Project management activities also belong in the WBS, e.g., *Develop Scope* is an activity (it consumes time), the verb is 'Develop,' and the deliverable is the *scope*. Many parts of the scope contribute activities. For example, an *assumption* may define that the home owner will obtain the permit for construction. In which case, the WBS should contain an activity called *Get Permit*. The deliverable is clear (the Permit).

WBS Rule #2

WBS activities are defined by active verbs.

Note the importance of the verb 'make' in *Make Invitations*, it immediately expresses the idea that we are going to *make* the invitations and not going to *purchase* ready-made invitations. If we had decided to buy ready-made invitations, the top-level box would say *Buy Invitations.*[2]

As another example, consider *Pour Foundation*. The verb 'pour' clarifies that the foundation is to be poured and not dropped in as a completed entity. Pouring also implies the need for a form to pour concrete into, the scheduling and arrival of a delivery truck, a time to harden, etc. All that derives just from the verb 'pour.' [3]

WBS Rule #3

The child activities together make up the parent activity, and only the parent activity.

When decomposing an activity, it is easy to add things into the project. Ensure that the decomposition only implements the contents of the parent, and no more.

For example, *Design Invitations* only involves *designing* graphics. If someone proposes *creating* graphics, this is scope creep. If you feel the urge to add something into the WBS, you should first request a change to the scope. If the ruling is that the change is a clarification, then you can go ahead. If it is an addition, do not proceed.

WBS Rule #4

The WBS is deliverable-oriented: all of the activities must produce a deliverable.

In Figure 9.1, all of the activities produce a deliverable, even the *Approve Invitations* activity: The Letter of Approval from the customer.

We have continually emphasized the idea that deliverables are tangible, e.g., the *Pour Foundation* activity produces the tangible concrete foundation. By concentrating on deliverables and their verbs, you remove ambiguity about the activity. Also, you will easily be able to tell when the activity *Pour Foundation* is complete.[4]

[2]The later versions of the PMBOK define all activities in terms of verbs. We've been campaigning for verbs for years and are delighted to see the world catch up with us.

[3]The WBS is enhanced by strong, active verbs and, unlike your English class, it is quite acceptable to repeat verbs. Always go for the precise and correct verb, even if you have to repeat it, e.g., *make invitations, make table settings*, etc.

[4]You won't be able to carve your initials in the concrete.

120

WBS Rule #5

There is no time ordering in the WBS.[5]

The WBS is just a list of activities. This means that when developing the WBS, you should never say things like "Printing comes *before* Mailing." Neither should you say "Mailing comes *after* Design." When designing the WBS, stay away from words like *before*, *after*, and *first*.[6]

WBS Rule #6

The 4 ± 2 *Activities Rule.*

Psychologists tell us that we can only hold about 4-5 ideas in our heads simultaneously. Since all of the activities in a layer are related, that means we should not have more than 5 or 6 of them in a layer. If you have more than that, you should combine them into more manageable pieces.

When developing a WBS, it is not unusual in the early stages for some layers to sprawl across the page. This is where creative design is required. What activities should be grouped together? Why should activities be combined? What will be the result of combining activities? There are reasonable answers to these questions, which we explore below when we talk about WBS design.

WBS Rule #7

The WBS is Progressively Elaborated.

The first version of the WBS is usually at a high level and, as project planning proceeds, more detail is added. Clarifying the design and detailing the deliverables is called *progressive elaboration*. Clarifying the planning of schedules and costs is also called *rolling wave planning*.

Excessive decomposition at inappropriate times, or in low priority sections, is unproductive. Therefore, not all levels need to be developed to the same level of detail, it is perfectly acceptable for the tree to be unbalanced. For example, in Figure 9.1, the activity *Design Invitations* is decomposed, but *Mail Invitations* is not. This is perfectly acceptable because *Mail Invitations* is pretty straightforward and needs no more decomposition.

The early work on the WBS tends to validate the scope by finding errors and missing activities. The later work on the WBS moves more towards design and begins to refine the project content and performance.

WBS Rule #8

Resist Obvious Details.

When developing the WBS, focus on the important issues, particularly the parts

[5]Sequencing of activities comes later when we construct the network diagram.

[6]It is quite acceptable, and even normal, to arrange the activities as we did in Figure 9.1, where the earlier stuff is on the left. It's just that you are not allowed to say it.

121

that are uncertain. Avoid the temptation to provide a lot of detail in areas that you know a lot about just because you know it.

For example, when developing the WBS for a party project, novices often elaborate the food and drink in excruciating detail. Once you have established that you are planning a "Beer and Pizza" party, it does not add value to list 12 kinds of beer and 6 types of pizza. Focus on the important issues, particularly the parts that are uncertain.

9.2 Some Bad WBS Practices

In Figure 9.2, we have deliberately committed a number of WBS no-nos.

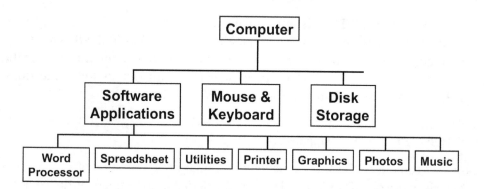

Figure 9.2: Some WBS No-Nos.

First, there are no verbs. The *Software Applications* activity contains a word processor, spreadsheet, and utilities, but we do not know whether we are to develop them or to buy them, which makes a huge difference. Also, the *Software Applications* activity is decomposed into too many child activities. It violates the 4 ± 2 rule.

The child activities mix apples and oranges: What is the *Printer* doing there? Since there is no verb, we do not know if it is printer software (in which case it might belong), or the physical printer (in which case it does not belong).

We might consider dividing the *Software Applications* node into *Applications* and *Utilities*. Then we have to decide which software goes where. Suppose the applications are expensive and require a careful evaluation of features vs. cost. On the other hand, suppose the utilities are generally low cost and we just have to select which ones we want. In that case, it makes sense in the WBS to separate the applications from the utilities.

That separation also improves project management because they are different types of activities requiring different skills and we can assign different people. This separation is an example of a WBS *design choice.*[7] and is an excellent example of how to go about the aggregating vs. decomposing process. It is about making the process easier to manage. Separating the complex software application evaluation from the simpler utilities acquisition put like things together.

We emphasize that the design of the WBS should facilitate the *management* of the project, not the design of the system.

9.3 Graphical vs. Outline WBS

There are two ways to present the WBS: graphical and outline. The graphical format is a good tool for the presentation of the status of the project to stakeholders and upper management. As details are added, the graphical format rapidly gets cumbersome and the outline format is preferable.

9.3.1 Graphical WBS

Figure 9.3 shows a high-level WBS for a kitchen remodeling project. In this form, it is called a *Graphical WBS.*

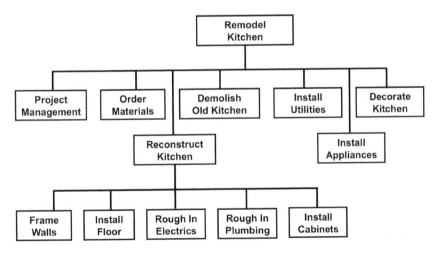

Figure 9.3: Graphical format WBS for a kitchen remodeling project.

[7]You should be careful with these, as they will haunt you for a long time.

123

At this point, we have a first pass for the WBS and it is now time to analyze it. The first step is to go back to the scope document and make sure that all of its requirements, features, and management processes are included in the WBS. Next, we examine all of the other existing documentation (Business Case, SOW, risk plans, etc.) and again ensure that all those requirements are in the WBS.[8]

The first layer decomposition has seven nodes. This is probably too many, so we should consider aggregating some. Therefore, we will ask some questions and give suggestions as to how to proceed.[9]

1. *Order Materials.* Separating this out makes sense if one person (or a single department) orders everything. The project manager can determine the status of all orders by asking one person. On the other hand, if the appliances are to be ordered by the customer, but the plumber and electrician order their own materials, it might not make sense to have a single ordering activity.

2. *Utilities.* These are scattered throughout the WBS. We have *Install Utilities* at the top level and plumbing and electrics at a lower level. We might consider moving the plumbing and electrics under utilities.

   Here are some issues to consider: Can the utilities be better *managed* if they are under one unified *Install Utilities* node? Or, is it better to leave them under *Reconstruct Kitchen*? Since the plumbers and electricians will almost certainly be separate sub-contractors, with their own skills, costs, schedules, and deliverables, perhaps it makes more sense to manage them under an *Install Utilities* node.

3. The floor and framing are carpentry activities and, so, belong together. In which case, they are probably acceptable where they are. Notice that we learned something: When we remove the plumbing and electric activities from *Reconstruct Kitchen*, what remains are activities for only carpenters. Therefore, a better name for the activity might be *Do Carpentry*.[10]

These examples illustrate important features of the WBS design process. Activities are continuously moved around, grouped, ungrouped, and renamed.[11] As you refine, add and decompose activities, the WBS quickly expands beyond the page. At this point, separate pages can be developed for activities that are relatively independent. For example, we could separate out the carpentry, and place it on a separate page. Since this is an important piece of the project, this page will make managing much easier.

---

[8] Notice the Project Management box in the WBS. It needs a verb, but it does contain deliverables: Scope, WBS, etc.

[9] There is no automatic process for decomposing a WBS, it is a creative process.

[10] We don't know the verb for *Carpentry*, so the boring "Do" will have to suffice.

[11] It is a good idea to begin the WBS design using sticky notes, which can be easily moved around.

9.3.2 Outline WBS

When the WBS becomes too complicated for a graphical representation, there is another option that is much better for presenting the details: The *Outline WBS Format*. and an example of this is shown in Figure 9.4.

```
0    Kitchen
     1.    Plan Project
           1.1      Obtain Loan
           1.2      Obtain Permit
     2.    Order Everything
           2.1      Select & Order Cabinets
           2.2      Select Appliances
     3.    Demolish Old Kitchen
     4.    Manage Utilities
           4.1      Install Plumbing
           4.2      Install Electrics
           4.3      Install Appliances
                    4.3.1    Install Gas Range
                    4.3.2    Install Refrigerator
                    4.3.3    Install Electric Appliances
     5.    Do Carpentry
           5.1      Install Floor
           5.2      Install Frame Walls
     6.    Decorate Kitchen
           6.1      Plaster Walls
           6.2      Paint Walls
```

Figure 9.4: Outline WBS Format for a kitchen remodeling project.

The outline format requires a numbering system, so that when we view an activity, we know where it belongs in the hierarchy. There are several ways to number the WBS[12] and our preferred method is shown in Figure 9.4, where each major subsystem in numbered sequentially. Another method is to number the kitchen as 1.0, but then everything has a '1.' in front of it—see Figure 9.5.[13]

One can also use letters for the major subsystems, which is useful when a large system is being developed, because you can use meaningful letters for subsystems. For example, in Figure 9.6, activities at the top system level are labeled with an 'A'. The software subsystem activities are labeled with an 'S', the radar activities with an 'R', etc. On a large system, this has the advantage of immediately indicating the area of expertise. When a staff member calls and says, activity R.2.6.4.3 is going to be late, the project manager at least knows it's in the radar subsystem.

[12] The simplest way to number a WBS is just to let *Microsoft Project* do it.

[13] You might object that the carpentry came after the utilities, which is illogical. However, we remind you that there is *no order* in a WBS. It is simply a list of activities.

125

```
1.0     Kitchen
  1.1     Plan Project
            1.1.1       Obtain Loan
            1.1.2       Obtain Permit
  1.2     Order Everything
            1.2.1       Select & Order Cabinets
            1.2.2       Select Appliances
  1.3     Demolish Old Kitchen
  1.4     Manage Utilities
```

Figure 9.5: Outline WBS numbered starting with 1.0.

```
A     Major System
  A.1     Collect System Requirements
  A.2     Design System
  A.3     Design Interfaces
S     Software
            S.1       Requirements Collection
            S.2       Design Software
            S.3       Code & Test
P     Project Management
R     Radar System
            R.1       Design Radar subsystem
            R.2       Design Radar Hardware
            R.3       Build & Test Radar System
T     Test System
            T.1       Test System
            T.2       Test Subsystems
            T.3       Test Interfaces
U       Train Users
X       Conduct Acceptance Tests
```

Figure 9.6: Outline WBS using letters for major subsystems.

9.4 WBS Design

In Figure 9.2, we provided some examples of the issues involved in the aggregating vs. decomposing process when designing a WBS. For example, separating the complex software application evaluation from the simpler utilities acquisition put like things together. Also, experts in software applications may not be experts in utilities, which provides another reason to divide them into separate entities.

We emphasize that the design of the WBS should facilitate the *management* of the project. Note that we are not facilitating the design of the system, a subtle but important distinction. The system designer has different goals, such as improving coherence (putting like things together), and reducing coupling (inter-dependencies).

9.4.1 Work Packages

The lowest level activities in the WBS are called *work packages*; they are the leaves of the tree and the definition is as follows:

> *Work packages are the lowest level items in the WBS and represent the level at which the activity's cost and duration can be reliably estimated and managed.*

For example, in the *Make Invitations* project in Figure 9.1, *Select Graphics* and *Mail Invitations* are work packages, since they are not decomposed further.

Initially, when the WBS is first constructed, the work packages identify:

- The outputs required, i.e., the deliverables.

- The work to be performed described by active verbs.

As project planning proceeds, and information becomes available, the WBS work packages accumulate more information:

The time to complete or the completion date.
A time-phased budget, i.e., the estimated cost.
The resources (personnel, time, and equipment) required.
A single person who is responsible.
Monitoring points (milestones) for measuring progress.
Documentation: scope cross-reference, technical requirements, etc.
Relevant contract information.

9.4.2 Work Package Size

The WBS should be decomposed until the activities are small enough to satisfy the following guide:

> **The $1 \rightarrow 2$ Rule:**
> *A work package should be able to be completed by $1 - 2$ people in $1 - 2$ weeks.*

The rationale for this rule is that if something goes wrong, the project manager will learn about it quickly. The problem may still remain, but the project manager will have options, such as changing staff assignments, requesting clarification, etc.

9.4.3 Control Accounts

People's hours must be tracked to ensure that the correct costs are assigned to the project. This requires recording the hours worked and assigning the resulting cost to the correct WBS activity. For example, in Figure 9.4, the person working on the *Install Refrigerator* activity may report their hours with the code: 4.3.2.[14]

Costs are tracked using *Control Accounts*, which are designated after the WBS has been constructed and are selected to track and manage the deliverables.

> *The WBS activity used for the project cost accounting is called the Control Account (CA). Each control account is assigned a unique code, or number, that links directly to the company's accounting system.*

Control Accounts are not the lowest level work packages, but usually contain an appropriately aggregated set of activities. For example, in Figure 9.4, the control accounts could be assigned at the level of *1. Plan Project, 2. Order Everything*, etc. Costs are allocated to all WBS activities, but are managed at the *Control Account* level.

Control accounts are often associated with departments responsible for the work, e.g., in Figure 9.4, *1. Plan Project* is assigned to the project management department; and *2. Order Everything* to the purchasing department.

9.4.4 WBS Dictionary

The detailed information about each activity in the WBS is recorded in the *WBS Dictionary*, which accumulates over time as the project proceeds. It contains deliverable information, costs and schedules, assigned personnel, acceptance criteria, technical requirements, and contract information. The definition of the WBS Dictionary is:

> *The WBS Dictionary is a detailed description of the work and technical documentation for each WBS element.*

Table 9.1 provides an example of a *WBS Dictionary* element for the PMA project.

9.4.5 WBS and the Cost Estimate

[14]Or, more likely, the company's information system will assign a number code that maps to the WBS item 4.3.2.

The WBS converts the scope into activities to be completed and is, therefore, the primary input to all activities that follow. Therefore, the accuracy of the cost and schedule estimates depends directly on the quality of the WBS.

Table 9.1: *A WBS Dictionary Element* for PMA Project

WBS Code	WBS Element
2.1	Create a Data Entry Form to Register New Members
	WBS Element Description The entry form should consist of first name, last name and email address. Additional information includes education, college, current job title. The form should have format validation for the email and test that the first name and last name are not blank. The QA department will test the form after it has been tested by the project team. QA will test for ADA compliance.
Milestone	Should be completed by November 30th.
Responsible	Joe Smith
Cost	8 hours, $400
Tests	Test the edit of all items. Test 'add new members.'

When designing the WBS, it is important to highlight items with a significant cost. For example, in Figure 23.7 the appliances were separated out: *4.3 Install Appliances*. The cost of the appliances was a major contributor to the cost and, therefore, it is useful for them to appear prominently in the WBS.[15]

This shows how the WBS is the foundation of all planning and estimation to follow, supports the assignment of work to specific team members, and is the link from the project to the company accounting system. During project execution, the WBS is used to report the status of the project to customers, management, and other stakeholders.

9.4.6 Requirements Traceability Matrix

After the Work Breakdown Structure (WBS) is completed a *Requirements Traceability Matrix* can be constructed. This matches the attributes in the *scope* (or the specification) to the WBS deliverables and allows for Verification and Validation of the requirements. Verification is the process that tests the *technical* validity of the requirements. Validation is the process that ensures the *value* of the individual requirements to the stakeholders.

For the PMA case, Table 9.2 shows a *Requirements Traceability Matrix*, which links the requirements to the WBS items.

A sample WBS for the PMA project is given in Figure 9.7.

[15]This, again, highlights the idea that the WBS is designed so as to improve the management of the project.

Table 9.2: *Requirements Traceability Matrix* for the PMA case study

Requirement	Status	Acceptance Criteria	WBS ID
Form to register new members	Completed	Form tested and approved by QA department	2.1
Email Newsletter to members	Not Started	Test designed for 3,000 emails	2.2

Figure 9.7: The graphical *WBS* for the PMA case.

130

10

COST ESTIMATION

The first 90% of the job took the first 90% of the money.
The remaining 10% of the job took the other 90% of the money.

Anonymous

Cost and schedule estimation are some of the hardest things to do on a project. They are a technically challenging topics and quite difficult in their own right. In addition, cost and schedule estimates are subject to many challenging issues.

10.1 It's an Estimate

One of the problems that make a discussion of cost estimation difficult for the project manager is that once you have told the stakeholders what the project cost estimated to be, that number is fixed forever in their mind.

No matter how many times you told them the number was "just a preliminary estimate," that number haunts you forever.[1] Once people hear the dollars or the delivery data, they conveniently forget you said it was "within ±25%."[2]

We all behave the same way, no matter how enlightened we think we are. Does the following sound familiar? You ask the plumber for an estimate to unblock your sink drain. "About $150" the plumber says. Then plumber opens up the pipes under the sink and groans. Eventually, you get a bill for $250.

[1] The project manager should remember that these same issues apply to the schedule estimate.

[2] If they heard anything, they only heard the *minus* 25%.

131

"But you said it would cost $150," you cry.

Now magnify that by a thousand and that is how your customer feels.[3]

In our experience, many people only poorly understand the concept of a draft document. They insist on correcting minor grammatical errors in something you clearly labeled, *Draft*. You were hoping for a conceptual review of whether the project was feasible. They came back with, "You should have asked if the project *were* feasible—it's subjunctive you know."

10.1.1 It's about the Future

**If I had asked people what they wanted,
they would have said faster horses.**

Henry Ford

Another issue that makes estimation difficult is that it is inherently a prediction about the future. Since projects have not been done before, there is little data to go on, and the more innovative the project, the less reliable the prediction. Some of the most famously innovative projects also have infamously incorrect price tags. Our two top personal favorites are the Sydney Opera House and Boston's "Big Dig."

10.1.2 The Dream Factor

The scope represents the customer's dreams and aspirations, which crash against the hard realities of cost and schedule. Figure 10.1 shows the spirit of this. The new project is always the shiny new idea without any apparent blemishes. The old project is slow, buggy, obsolete, and dirty.[4]

10.1.3 The Optimism Factor

People want to please, especially when giving a cost or schedule estimate to a customer. We want to give our customers a low number. A mature project manager will distinguish between doing what's right for the project, and the desire to please.

10.1.4 Cost Estimation Errors

The accuracy of a project estimate is a function of where you are in the project. Early on, you estimate the project cost as $10,000 with an error of 50%. That means the project might cost anywhere from $5,000 to $15,000. For projects, the lower

[3] Remember, in this book, you are the project manager. That tiny change to the scope document that hardly anyone noticed is now estimated to add thousands to the project. Imagine how your customer feels.

[4] And when the new project is finished, it often feels a lot like the old one.

132

Figure 10.1: Scope dreams often crash on the reality rocks of cost and schedule.

number is much less likely as cost over-runs occur more often than under-runs.[5] In fact, this is a well-known property of projects:

A project that starts to overrun stubbornly stays overrun.[6]

10.1.5 Marketing vs. Technical Estimates

There is an inherent tension between the marketing and technical departments over the budget and the schedule. Often, marketing has a good estimate what the customer is willing to spend and when they want it delivered. This may be completely different from the cost estimate and schedule derived from the scope by the technical team. Both organizations will appeal to the project manager:

Marketing: The technical bid is too high. We can't win with that.
Technical: We can't deliver the content if we use the marketing bid.

What the Marketing department proposes is a *target* cost and is often based on information about the customer's desires, or goals. If marketing knows that the customer has budgeted $100,000 for the project, they will press for the cost estimate

[5] Schedule delays are much more likely than early delivery.

[6] And in both the cost and schedule.

133

to come in at $100,000 (or less). The cost and schedule estimates derived from the specification may not bear any relation to the customer's budget.

The marketing department's *target* estimates should be carefully distinguished from project team's estimates. One way to deal with this is for the technical team to estimate the cost of a minimum system and, then, propose a series of optional add-ons. The customer can then prioritize the options they can afford.

10.1.6 Will it get canceled?

> Large increases in cost with questionable increase in performance
> can be tolerated only for racehorses and fancy women.
>
> *Lord Kelvin*

Large public sector projects are notorious for enormous cost and schedule growth because politicians sometimes believe that if they tell the truth about the cost, the public will not support the project and it will be canceled. This is a failure of nerve combined with a lousy cost justification argument. A good project manager should be able to make a financially compelling case for the project and to convince a variety of stakeholders.[7]

10.1.7 Protect the Valuables

Customers are understandably curious about how you came up with the estimates. It's their money and deadline and they feel entitled to investigate if you are taking advantage of them. It is a reasonable request. On the other hand, if you hand over your carefully calibrated cost estimation formula, you risk giving away your competitive edge.

We recommend you educate your customer in *general* cost and schedule estimation, especially in industry standards. That way, the customer can work from the scope to determine a reasonable cost estimate and a practical schedule. This will be an independent estimate and, if it is close to the one you have submitted, the customer should accept its validity.[8]

[7]A good PM can even convince politicians.

[8]Whether they like the answer is another issue.

10.2 Cost Estimates

> **It's tough to make predictions, especially about the future.**
>
> *Yogi Berra*

There are two types of cost estimates: high-level and low-level. High-level estimates are created early on in the planning cycle, while low-level estimates require more detail and are generated later. Any of the techniques of cost estimation described below can be used at any stage, the real difference is their purpose. An early, high-level estimate is also referred to as a macro or a top-down estimate and such estimates are made based on the *scope* document.

The first estimate for a project is not likely to be very accurate and is often referred to as a *Rough Order of Magnitude*, or *ROM*. The goal of the ROM estimate is to decide on the feasibility of the project. If the estimate and the budget are out of line, then adjustments can be made, either to the budget or, more likely, to the project content. The project manager should also begin lining up the cash-flow needs: Will it be necessary to borrow funds? When?

The early estimates establish the *budget* (the cost baseline) for the project, which is defined as the *Budget at Completion* (BAC). As soon as the project gets underway, costs will be reported and progress will be measured against the budget. If the budget is not well thought out, the project manager will have to continually ask for more money from the customer, which is not a good situation to be in.

> *Estimation is the process of forecasting the time and cost of completing project deliverables.*[9]

The questions of, "How long?" and "How much?" are intimately related. Usually, one estimates in person hours, not dollars. Estimates in person hours are independent of hourly rates (and inflation) and, so, are more reliable. For example, if it takes 8 hours to paint my office today, it will still take 8 hours to paint it next year. Next year, however, the painter's rates may increase and the job will cost more.

We wish to estimate in terms of some sort of constant productivity rate that is predictable. That is why almost all estimates are in terms of person-hours, not dollars. Dollars change, hours don't.[10] The estimate will be converted from hours to dollars for presentation to the customer.

It is important to realize that estimating the cost is an iterative process and the accuracy of the cost estimate increases as time goes by and more information accumulates. Early on, the cost estimate is a *Rough Order of Magnitude* estimate. History suggests that the variation in early cost estimates is often ±50%.[11]

As the project proceeds and the scope is refined and the cost estimate becomes more precise (and maybe, even, more accurate). As the accuracy improves, the estimate may be relabeled as a *Budget Estimate*. Eventually, when the project

---

[9] The PMBOK also adds "while balancing stakeholder expectations and the need for control." This is typical of junk added to definitions in the PMBOK. Balancing stakeholder expectations is a good idea, but technically irrelevant to the development of the cost estimate. The cost estimate is defined in terms of project parameters and the stakeholder needs come later in the negotiation about the budget.

[10] One of the more interesting estimates I learned many years ago (sorry, I don't remember where) is that the cost of a man's tailored suit is approximately equal to the price of an ounce of gold, and has been for over 700 years. That is a great example of a time-independent cost estimate.

[11] Data also suggest that the larger the project, the larger the initial error. Beware though, this is often a political error, in that people, particularly politicians, are often reluctant to disclose the true cost.

135

manager is confident about the project scope and potential risks, the cost estimate becomes a *Definitive Estimate.*[12]

Cost estimates include overhead costs (benefits, office, utilities, profit, etc.) and these are covered in section 10.12, Overhead Costs.

Depending upon the industry, worksheets may be available to help the team estimate the costs of activities. For example, for a construction project in the City of Boston, there are detailed worksheets available.[13]

Finally, we note that the cost estimate includes an allocation for known risks, which is called a *contingency* fund. However, the cost estimate does not include an allocation for unknown risks, which is called a *Management Reserve.* Both of these are covered in Chapter 17, Risk.

10.2.1 Alternative Approaches

An important aspect of cost estimation is the consideration of alternative implementation approaches in both the technical content and the managerial process. Exploration of alternatives will help to validate the cost estimate, as well as to develop multiple possible cost and schedule options.

An example of a technical alternative might be: Should a rapid prototype be developed to evaluate the performance characteristics of the proposed design?

An example of a process alternative might be: Should the project requirements be incrementally developed in concert with user feedback, or, should the scope be carefully defined and the project developed using the waterfall approach?

An example of a contractual alternative might be: Should an activity be built in-house or should its development be outsourced?

For example, for the PMA project, we might explore the following options:

[12]Only a foolish project manager would be so confident.

[13]See the NSP Preliminary Cost Estimate form at cityof-boston.gov in the dnd/ PDFs/ section.

[14]This is a classic "make versus buy" decision.

- Is a prototype website necessary for users to experience the look and feel of the site, or, are the requirements well understood and approved by users?

- Is the PMA project a candidate to be developed using agile development?

- Is the available staff qualified to build the website in-house, or, is it necessary to outsource the website development to an experienced subcontractor?[14]

10.2.2 Basis of Estimates

The *Basis of Estimates* is a document that contains a description of how the cost estimate was obtained for each WBS element. Such details are important to note and may be listed in an appendix to the cost estimate.

10.2.3 Estimation Accuracy

Figure10.2 shows the accuracy of the cost estimation process as the project proceeds. During the concept phase, the estimate is typically within +75% → −25%. During planning, the detailed estimate from the WBS is +25% → −10%. By the time the project is 30%-40% complete, the cost estimate is an excellent representation of the actual, final cost.[15] Notice the asymmetry: The project is more likely to overrun than under run.

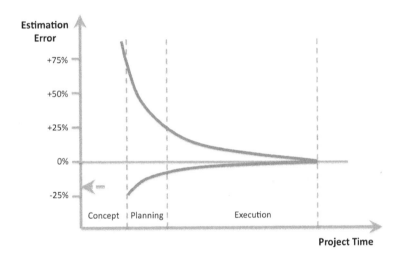

Figure 10.2: The accuracy of cost estimation during the project life cycle.

10.3   Types of Cost Estimates

There are two types of cost estimates:

1. Top-down (macro) estimate:

   The top-down estimate is made early on in the project, typically from the scope.[16] The estimate is typically derived using a mathematical relationship

[15]There are many projects for which the estimate is consistently incorrect. For example, the estimate for Boston's Big Dig was initially $2.6B in 1984, then $6.4B in 1992. The actual cost of $14.6B was not owned up to until 2002. However, the politicians were not telling the public the truth. The engineers always knew it was a $12-$14B program.

[16]Note that the estimate is made from the *scope*, but it will be dominated by *spec*, which specifies the project content.

between the scope items (parameters) and historical cost data. However, many other aspects of the *scope*, such as the schedule or assumptions, will affect the cost estimate. The estimate may be refined by analogy with other projects. Sometimes, a group of experts confer to reach a consensus.

There are several methods for performing a top-down cost estimate: A Parametric equation, section 10.5; The Delphi Technique, section 10.6.1; and reasoning by analogy, section 10.6.2.

2. Bottom-up (micro) estimate:

The bottom-up estimate is typically derived by estimating the cost of the individual activities in the WBS. Each element of the WBS (at some appropriate level) is independently estimated, and the layers summed to derive a total cost for the project.

The estimates may be derived through a mathematical relationship, even at the lowest levels of the WBS. The bottom-up estimation technique is discussed in section 10.7.

An important rule about cost estimates is that they should always be made for the "average" situation, the most likely case. You should never add contingencies, because that is handled in the risk analysis. It is tempting to add rainy day funds, but you will be adding unnecessary cost.[17]

10.4   Cost Estimate Examples

The cost of living has gone up another dollar a quart.

W. C. Fields

We show the general approach with some examples.

Go get some pizza

One of our favorite estimation formulas tells us how many pizzas to order:

$$N = 1 + \frac{3G}{8},$$ (10.1)

where G is the number of guests. With 10 guests, I need 4.75 pizzas, so rounding up, I order 5. I just have to multiply by the cost per pizza, and I have the cost.[18]

This is a quick and simple formula that does the job. It contains a parameter from the scope (number of guests) and is calibrated, i.e. it works in practice.[19] Every

[17]Besides, when your boss reviews your bid she will invariably uncover your rainy-day funds and immediately delete them.

[18]We are indebted to one of our students, Grant MacElhiney for telling us about this formula.

[19]Grant also said that it has worked for him for years, so it is calibrated. What more can you ask of a cost estimation formula?

138

industry has a standardized set of estimation parameters. You can't do business without them.

I want a Super-Yacht

Here's another example, which, despite its simplicity, also has all the features we need.[20] A super-yacht is defined as a yacht whose length is greater than 40 meters (>130 feet) long. The cost estimate is:

Sail: $1 million per meter
Power: £1 million per meter

How is this used? Someone saunters into the boat yard and casually remarks that they just saw a yacht they rather liked. It was about 150 feet long and they'd like to know how much it would cost to build one. You listen, rub your chin thoughtfully, and ask, *Power or sail?*[21]

Listen carefully to the accent, because the cost depends on the currency. *Sail*, they say in an American accent. You quickly divide the 150 feet by 3 to get 50 meters, and say,

"In which case, it's about $50 million."

Obviously, the eventual cost of the yacht will depend on a lot of factors, but for now you have established the ballpark. Assuming your client did not faint at the price, it is now probably a good idea to hedge that number,

"But, of course, the actual cost will depend on the quality of the outfitting."

This simple cost estimate formula actually has all the necessary features:

- *Parameters.* In this case there are two parameters: the length of the yacht, and whether it is power or sail. These two parameters are the major determinants of the eventual cost.

- *Accurate.* Accuracy depends on the situation, obviously, and there will be a lot of variation in super yacht costs. But this estimate is good enough to begin negotiations.[22]

- *Easy to use.* A good cost estimate is practical. You need to be able to be able to quickly give the client a decent answer.

- *Calibrated.* Somebody plotted a chart of super yacht costs vs. length.[23] Then they noticed that the line representing *$1 million per meter* was a decent fit to the data for sail. This rule must be derived by an expert in the field; someone with credibility and access to a decent sized data sample.

[20]This example comes from our colleague Steve Leybourne, a professor at BU, who studied the nature innovation in super yachts. See [25].

[21]Power yachts are about 50% more per meter than sail yachts.

[22]And, not incidentally, like all good "quick and dirty" estimates, it will immediately sort out the serious buyers.

[23]Actually, in this case, our colleague, Steve Leybourne– see [25].

139

- *Uncertain.* An "exact estimate" is an oxymoron. Estimates have uncertainties, which are important to understand.[24]

While few of us will get to purchase such a yacht, the same process is repeated for every project. If someone gives you an estimate for a project, you are entitled to ask, "On what basis did you estimate that?"

Cost estimates are used in strategic planning and feasibility studies. As the scope evolves (progressive elaboration), the cost estimate is refined (rolling wave planning), becoming more accurate.

10.5 Parametric Estimates

A dollar per horse per mile.

Paul Parnegoli

The above quotation by Paul Parnegoli was his cost estimation rule for transporting horses in his special truck, to and from Boston, to places like Kentucky Downs. As we shall learn, it is a parametric estimate.

A parametric estimate is a mathematical relationship between the cost (or schedule) of an element of the project and the project's parameters.

Most cost estimating tools have a parametric model inside. Parametric techniques are mathematical models that use project characteristics to compute project estimates. The estimates are usually for the cost, but may also be for the schedule. For example, a painter may use a parametric relation between the number of square feet to be painted and the hours required to do the job.

Parametric estimates consist of equations, constants, and parameters. The equation links the end result (e.g., the cost) to the constants and parameters. The values of the constants are determined by calibration using historical data. The parameters are system characteristics usually available in the specification or scope.

Equation 10.1 is an example of a parametric estimate. It is an equation that links the estimate (the number of pizzas required) to one parameter (the number of guests, G) and one constant, 3/8. This constant was determined by calibration: The equation was used in many different situations and the number of pizzas that showed up usually seemed to be about right.

[24]A good analyst would also list the standard deviation and the major factors that might increase or decrease the estimate.

Parametric techniques can be used as a fast and reliable way to obtain a cost estimate in the early stages of a project. Early on, the project parameters are usually determined from the specification.

However, parametric estimates are not confined to the early stages of a project. Even when performing a micro cost estimate deep down in the layers of the WBS, one still uses the parametric technique. For example, at the lowest level of the WBS, you may be asked to estimate the cost of a party project work package: *Mail Invitations*. You would multiply the cost of mailing an invitation by the number of guests, which is a parameter.[25]

It is important to realize that parametric estimates are used in both macro and micro cost estimates.

When facing an estimation task, the estimator should always have a particular model in mind. Most, if not all, estimation models use predictors. According to De Marco, "A predictor is an early-noted metric that has a strong correlation to some later results." [26]

10.5.1 Drinks and Hors D'Oeuvres

Here's another excellent example of a parametric cost estimate.[26] It demonstrates the idea that all industries need a cost estimation model for their business.[27]

At a reception, the cost of drinks is:

$$C = n \times h \times \$6.75. \tag{10.2}$$

The two parameters are n, which is the number of people at the event, and h, which is the number of hours the bar will be open. The constant, $6.75, is determined in two parts: $4.50 is the average cost of a drink and is multiplied by 1.5, which is the average number of drinks each person consumes per hour.

The cost of hors d'oeuvres is:

$$C = n \times h \times \$6.75. \tag{10.3}$$

The two parameters are n, the number of people at the event, and h, the number of hors d'oeuvres to be served. The constant, $6.75, is determined in two parts: $1.50 is the average cost of an hors d'oeuvre and is multiplied by 4.5, which is the average number of hors d'oeuvres each person consumes per hour.[28]

Therefore, the cost of drinks plus hors d'oeuvres is:

$$C = 2 \times n \times h \times \$6.75. \tag{10.4}$$

Elegant!

[25]We think there is really only one way to estimate anything, and that is using the parametric technique. If someone uses an analogous estimate, you are entitled to ask, "How analogous?" Any satisfying answer will have to use some parameters to compare the two cases.

[26]This example was provided by Andrew Korda, one of our undergraduate students.

[27]Thanks to Andrew Korda for this elegant parametric cost estimation example. Andrew took the undergraduate Project Management course in the Fall of 2012.

[28]We find it fascinating that the same constant arises in both cases, but for completely different reasons. The symmetry is charming.

10.5.2 Vijay's Parametric Model

The author[29] designed an excellent and sophisticated example of a parametric software cost estimation formula.[30] Here is Kanabar's formula for estimating the cost of a 4GT software project. The programming effort, *PE*, in person-hours, is.

$$PE = 10.2 \times \#Forms + 7.9 \times \#Reports + 4.9 \times \#Entities. \tag{10.5}$$

This is the programming effort only. The total effort, TE, for the project is:

$$TE \quad = \quad 3.1 \times PE. \tag{10.6}$$

The formula consists of several pieces. The parameters are the *number of forms*, the *number of reports*, and the *number of entities* (the data items). These can be estimated by examining the *spec*. The formula also contains several constants: 10.2, 7.9, and 4.9. These were determined by calibration using historical data.

The 4GT model first estimates the Programming Effort, which is 32% of the total effort. This data leads us to recommend a multiplier of 3.1 in the 4GT Model to obtain the total effort for a project.

There were three steps in the development of this parametric cost estimate formula:

1. Developing the parametric formula, which in terms of useful *spec* entities that can be counted, e.g., the number of forms.

2. The formula was calibrated to determine the constants, which required company data from similar projects.

3. Finally, the assumptions that apply to the model's use were listed, e.g., it applies to 4GT software developments only.

10.5.3 PMA Parametric Cost Estimate

Suppose PMA wants to add capabilities to their web site for managing papers submitted to a conference. The scope specifies the information for logging in; screens for referees to enter their data; listing the titles of papers; allowing referees to read their assigned papers; and tracking the referees' selections and rejections.[31]

PMA analyzed the scope and decided they need two login forms for names and addresses; two forms for the referee's background and expertise; and two forms to select and reject the papers, for a total of six forms. There is one report that prints out paper titles when the referee has completed her assignment.

[29]Vijay Kanabar.

[30]Technically, it's a 4GT Model, which, according to Pressman, encompasses a broad array of tools that automatically generates source code based on the developer's specification. [27]

[31]The scope would have more specific details, but this is sufficient for now.

As to data entities, PMA estimated that 50 are associated with the referee's name and address, 20 with their qualifications, and 20 with each paper (title, author data, subject area, accepted/rejected, etc.), for a total of 90 data entities.[32]

The cost estimate for the programming effort, PE, is:

$$\begin{aligned} PE &= 10.2 \times 6 + 7.9 \times 1 + 4.9 \times 90 \\ &= 61.2 + 7.9 + 441 = 510 \\ TE &= 3.1 \times PE = 1{,}581 \; person\ hours = 39.5 \; person\ weeks. \end{aligned} \tag{10.7}$$

At this point PMA has a cost estimate in person hours. PMA desires a schedule of six weeks and if they assign 4 people to the job, it will take $39.5/4 = 9.9$ weeks, while if they use 6 people, it will take $39.5/6 = 6.6$ weeks.[33]

We now convert to dollars by multiplying by the rates for the proposed mix of people to be employed on the job. Like many organizations, PMA has a standard job mix of people they use to bid on jobs—see Table 10.1.[34]

Table 10.1: PMA's job mix cost rates.

Job Title	Percent	Rate	Cost
Principal Engineer	10%	$100,000	$10,000
Senior Engineer	20%	$80,000	$16,000
Engineer	40%	$50,000	$20,000
Junior Engineer	10%	$30,000	$3,000
Clerical Support	10%	$20,000	$2,000
Total Person Year Cost			**$51,000**

Therefore, PMA estimates the cost of the job as 39.5 person-weeks at $51,000/52 per week = $38,740. They quote this as "around $39,000," since it is an estimate.

PMA analyzed the cost and noted that the largest contributors were the data items. Therefore, the number of data entities is *cost driver* for the project.

At this point PMA decided to go back and carefully re-estimate the number of data entities, because the accuracy of the estimate is very sensitive to that number. Do they really need 50 entities for the referee's name and address? After drawing some rough pictures of the screens, PMA decided to cut that to 20 entities, and re-estimated the cost of the project. This is an example of a *sensitivity analysis*.

When the PMA Board scrutinized the estimate during a review, they picked up on the fact that the number of data entities was driving the cost. They tried to cut the bid by assuming a lower number of data entities. At that point, PMA was able to defend their count of the data items.[35]

[32] Notice that there may be hundreds of papers, but that is not what is being counted. We are only to estimate the number of different data items.

[33] Of course that assumes that adding more people actually shortens the job. At some point, when you add people they just get in each other's way.

[34] Small organizations may simply bid the rate of the people who will be actually assigned to the project.

[35] Since you almost always have to cut the bid, this is a useful, practical skill.

143

10.5.4 Detailed PMA Parametric Estimate

Parametric estimation techniques can be used at all levels of the estimation process. Here is an example in which the method is used at a very detailed level of the WBS.

A form in the PMA web site has been assigned to a programmer and, during the detail design, the total number of data elements on the form and their properties were completely specified. The *Adjusted Specification Effort*, ASE, is the development effort for the whole form and is calculated as of the number of data element *specifications* multiplied by the *complexity* of the element. The specification of each data element is classified as follows:

- *Simple Element (SE)*. These are simple screen elements that do not have any complexity beyond data entry, e.g., a zip code, but with no implied retrieving of the town and state when the zip code is entered.

- *Basic Elements (BE)*. These data elements require some validation, and/or some simple additional processing. For example: checking the zip code for numeric values, and populating the city and state fields.

- *Detailed Elements (DE)*. These screen fields require implementation of a trigger or a stored procedure. For example: when the zip code is entered, the system accesses a shipping company's web site, and calculates the cost of shipping.

The cost estimation formula for the form is:

$$ASE = \#SE\ elements \times 10 + \#BE\ elements \times 24 + \#DE\ elements \times 250. \qquad (10.8)$$

The PMA web site form has 20 simple (SE), 5 basic (BE), and one form-function (DE). Therefore, the application development effort is:

$$ASE = 20 \times 10 + 5 \times 24 + 1 \times 250 = 570\ person\text{-}hours. \qquad (10.9)$$

This particular form will take about 570/40 ~ 14 person weeks of work.

When a department is assigned, the project manager will send over the form's specification and request a quotation for the work. The programming department manager will carry out the above calculation, and explain to the project manager that the job will take about 14 person-weeks of work. This is a simple form, and a junior programmer could be assigned, allowing the project manager to estimate the cost and schedule.

These examples show how the parametric technique is used at all levels of the project WBS—it is not confined to the higher levels.[36]

10.6 More Estimation Techniques

10.6.1 The Delphi Technique

Wideband Delphi is an expertise-based process for generating any kind of estimate. Delphi is an anonymous, group approach based on the theory that group opinions are fairly reliable, that extreme views get annulled, that informal one-on-one conversations are susceptible to bias and intimidation, and that an individual might not estimate frankly in the presence of managers, customers, or other stakeholders.

To begin, the project manager asks each person (or small sub-team) to estimate a series of quantities (costs or schedules). The teams are then informed about the other teams' estimates, and the process is repeated. The Delphi technique can be used when no historical data exists and is, therefore, useful when estimating a unique product or a project with no history data. Somewhat amazingly, the Delphi technique seems to converge to the right answer.

10.6.2 The Analogous Estimation Technique

In this case, one reasons by analogy with similar projects. One uses the values of parameters from a previous project for the scope, cost, or schedule as the basis for estimating the same parameter for the current project. The analogous estimate is often one of the first estimates to be performed, early on, as a rough guide. It is generally considered to be the least accurate method of estimating.

We all use this idea constantly when we estimate how long it will take to drive somewhere that we have driven to before. We know the previous estimate for the length of the trip and modify our estimate to allow for the things that might crop up. For example, driving to New York from Boston takes about 4 hours.[37] But that 4-hour trip can change depending on random events (accidents in Southern Connecticut) and systematic events.[38]

An interesting analogous estimate is the average cost-per-pound to launch something into space: [39]

Low Earth Orbit:	$3,600	→	$4,600
Geosynchronous Orbit	$9,200	→	$11,000

[36] By the way, the *Practice standard for Project Estimating* says that parametric techniques are useful at "level one and level two" of the WBS. Actually, as you can see from this example, parametric models are actually used at *all levels* of the WBS.

[37] Both authors used to have children living in New York, so we know this trip well, satisfying the constraint that only experienced people should estimate.

[38] Friday and Sunday traffic is always much worse.

[39] The data is summarized in an article by Frank Sietzen Jr. in *Space Ref* [28]. The actual data comes from an Appendix to a technical report by Barry Watts at the Center for Strategic and Budgetary Assessments in 2001. [29]

145

An analogous estimate is a very rough, preliminary, and parametric, and is only as good as the degree to which it is *analogous*. The new project must be similar to the baseline project and the parameters used for comparison must be appropriate.[40]

10.7 Bottom-Up Cost Estimate

This is sometimes referred to as a *Micro Cost Estimate* and is typically carried out using the WBS. The more detailed the WBS level that is used, the more accurate will be the estimate. When performed on work packages, which are at the lowest level of the WBS, the estimate is about as accurate as possible.

In bottom-up WBS estimation, the team focuses on precisely estimating the costs of the individual activities. Once they are estimated, the costs are rolled up, i.e., the costs of each level of the WBS are summed to produce an estimate for the entire project.

Figure 10.3 shows a summary snap shot of an estimate for the PMA Project. The total estimated effort for the project is 522 work-hours.

Task Name	Work
PMA PROJECT	522 hrs
Initiation Processes	24 hrs
Review Inputs to Initiation	12 hrs
Create Project Statement of Work	12 hrs
Produce Outputs from Initiation	12 hrs
Develop Project Charter (3.2.1.1)	6 hrs
Develop Stakeholder Register	6 hrs
Initiation Processes COMPLETE	0 hrs
Planning Processes (3.2.2.1)	143 hrs
Scope Management Processes	50 hrs
Complete Scope Definition (3.2.2.3)	30 hrs
Create WBS to level of Work Packages (3.2.2.4)	20 hrs
Activity Planning	20 hrs

Figure 10.3: A portion of the micro (or, bottom-up) estimate for the PMA project derived using Microsoft Project.

Bottom-up estimation is generally considered to be more accurate than top-down estimation because it is based on the WBS, which is a refined version of the scope. The major risk is that the project manager is so focused on the details that he or she might overlook the fact that the WBS is missing some key features.

[40]The parameters should also be those that actually drive the cost.

146

Table 10.3: PMA Project Time-Phased Costs by Resource, from Microsoft Project.

Resource	1/3/10	1/10/10	1/17/10	1/24/10
Management	$1,200			$400
Project Manager	$1,60		$2,000	$2,000
Analyst	$840	$2,800	$1,680	$1,400
Tester	$2,800	$2,800	$2,800	$2,800
Total	$6,440	$5,600	$6,480	$6,600

10.9   Cash Flow

The next step is to add all of the cash inflows and outflows over time. Money flows in when the customer makes payments, which is usually when specific milestones are completed. Money flows out when workers, subcontractors, and suppliers are paid. This requires a detailed cash flow analysis, because accumulating bills and invoices may require the project manager to borrow funds to pay the bills. Therefore, synchronizing cash flow is as important as the budget.

As an example, we present the project costs and payments for the PMA project website in Figure 10.4, which shows the outflow of cash as payments are made to the team (black). It also shows the inflow of cash from the sponsor (grey). The inflows are separated in time because they are tied to deliverables. For example, there is a payment from the sponsor upon signing of the contract (week 0). The payment in week 4 is for the successful completion of the scope.

In Figure 10.5, we have added the weekly cash flows to produce the cumulative net cash position over time (shaded). The cash flow is initially positive due to the payment at contract signing. The net cash position fluctuates as team members are paid, deliverables are completed, and sponsor payments are received.

In weeks 7 and 10, the net cash position turns negative and the project manager will have to borrow money to pay the bills. In weeks 12-17, the project manager will need a line of credit approaching $20,000. Note that the project will eventually end up with a positive balance, but not until well after week 20.

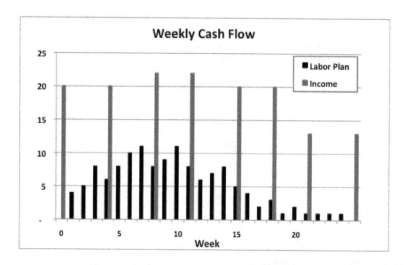

Figure 10.4: The time-phased budget for the PMA project

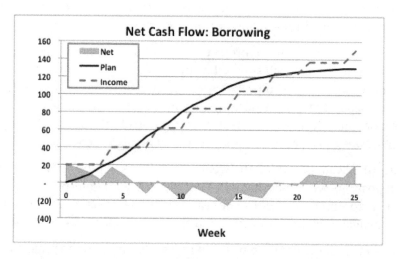

Figure 10.5: The cumulative net cash position for the PMA project

10.10 Contingencies and Management Reserves

Cost and schedule estimates may include *contingency reserves* or *contingency allowances*. Both cost and schedule reserves should be allocated to specific, identified risks. The cost and schedule impacts of the risks should be analyzed as part of the quantitative risk analysis, see Chapter 17, Risks.

Contingency Reserves (for cost or schedule or both) may be added to individual activities or managed centrally for the entire project.[45] As the project proceeds and more information becomes available, the reserves may be used, reduced, or eliminated. The policy for using contingencies should be clearly documented in the project management plan.

The *Management Reserves* are costs and times that are typically *not* included in the cost and schedule baseline. They are withheld and managed by the project manager to be applied to unforeseen work that is within scope.[46] Since the *Management Reserves* are assigned to "unknown unknowns," it is difficult to estimate them. When the project manager decides to use some of the *Management Reserves*, since it is not included in the baseline, the request should go through the formal change control process.

It is important to distinguish between contingencies and reserves. Contingencies are included in the baseline because they are specifically allocated to identified risks. While not all risks will materialize, if the likelihoods and impacts have been reasonably analyzed, the contingency funds and the contingency times should cover the risks that do occur. On the other hand, management reserves are not included in the baseline because they are allocated to unknown events, which are hard to estimate with any accuracy.[47]

The occurrence of risk events can impact the project cost and schedule. There are usually considered to be two types of risks: *Known-unknowns* and *unknown-unknowns*. The known-unknowns are listed in the *Risk Register* and can be quantified.[48] The unknown-unknowns are those events that are totally unexpected and are much more difficult to deal with.[49]

During the process of risk quantification, the team calculates and sets aside contingency reserves for known-unknowns. These reserves can be integrated into the project budget baseline. The PMBOK suggests that funds also be allocated for unknown-unknowns, depending upon the risks and uncertainty existing in the project.[50] A project manager may keep a separate account with the contingency funds to be spent as needed.

10.11 PERT

How do we estimate costs and schedules when there is uncertainty? Usually, we use the concept of the standard deviation, which measures the likely spread in a sample of numbers. For example, if we toss a coin 100 times, we expect *on average* that we will get 50 heads. Of course, in reality, we also know that we may get 46 heads, but we would be surprised to get 100 heads.

[45] Adding cost or time "in case" is unnecessary padding.

[46] For those "unknown unknowns."

[47] Management will often eliminate reserves, on principal, as they raise the cost and delay the schedule without adequate justification.

[48] Well, it is assumed that they can be quantified.

[49] "No one could have expected that .... (insert your favorite event here)."

[50] Unfortunately, it is very difficult to convince upper management to set aside funds for things you don't know anything about.

151

Unfortunately, the normal distribution doesn't work for project management because once projects start to be overrun and late, they stay overrun and late. Therefore, project management costs and schedules are *not* symmetric. Since the normal distribution is symmetric, we cannot use it. Instead we use something called the *beta*, β, distribution.

To estimate an effort, a cost, or a schedule, a project manager can use the three-point technique, also called the PERT Weighted Average (or simply, PERT). PERT is an acronym for Program Evaluation and Review Technique, and was developed as a quick estimating strategy in the 1950s for the Polaris Missile System. One of its main advantages is that it uses very simple mathematics.[51]

We begin by assuming that each activity duration has a range of values and that these durations statistically follow a beta distribution, see Figure 10.6.[52]

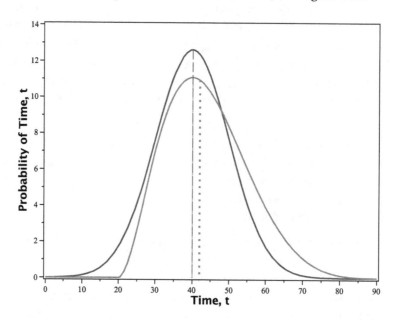

Figure 10.6: A comparison of the β and normal distributions for projects with the same total cost. β is asymmetric, with less likelihood of being early, and more likely to take longer.

---

[51] This was long before electronic calculators.

[52] We are using durations as the example, but PERT can be used to estimate any quantity.

In the PERT technique we use three data points:

- *Pessimistic estimate, p.* The pessimistic estimate is used to come up with a worst-case scenario–if all the risks materialize and everything that could go wrong did go wrong. If the project were repeated, 1% of the time this pessimistic estimate of the activity duration would be realized.[53]

- *Most likely estimate, m.* If the project were repeated, this would be the activity duration that occurred the most often. (In statistics, it is called the *mode*.)

- *Optimistic estimate, o.* The optimistic estimate is defined as the shortest activity duration one might expect to experience. If the project were repeated, this would occur 1% of the time.[54]

The formula to calculate the PERT *mean*, μ, is:

$$\mu = \frac{o + 4m + p}{6}. \tag{10.10}$$

The variability in the activity duration estimates is represented by the PERT *standard deviation*, σ:

$$\sigma = \frac{p - o}{6}. \tag{10.11}$$

The PERT standard deviation, σ is used with the PERT mean, μ to determine how diverse the range in the estimate is likely to be and allows the assignment of a degree of confidence to the estimate of the mean.[55]

The confidence intervals for the σ are as follows:

1σ	$\rightarrow$	68%	The actual schedule has a 68% chance to be within $\pm 1\sigma$.
2σ	$\rightarrow$	95%	The actual schedule has a 95% chance to be within $\pm 2\sigma$.
3σ	$\rightarrow$	99.7%	The actual schedule has a 99.7% chance to be within $\pm 3\sigma$.

10.11.1 PERT Interview Example

Suppose we are going for an interview. We estimate the drive is most likely to take 60 minutes. Then we consider the worst case, and decide that if there is snow, it might take 120 minutes. On the other hand, if there is no traffic, we could possibly do it in 45 minutes. These values are shown in table 10.4.

The PERT mean, μ, is:

$$\mu = \frac{o + 4m + p}{6} = \frac{45 + 4 \times 60 + 120}{6} = 67.5 \tag{10.12}$$

[53]This is the Murphy's Law estimate.

[54]This is the wishful thinking estimate.

[55]Both the PERT mean and standard deviation formulas are approximations to a *beta distribution*, which is more appropriate for projects, in that once a project starts to be late, it stays late. The two PERT formulas are accurate enough for practical work and their simplicity makes them useful.

Table 10.4: Driving to an interview: The PERT optimistic, pessimistic, and most likely estimates.

Optimistic	o	1% chance	45 min
Pessimistic	p	1% chance	120 min
Most Likely	m		60 min

The variability in driving times is represented by the standard deviation, σ:

$$\sigma = \frac{p-o}{6} = \frac{120-45}{6} = 12.5 \qquad (10.13)$$

Our best guess for the time to drive to the job interview is 68 ± 13 minutes. But that only gives us a 66% chance of arriving on time.[56] However, this is a job interview and we want to reduce the chance that we arrive late, so we might choose a 95% confidence level. Therefore, we would use 2σ: $68 + 26$ minutes, i.e., we should allow 94 minutes.[57]

Table 10.5: PERT interview chances of being on time.

$1\,\sigma$	$68 + 13 = 81$ min.	66% chance of being on time.
$2\,\sigma$	$68 + 2 \times 13 = 94$ min.	95% chance of being on time.
$3\,\sigma$	$68 + 3 \times 13 = 107$ min.	99.5% chance of being on time.

PERT applies to many different types of estimates, not just activity durations. It can be used to estimate costs, schedules, or personnel requirements.[58]

10.11.2   PERT Example for the PMA Case

The team estimates the time to develop a website: Most likely, the prototype will take 2 months. Pessimistically, if things go wrong, we estimate that development will take 5 months. Optimistically, the prototype can be completed in one month. Substituting the above numbers in the PERT mean equation gives:

$$\mu = \frac{o+4m+p}{6} = \frac{1+4\times 2+5}{6} = 2.3 \; months. \qquad (10.14)$$

The variability in the activity duration estimates is σ:

$$\sigma = \frac{p-o}{6} = \frac{5-1}{6} = 0.66 \; months. \qquad (10.15)$$

[56] One of the characteristics of PERT estimation is that schedule accelerations are much more unlikely than delays. This is shown in the above example, which shows how the schedule acceleration tends to become unreliable for more than 1 or 2 σ. This is one of the limitations of the beta distribution.

[57] Personally, if I really were going to a job interview, I'd leave 1 hour and 47 minutes for the trip (3σ, 99.5%); show up early and walk around outside if need be.

[58] Vijay is famous for teaching PERT in the classroom by having students estimate the weight of an Indian elephant. Amazingly, it works, even though the students do not know much about elephants. The key is to spread out the o and p values.

154

Therefore, we would quote our estimate for the schedule as:

$$Project\ Schedule\ Estimate = 2.3 \pm 0.7\ months. \qquad (10.16)$$

For the PMA project, we would like to have a 95% confidence estimate for the project schedule, i.e., 2σ. We therefore quote the following schedule estimate: The project schedule estimate is 4 months, with 95% confidence.

10.12 Overhead Costs

> **Beware of the little expenses; a small leak will sink a great ship.**
>
> *Benjamin Franklin*

Overhead costs are the costs of running the business. A team member needs a desk, a computer and a place to work, which require utilities (heat and light). Also, if a team member works on several projects, the company needs a way to divide up the expenses fairly. If someone works 90% on project A, and 10% on project B, then project B should only pay for 10% of the heating bill.

The sum of all the company's expenses is called the *total overhead*. The process of allocating charges fairly across projects is to calculate a percentage overhead that is applied to the direct labor for each project. The largest overhead cost is almost always the occupancy (mortgage or rent, utilities, supplies, etc.).[59]

It all begins with the direct labor, which are the salary payments to the staff. When you pay a staff member $1, what does it cost the customer?[60]

Direct labor (DL) is the cost to pay the staff.

Charges for work directly associated with the project are called direct costs.

Direct Costs are items that are chargeable to a specific work package.

Direct costs come in two categories: labor (i.e., staff work), and materials and equipment. Only labor performed actually working on the project can be charged to the project. The same applies to materials and equipment: only equipment used directly on the project can be charged to the project. For example, the cost of renting a backhoe used to dig a hole for a construction project is a legitimate cost

[59] A mentor once told me that 90% of companies fail, not because of profitability, but because of cash flow, and 90% of cash flow problems are due to occupancy.

[60] Somewhat surprisingly, usually between $2 and $3.

155

and will be paid for by the project. Expenses that can be legitimately charged to the project are called *allowable expenses*.

Not all staff time is chargeable to the project. Sometimes, team members perform non-project related work, such as company assignments, attending professional development conferences, and even the dreaded committee work. This is called *indirect labor* and the customer will not pay for it.[61]

10.12.1 What Does $1 Cost?

The *total overhead rate* is the sum of all the costs other than direct labor: benefits (vacation, sick time, and health insurance), office costs (rent, utilities, and computers), the company bureaucracy (payroll, accounting, legal, and human resources), and profit. The total overhead rate is defined as the multiplier from $1 of direct labor to the final amount charged to the customer.

Suppose the *total overhead rate* is quoted as 2.2. For every dollar of direct labor applied to the project, the customer is billed $2.20. For example, if you make $17.00 per hour and work 40 hours, the bill to the customer is $40 \times \$17 \times 2.2 = \$1,496$. In this section, we show you how to calculate that important number, the 2.2.[62]

The *total overhead rate* is a unique characteristic of every company and is an official, audited number that applies to everything the company does. The *total overhead rate* is often public because it is an integral part of both the bidding and billing processes. The *total overhead rate* is audited to ensure that only legitimate costs are included, but the details are not made public because they contain sensitive information.[63]

Every company must know its overhead rate, if for no other reason than to know when it is making a profit. Even non-profits and charities need to clearly understand the details of overhead calculations. The overhead rate is calculated each year before the fiscal year starts. The costs for the previous year are audited, the proposed costs for the upcoming year are estimated, and the overhead rate is established.

10.12.2 Calculating the Overhead Rate

> **The real problem is not the overhead.**
> **What is really stifling is the underfoot.**
>
> ――――――――――――――――――
>
> *Bill Carlson*

[61]The PM must understand the categories of allowable and non-allowable expenses.

[62]This is also referred to as the *fully burdened* or *fully loaded* rate.

[63]A low overhead rate is a competitive advantage.

The process for calculating the overhead rate is the same in all organizations. Suppose you are thinking of starting the Small Beer Company and want to determine if you should quit your job. Here's how you would go about it.

The first step is to make a cost budget for the entire year. The Small Beer Company has estimated they need the following staff: 3 senior partners, who will make $40,000 per year; and 4 semi-skilled brewers who will make $20,000 per year.

Everyone is allocated 2 weeks' vacation, 8 holidays, and 5 sick days. All employees have a pension plan that costs the company 6% of the labor cost and a medical plan that costs 25% of the labor cost.

The partners estimate they need to borrow $250,000 for the beer making equipment and they plan to pay off the loan in 5 years. They require 20,000 square feet of space, rented at $0.50 per square foot per year. Utilities are estimated at 33% of the space rental. Office supplies, computers, etc., are estimated at $10,000 per year. Payroll, legal, and other corporate expenses are estimated at 5% per year, the G&A.

One of the partners performed a preliminary marketing study and believes their specialty beer will be competitive at $30.00 per case. Each case of beer contains $10 worth of ingredients. The preliminary marketing study also suggests that, initially, they can sell around 20,000 cases per year. To be worth the effort and sacrifice, the partners plan for a profit margin of 25%.

The overhead calculation is shown in Table 10.6 and it begins with the direct labor: The yearly direct labor for the partners is $3 \times \$40,000 = \$120,000$. The direct labor for the brewers is $4 \times \$20,000 = \$80,000$, so the total direct labor is $\$200,000$.

Next, we add all the fringe benefits, such as vacation time and sick pay. For example, the employees receive 10 days' vacation. They work 52 weeks, 5 days per week, so the percentage vacation time is $10/(52 * 5) * 100 = 3.8\%$. Similar calculations are performed for the holidays and sick pay.

We can now calculate the *fringe percentage*. The total cost of the fringe package is $79,692 and, as a percentage of the direct labor, is: $79,692/$200,000 = 39.8\%$. For every dollar paid to an employee, there is a cost of $0.398 for the fringe benefits.

Next we calculate the *overhead rate*.[64] The major occupancy items are the equipment, rent, and supplies. The total cost of all occupancy items is $77,300, which, as a percentage of the Direct Labor plus Fringe, is:[65]

$$\textbf{Overhead Percentage} = \frac{\textit{Overhead Expenses}}{\textit{Direct Labor} + \textit{Fringe}} = \frac{77,300}{279,692} = 27.6\%. \qquad (10.17)$$

The General and Administrative Costs (G&A) are the central corporate expenses, such as payroll, accounting, human resources, and legal. Typically, these are ex-

[64]This is distinct from the *total overhead rate*.

[65]Notice that the overhead rate is calculated as a percentage of the Direct Labor **plus** Fringe.

157

Table 10.6: The overhead calculation for the Small Beer Company.

Direct Labor					
	Partners	3	$40,000	$120,000	
	Labor	4	$20,000	$80,000	
	Total DL				**$200,000**
Fringe					
	Vacation	10 days	3.8%	$7,692	
	Holidays	8 days	3.1%	$6,154	
	Sick Pay	5 days	1.9%	$3,846	
	Medical		25%	$50,000	
	Pension		6%	$12,000	
	DL+Fr % =	79.69/200	39.8%	$79,692	
	DL + Fringe				**$279,692**
Overhead					
	Equipment			$50,000	
	Interest	8%		$4,000	
	20K sq ft	$0.5 / sqft		$10,000	
	Utilities	33% of Rent		$3,300	
	Office Supplies			$10,000	
	OH% =	77.3/279.7	27.6%	$77,300	
	DL+Fr+OH				**$356,992**
G&A					
	Payroll, Accounting, & Legal			$17,850	
	G&A% =	17.85/357.0	5.0%		
	DL+Fr+OH+G&A				**$374,842**
Total Cost					**$374,842**
Sales					
	Plan	20,000 cases	$30.00	$600,000	
	Cost of Goods	Ingred.	$10/case	$200,000	
Gross Profit					**$400,000**
Net Profit			6.3%	**$25,158**	
Planned Profit			25%	**$100,000**	

[66] A sharp-eyed student will again notice that we have used a non-project example; it's another manufacturing case. That is because this case has all the pieces that go into an overhead calculation. Your project might not have a Cost-of-Goods, but if it does, at least you'll know where to put it.

pressed as a percentage of the Direct Labor plus Fringe plus Overhead. The Small Beer Company allocated 5%, i.e., 5% of DL+Fr+OH = 5% × $356,992 = $17,850.

We now have the total costs to run the Small Beer Company for a year.[66] To pay these costs, the company needs sales. The marketing study suggested that they could sell 20,000 cases at $30.00 each, for gross sales of $600,000. Subtracting the cost of making that beer ($200,000) leaves a gross profit of $400,000.

The net profit is the gross profit minus the total costs:

$$\textbf{Net Profit} = \$400,000 - \$374,482 = \$25,158. \qquad (10.18)$$

The percentage profit is $25,158/400,000 = 6.3\%$ and this is the best estimate of the profit for the first year. It is a lot less than the planned 25%.[67] We now have the overhead percentages, which are summarized in Table 10.7.

Notice that if the overhead costs go up (e.g., the landlord demands a rent increase), the profit will fall. Also, if the sales do not meet their target while the costs remain the same, the profit will be reduced. Thus, the overhead calculation is a critical component of planning.

Table 10.7: The overhead summary for the Small Beer Company.

Direct Labor			$1.00
Fringe	39.8%	DL*1.398	$1.40
Overhead	27.6%	1.276*(DL+Fr)	$1.79
G&A	5%	1.05*(DL+Fr+OH)	$1.88
Total Cost			$1.88
Profit	25%	1.25*(DL+Fr+OH+G&A)	$2.35

10.12.3 Cost vs. Price

Price is what you pay. Value is what you get.

Warren Buffett

Suppose a friend calls asks you to create a special brew for a party.[68] You estimate the labor cost $10,000 and the total project cost immediately follows from the overhead in Table 10.8.

We emphasize that the *cost* of the special brew is $18,730, which is different from the *price*, which is what we charge the customer. For example, this special brew might be a lot of bother and interfere with normal operations. In which case, we might inflate the price to make it worthwhile: We explain to our friend that the

[67] This is quite typical. In fact, the first pass often indicates a loss, never mind a smaller than desired profit. This is where the work really begins: how to get more sales at less cost.

[68] A sharp-eyed student will notice that this is (finally) a project: a unique brew, never been done before, one time, etc.

159

Table 10.8: The estimated cost for the special brew from the Small Beer Company.

Direct Labor		$10,000
Fringe	39.8%	$13,980
Overhead	27.6%	$17,838
G& A	5.0%	$18,730

price is $30,000. On the other hand, if this as an opportunity to get into an exciting new area, we might price the brew below cost at $15,000. We are planning to lose $3,730.[69]

This highlights the important distinction between the cost and the price. The cost is fixed, while the price can be any number at all.[70] You should be quite willing to do the job for $15,000, but you should make it absolutely clear that the company will lose $3,730.

What often happens is that management says, "We'll do the special brew project, just try to do it for $15,000." This is a nasty trap, because you might think it is OK to lose $3,730.[71]

At this point, the project manager should write a charter for the unique brew project, explaining the new venture and its excellent potential for increasing sales.[72] Sneak into the charter that the company will invest $3,730 and ask everyone to sign it.[73]

10.13 Cost Estimation Summary

We summarize the estimation process as follows:

People familiar with the project make the estimate.
Use several people to make independent estimates.
Use normal conditions, efficient methods, and standard resources.
Don't make allowances for contingencies.
Use consistent time units.
Treat each task as independent.

10.13.1 PMI and Estimating

The Project Management Institute released a *Practice Standard for Project Estimating* in 2010. [30] This standard provides guidance for sound estimating principles for the life of a project and treats estimating as a living process.[74]

[69]Assuming, of course, the labor estimate is correct.

[70]The Marketing department often wants to win the job by bidding low.

[71]In fact, a more correct reading of upper management's position is *"We expect you to complete the project for $15,000."*

[72]Remember, it is perfectly standard for everyone to sign the charter; you are not asking anything unusual.

[73]Then stand back and wait for the sparks to fly.

[74]This is the first edition, and like many first attempts, it is a bit weak. In our opinion, the estimation examples are not very insightful. For a detailed analysis of the standard, see [31].

11

SCHEDULE ESTIMATION

What's here? The portrait of a blinking idiot.
Presenting me a schedule!

William Shakespeare, The Merchant of Venice

In this chapter, we describe the methods for estimating the project's *schedule*. But, first, we have to distinguish between the schedule and the duration. The Merriam Webster definition of schedule is: [32]

Procedural plan that indicates the time and sequence of each operation.

A *schedule* includes the idea of a *sequence* of operations, while the definition of the *duration* is *the time during which something exists or lasts*. Therefore, the schedule is a more general concept than the duration, which is simply a span of time.

11.1 Schedule Estimation Methods

11.1.1 Parametric Methods

While every industry has a cost estimation method, there are very few parametric formulas for estimating the project's duration and mostly apply to software projects.

One example of a duration estimation formula is the COCOMO model for software development. [33] The basic COCOMO equations for a straightforward software project, such as the PMA web site, take the form:

$$E = 2.4 \times K^{1.5} \qquad \text{person-months}$$
$$D = 2.5 \times E^{0.38} \qquad \text{months}, \qquad (11.1)$$

where E is the staff effort, K is the estimated number of delivered lines of code (expressed in thousands), and D is the development time. The COCOMO model in eq. 11.1 is appropriate for quick, rough estimates and the parameters are appropriate for a project with a small team with good experience, working with less than rigid requirements.[1]

11.1.2   From the Cost Estimate

If a parametric schedule estimate is not available, the project manager can use the cost estimate to derive a duration estimate. Most parametric cost estimation formulas estimate the cost in person-hours (or other time units, such as weeks or months). To determine an estimate for the project's duration, the project manager simply divides by the number of people assigned to the job.

For example, Vijay's parametric cost estimate for the PMA project was 40 person-weeks. Therefore, one person working alone can complete the job in 40 weeks, while two people should be able to complete the job in 20 weeks.

Adding more and more people should shorten the project duration, at least theoretically. At some point, however, they start getting in each other's way and adding people actually delays the project.[2]

When a parametric schedule estimate is not available, the general approach is to conduct a cost estimation first. Then, the duration is derived from the cost estimate, depending on the availability and assignment of personnel.

11.1.3   From the WBS

Parametric methods can be used early in the project's life cycle. Once the WBS is available, a detailed schedule estimate can be produced using the *network diagram*. The *critical path*, which is the most important concept in all of project management, also emerges from the network diagram.

The *network diagram* requires, as input, an estimate of the duration of each WBS activity.[3] If the WBS has been decomposed all the way down to work packages,

[1] There are different sets of parameters for other types of software.

[2] This is the infamous Brooke's Law: Adding people to a late software project makes it later. [34]

[3] This is a bit of a catch-22, because to estimate the project duration requires activity durations.

estimating the individual durations should be reasonably accurate, because the Work packages satisfy **The** $1 \rightarrow 2$ **Rule:** (see section 9.4.2). In which case, the WBS activities should be small enough to estimate accurately.[4] If the WBS exists at a high level, then the accuracy of the schedule estimate will reflect the accuracy of the estimates of the activity durations.

11.2 Estimating the Schedule

Developing the schedule from the WBS consists of the following activities:[5]

- *Define Activities.* The WBS work packages are *activities* that produce the deliverables. WBS activities are decomposed to the point where their cost and duration can be *estimated.*

- *Sequence Activities.* The next step is to define the order in which the activities must be carried out and the relationships between them.

- *Estimate Activity Resources.* The types and quantities of resources required to complete the activity are estimated. This includes people and materials, such as cash, equipment, and supplies.

- *Estimate Activity Durations.* The time required to complete each individual activity is estimated, the *duration.*[6]

- *Develop Schedule.* All of the above data are combined to develop the project schedule. The schedule is an output of the network diagram, which is the focus of Section 11.3, Network. The critical path emerges.

- *Control Schedule.* As the project proceeds, the project manager *monitors* the schedule as it evolves. This includes determining the impact of changes on the actual (vs. planned) schedule.

In practice, the above actions may not be carried out in the order presented. For example, the WBS may be decomposed until the activity durations can be estimated. After that, the sequencing may take place followed by the development of the detailed schedule. The duration can be shortened by adding personnel and, so, the resources may be assigned last. Therefore, developing a schedule is a non-linear, iterative process and the above list should be considered a checklist of tasks to complete, rather than a sequence of steps.

[4] Also, the fact that there are many of them means the statistics are probably on your side, i.e., hopefully, the plus and minus errors will cancel.

[5] We were pleased to see that *Time Management* was finally replaced in the PMBOK with *Schedule Management.* You can't manage *time.* No one understands what time is, let alone explain how to manage it. But you can manage the schedule.

[6] The estimation process is covered in Chapter 12, Earned Value.

11.2.1 Define Activities

The activities are first defined. An illustration of an *Activity List* for the PMA project is presented in Table 11.1.

Table 11.1: *Activity List* for the PMA Case

Initial Design of Membership Form
Create the Requirement Specification
Create User Interface Design
Create Database Table to Store Membership Data
Review Specification and Prepare Test Cases
Review User Interface Design documentation
Documentation of all Systems Documentation
Update Project Management Documentation
Completion of Initial Design Phase

11.2.2 Sequence Activities

The WBS is a deliverable-oriented list of activities and we emphasized that there is no order to the activities in the WBS. Therefore, the next step in constructing the schedule is to determine the order in which to complete the activities, which is called sequencing. To do so, we need to specify which activities need to be completed before others can start and which activities can be completed in parallel.

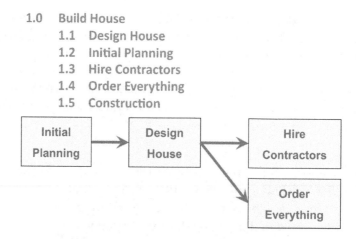

Figure 11.1: From WBS to ordered activities.

Figure 11.1 shows how use the WBS to create an ordered collection of activities. It was decided that initial planning should come before the design. Also, once the design is in place, hiring contractors and ordering can be conducted in parallel.

11.2.3 Estimate Activity Resources

The human mind is our fundamental resource.

John F. Kennedy

Here is where you estimate the types and quantities of resources required for each activity. Resources include people (the team, external consultants, subject matter experts, etc.), material, equipment, and supplies.

Table 11.2 shows examples of resource estimation for the PMA project. Note that the resource types are matched with the activities using them.

Table 11.2: Some examples of *Estimate Activity Resources* for the PMA case.

Activity	Resource Type	Quantity
Create Requirement Specification	Business Analyst	2
Create User Interface Design	Systems Analyst	1
Create Database Table	Database Developer	1
Review Specification and Prepare Test Cases	Test Developer	1
Review User Interface Design Documentation	Design Specialist	1
Writing Systems Documentation	Programmer	1
Update Project Management Documentation	Project Manager	1
Database & Programming Activities	High End Work Stations	6

Resource Breakdown Structure

The *Resource Breakdown Structure* (RBS) hierarchically categorizes the available resources according to different functions, types, or categories. As an illustration, Figure 11.2 presents an RBS in hierarchical format for the PMA project.

11.2.4 Estimate Activity Durations

This is where the time to complete an activity is estimated. The required resources are considered to be an input.

```
0    Project PMA RBS
     1.    Personnel Resources
           1.1       Business Analyst (2)
           1.2       Database Developer (1)
           1.3       Test Developer (1)
           1.4       Design Specialist (1)
           1.5       Programmer (4)
           1.6       Project Manager (1)
     2.    Equipment
           2.1       High End Workstations (6)
           2.2       Printers (3)
     3.    Materials
           3.1       DVDs, USBs, etc.
           3.2       Books, Online Tutorials, etc.
     4.    Services
           4.1       Web Hosting
           4.2       High Speed Networks
```

Figure 11.2: *Resource Breakdown Structure* for the PMA case.

There is considerable debate as to whether the activity resources are estimated before or after the activity durations. We have presented the standard PMBOK approach, which says that resources are estimated before durations. The argument to support this is that you can't realistically estimate how long it takes to do a job unless you know the skills of the person working on it.

However, many organizations have an estimating procedure that estimates activity hours directly from the parameters in the scope and then use a standardized mix of labor rates to determine the cost. For example, a painter may estimate the time to paint a room based on the number of square feet. The cost is then determined by multiplying by their average hourly cost.

Software cost estimation does not follow the PMBOK either. Typically, one first determines the program parameters (e.g., lines of code, or forms and screens) and then derives the estimated number of hours to complete the job. After that, an allowance is made for the type of staff assigned.

[7]This is an important knowledge area and we have dedicated an entire chapter to duration (and cost) estimating–Chapter 10—Cost.

Many techniques are available for estimating the duration of an activity, including both top-down and bottom-up. Popular methods for estimating durations include parametric estimating, analogous or experience-based estimating, the three-point (PERT) method, and the Delphi approach.[7]

[8]Note that activities with zero duration are considered to be *milestones.*

An example of *Activity Durations* is shown in Table 11.3 for the PMA case.[8]

166

Table 11.3: *Activity Durations* for the PMA case

Activity	Duration (days)
Design	
Review preliminary software specifications	2
Develop functional specifications	5
Develop prototype based on functional specifications	4
Develop prototype based on functional specifications	4
Review functional specifications	2
Incorporate feedback into functional specifications	1
Obtain approval to proceed	0.5
Design complete	0
Development	
Review functional specifications	1
Identify modular/tiered design parameters	1
Assign development staff	1
Develop code	15
Developer testing (primary debugging)	15
Development complete	0

11.3 The Network Diagram

**Even if you are on the right track,
you'll get run over if you just sit there.**

Will Rogers

After sequencing the activities and estimating their duration, we have all the information necessary to construct the *network diagram.*

To demonstrate how to construct a network diagram, we use a simple example that includes everything you need to know about network diagrams. No matter what network you find yourself confronted with, no matter how large or complicated it looks, it will not contain any concepts that are not in the simple example presented here. If you understand this example, you need not be afraid of any network.

11.3.1 Network Activities

It's dinnertime, and you decide to have chicken for dinner.[9] Some quick planning ensues, and you realize that you need to complete four *activities,*[10] each with a duration estimate (in minutes):

[9]A student paying attention will say, "Wait. This is not a project, it's routine. Quite correct. However, we have selected a *simple* example to illustrate the network diagram, preferring clarity.

[10]Remember, the definition of an activity is that it consumes time.

1. Marinate the chicken (15 min).

2. Cook chicken (20 min).

3. Microwave the vegetables (10 min).

4. Serve (5 min).

Next, we must sequence the activities so that they are completed in the correct order, e.g., cooking cannot happen before marinating. We also realize that cooking the chicken takes place in the oven, while the vegetables are microwaved. Therefore, these activities can happen in parallel. Finally, the 'serve' activity cannot take place until both the microwave and cooking activities are completed.

This is called activity sequencing and requires the determination of the *predecessors* for each activity. Predecessor activities are those that must be completed before an activity can start. The predecessors are added to the table of activities, as shown in Table 11.3.1.

Table 11.4: Table of activities, durations, and predecessors.

ID	Activity	Duration	Predecessors
A	Marinate	15	None
B	Cook Chicken	20	A
C	μWave	10	A
D	Serve	5	B, C

The first column identifies the activity, by giving it a label (or number), called the *activity identification* (ID). The *ID* is a unique number and you can use any convenient system to identify the activities. For example, in a complex diagram with sub-activities, you may use 1.1, 1.2.1.2, etc.

The second column is the name of the activity, which was defined in the WBS, and the third column lists the activity's estimated duration. During the planning stage, which is where we are in the project cycle, the durations are estimates. When the project moves into implementation, these will change to actual durations.

The fourth column lists the predecessor activities. Serving cannot happen until both microwaving and cooking are completed. Therefore, activity D (serving) cannot begin until activities B (cooking) and C (microwaving) are completed. We say that B and C are predecessors to D.

It is important to list only the *immediate* predecessors. For example, *marinate* is a predecessor to *serving* but is not listed in Table 11.3.1. When determining the predecessors to *serving*, we ask, "What activities must be completed before the 'serve' activity can start?" The answer is just cooking and microwaving.[11]

11.3.2 Network Nodes

Using Table 11.3.1, we next construct a rough network diagram—see Figure 11.3. This is a useful step, as it allows you to lay out the diagram and arrange the activities on the page.[12] The circles in the diagram are called nodes.

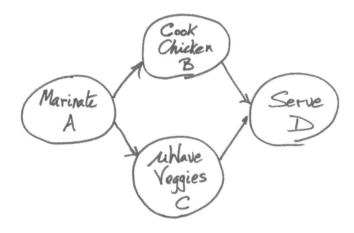

Figure 11.3: Rough Network Diagram.

11.3.3 Arrows and Predecessors

The arrows in Figure 11.3 have a well-defined meaning:

> *The arrow from A to B means that activity B cannot start until activity A is completed.*

A is said to be a *predecessor* of B. This definition of the predecessor is very precise. In fact, the entire network is constructed from this definition.

Activity, A, the marinating activity, has no predecessors. Once we start the project, marinating starts.

As soon as marinating is completed, two more activities can start: cooking and microwaving. The arrows from A to B, and A to C have very specific, well-defined

[11] This considerably simplifies the determination of the predecessors.

[12] We encourage you to draw this out first to figure out where the nodes go before attempting the forward pass.

169

meanings: The arrow from A to B means that B cannot start until A has finished. The arrow from A to C means that C cannot start until A has finished.

The arrows from B to D, and C to D also have the same, very specific, well-defined meanings. The two arrows going into the node D mean that D cannot start until *both B and C have finished.* That is, D cannot start until both B and C are complete.

We emphasize that all this is contained in the definition of the arrows. In practical terms, the two arrows going into D mean that serving cannot take place until both the chicken is cooked, and the vegetables come out of the microwave.

These predecessor (or ordering) relations are shown in Table 11.3.1. When the arrow is used in this way, it is called a finish-to-start constraint.

11.3.4   The Activity Properties Box

Each activity is described by an activity properties box—see Table 11.5. We replace each of the nodes in Figure 11.3 with an activity property box. Drawing the rough network diagram first helps to create a clear network diagram by showing where there is room for the activity property boxes.

Table 11.5: The activity properties box.

Earliest Start	ID	Earliest Finish
Slack	Description	Slack
Latest Start	Duration	Latest Finish

Let's fill in this box for activity 'A.' The identification (ID) is A, the description is "Marinate Chicken," and the duration is 15 minutes. The next box to be filled in is *Earliest Start.* A is the first activity in the project and so it starts at time zero. The earliest time that A can start is zero, so we put zero in the top left-hand box.

We now ask the following question:

> *If the earliest start for A is zero, and A takes 15 minutes to complete, what is the earliest finish for A?*

It should be clear that the earliest finish for A is 15, which is shown in Table 11.6.

Table 11.6: Table of *earliest* properties for A.

0	A	15
	Marinate Chicken	
	15	

11.3.5 The Forward Pass

At what time will we serve dinner? Or, how long is our project?

This question is answered by completing what is known as the forward pass, which proceeds as follows. The definition of the arrow from A to B means that activity B cannot start until A has finished. Therefore, the earliest that B can start is the same as the earliest finish for A. Therefore, the earliest start for B is 15.

We now ask the same question of B that we asked of A:

> *If the earliest start for B is 15, and B takes 20 minutes to complete, what is the earliest finish for B?*

It should be clear that the earliest finish for B is $35 = 20 + 15$, which is shown in Table 11.7.

Table 11.7: Table of *earliest* properties for B.

15	B	35
	Cook Chicken	
	20	

We now continue this *forward pass* process by completing the table for C, which is shown in Table 11.8.

A complication in the forward pass occurs when two arrows go into an activity, such as D—see Figure 11.4. The arrows from B to D and C to D mean that D cannot begin until both B and C have finished. In practical terms, the arrows represent the idea that serving cannot start until both cooking and microwaving have finished.

The earliest finish for B is 35, and the earliest finish for C is 25. Therefore, B finishes last at 35, and D has to wait around for that, so the earliest start for D is

Table 11.8: Table of *earliest* properties for C.

15	C	25
	μWave	
	Vegetables	
	10	

35. The earliest start for serving is the latest of the earliest finishes for cooking and microwaving, i.e., after whichever activity is the *last to finish*.

Since D takes 5, the earliest finish for D is 40. Since D is the last activity in the project, the earliest finish for the entire project is also 40.

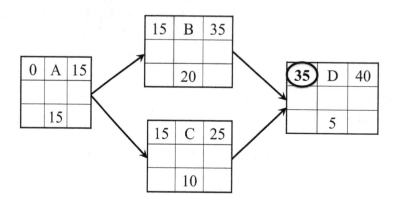

Figure 11.4: The completed *Forward Pass*.

We know the earliest finish date for the project.

When two arrows go into an activity, it is called a *merge activity*. A merge activity cannot start until both preceding activities are complete and, so, the earliest start time for a merge activity is the latest of the earliest finishes of its preceding activities.[13]

This completes the forward pass. The only issue is that, since B will take longer than C, there is some spare time between the finish of C and the beginning of D—the vegetables are going to be sitting around for a while.

The power of the forward pass is that it determines the earliest finish for the entire project. If we start cooking at 6 pm, the earliest we can expect to finish serving is 40 minutes later.

[13] This definition is almost impossible to remember, so when facing a test, we suggest you just draw Figure 11.6.

11.3.6   The Backward Pass

Life can only be understood backward, but it must be lived forward.

Søren Kierkegaard

To start the backward pass, we go to the latest finish for the last activity in the network, which is activity D, serve. Note that D is the last activity in the project, so the latest finish for D is the *latest finish for the entire project*. To fill in the correct value for this box, we ask a deceptively simple-looking question:

What is the latest finish for the project?

Actually, this is a trick question and you might want to think about it before continuing. The answer is below.[14]

Assume we start cooking at 6 pm and suppose we want to watch a TV show that starts at 6:30 pm. We will miss the start of the show because the earliest time the serving will finish is 6:40 pm. We estimated the activity durations and constructed the forward pass without knowing how long the project would take. The fact that we want to watch a show at 6:30 pm is now a problem.

In practice, this is not at all unusual as customers almost always have a finish date in mind when they conceive the project. When the earliest finish time emerges from the forward pass, often, it is after the customer's preferred end date.

At this point, the project manager has several options, including doing some activities in parallel, reducing the time for activities by adding staff, and re-negotiating the end date with the customer, but these are topics for a later discussion. For now, we will proceed with the backward pass by inserting 40 as the latest finish for D. In section 11.4.1, we will show what happens when another value is used.

We ask the question:

If the latest finish for D is 40, and its duration is 5, what is the latest start?

It should be clear that the latest start for D is 35 ($40 - 5 = 35$), which allows us to complete the *latest* properties for D, see Table 11.9.

D can start as soon as both B and C have finished (this is the meaning of the arrows from B and C to D). Therefore, since the latest start for D is 35, the latest finish for both B and C is also 35.

[14]The end date for the project is .... *Whenever the customer wants it.*

Table 11.9: Table of *latest* properties for D.

35	D	40
	Serve	
35	5	40

For B, the duration is 20, and since the latest finish is 35, the latest start is 15 (35 − 20 = 15). Similarly, the latest start for C is 25 (35 − 10 = 25). The latest start for B is 15 and for C is 25.

The arrows from A to B and A to C mean that activities B and C can begin once A is completed. B has the earliest of the latest starts of B and C. Therefore, since the latest start for B is 15, the latest finish for A must also be 15. If the latest start for C (25) were inserted as the latest finish for A, this would violate the condition that B's latest start is 15.

For A, the duration is 15 and, since the latest finish is 15, the latest start is 0 (15 − 15 = 0). Since A is the first activity, we have arrived at the latest start for the entire project. This completes the backward pass, which is shown in Figure 11.5.

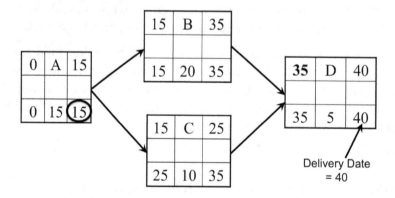

Figure 11.5: The completed *Backward Pass*.

[15]This definition is almost impossible to remember, so when facing a test, we suggest you just draw Figure 11.6.

The complication in the backward pass is when two arrows come out of an activity, which is called a burst activity. For the latest start time of a burst activity we used the earliest of the latest finish times.[15]

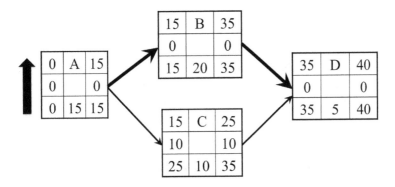

Figure 11.6: The network diagram, showing the *slack* and the *critical path.*

11.3.7 Finish-to-Start Constraints

The definition of the arrow is an example of a *finish-to-start* constraint. That is, we defined the arrow from A → B as meaning that B cannot start until A is complete. This is what is meant by the *finish-to-start* constraint.

There are other types of constraints, such as the *finish-to-finish* constraint. However, we believe that these other types of constraints are very difficult to understand and are a constant source of confusion. We suggest that you avoid them.

11.3.8 Slack

The *slack*, which is also referred to as the *float*, is defined as:

$$Slack = Latest\ Finish\ \text{-}\ Earliest\ Finish\ (LF-EF)$$
or
$$Slack = Latest\ Start\ \text{-}\ Earliest\ Start\ (LS-ES)$$

The easy way to remember the above formula is indicated in Figure 11.6 by the vertical arrow to the left of the diagram: To calculate the slack, one subtracts the top number from the bottom number.[16]

The values for the slack are shown in Figure 11.6. For example, for activity C, the latest finish, LF, is 35 (bottom) and the earliest finish, EF, is 25 (top), so the slack is $LF-EF = 35-25 = 10$ (bottom - top). Similarly, the slack can be calculated from the latest start minus the earliest start, $LS-ES = 25-15 = 10$.[17]

[16]The PMBOK uses the term "total float," which we dislike for several reasons. First, *total* implies a sum, which it is not, it only applies to a single activity.

Also, *slack*, which means loose (like a rope), seems a better description, as in, "a slack schedule."

[17]We emphasize that you really should calculate both slacks, because when you make an error in the backward pass calculation (which is where most people err) the two slacks come out different. Making sure that the two slacks are the same eliminates a lot of errors.

175

11.4 The Critical Path

If we examine Figure 11.6, we note that there is something special about the path: $A \rightarrow B \rightarrow D$. All of the activities on the path have the *least* slack (in this case, the slack is zero). If any of A, B, or D is delayed, the whole project will be delayed. There is slack in C, so if C finishes a little late, it will not delay the project.

The path $A \rightarrow B \rightarrow D$ is called the *critical path*.

The Critical Path is the most important concept in project management.

In Figure 11.6, the path $A \rightarrow B \rightarrow D$ has two very important properties:

- The critical path is the *longest path* through the network.[18]

- The critical path is the *shortest time* in which the project can be completed.

The activities A, B, and D are *critical* because if anything delays any one of them, the entire project will be delayed. If the cooking takes 40 minutes, rather than the 30 that was planned, serving will finish 10 minutes later than scheduled.

Microwaving the vegetables does not lie on the critical path, and so it can be delayed without affecting the project schedule. If microwaving begins as soon as the marinating is completed, and even if it takes an extra 8 minutes, it will still not delay the project. Activity C is said to have some slack.

The formal definition of the critical path is:

The critical path is the path that has the least slack in common.

Note that there may be more than one critical path. If the duration for activity C were 20 minutes, then there would be 2 critical paths: $A \rightarrow B \rightarrow D$ and $A \rightarrow C \rightarrow D$. This means that we should also allow the definition of the critical path to be ... *the path(s) that has (have) the least slack in common.*[19]

The microwaving activity has a slack = 10 minutes, and so it can be started up 10 minutes later and still not delay the serving activity. C can be started later or take longer, but as long as the combination does not exceed the 10 minutes of slack, the project will not be delayed.

Of course, if microwaving takes more than 10 minutes, it will now be on the critical path. If we forgot to turn on the microwave and only realized it after 15 minutes, then activity C ends up on the critical path and will delay the serving activity.

[18] People who do not actually understand networks often say, "the CP is the shortest path."

[19] The inclusion of the plural form, "path(s)", makes the definition of the critical path so ugly that we have left it out of our definition. It is formally correct, so just remember that it might be "paths."

Warning:

A "task" is the word that Microsoft Project uses for an activity. Tasks are essentially equivalent to *activities* as we have defined them.[20]

11.4.1 Please Finish Earlier

> **The show doesn't go on because it's ready. It goes on at 11:30.**
>
> *Lorne Michaels*

Our project started at 6 pm and we now know that the earliest finish is 40 minutes later. But, we probably did not know that when we started the network diagram.

Let's suppose we want to watch a TV program that starts at 6:30 pm. therefore, when we start the backward pass, we should insert 30 in the latest finish for D. Since D is the last activity, it represents the end of the project. Therefore, we enter 30 into the latest finish for node D in Figure 11.7.

We now repeat the backward pass. The latest finish for D is 30, and its duration is 5, so the latest start is 25.

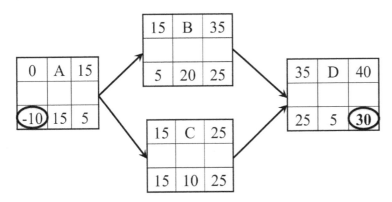

Figure 11.7: The completed backward pass with an earlier project finish date.

Since the latest start for D is now 25, the latest finish for both B and C is also 25. For B, the duration is 20, and since the latest finish is 25, the latest start is 5 ($25 - 20 = 5$). Similarly, the latest start for C is 15 ($15 - 10 = 15$).

The latest start for B is 5 and for C is 15, so the latest finish for A is 5. For A, the duration is 15, and since the latest finish is 5, the latest start is *minus 10* ($5 - 15 = -10$). The latest start for the project is at time *minus 10*.

[20]The word "task" is not used in the PMBOK.

177

This simply says that to finish at 6:30 pm, we need to start 10 minutes earlier than 6 pm, i.e., at 5:50 pm. If the project has not started yet, then this is workable. If the project started at 6 pm and you started the network diagram at 6 pm, then you are in trouble: You are going to miss the first 10 minutes of your TV show.[21]

11.4.2 Milestones

Milestones, or events, denote important points in time in the project's schedule, such as the completion of an activity or a deliverable. Examples of milestones are: the completion of the scope, the receipt of planning permission, and the acceptance by the customer of a deliverable.

Milestones are activities with zero duration.

This is a technical definition that allows milestones to be considered as *activities* that can be included on the network diagram. Activities are linked by predecessors and successors and, because of the above definition, milestones can also be linked.

For example, we wish to create a milestone for the completion of the scope, which is a major event and should be made visible to stakeholders. We define the milestone, *Complete Scope*, as an activity that is a successor to *Develop Scope*. Or, equivalently, *Develop Scope* is a predecessor to *Complete Scope*.

Software systems, such as Microsoft Project, designate milestones with a different symbol to make them visible. Milestones are indicated on a network diagram as triangles with zero duration. Milestones do not affect the project schedule, even though they may appear along the critical path. In our cooking example, we might create a milestone called *Finished Cooking* at the point at which the serving activity starts. If cooking is delayed, then the milestone will be delayed.

Explanations of the project's schedule to customers, stakeholders, and upper management are usually clearer when presented in terms of milestones. When milestones represent the completion of important activities, they are an excellent way to show the project's status.[22]

11.4.3 Managing the Critical Path

Lost time is never found again.

Benjamin Franklin

[21] The PMBOK says that the critical path is "normally characterized by zero total float." This again introduces confusion over the total path float vs. the individual activity floats. Also, in our experience, critical path activities rarely have zero slack.

[22] The PMBOK actually says that since milestones are easier to understand, it is better to present to upper management this way.

178

By far the most important feature of any network diagram is its critical path. It is not at all unusual for the activities to change during a project and their delivery may occur either earlier or later than originally planned. As soon as any change occurs on the project, the project manager should immediately check the impact on the critical path.

Suppose your boss comes into your office and asks if he can borrow Mary for a few days. What do you do? *Check the critical path.*[23]

If Mary's assigned activity is not on the critical path, you can lend her out, and you gain credibility as a team player. If Mary's activity is critical, then you have an excellent excuse for declining to lend her out. On the other hand, you might suggest that Joe, whose activity is not on the critical path, would make a suitable substitute for Mary. You gain even more credibility as a smart team player.

Many project management decisions are made easier when viewed in terms of their impact on the critical path. Consider the following recommendations:

- *Assign the best people to critical activities.* Often, this is **not** the case. Companies usually assign difficult activities to the most senior staff. Personally, we suggest assigning senior staff to the critical activities, even if they are the simplest. That way, if they finish early you pick up some valuable time.

- *Prioritize critical activities.* Every day when you come in, check the status of critical path activities. Smooth their way.

- *Conduct risk assessment on critical activities.* Once you start making up risks, it is easy to get carried away. Assess the critical path risks first.

- *Regularly visit people working on critical activities.* Buy them coffee. Keep them happy.

- *Assign the best computers and equipment to critical activities.* When a shiny, new, super-fast computer arrives, don't give it to the boss, give it to the person working on the critical path.

- *Roll up the non-critical activities.* An entire non-critical branch of the network can be lumped together as a single entity for management purposes. This unclutters the network diagram and makes it easy to quickly pass over non-critical issues. Management typically prefers only to deal with problems.[24]

All of these management actions depend on knowing and understanding the critical path. The critical path typically includes only a small fraction of the activities in a

[23] Actually, we say the correct response to any request is always, "I'll get back to you." Then check the critical path.

[24] Of course, if any of those noncritical activities are delayed enough to affect the CP, they can quickly turn into real problems. Many late activities on a noncritical path can quickly turn it into a critical path.

179

project.[25] This is useful, since it means the project manager can easily prioritize management decisions to ensure the critical path is not adversely affected.

11.4.4 Analyzing the Critical Path

The real work on the critical path begins once it is created. Some examples of typical issues are discussed below:

- *Why is Microwave the Vegetables a successor of Marinate?*[26] We could actually start microwaving the vegetables as soon as the project starts, in parallel with marinating. While this does not make a lot of sense, it is a good example of the kinds of issues that arise when one conducts a detailed and thorough analysis of the critical path.

  Microwave the Vegetables need not necessarily have *Marinate* as a predecessor because one could perform both at the same time. This is another good example of careful analysis.

  To deal with this, one can add another constraint, such as, "The vegetables should be hot when served." This would delay the start of the microwaving.

- *Is the network sensitive?* When many activities fall on the critical path, the schedule is sensitive to delays. The project manager should decrease the sensitivity by moving activities around and breaking them up.[27]

- *A few long tasks dominate.* In this case, the long tasks should be divided into smaller activities. Many smaller activities can often be re-assembled in different ways and processed in parallel, shortening the schedule.

11.4.5 Time Reserves

The activity durations are estimates and the actual durations are likely to vary during execution.[28] Therefore, extra time may be added to the duration estimate to allow for a *schedule contingency*. These are called *time reserves*, or *time buffers*. *Time reserves* should be allocated to specific, identified risks.[29]

Schedule reserves may be added to the activity duration either as a specific duration or as a percentage.[30] Contingencies are not usually included in the network diagram but managed centrally by the project manager. As the project proceeds and more information becomes available, the schedule reserves may be used, reduced, or eliminated. The policy for using the schedule reserves should be clearly documented in the schedule section of the project management plan.

[25] How do we know that the critical path typically includes only a small fraction of the activities in a project? Boris Cailloux, one of our undergraduate students, found the original reference and it is fascinating. The statement occurs in a 1963 *Harvard Business Review* article entitled "The ABC's of the Critical Path Method" by F. K. Levy, G. L. Thompson and J. D. Wiest.

Project management arose in military applications and this was one of the first, generally available, public articles. Almost casually, they say, "In many projects studied, it has been found that only a small fraction of the jobs are critical." We see that there is not much support for such a strong statement but given that it was 1963, they can be excused.

Thus was born the urban legend. Thank you, Boris.

[26] We overlooked this interesting issue in the first edition and our students immediately caught it. Well done!

[27] See *Microwave Veggies* for an example of changing the constraints.

[28] Usually, they overrun.

[29] The schedule impact of the risks should be analyzed as part of the risk analysis.

[30] Adding time "in case" is unnecessary padding.

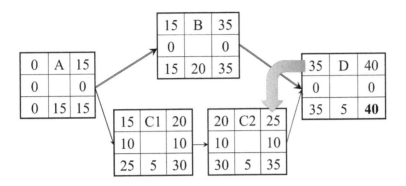

Figure 11.8: A network diagram with *Free Slack*: $ES(D) - EF(C2)$.

11.4.6   *Free* Slack

We now make a small change to the network diagram: We divide activity C into two parts (C1 and C2)—see Figure 11.8 and this small change has an interesting impact. We have not changed the critical path, so we have not changed the project schedule. Nevertheless, there is now something very special about activity, C2.

> *Activity C2 can be delayed without affecting any other activity in the network.*

This is an incredibly useful property of C2, and it is called *free slack*.[31]

It is true that C1 can be delayed and not affect the project schedule, but a delay in C1 will delay the start of C2. Therefore, if C1 is delayed, the people and resources associated with C2 will be affected.

For example, suppose that activity C2 is *Pour Foundation* and requires the delivery of concrete by an expensive and carefully scheduled truck. If C1 is delayed, the concrete truck will have to be postponed, perhaps causing further delays and expensive penalties.[32]

On the other hand, C2 can be delayed without affecting any other activity. For example, if activity, D, requires the expensive concrete truck, a delay in C2 will not impact the concrete truck.

[31] It is also called *free float*, but we have the same reservations as expressed earlier about the use of the word 'float.'

[32] C1 is not on the critical path but it is a very important activity. Note the distinction: C1 is important, but not critical.

181

Definition of Free Slack

There are two ways to define *free slack*. The practical method that can be used when analyzing a network diagram is:

> *An activity has free slack if it occurs at the end of a non-critical chain in the network diagram.*

A more technical definition of free slack is:[33]

> **Free** slack occurs in the last activity in a non-critical chain and is the difference between the ES of the activity that follows it and the EF of the activity, i.e.,

$$FS = ES^+ - EF. \tag{11.2}$$

The Value of Free Slack

A theme that emerged from the analysis of the network diagram and, particularly, the critical path was the idea that, during the project, changes are inevitable. When your boss calls asking to use Alice on another project, your immediate response should be, "I'll get back to you."

You look at the critical path. If Alice is working on activity C2, an activity with free slack, you call back and say "Sure."[34] On the other hand, if Alice is working on a critical activity, you have several options:

1. Say, 'No.'

2. Let Alice go and move someone from C2 to Alice's activity.

3. Let Alice go, but explain to your boss that there will be a schedule slip.[35]

4. Let Alice go, but explain to your boss that there will be a cost overrun.[36]

Free Slack is the project manager's friend. Once a network diagram is completed, the project manager should identify all the activities with *free slack*.[37]

[33] This is another definition that's hard to remember. Just remember where the arrow is in Figure 11.8: From the EF of the activity at the end of the chain to the ES of the next one.

[34] You are a team player.

[35] Yawn.

[36] What?!

[37] Put them in your pocket and save them for a rainy day.

182

11.4.7 Schedule Compression

There are several techniques for schedule compression and the most effective is to reduce the scope. There is a tendency for project managers to insist maintaining the scope, the cost and the schedule, which is, usually, unrealistic. A discussion with the stakeholders on the relative priorities of scope content, cost, and schedule may give the project manager options for schedule compression.

If the content cannot be reduced, the following techniques for schedule compression can be explored:

- *Crashing:* In *crashing,* one adds resources to activities to shorten their planned duration. The activities must be on the critical path. Examples of adding resources include adding staff, allowing overtime, and paying to expedite deliveries.

  If an activity has a planned duration of four weeks for one person, then it may be reasonable to expect it to be completed in two weeks by two people. However, just adding people will often delay a project rather than accelerate it.[38] Therefore, *crashing* may increase risks and costs without achieving the desired schedule compression.

- *Fast Tracking:* In *fast tracking,* activities that are normally specified to be sequential are worked on in parallel. This usually means that a later activity is started before all of its prerequisites are completed. The activities must be on the critical path.

  For example, one might start designing the project before the scope is complete. This will work if the scope sections to be designed are almost complete. The risk with *fast tracking* is that changes to the scope may result in rework of the design, causing delays and cost increases. Therefore, *fast tracking* requires close coordination between the activities.

11.5 Network Issues

There are a number of issues that affect networks.

11.5.1 Activity Sequence Relationships

Identifying the activity sequence relationships defines the logical flow of work. Predecessor and successor activities are constraints on the sequence in which activities must be performed. They dictate the order of activities.

[38] Brook's Law: Adding people to a late project makes it later.

- *Predecessor Activities.* These must finish before any following activities can begin. (A is the predecessor to B in figure 11.6.)

- *Successor Activities.* These follow immediately after other activities. (B is the successor to A in figure 11.6.)

- *Concurrent, or parallel, activities.* These can be worked on at the same time, which shortens the schedule. (In Figure 11.6, activities B and C can be performed in parallel—cooking the chicken and microwaving the vegetables can be performed at the same time.

- *Merge Activities.* These have at least two preceding activities on which they depend. In Figure 11.6, activity D is a merge activity (B and C merge into D).

- *Burst Activities.* These have at least two succeeding activities on which they depend. In Figure 11.6, activity A is a burst activity (B and C burst from A).

Dependencies dictate when or how an activity must be performed, and there are three types:

- *Mandatory Dependencies.* These are restrictions specific to one or more activities. Mandatory dependencies never change. Sometimes, mandatory dependencies are referred to as *hard logic.*

  For example, a mandatory dependency occurs in our cooking example because we specified that marinating must be completed before cooking can begin. When building a house: the permit must be obtained before construction can start; and the foundation must be finished before the walls can be erected.

- *Discretionary Dependencies.* These are *preferred* ways of doing the project. Because they are *discretionary,* they may change as priorities change.[39]

  For example, in our cooking example, we may choose to complete the microwaving the vegetables activity after the chicken finishes cooking. That way, the vegetables are still hot. We may equally well decide that the vegetables need to be cooked as quickly as possible, in which case we would start them as soon as the chicken is marinated. The choice is at our discretion.

- *External Dependencies.* These are restrictions that result from activities outside the project itself. Usually, neither the project manager nor team members can control external dependencies. External dependencies may be either mandatory or discretionary.

[39]Discretion is the better part of valor, and so the best way to perform the task is often the way that keeps the stakeholders happy.

184

For example, obtaining a construction permit is an external, mandatory dependency. It is external, since the regulation comes from the town, and it is mandatory before construction can start.

Both mandatory and discretionary dependencies should be used with care, since they can affect the sequence of activities. Often there are assumptions involved, and these should be clarified and documented because the justification for the assumptions may change as the project evolves.

An example of an internal discretionary dependency is to insist that the vegetables and the chicken finish at the same time, so that they are hot.

11.5.2 Lags

The classic situation where a lag is used is in purchasing an item. Suppose you decide to buy a computer part and the delivery time is ten working days. The time estimate for the *Order Part* activity might be one day (the time it would take to fill out the purchase request form, get signatures, etc.). Therefore, the duration for the *Order Part* activity should be 1 day.

Then you sit around for 10 days, waiting for the part. If you put 11 days in the network (1 to purchase the part and 10 for delivery), then the system will compute the cost of 11 days of work, when only one is really required. The 10 days of waiting should not be charged as a labor cost.

What is also important when adding up the costs is that the *Order Part* activity only consumes one day's worth of labor, the waiting activity costs nothing.

However, any activities that cannot start until the part arrives must wait for the delivery, which takes 10 days. To properly handle this in the network diagram, you introduce a lag into the buying activity—see Figure 11.9.

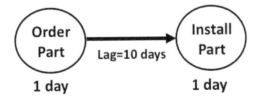

Figure 11.9: A classic lag: Ordering takes one day, but waiting for the part to arrive takes another 10 days.

The definition of a lag is:

In a finish-to-start dependency, a lag is the time between the finish of a predecessor activity in a network diagram and the start of its successor activity.

The software for constructing network diagrams often buries the lag inside the arrow, where it is hidden. Therefore, our preference is not to use lags, but to explicitly create a *Wait* activity in the network diagram, see Figure 11.10. This clarifies the delay, and explicitly presents it to everyone. Especially if it is a significant item on the critical path, you would want everyone to know what the delay is. Also, you might not be able to affect the delay (e.g., manufacturing and shipping times), and so need to highlight it in the discussions.

Figure 11.10: Network with a *Wait for Part* activity instead of a lag.

If the *wait* activity is on the critical path, it will be visible. If the project manager needs to shorten the project duration, it may be cost effective to pay for express shipping to shorten the delivery time. Thus, a *wait* activity in Figure 11.10 improves communication and gives the project manager options.

11.5.3 Leads

A *lead* allows an activity to begin early.[40] For example, when writing a document, you might allow editors in the proofing department to start a week before the document is complete and formally delivered by the writers. This is a risky action. The benefit is that some schedule compression might accrue because proofing starts early. This must be balanced against the risk that the document might change substantially before delivery and the proofing team might have to redo their work.

Leads and lags affect the timing of activities and, therefore, the critical path.[41] In fact, they may make the calculation of a critical path a bit tricky. Software packages may bury leads and lags inside tasks, which makes the resulting critical path difficult to understand.

[40]A *lead* can be thought of as a negative lag.

[41]We try to stay away from leads all together.

186

11.5.4 Loops and Conditional Branches

A document that requires multiple drafts might be considered as an example that could use loops in its sequencing as shown in Figure 11.11. Suppose Chapter #1 is written and delivered, so that the activity is complete.

The next activity is *Edit Chapter #1*, but there is a request for re-writes. This might be considered as a loop in the network diagram because *Write Chapter #1* is being re-executed. Such loops are not allowed in network diagrams and the arrow from *Edit → Write* in Figure 11.11 is considered an illegal construct.

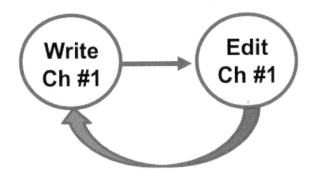

Figure 11.11: An illegal loop in a network diagram.

From a project perspective, a much better way to describe the activities is by the following sequence of activities: *Write Chapter #1*, *Edit Chapter #1*, and *Re-Write Chapter #1*.

Since the activities of writing, editing and, even, re-writing, require different skills, they can (and probably should) be assigned to different staff members. The initial writing may require an expert, but editing skills are quite different. After that, the re-write might be accomplished by a junior staff member. By not writing the activities in a loop, we more clearly define the work required and retain flexibility in assigning staff. Therefore, for the project manager, it is much better not to use a loop.

A conditional branch is one that has an "if" statement in it. An example of a *conditional activity* is: "Activity *P* is completed if activity *Q* is successful."

Both loops and conditional branches tend to complicate the network. If you really want to include looping and branches, you can use the *Graphical Evaluation and Review Technique* (GERT).[42]

[42] Typically, both loops and conditional branches complicate the reading of network diagrams and confuse the readers more than they help. We avoid them like the plague.

11.5.5 AOA and AON

Two approaches are used to describe project networks and the one we have used so far is called *Activity on Node* (AON). AON is also called the *precedence diagramming method* (PDM) and is used by most project management software packages. In practice, AON has come to dominate most project management network diagrams.

The network diagrams in this chapter all used AON. Each activity is associated with a node and represented by a circle in the diagram. The activities consume time, which is represented by the nodes.[43] The arrows do not consume time, they represent predecessor and successor relationships.

There is another method called *Activity-on-Arrow*, (AOA) in which activities are denoted by arrows. If Figure 11.3 were rewritten in terms of AOA, it would become:

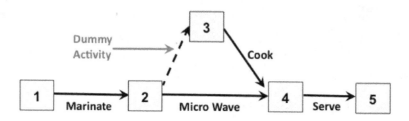

Figure 11.12: An *activity on arrow* (AOA) diagram, equivalent to Figure 11.3.

In an AOA diagram, the activities (and therefore, time) are denoted as arrows and are labeled by the numbers of the nodes they connect. In the AOA diagram, the nodes consume no time. For example, the activity *Marinate* is represented by the arrow from $1 \rightarrow 2$, as it goes from node 1 to node 2. The activity *Cook* is $3 \rightarrow 4$.

The complication that occurs in an AOA diagram is the need for *dummy* activities. In order to designate that *Cook* (arrow $3 \rightarrow 4$) cannot start until *Marinate* (arrow $1 \rightarrow 2$) is finished, the dummy activity $2 \rightarrow 3$ (the dotted line in Figure 11.12) must be added to the network.

Some analysts claim that the AOA form is easier to read and draw. We believe that the addition of the dummy activities tends to make AOA more difficult to understand and construct.[44] What is true, however, is that AON has come to dominate the world of project management.

[43] Remember, the definition of an activity is that it consumes time.

[44] Personally, we think that any system that requires adding something called a *Dummy* is pretty dumb. On the other hand, one of our colleagues thinks that AOA is the *only* thing to use. You decide.

11.6   Another Network Example

We present a more complex network to illustrate the project management concepts associated with analyzing the network and, in particular, the critical path. The table of predecessors and durations is in Table 11.10.[45]

Table 11.10: Network Example: Table of activities, durations, and predecessors.

ID	Predecessors	Duration
A	None	10
B	A	6
C	A	8
D	None	17
E	B, C	5
F	C	3
G	B	4
H	D, E, F, G	2

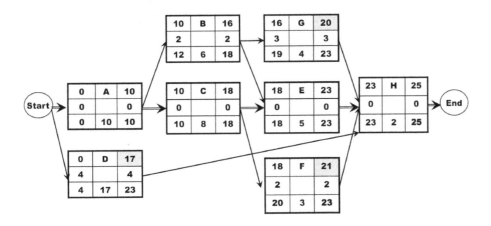

Figure 11.13: An example of a network diagram.

Once a network diagram is produced, the job of the project manager is to *analyze* it. The network diagram is shown in Figure 11.13 and we note the following issues:

- We have inserted start and end nodes, which all projects should have. Sometimes an activity can be started at any time, but without a start node, it cannot be linked to the network. An activity without an input arrow or an output arrow is called a 'dangling' activity.

[45]Students are encouraged to develop the network diagram from Table 11.10 without looking at Figure 11.13.

Activity D has no predecessor and, so, can be started at any time. Therefore, we connected D to the *Start* node, otherwise it would be dangling.[46]

- Start and stop nodes allow us to create milestones for the start and end of the project, so they are important planning tools. All projects need both a start date and an end date, and the start and end nodes are a convenient place to put them.

- We explicitly include two boxes for calculations of the slack. It may seem redundant because the two slack values should, indeed, be the same. However, a mistake in the backward pass often shows up as a difference in the two slack values.

- Arrows may cross. This is allowed and, in fact, it is difficult to draw this diagram without having some arrows cross.[47]

- The critical path is highlighted with thick arrows, which makes it obvious and easier to manage.

- The critical path has four activities out of a total of eight, so it contains only 50% of the activities. Although this is only a small network, we begin to see that the critical path contains only a fraction of the activities.[48]

- Activities with shaded boxes have *free slack*. Activity D has free slack, even though it is the only activity in the non-critical chain, i.e., between Start and activity H.

- Activity G has free slack because it is at the end of the non-critical B → G chain.

- The network is somewhat *sensitive*, because the non-critical path B → G has a small amount of slack. Therefore, small delay in either B or G will turn that path into a critical path.

- Although it is not explicitly stated, activity D represents a roll-up of a collection of non-critical activities. That is, there is an entire sub-network represented by D with a total time of 17. When presenting the project status to stakeholders, this helps to clarify the important schedule issues because all the clutter of the D subnetwork is hidden.

- Activity G is the *lag* in activity B. For example, suppose activity B is the selection and purchase of an item, and G represents the delivery time of 4 days. By explicitly adding the activity G we see the delay when waiting for

[46] Every activity must be connected at both ends.

[47] Make it clear rather than obsessing about crossing arrows.

[48] Worry about these and then go home early.

the item to arrive.[49] Since G is not on the critical path, a small delay in the delivery time is not a problem.

11.7   From Network Diagram to Cost Profile

We need just two more pieces of information to complete the estimation process: the *staffing profile*, which is the required personnel over time, and the *cost profile*, which is the funds required over time.

The network in Figure 11.13 shows the order in which activities must be executed, but it is not, in any way, a true time-axis with incremental time units. What we need is a chart with a genuine x-axis that measures time and with a y-axis that measures the number of people working at that time.

Figure 11.14 is an example of how to calculate a staffing profile. We assume that the time units are in weeks and label the x-axis in weeks, starting at the project inception, which is the zero point, and ending at the project duration, see Figure 11.14. We then place the activities, each beginning at their correct starting time coordinate and spanning their correct duration. For example, activity *A* starts at week #1 and lasts for 10 units; activity *B* starts at week #11 and lasts for 6 weeks.

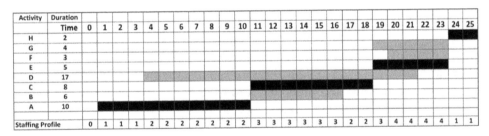

Figure 11.14: The draft staffing profile.

It is useful to highlight the critical path activities, which we have colored black. The grey activities are not critical, which means they have slack. Therefore, we have flexibility as to where we place them. For example, activity *B* has a slack of 2 and could start at weeks #11, #12, or #13 and not delay the project.

Therefore, we need some sort of rule to decide how to place the non-critical activities. In Figure 11.14, we used the simple rule that activities start as soon as they can, i.e. immediately after their predecessors are complete.

The project manager wants to have as stable a staff level as possible over time because it is difficult to acquire people for only short periods and then release them.

[49]We much prefer this approach to burying the lag in activity B.

191

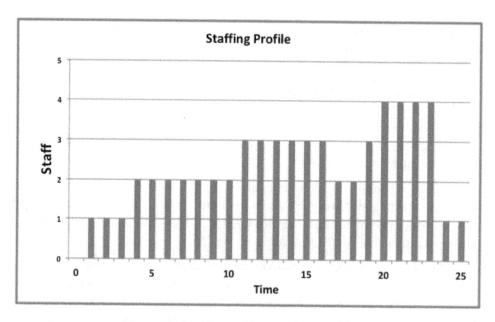

Figure 11.15: The staffing profile over time.

Therefore, adding staff assignments to Figure 11.14 is useful for showing who will be working when.

Many software systems have algorithms for leveling the staff profile. However, the algorithms are difficult to understand and the impact of leveling can be unpredictable. For example, some leveling algorithms assume that it is acceptable to delay the project.[50]

Once the project manager approves the individual staff assignments, the next step is to add up the staff requirements in each week to get the total staff required in each week. This is shown in Figure 11.15.

Finally, we calculate the costs in each week, or funding profile. If we assume that each activity is staffed with one person, multiplying by the average labor rate gives the required funds per week. If more than one person is assigned to an activity, a corresponding adjustment is required.

[50]We suggest that project managers do their own leveling. The project manager usually understands where the issues are and the personnel involved. Also, moving just a few people around often solves the problem.

11.8   The Schedule for the PMA Case

For the PMA case, the piece of the network diagram in Figure 11.16 shows that the activity *Review Functional Specification* is on the critical path.

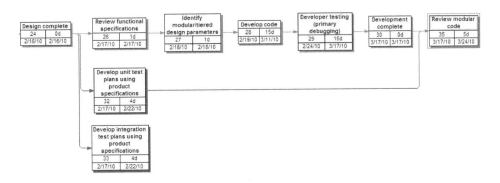

Figure 11.16: A portion of the network diagram for the PMA case.

Further, three activities can start upon completion of the design phase, and we can now see their start and completion times, their durations, and the resources required. As the start and completion times for the activities emerge, we can add these dates to the WBS Dictionary.

Modern software systems make it relatively easy to generate such network diagrams.[51] The project schedule shown in the network diagram is called a Gantt chart, and it is widely used to communicate the schedule information. A Gantt chart is easily understandable by anyone, even if they have no formal training in network diagrams. For the PMA project, an example of a Gantt chart is shown in Figure 11.17 .

Schedule Baseline

Once the schedule has been estimated, it should be saved as a *Schedule Baseline* and communicated to all stakeholders and an official sign-off obtained.

> *The Schedule Baseline is a specific version of the project schedule that is accepted and approved by the team, with committed start and finish dates.*

In Figure 11.18 we illustrate the schedule baseline graphically using the Timeline Tool from *Microsoft Project*. Typically, however, it is the Gantt chart that is submitted to stakeholders to communicate the schedule baseline.

---

[51]We insist there is no excuse for not using them.

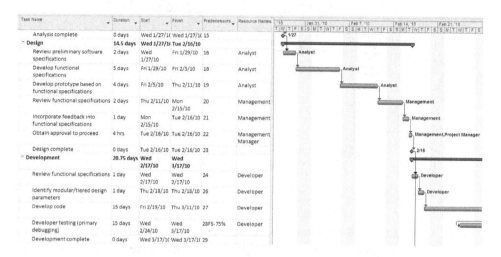

Figure 11.17: A portion of the Gantt chart for the PMA case.

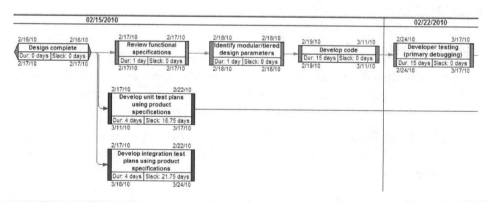

Figure 11.18: A portion of the Timeline diagram for the PMA case.

12

EARNED VALUE

> **The more education a woman has, the wider the gap
> between men's and women's earnings for the same work.**
>
> *Sandra Day O'Connor*

Earned Value Management (EVM) is the fundamental tool for managing the cost and schedule.[1] In this chapter, we present the fundamental methods for cost and schedule *tracking*: determining whether the project is within budget and on schedule.[2] Fortunately, the basic ideas are relatively straightforward and use mathematics no more complicated than percentages.

12.1 How ya doin'?

This is the question everyone wants the answer to. Customers, upper management, stakeholders, and the project team all want to know if you are within budget and on schedule. They all expect you, as the project manager, to be able to give an accurate assessment of the final cost and schedule, as compared to the initial estimates. How do you determine that?

We begin with a simple example: We are asked to write a 50 page document. We look at the requirements and estimate that we can deliver 5 pages per day for 10 days.

[1] We believe that the two most important technical concepts in project management are the critical path and earned value.

[2] As distinct from *estimation*, which was the topic of the previous two chapters.

195

We explain to the customer that we earn $10 per hour and agree to work 10 hours per day.[3] We are paid for all the hours worked and, at the end of each day, report the number of pages written, the hours worked, and the cost.

Therefore, we have a plan, which is to complete 10 pages per day for 5 days for a total estimated cost of $500. This is our budget.

Then, we started the project and here's what happened:

Day #1   We worked 10 hours and wrote 5 pages. The customer accepted the pages and paid us the agreed amount for the day's work: $100. We are clearly on budget and on schedule.

Day #2   We again worked 10 hours and produced the planned 5 pages. The customer paid us $100. We are still on budget and schedule.

Day #3   We ran into a problem and only delivered 2 pages. Also, we worked an extra 2 hours trying to fix the problem. (We worked 12 hours.) Since we get paid $10 per hour, we submitted a bill for $120.

We are over budget.

But is our cost overrun significant? Should we be worried? Can we make it up?

So far, the total actual cost of the project is $320, but we have only delivered 12 of the planned 15 pages. How can we measure our *true* progress?

Let's go back and carefully analyze the *plan*: We estimated that we could deliver 5 pages per day and get paid $100 per day. Therefore, each page has a *planned value* of $20. After 3 days, we planned to deliver 15 pages, so the value of the work we planned to deliver is $15 \times $20 = 300. We refer to this as the *Planned Value* on day #3 and write it as, $PV(3) = 300.

Now let's look at the *Actual Cost*: We have actually spent $320 and there is no arguing with this, it is simply the invoiced amount, which we write as, $AC(3) = 320.

We only produced 12 of the planned 15 pages, so the actual cost applies to the 12 pages delivered, not the planned 15 pages. Therefore, we need to determine the *value* of the delivered work. We are simply going to define the *value* of the work completed, at any time, as the percentage of the plan completed at that time.

At the end of day #3, the plan was to have delivered 15 pages at a cost of $20 each, $PV(3) = 300. We have actually delivered 12 pages, or $12/15 = 80\%$ of the plan. Therefore, the *value* of the completed work is defined to be, $80\% \times $300 = 240. We call this the *earned value* on day #3, and write it as, $EV(3) = 240. It is the value of the work we have actually delivered.

[3]We are keeping the numbers as simple as possible.

The *value* of the work completed (the *earned value* of the 12 pages) is $240, but the actual cost for those 12 pages of work was $320. That is, we completed $240 worth of work (12 pages), but at a cost of $320. Therefore, in monetary units, our cost efficiency is: $240/$320 = 75%.

From a cost perspective, at the end of day #3, we are working at an efficiency of 75%. The cost efficiency goes by the name, *Cost Performance Index (CPI)*.

Since we are working at less than 100% cost efficiency, it is reasonable to project that the final cost will be higher than the budget of $500. In fact, if we continue to work at this same efficiency, we can project an estimate of the final cost at the completion of the project as the budget divided by our efficiency.

The revised final cost estimate is the *Cost Estimate At Completion* (CEAC):[4]

$$CEAC = \frac{Budget}{CPI} = \frac{\$500}{0.75} = \$667. \tag{12.1}$$

This simple example illustrates all of the features of a *cost tracking* calculation:

1. We started with a planned value for the work over time. This was the budget estimate over time: 5 pages per day and $10 per hour = $100 per day.

2. Next, we designated a time at which we wish to *track* the progress. In this case, we decided to measure the progress on day #3.

3. We used a *cumulative* measure of progress. That is, on day #3, we reported the total number of pages delivered (12) and the total cost ($320). We did not report that, on day #3, we spent $120 to produce 2 pages.

4. We used a *physical measure* of progress. That is, we measured progress in terms of completed deliverables (in this case, pages). An important feature of cost tracking is that every deliverable should be measured in physical units in order to determine real progress.[5] This is discussed in detail in section 12.4.2.

5. The cost efficiency was less than 1.0 and we determined that this meant the project was over budget.

6. From the cost efficiency, we estimated the final cost. Assuming that we continue to perform at the current rate, we estimated the Cost Estimate At Completion (CEAC), which turns out to be an easy-to-compute and remarkably accurate estimate after only about 20% of the project.

[4]There are a number of assumptions in this estimate and we will examine them in detail.

[5]Eventually, the progress will be converted into monetary units, but the actual progress should first be measured in physical units, e.g., pages completed.

197

We emphasize that cost *tracking* calculations use a *cumulative* measure of cost progress. This makes sense, because we did 2 days of work, which was on budget, and it was only on day #3 that we ran into problems. We should get credit for the on-budget work in the first 2 days. Therefore, a reasonable measure of our cost progress is the cumulative value of the completed work, i.e., 12 pages at a cost efficiency of 75% ($240 worth of completed deliverables which cost $320).

Now let's examine the schedule.

At the end of day #3, we were supposed to have completed 15 pages and we have only delivered 12. Obviously, it will take more time to finish the work we are supposed to have completed by now.

We are behind schedule.

But how much are we behind schedule? We were supposed to complete 15 pages (our planned deliverables), but we have only completed 12 (our actual deliverables). So, a measure of our schedule progress is that we have completed only 12/15 = 80% of the planned deliverables due on day #3, i.e., we have actually completed 80% of the planned work.

Our schedule efficiency is 80%.

From a schedule perspective, at the end of day #3, we are working at an efficiency of 80%. The schedule efficiency goes by the name, *Schedule Performance Index (SPI)*. We determined that the schedule efficiency was less than 1.0, which meant that the project was behind schedule.[6]

Unfortunately, we cannot use this schedule efficiency to compute an estimate of the final project duration. That is, we cannot use the *SPI* in a formula equivalent to equation 12.1. We will explore this issue in detail and show the correct approach for calculating the final duration in section 13.2, Duration Estimation.

For now, however, a schedule efficiency of less than 100% indicates that the project is *behind* schedule.

This simple schedule example illustrates the features of the *schedule tracking* calculation. It uses the earned value data, which is the same data as was used for cost tracking, to calculate the schedule efficiency. The schedule efficiency is a useful *indicator* of the schedule status early in the project.[7]

There are some technical details with both the cost and schedule predictions. First, the project manager must be aware of the quality of the work. We should not get credit for completing pages if the customer rejects by them and they have to be re-written. Therefore, when performing tracking calculations, we assume that completed deliverables are of acceptable quality.

[6]Note that we have not used any cost data in the assessment of the schedule. The assessment of the schedule is independent of whether the work was completed over or under budget.

[7]It is an *indicator*, not a predictor of the schedule.

198

Also, we measured progress in pages, establishing that we measure progress in terms of the physical attributes of the deliverables. In general, it is much easier to understand progress in terms of a physical measure of the deliverables. It is easier to measure, and understand the implications, of the number of pages written than it is to understand the dollars spent. This is discussed in detail in section 12.4.2.

12.2 Formal Definitions

We now provide the formal definitions of all of the quantities:

12.2.1 Planned Value, PV

The Planned Value, PV, is the cumulative time-phased budget.[8]

In the above example, the planned value of the work is $20 per page, or $100 per day for 5 days.

12.2.2 Budget at Completion, BAC

The Budget at Completion is the total planned budget for the project.

The PV at the end of the project is called the Budget at Completion (BAC).

In the above example, the budget at completion is the total planned budget for the project, which is, $500.

12.2.3 Earned Value, EV

The Earned Value, EV, is the cumulative value of work performed.

We emphasize that the EV is the *cumulative* value of the work completed.

EV can be measured both instantaneously and cumulatively.[9] An instantaneous EV measurement would be: On day #3, we completed 2 planned pages. In monetary units, we actually completed $40 worth of work on day #3.

12.2.4 Actual Cost, AC

The Actual Cost, AC, is the total cost incurred to date.

[8]The PMBOK definition also includes the idea that the budget is authorized, and allocated over the life of the project. All that just clutters the definition. Somewhat strangely, the word cumulative is left out of the PMBOK definition.

[9]The PMBOK uses the word *incrementally*, rather than *instantaneously*. We believe that an *instantaneous* measurement is a more correct description of what is being performed, since we are measuring the EV at that instant. An *increment* is a change, which is not what we are measuring, unless you regard day #3 as the increment.

199

AC includes all expenditures, including labor costs, overhead costs, equipment rentals, purchases, and subcontractor costs.

While *AC* is a cumulative measure, it can also be measured instantaneously. An instantaneous measurement of the cost is: On day #3, we spent $120.

12.2.5   Cost Variance, CV

The cost variance is the earned value minus the actual cost.

$$CV = EV - AC. \tag{12.2}$$

The cost variance is a measure of the cost performance of the project. When the value of the work actually completed (i.e., work earned, *EV*) is less than the actual cost spent, *AC*, the project is over budget. Simply put, you have spent more than you were supposed to on the work you have actually completed. Therefore, when *EV* < *AC*, the project is over budget and *CV* is negative.

In the above example, at the end of day #3, we have spent $320, and have completed $240 worth of work (12 of 15 pages). Therefore, the *CV* is negative:

$$CV = EV - AC = \$240 - \$320 = -\$80. \tag{12.3}$$

When the project is complete, *CV* measures the total cost overrun or under run. At the end of the project,

$$CV_{end} = Budget - AC_{end}. \tag{12.4}$$

Suppose that the budget for the project was $1,000 (the budget at completion, BAC). If at the end of the project you have spent $1,200, the *Cost Variance* is:

$$CV_{end} = BAC - AC_{end} = \$1,000 - \$1,200 = -\$200. \tag{12.5}$$

12.2.6   Schedule Variance, SV

> **The sooner you fall behind,
> the more time you'll have to catch up.**
>
> *Steven Wright*

The schedule variance is the earned value minus the planned value.

$$SV = EV - PV. \tag{12.6}$$

The schedule variance is a measure of the schedule performance of the project. When the work actually completed (i.e., the earned value, EV) is less than what was planned (PV), the project is behind schedule. Simply put, you have not done what you were contracted to have done, so you are behind schedule.

Therefore, when $EV < PV$, the project is behind schedule and SV is negative.[10]

In the above example, at the end of day #3, we were supposed to have completed $300 worth of work, and we have actually completed $240 worth of work (12 of 15 pages). Therefore, the SV is negative:

$$SV = EV - PV = \$240 - \$300 = -\$60. \tag{12.7}$$

Notice the weird set of units here. Your boss calls and says, "I hear you are behind schedule. How much are you behind?"

You answer, "I am $60 behind schedule."

Your boss is perfectly entitled to ask, "How can you be $60 behind schedule? How much is that in days?"[11]

When the project is complete, all deliverables will be complete: All planned work is finished. Therefore, at the end of the project $EV = PV$, and $SV = 0$. If the project is behind schedule, this may happen after the planned delivery date.

12.2.7 Cost Performance Index, CPI

The cost performance index (CPI) is a measure of the cost efficiency with which the money is being spent on the project. It is one of the most important concepts in all of project management. The CPI is:

$$CPI = \frac{\text{Earned Value}}{\text{Actual Cost}} = \frac{EV}{AC}. \tag{12.8}$$

When $CPI < 1$, the project is over budget, when $CPI > 1$, the project is under budget, and when $CPI = 1$, the project is exactly on budget.

In the above example, on day #3 I have actually spent $320. There is no arguing with this, it is simply the invoiced amount, $AC(3) = \$320$. The value of the work accomplished (the earned value) is $240. Therefore, CPI is:

$$CPI = \frac{EV}{AC} = \frac{240}{320} = 0.75. \tag{12.9}$$

From a cost perspective, after day #3 I am working at an efficiency of 75% and I am over budget ($CPI < 1$).

[10]We feel obliged to point out that there are serious problems with the SV concept. First, it is not actually a variance in the statistical sense; it is really a difference. Also, it is measured in dollars, which is a strange set of units for a schedule variance.

[11]And you do not know how many days behind you are, because SV is measured in dollars.

12.2.8   Schedule Performance Index, SPI

The *schedule performance index* measures the efficiency with which the schedule is progressing.

$$SPI = \frac{\text{Earned Value}}{\text{Planned Value}} = \frac{EV}{PV}. \tag{12.10}$$

When $SPI < 1$, the project is behind schedule, when $SPI > 1$, the project is ahead of schedule, and when $SPI = 1$, the project is exactly on schedule.[12]

In the above example, on day #3 I planned $300 worth of work. The value of the work accomplished (the earned value) is $240. Therefore, the SPI is:

$$SPI = \frac{EV}{PV} = \frac{\$240}{\$300} = 0.80. \tag{12.11}$$

From a schedule perspective, after day #3, I am working at an efficiency of 80%.

12.2.9   The Cost Estimate at Completion, CEAC

What every stakeholder wants to know, is: *What will be the final cost?*

When you are in the middle of the project and have accumulated some cost data, you can estimate the final cost, which is called the cost estimate at completion (*CEAC*). There are two ways to estimate the *CEAC*.

The Average CPI Method

A quick and easy way to estimate the final cost is to select an appropriate, average *CPI* for the project and then,

$$CEAC = \frac{BAC}{\langle CPI \rangle}, \tag{12.12}$$

where $\langle CPI \rangle$ denotes the average *CPI* for the project. If you think you have a decent estimate of this, then equation 12.12 provides an excellent estimate for the final cost of the project.[13]

Here's an example of how to use the *CEAC*. Consider a book project where we agree to write 10 chapters, each with an estimated cost of $100. Therefore, *Budget at Completion, BAC* = $1,000.

When the project started, we delivered the first chapter on time, but we immediately ran into problems and the actual cost was $133. We also delivered the second chapter on time, but at a cost of $138.

[12]At the end of a project, the $SPI \rightarrow 1$, always, so the SPI inevitably rises towards the end of the project. This does not actually mean the efficiency is improving; it is just an inherent property of the SPI. This makes the use of SPI problematic after about the 50% point.

[13]We note that equation 12.12 assumes that the average *CPI* is constant and that the average value is a reasonable representation of the *CPI* for the entire project.

202

The planned value after month 2 is $PV(2) = \$100 + \$100 = \$200$. The actual cost is $AC(2) = \$135 + \$138 = \$271$. Therefore, after two months, the $CPI(2) = \$200/\$271 = 0.74$. We can now estimate the $CEAC$:

$$CEAC = \frac{BAC}{\langle CPI \rangle} = \frac{\$1,000}{0.74} = \$1,351. \qquad (12.13)$$

We are working at a cost efficiency of around, $CPI = 74\%$. Therefore, the project manager should report that the new estimated final cost is around $\$1,350$. If the team believes they can increase their production, then perhaps the project manager can convince the customer that they will improve on the above estimate.[14]

Since we obtained this future cost estimate after delivering only two chapters, there is some uncertainty about its accuracy. However, cost data from thousands of projects suggests that their rates tend to remain fairly constant and, therefore, $\$1,350$ is probably a good estimate of the final cost.

Should you report this preliminary estimate of an overrun to the customer? The customer probably has strong views of the relative importance of the cost, schedule, and quality of deliverables. We believe that it is a good idea to report this data to the customer with options.

For example, if the customer's budget is tight, then the content may need to be adjusted and the customer could be offered a prioritized list of content options to select from. If the customer's priority is the schedule, the current approach of keeping to schedule by performing extra work may be maintained.[15]

We note that our cost efficiency to date is measured by the current $CPI(t)$. If the $CPI = 1$, then we are on budget, and we can expect to complete the work at that rate in the future.

On the other hand, suppose the $CPI = 0.5$, which says we are only performing at a 50% efficiency rate on the cost. For the remaining work, therefore, we should double the estimate of the cost to complete it. This is accomplished in equation 12.12 by dividing the work remaining by the current CPI.

This is perfectly fine, as long as the current value of the CPI is a sound representation of the efficiency we can expect on the remaining work. If so, then equation 12.15 will give a reasonable value for the $CEAC$. On the other hand, if the CPI is declining, as it often is, the estimate in equation 12.15 will increase. Therefore, if the CPI is declining, equation 12.15 gives an *optimistic* estimate of the cost.[16]

[14] But you'd better have a really good, credible reason. Remember, the customer probably has the same data you have.

[15] It is really bad project management to exhort the team to stay on schedule and lower the cost. It won't happen.

[16] A declining CPI means that the estimate is as low as it will get; it's an optimistic estimate. The situation, however, is pessimistic.

The Expanded CEAC Formula

A more complete analysis proceeds as follows: The expenses to date cannot be argued with, they are what they are, and have probably been invoiced. Therefore, what is needed is the *Estimate to Complete (ETC)* the project. To calculate the *ETC*, we estimate the remaining work and then assume that it will be completed at the current cost efficiency. That is,

$$ETC(t) = \frac{BAC - EV(t)}{CPI(t)}. \tag{12.14}$$

The remaining work is the numerator in equation 12.14: the budget (for the entire project) minus the work completed to date, which is represented by the earned value, $EV(t)$.[17] Therefore, the *cost estimate at completion* is the actual cost to date, $AC(t)$, plus the estimate to complete:

$$CEAC(t) = AC(t) + \frac{BAC - EV(t)}{CPI(t)}. \tag{12.15}$$

At any time, t, we can estimate the final project cost using equation 12.15 as follows: At the current time, we have spent a specific, actual amount, indicated as $AC(t)$. One cannot argue with this amount, it is the actual amount spent to date.

Next, we have to estimate the cost to complete the project. The remaining work is the total work to be done, which is the total work to be completed, BAC, minus the work completed, which is the earned value to date, $EV(t)$. So, the remaining work is: $BAC - EV(t)$. This is the numerator in equation 12.15.

We note that there are two formulas for the *Cost Estimate at Completion, CEAC*: 12.12 and 12.15. However, they are algebraically identical and give exactly the same answer. To show that equations 12.12 and 12.15 are equivalent, consider 12.12 and substitute for $CPI = EV/AC$:

$$EAC(t) = AC(t) + \frac{BAC - EV(t)}{CPI(t)} = AC(t) + \frac{BAC}{CPI(t)} - EV(t)\frac{AC(t)}{EV(t)} = \frac{BAC}{CPI(t)}, \tag{12.16}$$

which is equation 12.12. Equation 12.12 is easier to use, while equation 12.15 provides a detailed look at how the CEAC is arrived at and the assumptions involved.[18]

Another CEAC?

The PMBOK lists another formula for the CEAC:

$$CEAC = AC + \frac{BAC - EV}{CPI \times SPI}, \tag{12.17}$$

[17]Remember, $EV(t)$ is the percentage of the plan completed.

[18]The PM should always be aware of the assumptions involved in any calculation.

with the explanation, "If both the *CPI* and *SPI* influence the remaining work."

In our opinion, this is a terrible formula. There is no theoretical justification for this formula whatsoever. Worse, there is little practical evaluation of its use in the literature, which means a project manager can have no confidence it its use. Also, why should a schedule delay increase the cost? The schedule is independent of the cost and the *SPI* cannot be used to predict a duration.

Finally, equation 12.12 has been shown to correctly predict final cost for thousands of projects as early as 15% to 20% through. Therefore, it makes no sense to divide the correct answer by $SPI \neq 1.0$ to get an incorrect answer.

12.3 Simple Example

We now cover the same example as above only this time we use the formally correct terminology. Before we begin, it is important to stress that you should always measure the physical status of deliverables.[19] This is why we chose, in this example, to measure the deliverables in pages completed.

The budget for the project is 5 pages per day for 5 days at $100 per day. The budget at completion is, $BAC = \$500$.

We first specify the current time, t, which is when the calculation is performed: We are reporting the status of the project on day #3, which we denote as, $t = 3$.

The project status data are typically presented in table form, as in Table 12.1.

On Day #1, we planned to complete $100 worth of work (5 pages), which we write as, $PV(1) = \$100$. We actually completed that work and so we *earn* 100% of the planned value, i.e., we earn 100% of $100, which we write as $EV(1) = \$100$. The same is true on Day #2 and Table 12.1 lists the values for $PV(2)$ and $EV(2)$.

The *Planned Value* is the budget of the work that is planned to be complete at time, t. Note that this is value of the *cumulative* total planned work to date.

Table 12.1: The EVM Data for the Simple Example.

Day	Daily Planned	Daily Earned	Daily Actual	Cumulative Planned PV	Cumulative Earned EV	Cumulative Actual AC	CPI	SPI
1	$100	$100	$100	$100	$100	$100	1.00	1.00
2	$100	$100	$100	$200	$200	$200	1.00	1.00
3	$100	$40	$120	$300	$240	$320	0.75	0.80

[19]After a little thought, you will realize that until it is delivered, to the project manager, it does not exist.

Now we come to day #3, when we planned to have completed another $100 worth of work for a total planned value, $PV(3) = \$300$.

On Day #3, we ran into a problem and only delivered 2 of the planned 5 pages. We only delivered 2/5 of the planned work and, so, only *earned* $2/5 = 40\%$ of the planned value, which is $40\% of \$100 = \$40$. Therefore, the cumulative *earned value* for day #3 is, $EV(3) = \$240$.

On Day #3, when we ran into the problem, we worked an extra 2 hours trying to fix it. We worked 12 hours and, since we get paid $10 per hour, we submitted a bill to the customer for 12 hours, the actual cost, which is $AC(3) = \$120$.

We can now calculate the cost and schedule performance indexes for the project:

- *Cost Performance Index (CPI):* The *earned value* on day #3 (12 of 15 pages) is, $EV(3) = \$240$ and the actual cost is, $AC(3) = \$320$. Therefore, the CPI is:

$$CPI = \frac{Earned\ Value}{Actual\ Cost} = \frac{\$240}{\$320} = 0.75. \tag{12.18}$$

Since the $CPI < 1$, we are over budget.

On day #3, we completed 2 out of 5 pages, which was worth $40. We actually spent $120 and, so, our *instantaneous* cost efficiency is: $40/\$120 = 33\%$. This is distinct from our *cumulative* cost efficiency, which is 75%.

- *Schedule Performance Index (SPI):* The *earned value* on day #3 (12 of 15 pages) is, $EV(3) = \$240$ and the planned value is, $PV(3) = \$300$. Therefore, the SPI is:

$$SPI = \frac{Earned\ Value}{Planned\ Value} = \frac{\$240}{\$300} = 0.80. \tag{12.19}$$

Since the $SPI < 1$, we are behind schedule.

On day #3, we completed 2 out of 5 pages and, so, our *instantaneous* schedule efficiency is 40%. This is distinct from our *cumulative* schedule efficiency, which is 80%.

Finally, we can calculate the *Cost Estimate At Completion (CEAC)*:

$$CEAC = \frac{Budget}{CPI} = \frac{\$500}{0.75} = \$667. \tag{12.20}$$

We are around $167 over our budget of $500, which is about 33%.

12.4 Notes on Earned Value

The most important quantity in the above calculations is the **Earned Value**.[20]

The power of earned value is that it provides measures of efficiency for the work accomplished: Earned Value provides a measure of the efficiency with which we are completing the project. We will make this more formal with the concepts of cost and schedule variance, and cost and schedule performance indexes.

To calculate this measure of efficiency, we only needed three quantities, planned value, PV, actual cost, AC, and earned value, EV. A little thought shows that these are the minimum data that the project manager reports to the customer. The plan was agreed to upon contract signing and is, therefore, readily available. Table 12.1 is the minimum information that a project manager should present to the stakeholders: What you planned, what you delivered, and what it cost.

The project begins with a plan. The cost is always regularly reported to the customer, because otherwise the team does not get paid. Finally, the project manager reports progress on deliverables, which is nothing more than the earned value. For example, at the end of day #3, we would have reported the number of pages completed and the costs. Therefore, the project manager should assume that the customer has all of the cost and schedule tracking data.

The customer also has all the data needed to estimate the cost and schedule efficiencies and, most importantly, the cost estimate at completion.[21]

12.4.1 The End of the Project

At the end of the project, if all the work is successfully completed, the earned value is equal to the planned value. This is most easily seen in a simple example.

Suppose the project is to deliver 4 pages, one per day, and each page costs $1 ($BAC = \$4$). Suppose we deliver 1 page every two days, instead of the planned 1 page per day. It will take us 8 days to complete the 4 pages. The planned and earned values are shown in Table 12.2 and the SPI is plotted in Figure 12.1.

At the end of the project, we have delivered all of the required pages and our total earned value is $4: We earn the value of the completed deliverables and, when we have delivered them all, we earn 100% of the planned value. Therefore, at the end of the project, $EV(t_{end}) = PV(t_{end})$ and $SPI = 1$.

However, this occurs after the planned end of the project and, here, that is not until day #8. Notice that $PV(4) = \$4$, while $EV(4) = \$2$. It is not until the end of the project, $t = 8$, when $PV(8) = EV(8) = \$4$.

[20]We emphasize that Earned Value Management uses *cumulative* quantities. We added the instantaneous quantities in this discussion to clarify the distinction.

[21]This is why we say that when customers learn to use *Earned Value*, we will no longer be able to hide the true project status!

207

Table 12.2: The SPI for the 4 page project.

| | Daily | | Cumulative | | |
Day	Planned	Earned	Planned	Earned	SPI
1	$1.00	$0.00	$1.00	$0.00	0.00
2	$1.00	$1.00	$2.00	$1.00	0.50
3	$1.00	$0.00	$3.00	$1.00	0.33
4	$1.00	$1.00	$4.00	$2.00	0.50
5	$0.00	$0.00	$4.00	$2.00	0.50
6	$0.00	$1.00	$4.00	$3.00	0.75
7	$0.00	$0.00	$4.00	$3.00	0.75
8	$0.00	$1.00	$4.00	$4.00	1.00

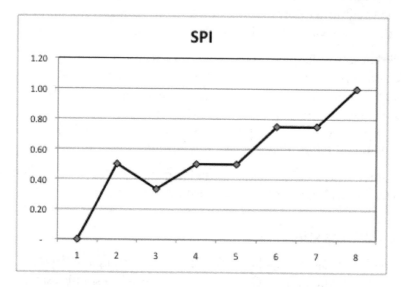

Figure 12.1: *SPI* for the 4 page project. The $SPI \to 1$ at the end of the project, which, here, is on day #8.

In a real sense, the schedule efficiency was 50% *at all times*, because we were completing 0.5 pages per day. However, the shape of the *SPI* curve does not reflect a constant rate of page delivery, it continuously rises towards the end of the project, see Figure 12.1.

This illustrates some of the pitfalls in the use of *SPI* curves. The *SPI* is only actually useful in the early stages of a project and should only be considered as an indicator of the status of the schedule. The project manager cannot take any credit for the "improving" SPI in Figure 12.1, it is an artifact of the definition of the SPI. Chapter 11, Schedule Estimation, is devoted to the solution to this problem.

12.4.2 Measuring Progress

The CPI formula has two terms, AC and EV. The actual cost can only be measured in dollars[22] and so, to calculate the CPI, the earned value must also be measured in dollars; we need all quantities in the same units. Therefore, EV must be converted into dollars.

Sometimes, the topic of earned value is presented as if value is only measured in monetary units.[23] It is not. Progress should be measured in physical units and converted to monetary units.

If we hire a painter to paint a room, the progress is easily measured in square feet actually painted. At the end of each day, we can see how much of the room is painted. Suppose the wall is 10' tall by 10' long (area = 100 square feet). The painter discovers that he cannot reach above 8' and needs to borrow a ladder to complete the work. At the end of the day, he has only completed the lower 8' by 10' = 80 square feet, which is 80/100 of the area = 80%.

Therefore, the value of the work earned is only 80% of the planned work. It is hard to argue with this simple measure of progress: the area actually painted. The painter might argue that his efficiency is actually better, and he could have finished the wall if he had a ladder. He might argue that it is unfair to say his efficiency only 80%. As a project manager, however, we are only interested in *measurable* progress. It really does not matter how fast the painter *might* have finished the work, the *actual* progress was only 80% of planned.

The painter may say that tomorrow, he will "make it up" because now he has the ladder. Currently, however, he is over budget and behind schedule.

If the painter agreed to a fixed price contract, he may be motivated to catch up and finish on time. Alternatively, he may say that the ladder was not his responsibility and that he expects to receive more money because the delay was not his fault. If the painter is working on a Time and Materials contract, he has no incentive to work harder to catch up.

This illustrates several issues. Mathematically, it is easy to see that the painter has only accomplished 80% of the planned work and that he is behind schedule and over budget. But, even this simple example shows that the project manager will quickly become embroiled in the contractual issues.

[22] Assuming you get paid in dollars and not euros.

[23] For example, the PMBOK says that EV is the "value of work performed expressed in terms of the approved budget," i.e., it is assumed to be measured in dollars.

Mathematically, the CPI is simply a ratio; there is not much to it. However, even in this simple painting example, we see immediately that the cost estimate can be interpreted in different ways. We refer to this as the *political* aspect of cost estimation, which complicates the discussion.

Some manuals on the use of the earned value are hundreds of pages thick and propose a process involving dozens of steps. Much of the complication and bureaucracy is an attempt to define carefully how to collect data and how to interpret the results, i.e., they attempt to remove the political aspects.[24] We believe that a better approach is to understand the fundamental assumptions involved in calculating the $CEAC$ and to carefully analyze its implications on each project.

We claim that on any project, if you give it a little thought, the deliverables can be measured in physical units, e.g.,

Miles of roadway completed.
Number of steel girders erected.
Cubic yards of tunnel dug out. Cubic yards of concrete poured.
Software modules designed, tested, documented, and delivered.
Web pages operational.
Scope pages delivered.
Book chapters delivered to the publisher.

12.5   The Re-Paving Project

Data is what distinguishes the dilettante from the artist.

George V. Higgins

We now work through an example of using *Earned Value Management* to estimate the final cost and schedule. The state has decided to repave a road, which is 7.7 miles long. The plan is to complete the job in 10 months with an estimated cost, for the whole project, of $1,470,000.

12.5.1   Month Three

The following table represents the status of the project in month three:

We claim that this table is the minimum that any project manager would report to the client on a monthly basis. It consists of the work completed (in miles) and the costs incurred.[25]

[24] In our opinion, such unwieldy documents have given *Earned Value Management* a bad name.

[25] We immediately see that unlike its bad press, EVM actually does not require any extra bookkeeping.

210

Table 12.3: The status of the repaving project after month 3.

Month	Miles Completed Planned	Actual	Costs Planned	Actual
1	0.77	0.77	$147,000	$147,000
2	0.77	0.62	$147,000	$161,711
3	0.77	0.64	$147,000	$158,492

From this data we can calculate the earned value as follows: The planned amount to be paved each month is 0.77 miles and the planned cost for this is $147,000. The planned cost per mile is therefore:

$$\text{Planned Cost per mile} = \frac{\$147,000}{0.77} = \$190,909. \quad (12.21)$$

In month one, we complete all of the planned 0.77 miles on time and on budget. Our earned value in month one is, therefore, 100% of the plan, which is $EV(1) = 0.77$ miles, or in dollars, $EV(1) = \$147,000$.

In month two, we only completed 0.62 miles, which is $0.62/0.77 = 86\%$ of the plan and, so, our earned value is $EV(2) = 0.62/0.77 \times \$147,000 = \$118,364$. The actual cost is $\$161,711$, which means we have spent more than was planned to accomplish less than was planned. In Table 12.5, we augment the Table 12.4 with cumulative data.

Table 12.4: The repaving project after month 3 with cumulative data.

Month	Costs Planned	Actual	Earned	Cumulative Costs PV	AC	EV
1	$147,000	$147,000	$147,000	$147,000	$147,000	$147,000
2	$147,000	$161,711	$118,364	$294,000	$308,711	$265,364
3	$147,000	$158,492	$122,182	$441,000	$467,203	$387,546

From this we can now compute the *CPI, SPI,* and *CEAC*, see Table 12.5. Remember, the formula for CEAC is equation 12.12. For example, the month two calculation for $CEAC(2)$ is:

$$CEAC(2) = \frac{\$1,470,000}{0.86} = \$1,710,126. \quad (12.22)$$

Table 12.5: CPI, SPI, and $CEAC$ for the repaving project after month 3.

Month	CPI	SPI	CEAC
1	1.00	1.00	$1,470,000
2	0.86	0.90	$1,710,126
3	0.83	0.88	$1,772,149

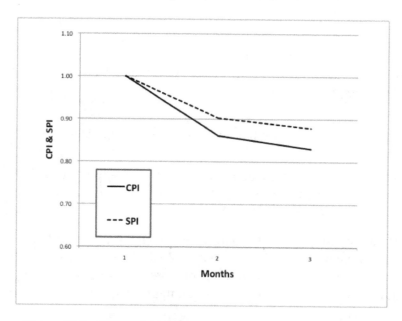

Figure 12.2: CPI and SPI in month 3 for the repaving project.

In month 2, the best estimate for the final cost, based on the expenditures and the efficiency to date, is: $1,710,126. The variance at completion for month 2 is:

$$VAC(2) = BAC - EAC(2) = \$1,470,000 - \$1,710,126 = -\$240,126. \qquad (12.23)$$

In month 2, we are already two hundred and forty thousand dollars over budget.

It is interesting at this stage to plot the CPI and SPI, which are shown in Figure 12.2. We have selected the current CPI as the one to use in the formula for $CEAC$. However, which value of CPI should we actually use?[26]

Figure 12.2 shows that the CPI is declining. We are entitled to ask, therefore, if the current $CPI(3)$ is a good representation of the overall CPI of the project.[27]

[26]Immediately introducing the idea that which CPI the PM should select for the cost estimate is a *political* decision.

[27]In fact, one might argue that because the CPI is declining, the current value is an *optimistic* estimate and our estimate of the final cost should be higher.

The customer might well ask how you intend to get back on track.[28] Here we see the importance of *EVM*. Using a few simple concepts, in month three we estimated the final cost, and it is problematic.[29]

12.5.2 Plot Everything

We recommend that the project manager plot all quantities, because plots explain what is happening far better than do tables. For example, Figure 12.3 shows the actual miles completed, which quickly reaches around 0.6 miles per month. We can easily determine that we are not going to achieve the planned 0.77 miles per month.

Figure 12.4 shows that in the first few months, the *CPI* falls and then levels off. After a few months, the *CPI* is pretty well established. This means that the final cost estimate, the *CEAC*, quickly converged to an accurate estimate for the final value. The plot of the *CEAC* is shown in Figure 12.5 and, by month 3, the *CEAC* has converged to the correct final cost.

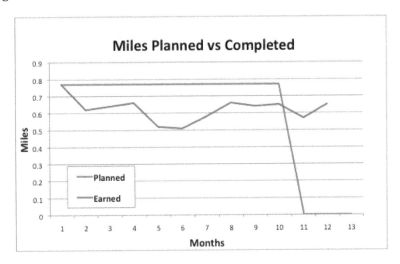

Figure 12.3: Miles (planned and completed) for the repaving project.

In fact, data from thousands of projects shows that the *CEAC* is an excellent predictor of the true cost after about 20% of the project. We also note that when the *CPI* is declining, the *CEAC* a lower bound on the cost.[30]

The behavior of the *SPI* in Figure 12.4 is slightly different. In the first few months, the *SPI* also falls, but, towards the end of the project, it converges to 1.0.[31]

[28] Remember, this chart is easy to plot. If the project manager reported the miles completed and the costs to date, the customer has everything necessary to plot the chart.

[29] The only good news is that it may be early enough for the project manager to take corrective action.

[30] Christensen has conducted several landmark studies on the accuracy of the *CPI*. Using Department of Defense data he found that, "without exception, the CPI does not improve during the period 15% to 85% of the contract."[35, 36]

[31] As it must.

213

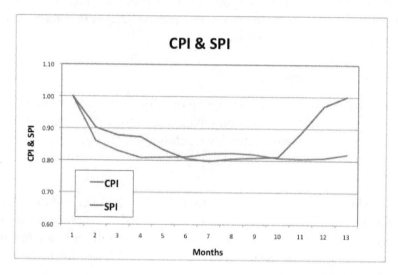

Figure 12.4: CPI and SPI for the repaving project.

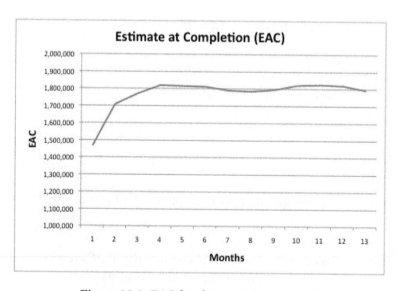

Figure 12.5: EAC for the repaving project.

12.6 Using Earned Value Management

> **The only way to enjoy anything in this life is to earn it first.**
>
> *Ginger Rogers*

Earned Value Management (EVM) has been established as a valuable tool, but, out in the real world, it is often much neglected and, even, maligned. EVM provides early warning signals of project trouble and its predictions are reliable as early as 15% into the project.[32]

So why doesn't everyone use it? There are many excuses, for example: [38]

- "It is not needed on small projects."

  OK, so let me get this straight. Just because you are working on a small project, you do not want to know if your project is late or over budget. Hmm.

- "It is too hard to use."

  You have to report the cost and completed deliverables to your customer every month. Why not divide the cost of the deliverables by the actual cost to determine the CPI? That doesn't sound too hard.

- "The terminology is complex and the rules are overly restrictive."

  There are two quantities, the *CPI* and the *SPI* and they are simply percentages. Reporting those every month doesn't seem very complex. Since you have to report those to the customer anyway, why is this so "restrictive?"

We suspect the real reason that people don't want to use EVM is that their customers will discover the truth about their projects.[33]

12.6.1 Using Hours

Many companies and organizations do not track dollars spent, but only "hours worked." In this case, it is still possible to use Earned Value, one simply calculates everything in hours.

A project must be defined in terms of deliverables and each has a number of *planned hours* over time. As the project proceeds, the hours spent define the *actual cost*. As deliverables are completed, they *earn* the percentage of the planned value of the deliverable in *hours*.

[32] For a theoretical justification of this statement, see [37].

[33] We have repeatedly suggested, both here and in talks, that the real problem with EVM is that customers will find out the truth.

215

As an example, consider a project that is estimated to require 30 hours per month for 6 months and, so, the budget is 180 hours. After month 3, the data are presented in data in Table 12.6. All of the EVM quantities are calculated, but without any mention of monetary units.

Table 12.6: EVM quantities and calculations in hours.

Month	Plan	Monthly Earned	Actual	Cumulative Plan	Earned	Actual	CPI	SPI	CEAC
1	30	20	33	30	20	33	0.61	0.67	269
2	30	25	35	60	45	68	0.66	0.75	272
3	30	20	28	90	65	96	0.68	0.72	265

For example, in month 2, the deliverable was planned to take 30 hours, but only 2/3 of the deliverable was finished and, therefore, only 66% of the plan was earned, $EV(2) = 2/3 \times 30 = 20$ *hours*.

Table 12.6 shows that the project is both over budget and behind schedule. To finish the project will require somewhere in the region of 270 hours, which is 90 more hours than the plan of 180 hours.

The essential point is that EVM does not require monetary units, all calculations can be performed in any units that measure the deliverables.

12.6.2 No Progress

Figure 12.6 shows what happens when a project does not start well. The project was supposed to complete many small deliverables at a constant rate. In the early stages, a small fraction of the deliverables was completed, and each one was completed on budget. Therefore, $AC = EV$, and $CPI = 1.0$, as shown in Figure 12.6.

The project is on budget.

Where are the trouble signs? The problem is that there is not much progress and this is indicated in the SPI curve in Figure 12.6, where the $SPI = 0.4$. Only 40% of the deliverables are being completed in the early stages of the project. (The $PV = 100$, but the $EV = 40$.) In fact, this project continued at the 40% completion rate all along, right up until week 24 when the project was completed.

Notice that the SPI eventually begins to increase, which has nothing to do with the actual progress. The productivity is constant: 40% of the deliverables are completed each week. Nevertheless, the SPI is useful, particularly early on, when the lack of progress is shown in the SPI, not the CPI.[34]

[34]One should not allow the project manager on such a project to claim that the rising SPI means progress.

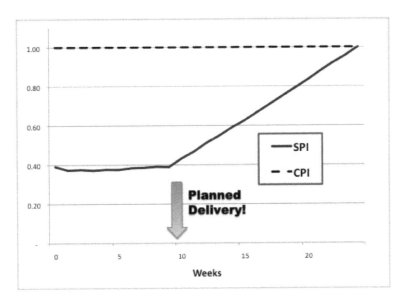

Figure 12.6: CPI and SPI when there is not much progress.

12.6.3 Throw Money At It

Figure 12.7 shows what happens when a project gets into schedule trouble and the project manager decides to throw money at it to get it back on schedule. This project was *schedule dominated*, meaning that the stakeholders would not tolerate a delay. In the early stages, the project is on schedule, but slightly over budget, which can be seen in Figure 12.7: *SPI* ~ 1.0, and *CPI* ~ 0.96.

The project is on schedule.

Around week 8, the project runs into trouble and a few deliverables are late. The *SPI* falls to around 0.96. The project manager immediately recognizes the trouble and spends extra money to get the project back on schedule. This is shown in Figure 12.7, where the *SPI* climbs back to 1.0, and the *CPI* falls to around 0.88.

This is a useful pattern to recognize. The *SPI* falls and then climbs back to where it was. Meanwhile the *CPI* falls to a new average level. The decline in the *CPI* shows that money was thrown at the project to get it back on schedule.[35]

12.6.4 Rotten Quality

Finally, we note that Earned Value Management will not help with the *quality* of the deliverables. It not unusual for the first few deliverables to be completed on time

[35]Whether the money is well spent, we leave to the reader to decide when they uncover such a pattern.

217

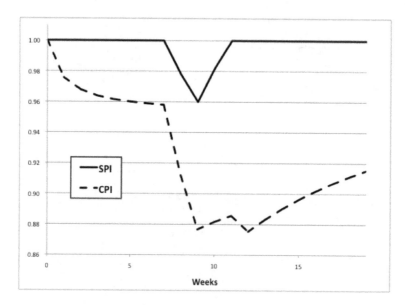

Figure 12.7: CPI and SPI when the project manager throws money at it to get back on schedule.

and within budget, but for a thorough review to uncover errors and missing pieces. The $CPI = 1.0$ (on budget), and the $SPI = 1.0$ (on schedule), but the quality stinks.

In this case, one has not actually *earned* the value of the planned deliverable. A good project manager assigns the earned value of the deliverable only after a thorough review of the quality of the deliverable and its acceptance by the customer.

Earned Value does not tell you what is wrong, or what is causing the problem. Neither does it tell you how to fix it. Think of Earned Value Management as a Thermometer that merely *indicates* when there is a problem. The project manager needs to investigate the *cause* of the problem.

12.6.5 Importance at Major Milestones

Earned Value is particularly important at major milestones. Customers will want to see a measure of progress at these important events. At major milestones, the discussion is not going to be about the money spent, but the accomplishment of something useful.[36]

[36]Earned Value doesn't deliver a project, people do.

For example, for the PMA case study, we illustrate a *Variance Analysis* with a sample report shown in Table12.7. This is an example of using one report to cover multiple topics, which is efficient and helps eliminate errors by reducing redundancy.

Table 12.7: Variance Analysis and Work Performance Results

Project: Date:	PMA 05/20/2011	
Planned: **Schedule:**	**Actual** **Schedule**	**Variance**
Package 1: 20 out of 47 project deliverable reports, documents expected completed by 4/15 Planned Value: $PV = \$4,000$	Only 13 deliverables were completed by 4/15/2011 Earned Value: $EV = \$3,000$	 Schedule Variance: $SV = -\$1,000$
Package 2: First iteration of website scheduled to be completed by 4/15 $PV = \$2,500$	Only 80% of the site pages complete $EV = \$2,000$	 Schedule variance: $SV = -\$500$
Total PV = $6,500	Total EV = $5,000	Variance: $1,500 $SPI = 0.77$ **Behind schedule.**

Root Cause:
(#1) One member of the team was on medical leave of absence.
(#2) Detailed Design delayed by team member on a different page

Planned Response:
New team member requested to pick up the slack.
All documents will be updated to reflect this change.
Existing team will work extra hours until the new resource is up to speed.

12.6.6 Non-Profits

You might get lulled into the idea that earned value is only about dollars. It is not, it is really about deliverables. While the easiest way to measure deliverables is indeed in dollars, it is not the only way.

Suppose you are working on a non-profit project and the staff is all volunteers. You are not paying them and, because you cannot measure their actual labor costs, you might assume that you cannot use earned value. This is not so, as the following example illustrates.

You decide to hold a golf charity event with the goal of raising $5,000.[37] The plan is to accumulate sponsors, each of whom is to donate $50.

In the first week, you get 9 sponsors. Are you ahead or behind schedule?

You do not actually know because it depends on how many volunteers showed up.[38] You need a project management plan.

Let's provide some details. You decide to use volunteers on Saturday mornings to call sponsors and solicit pledges of $50. You need 100 sponsors and your project schedule allows ten weeks to get them. Therefore, you plan on using five volunteers each week who are assigned the goal of obtaining two sponsors each per week.

The first week only three volunteers show up and they exact pledges from nine sponsors. You can now perform the earned value calculation, as follows: The plan was for 5 volunteers to show up and entice 2 sponsors each for a planned 10 sponsors. The sponsors are the deliverables, so we can assign the planned value $PV = 10$. The number of sponsors actually obtained was 9, so the number of sponsors earned on the first week was $EV = 9$.[39]

The actual cost is a little tricky, but think of it as follows: Only 3 volunteers showed up, so they consumed only 3 people's worth of the sponsors (the deliverables). That is, they consumed 6 sponsors (3 volunteers × two sponsors each = 6), so the "actual cost" is $AC = 6$. Table 12.8 summarizes the results.

Table 12.8: The status of the non-profit golf fund-raiser project after week 1.

Week	PV	EV	AC	CPI	SPI
1	10	9	6	1.5	0.9

[37]A real project from one of our students who wrote an excellent paper on the use of earned value to track his volunteers.

[38]This is the non-profit version of the "How ya doin'?" problem.

[39]Once again, the earned value is the percentage of the plan that is completed.

[40]Supporting our claim that there is no excuse for not using earned value.

At the end of week 1, the CPI is significantly greater than 1. This makes sense because the earned work (9 sponsors) was accomplished by only 3 people. Three people are supposed to obtain 6 sponsors, so the fact that they actually obtained 9 is a 50% improvement, as shown by the $CPI = 1.5$. The $SPI = 0.9$, which shows the project behind schedule. This also makes sense because at the end of week 1, the plan was to have 10 sponsors and we only have 9.

This simple example shows that by tracking deliverables (in this case, sponsors), non-profits can use earned value to track a project that doesn't use money.[40]

		Weekly		Cumulative						
Week	Plan	EV	Actual Cost	C Plan	C Earned	C Actual	CPI	SPI	EAC	TCPI
0	-	-	-	-	-	-				
1	0.7	1.0	0.5	0.7	1.0	0.5	2.00	1.47	$600	1.00
2	1.4	1.0	0.8	2.0	2.0	1.3	1.54	0.98	$780	1.00
3	2.0	1.0	0.6	4.1	2.0	1.9	1.05	0.49	$1,140	1.00
4	2.7	2.0	0.5	6.8	3.0	2.4	1.25	0.44	$960	1.00
5	3.4	1.0	1.0	10.2	3.0	3.4	0.88	0.30	$1,360	1.00
6	4.0	2.0	2.0	14.2	5.0	5.4	0.93	0.35	$1,296	1.00
7	4.7	2.0	3.0	18.9	7.0	8.4	0.83	0.37	$1,440	1.00
8	5.3	4.0	4.0	24.2	11.0	12.4	0.89	0.45	$1,353	1.00
9	6.0	4.0	5.0	30.2	15.0	17.4	0.86	0.50	$1,392	1.00
10	6.6	4.0	6.0	36.8	19.0	23.4	0.81	0.52	$1,478	1.00
11	7.2	6.0	7.0	44.1	25.0	30.4	0.82	0.57	$1,459	1.00
12	7.8	6.0	8.0	51.9	31.0	38.4	0.81	0.60	$1,486	1.01

Figure 12.8: Column layout of Earned Value quantities in Excel.

12.7 Large Project Example

What is the best way to implement EV? *Use Excel.*[41]

All the project management tools support EV, including *Microsoft Project.* However, they tend to make the EV process very complicated and unwieldy. In our opinion, it is much more practical to use *Excel.* Tables 12.4 and 12.5 can form the basis of a clear presentation.

We present the cost and schedule data for a large, complex project.[42] The budget for the project was 1,200 person-weeks and the planned expenditures are plotted in Figure 12.9. The project was planned to be completed in 105 weeks.

Figure 12.8 shows an effective layout for the data in Excel. The columns list the weekly planned, earned, and actual costs, which, in this case, are for the number of people working on the project. Next the cumulative data are calculated. In this format, it is easy to add the interesting quantities to the right of those columns, such as the Cost Estimate at Completion (CEAC), TCPI, etc.

You can produce beautiful charts quite easily. For example, see Figure 12.9, which shows the weekly data for the entire project. Such charts enhance the project manager's credibility and demonstrate competence to stakeholders.[43]

A characteristic of the weekly data is that it shows erratic deviations and these usually reflect management decisions. For example, in week #15, the customer had funding problems and the project manager had to reduce staff for a few weeks. The W-like patterns around weeks #60 and #110 reflect the drop in hours worked around the holidays.

[41] While Microsoft Project includes earned value, it is very difficult to implement. Excel is much easier to use and produces much nicer charts.

[42] The details can be found in [39, 37]

[43] The opposite is also true: Ugly and poorly constructed charts with careless errors demonstrate project management incompetence.

221

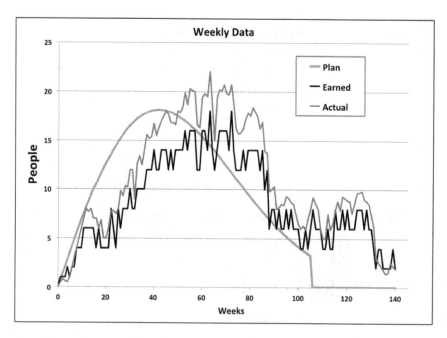

Figure 12.9: Weekly data chart showing management decisions.

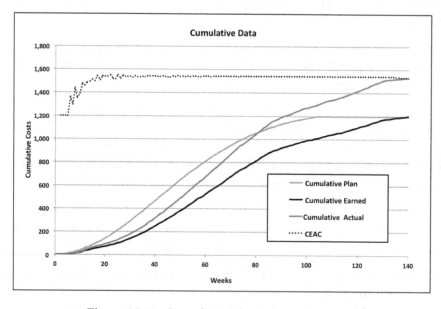

Figure 12.10: Cumulative data plot with CEAC.

The spikes and flat portions of the earned value curve represent the fact that value is only earned when deliverables are completed. In this case, value was earned when software modules were tested and approved. Therefore, the earned value tends to accumulate in lumps.

In week #90, the project manager panicked. With 17 people working on the project, the expenditure rate was high and the project manager reduced staff. Unfortunately, this is was too soon and staff had to be added around week #110.

Figure 12.10 shows the cumulative data, corresponding to Figure 12.9. We can see the immediate effect of the cumulative data is to smooth out the curves. All of the erratic (lumpy) behavior in the earned value and actual costs are smoothed out.

The cumulative data shows that the project was completed in 140 weeks, about 35 weeks late, or 33%. The total cost was planned to be 1,200 person-weeks, but ended up at 1,534 person-weeks, a growth of 28%.

It is useful to add the *Cost Estimate at Completion (CEAC)* to the cumulative chart, and this is shown in Figure 12.10. The *CEAC* is simply the budget, which is constant, divided by the *CPI* and the erratic behavior in the *CEAC* is due to the fluctuations in the *CPI*.

Next, we plot the *CPI* and *SPI*, which are shown in Figure 12.11. In the early stages of the project, modules are delivered, value is accumulated in lumps. Since the earned value data is small, the variations in the cumulative total are comparatively large. This, in turn, means that the early values of both the *CPI* and *SPI* are erratic. However, the *CPI* settles down quite quickly to a constant value.

By week #20, the *CPI* has smoothed out and the *CEAC* has also. Therefore, by week #20, we have a good estimate of the final cost. This is quite remarkable, as we are only 20 weeks into project, and we know the final cost is approximately 1,500 person-weeks, a 25% overrun.

However, we do not know, as yet, how to estimate the final duration. We do know that the *SPI* 0.5, so we know the project is significantly delayed. The *SPI* in Figure 12.11 is particularly interesting. The *SPI* is not at all constant, it gradually rises from a low of 0.3 to 1.0 at the end of the project.[44] Also, the delay in the project around week #10 had a dramatic effect on the *SPI*.

We do not know, as yet, how to estimate the final duration. For this project, we will show you how to do that in Chapter 13, section 13.2.1, *Duration Estimation.*

---

[44] The *SPI* always rises to 1.0 at the end of the project.

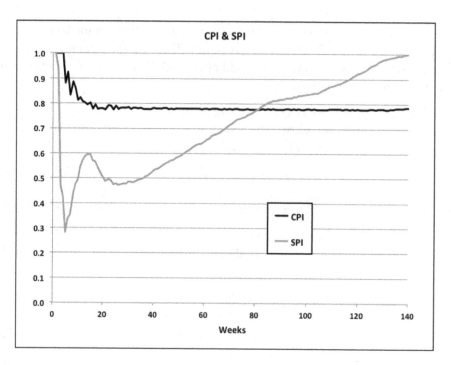

Figure 12.11: A plot of the *CPI* and *SPI*.

12.8 Further Reading

Fleming and Koppelman basically invented the modern formulation of Earned Value. [40] [41] Frank Anbari wrote the definitive summary of the state of the art of EVM. [42]

Christensen & Heise found that EVM provides reliable early warning signals of project trouble as early as 15% into a project. Contracts from the Defense Acquisition Executive Database (DAES) indicate that *without exception, the cumulative CPI does not significantly improve during the period of 15% through 85% of the contract performance; in fact it tends to decline.* [35]

Christensen summarizes this succinctly by saying, "Usually, on a project, things will only get worse."[45]

For one solution to the *SPI* time-dependence, see [37].

Warburton and Cioffi wrote a paper that established how to estimate the duration. They derived the duration estimation formula that is covered in Chapter 13, Cost and Schedule Tracking. See [39].

[45]We particularly like Christensen's writing, he tells it like it is.

224

13

COST AND SCHEDULE TRACKING

**If you guys were women, you'd all be pregnant.
You just can't say no.**

Congresswoman Pat Schroeder

Everyone wants to know what it will cost and how long it will take. Your job, as the project manager, is to figure that out and to explain it to anyone who will listen.[1]

In the previous chapter, we covered Earned Value Management, which provided the fundamental techniques for cost and schedule tracking. In this chapter, we focus on how to use those tools to communicate project status to stakeholders.

While this chapter introduces new skills (especially, duration estimation), the focus is on analyzing the cost and schedule data, understanding what it means, and communicating the project status to the stakeholders.[2] To do that, we:

- Explain what data you will need to collect.

- Show you how to estimate the final cost and schedule.

- Demonstrate the use of the relevant tools and explain their shortcomings.

- Explain the assumptions, ambiguities, risks, and uncertainties.[3]

- Illustrate how to communicate the estimates effectively.

[1]And to some who won't listen.

[2]In this chapter, we are explicitly ignoring the technical status, which is covered in Chapters 14 and 17.

[3]Because a lot of this is guesswork.

13.1 TCPI

**Once our customers start using TCPI,
we will no longer be able to fudge the cost!**

Roger Warburton

The fourth edition of the PMBOK added a simple idea that could change the world. The topic carries an unwieldy name: The *To-Complete Performance Index*, or *TCPI*. While *TCPI* sounds very similar to *CPI*, it is, actually, a very different idea:

- *CPI* is about *your* view of your project and describes the *past*.

- *TCPI* is about the *customer's* view of your project and describes the *future*.

When you present the status of your project to your customer, you typically report three things: what you planned to do, what you actually did, and what it cost. In the technical language of Earned Value Management, you report the planned value, the earned value, and the actual cost. Therefore, your customer can calculate your *CPI* and *SPI*.[4] However, as more customers become smarter in project management techniques, they will also calculate the *TCPI*, which will tell them how much trouble your project is in.

We already have *CPI* and *SPI*, so what else do we need? *TCPI* is not just another formula to measure the status of a project, it is a revolution waiting to happen, but, surprisingly, it's a political and ethical revolution.[5]

The *To-Complete Performance Index* is defined as follows:

> *TCPI is the projection of cost performance that must be achieved on the remaining work to meet a specified management goal, such as the planned budget, the BAC.*

The equation for the *TCPI*, using the *BAC*, is:

$$TCPI = \frac{\text{Work Remaining}}{\text{Funds Remaining}} = \frac{BAC - EV(t)}{BAC - AC(t)}. \tag{13.1}$$

[4] From your data and without your help.

[5] The ethical issue is whether you have the responsibility to tell the customer the truth.

These definitions are pretty cryptic, so we'll provide an example to explain the point of *TCPI*.

Here's an illustration of the problem: You're a couple of months into a project, the first few deliverables have been completed and you diligently calculate the $CPI = 0.9$. Noticing that the $CPI < 1.0$, your customer asks about your plans to deal with the cost overrun.

"No problem, we'll make it up," you say.

Unfortunately, once your customer computes the *TCPI*, that answer is not going to work anymore. Let us show you why.

13.1.1 TCPI Example

Suppose we are writing a book and we propose 10 chapters (the scope). We estimate the cost and negotiate the following deal with the publisher, who is the customer: The planned cost of each chapter is $100 and we promise to deliver one chapter per week for 10 weeks. Therefore, the *Budget at Completion, BAC*, is the planned (estimated) cost of the book, which is $1,000.

We started the project and dutifully delivered the first 3 chapters on time. While we kept to the schedule, we had to put in some over-time to complete each chapter and this added some extra cost. Table 13.1 shows the status of the project at the end of month three.

Table 13.1: The status of the book project after month 3.

Month	1	2	3
Planned Value	$100	$100	$100
Earned Value	$100	$100	$100
Actual Cost	$125	$125	$125
Cumulative Earned Value (EV)	$100	$200	$300
Cumulative Actual Cost (AC)	$125	$250	$375
CPI = EV/AC	0.80	0.80	0.80

Line 1 of Table 13.1 shows the planned costs for the first three months. We delivered the first 3 chapters on time and, so, according to the standard earned value approach, we *earn* the planned value for those deliverables (the second line of the table). Line 3 of the table shows the actual costs incurred, which are larger than the planned costs because of the extra work performed.

We dutifully calculated the $CPI = 0.8$, which showed we ran a little over budget, but at this stage we might just shrug it off, telling the publisher,

"No problem, we'll make it up later."

Now let's add the *TCPI* calculation. The work remaining is the total work minus the work accomplished to date:

$$BAC - EV(3) = \$1{,}000 - \$300 = \$700. \tag{13.2}$$

It is important to note that the work remaining is defined as the *earned value remaining*. The total earned value for the project is $1,000 (the *BAC*) and we have completed three deliverables, so the earned value *remaining* is, $700.[6]

The funds remaining are simply the total budget minus the actual costs expended:

$$BAC - AC(3) = \$1{,}000 - \$375 = \$625. \tag{13.3}$$

We now calculate the *TCPI* at month 3 according to equation 13.1:

$$TCPI(3) = \frac{1{,}000 - 300}{1{,}000 - 375} = \frac{700}{625} = 1.12. \tag{13.4}$$

The interpretation of the *TCPI* is as follows: To complete the project within the assigned budget, you have to work at a rate of 1.12 times your plan, which is 112% of your plan. That is, your productivity needs to be 12% greater than you had planned.

We just need a 12% improvement? No big deal, we'll make it up later.[7]

However, we should not be quite so casual. So far, we are working at a cost efficiency, defined by the *CPI*, of 80%. (Our $CPI = 0.80$.) We need to get our production rate up to 112%. Therefore, to deliver on budget, we need to improve our efficiency from 80% to 112%, a 32% growth in productivity. Maybe we should worry.

[6]Remember, when a deliverable is complete, you earn the *planned* value, not the actual cost.

[7]Isn't that what we tell the customer?

[8]In reality, this is not an uncommon occurrence. There is ample data showing that projects tend to perform at a constant rate. "A project that starts late, stays late." [36]

Two Months Later

Let's now consider the situation at the end of month 5. We delivered 2 more chapters on time and at the same cost. The status is shown in Table 13.2.

We delivered chapters 4 and 5 on time, so we again *earn* the planned value for those (the second line of the table). Our cost efficiency is constant, $CPI = 0.8$.[8]

Let's now perform the *TCPI* calculation at the end of month 5. The work remaining is: $BAC - EV(5) = \$1{,}000 - \$500 = \$500$. The funds remaining are: $BAC - AC(5) = \$1{,}000 - \$625 = \$375$. The *TCPI*, according to equation 13.1, is:

$$TCPI(5) = \frac{1{,}000 - 500}{1{,}000 - 625} = \frac{500}{375} = 1.33. \tag{13.5}$$

Table 13.2: The status of the book project after month 5.

Month	1	2	3	4	5
Planned Value	$100	$100	$100	$100	$100
Earned Value	$100	$100	$100	$100	$100
Actual Cost	$125	$125	$125	$125	$125
Cumulative Earned Value (EV)	$100	$200	$300	$400	$500
Cumulative Actual Cost (AC)	$125	$250	$375	$500	$625
CPI = EV/AC	0.80	0.80	0.80	0.80	0.80

To complete the project within budget, we must now work at a rate of 133% of our plan, i.e., 33% greater than we planned. Since our actual production rate remains at only 80% of what we planned, we need to raise our production from our current performance rate of 80% to the necessary rate of 133%.

We need a 53% improvement in our production rate.

At this point, it is getting extremely difficult to justify our position: "No big deal, we'll make it up." If our customer computes the *TCPI*, she will have every reason to be concerned.

The TCPI does not Lie

> **I cannot help it–in spite of myself, infinity torments me.**
>
> *Alfred De Musset*

In fact, things get rapidly much worse. In month 6, the *TCPI* reaches the value, *TCPI*(6) = 1.6, suggesting we need an 80% improvement to meet the planned budget. The point is that *TCPI* continues to rise, and very rapidly.

The story does not end here—it gets even more interesting. Figure 13.1 shows a plot of the *TCPI* for the book project if things continue at the same production rate. The *TCPI* goes to infinity in month 8!

No matter how optimistic you are, no matter what miracle you think you have up your sleeve, and no matter how great an improvement you think you can induce from your team, the *TCPI* will eventually overtake that performance. The *TCPI* will show your customer that your project will inevitably reach a point where you just cannot deliver on budget. You can't fight infinity.[9]

[9] We actually think it is rather cool that a well-defined project management quantity legitimately approaches infinity.

229

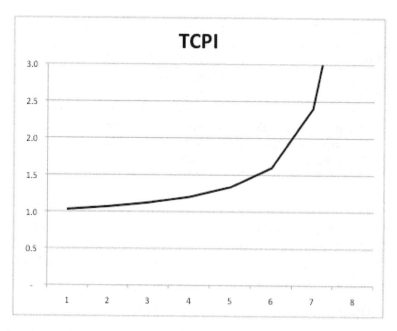

Figure 13.1: The *TCPI* is the cost performance required to complete the rest of the project on budget. The *TCPI* rises dramatically and goes to infinity in month 8.

PMBOK to the Rescue

At this point, the PMBOK suggests a fix. Buried in the *TCPI* paragraph is the apparently innocuous comment:

> *If it becomes obvious that the BAC is no longer viable, the project manager develops a forecast cost estimate at completion (CEAC). Once approved, the CEAC effectively supersedes the BAC as the cost performance goal.*

This is a fancy way of saying that the *TCPI* formula changes to:

$$TCPI = \frac{BAC - EV(t)}{BAC - AC(t)} \rightarrow \frac{BAC - EV(t)}{CEAC - AC(t)}. \tag{13.6}$$

The subtle change is that the *EAC* is in the denominator instead of *BAC* and this is referred to as the *CEAC version* of the *TCPI* formula. Let's see what happens when we use it. First, we need to determine the $CEAC$:

$$CEAC = \frac{BAC}{CPI} = \frac{\$1,000}{0.80} = \$1,250. \tag{13.7}$$

We can now calculate the new $TCPI$ using the right hand version of equation 13.6. At the end of month 5, we have:

$$TCPI(5) = \frac{BAC - EV(5)}{CEAC - AC(5)} = \frac{1,000 - 500}{1,250 - 675} = \frac{500}{625} = 0.80. \tag{13.8}$$

The new $TCPI$ is equal to the CPI. Remember, the $TCPI$ is the "performance that must be achieved on the remaining work to meet a specified management goal." Equation 13.8 simply says that our remaining performance need only be at the rate of $TCPI = 0.8$ to meet our cost goal, which is the newly revised budget of $1,250.

In other words, we have been forced to admit that our productivity is really at the level of the CPI (80% of our plan) and that the project will really cost $1,250. Therefore, if we continue to produce at our past rate, we will meet the revised $CEAC$ goal.[10]

Let's review the process. We calculated the $TCPI$ at each time and its rapid and relentless rise meant that, eventually, we were *forced* to admit that the original budget was no longer viable. We then calculated the new $CEAC$ using our ongoing, established CPI, and this brought our $TCPI$ and CPI into agreement.

All of this comes down to a relatively simple idea: As a project manager, you will eventually have to admit that your productivity is really at the level of the CPI and, that if you produce at that rate, the final project cost will be the revised $CEAC$.

13.1.2 TCPI = CPI?

When we admitted that the BAC was no longer a viable goal, we used the $CEAC$ version of the $TCPI$, which turned out to be equal to the CPI. Is this a coincidence? Actually, no, it is a direct consequence of the $CEAC$ version of the $TCPI$ formula.

If we substitute the $CEAC$ from equation 12.12 into the $TCPI$ formula, we get:

$$TCPI = \frac{BAC - EV(t)}{CEAC - AC(t)} = \frac{BAC - EV(t)}{AC(t) + \frac{BAC - EV(t)}{CPI(t)} - AC(t)} = CPI. \tag{13.9}$$

The $CEAC$ version of the $TCPI$ formula is an identity: $TCPI = CPI$. Presumably, this is what the PMBOK means by: "If it becomes obvious that the BAC is no longer viable .... the $CEAC$ effectively supersedes the BAC as the cost performance goal."

[10]Somewhat ironically, we could actually have determined this value for the overrun in month *one* from the $CEAC$ formula, equation 12.12.

This reinforces the idea that if we own up to the cost overrun, the cost efficiency that is required for the rest of the project (the *TCPI*) is simply our current performance level, which is the *CPI*. The *TCPI* has the remarkable property that if we own up to the cost overrun, we can proceed at our current efficiency (our current *CPI*) and hit the new cost target—the *CEAC*.

13.1.3 Oh-Oh. The Customer Knows

Kirk:	**You're not exactly catching us at our best.**
Spock:	**That much is certain.**

Star Trek IV

One of Albert Einstein's oft-quoted sayings was, "insanity is doing the same thing over and over and expecting a different result."[11] As project managers, we are often guilty of this kind of insanity when we measure a few values for $CPI < 1$ and, then, convince ourselves (and even worse, our customers) that all will be well.

PM:	*We've run into some problems and our CPI = 0.9.*
	Nevertheless, we still believe that we can deliver on budget.
Customer:	*Oh Yeah? I've computed your TCPI = 1.2.*
	How are you going to get 30% increase in productivity?

See what we mean? If your customers start computing the *TCPI*, it's going to change the world. *TCPI* makes your customers tougher and smarter.[12]

Also, the *TCPI* will eventually go to *infinity*, which means you'll never catch up. You just can't win. You may as well learn to compute the *CEAC* as early as possible and tell the stakeholders the truth about the estimated final cost. Also, since you reported the plan, deliverables completed, and actual costs, the customer can compute the *CEAC* without your help.

13.1.4 Advice on Overruns

In our experience, project managers are often reluctant to accept the reality of an overrun. When the *CPI* calculation consistently predicts a significant overrun, it is advisable to let everyone adjust gradually to the new reality. The following modification of the Kübler-Ross model, which deals with grief, might help. [43]

The Stages of Grief:

1. *Denial*: The reality of the overrun is hard to face. People tend to ignore the data and develop a false, preferable reality in which the project is on budget.

[11] The expression probably dates from much earlier, but Einstein quoted it a lot and, so, we credit him with it.

[12] We keep insisting that your customer can calculate the *TCPI*, and all other EVM quantities, from your monthly reports of deliverables and costs. You cannot hide.

2. *Anger*: Why my project? It's not fair! Because the anger gets in the way, no one wants to talk about it.

3. *Bargaining*: We'll do anything. There must be something we can do. Perhaps we can buy more time.

4. *Depression*: Things are really bad on the project, so why bother doing anything? The overrun is certain and there is not much we can do about it.[13]

5. *Acceptance*: Maybe it's going to be okay. We can't fight it, so we may as well prepare for it. We have to come to terms with the reality of the overrun.[14]

Once the team has gone through the grief stages, there is another roadblock: The customer, who is often even more reluctant than the team to deal with the overrun. After all, it's not the customer's fault. The project manager should plan to give the customer some time to go through the same stages of denial, anger, etc.[15]

13.2   Duration Estimation

> **I am definitely going to take a course on time management ... just as soon as I can work it into my schedule.**
>
> *Louis E. Boone*

In chapter 12, we defined the schedule variance, *SV*, and the schedule performance index, *SPI*, both of which are advertised as indicating whether the project is on schedule or not. While both *indicate* a delay, neither *SV* nor *SPI* can be used to estimate the final project duration.[16]

Also, many people are confused by the completely non-intuitive measurement of a schedule delay, represented by the *schedule variance*, as:

$$SV = EV - PV = \$10,000 - \$12,000 = -\$2,000. \qquad (13.10)$$

The conventional wisdom that, because *SV* is negative, the project is "$2,000 behind schedule."[17] Therefore, we need a way to estimate the final duration in time units, not dollars.[18]

There is also confusion at the end of the project where the earned value and the planned value are equal. When all value that has been planned has been earned, *SV* = 0. That is, the measure of the project's lateness is zero, even if the project's completion is far beyond the planned date.

[13] There is often some progress at this stage, as the team begins to accept the situation.

[14] This stage often comes with a calm, more stable mindset.

[15] It is also unreasonable to expect the stakeholders to accept the overrun in the first discussion.

[16] We did not present a formula equivalent to the cost estimate at completion because there isn't one.

[17] Shouldn't schedule overruns really be measured in time units (days, weeks, or months), not monetary units?

[18] Lipke deserves credit for convincing the project management community that "Schedule is Different" [44] and defining the concept of *Earned Schedule* (ES). However, his formulation of ES is not without its problems–see Book [45].

13.2.1 Estimating the Duration

**We've been running a little behind schedule,
but only by about 15 years or so.**

Matt Groening

Given some early project data, we want to determine if the project is on schedule or not. To do that, we have to estimate the final duration. First, we need to distinguish between the schedule and the duration.

13.2.2 Formally Defining the Earned Duration

We continue to use the same data as we used for the calculation of the *CEAC: PV(t)*, $EV(t)$, and $AC(t)$. We define the planned end point of the project as T_p and assume that, during execution, it ends at the actual time, T_a.

If the project is delayed, $T_a > T_p$, and if the project is accelerated, $T_a < T_p$. The total planned cost is the budget at completion, which is the planned value at the end of the project, i.e., $BAC = PV(T_p)$.

We next plot the cumulative planned value, $PV(t)$, and the cumulative earned value, $EV(t)$, see Figure 13.2.[19] When a project is delayed, the earned value curve falls behind the planned value curve, which is illustrated in Figure 13.2.

The earned duration, $T_e(t)$, is defined using the following graphical construction:

At any given time, t, the earned duration, $T_e(t)$, corresponds to the project duration at which the current earned value, $EV(t)$, is projected back to meet the planned value curve, which is at $PV(t - \delta(t))$.

At the current time, t, the delay, $\delta(t)$, is defined as the time difference represented by the horizontal projection back from the point on the earned value curve at t to its intersection with the planned value curve:

$$EV(t) = PV[t - \delta(t)]. \tag{13.11}$$

Positive values for $\delta(t)$ represent accelerations while negative values represent delays. We now define the *Earned Duration*, $T_e(t)$, as the time from the start of the project to that of the above intersection. The intersection time is defined by,

$$T_e(t) = t - \delta(t). \tag{13.12}$$

[19]We add the '(t)' to the quantities to remind the reader which ones are functions of time.

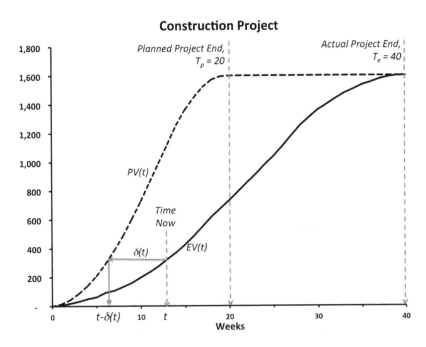

Figure 13.2: The *delay* construction: The schedule delay at time, t, is $\delta(t)$, which is determined by the arrow from $EV(t)$ to $PV(t - \delta(t))$. The earned duration, $T_e(t)$, is defined as $T_e = t - \delta(t)$.

Thus, we have created a duration triad: planned total duration, T_p; actual total duration, T_a; and, at any given time, t, the earned duration, $T_e(t)$. These durations are directly analogous to the quantities that compose the EVM cost triad: planned value, earned value, and actual cost.[20]

We continue to follow standard EVM, which says that as each activity is completed, it earns its planned value, even if there is a cost increase or a delay in completing the activity, e.g., if additional resources have to be applied.

13.2.3 The Duration Estimation Formula

The formula for the estimate of the revised final duration, T_a, is:

$$T_a = \frac{t T_p}{T_e(t)}, \qquad (13.13)$$

where t, is the current time at which we want to estimate the final duration, T_p is the planned duration, and $T_e(t)$ is the earned duration.

[20]These definitions are completely general and can be applied to any cost profile. Most definitions of *Earned Schedule* only apply to linear $PV(t)$ and $EV(t)$ cost curves.

235

We now show how to use equation 13.13 to estimate the revised final duration at the current time, $t = 4$. Suppose the planned schedule for the project is, $T_p = 20$, and we determine the intersection as, $T_e(t) = t - \delta(t) = 3$. The estimate of the actual duration, T_a, is:

$$T_a = \frac{tT_p}{T_e(t)} = \frac{4 \times 20}{3} = 26.6. \tag{13.14}$$

Our new duration estimate is 27 weeks, compared to our plan, which was, $T_p = 20$ weeks. This means we are estimating that we will be 7 weeks late.[21]

The T_a equation is pretty easy to use and, in practice, gives a good estimate of the final duration.[22]

13.2.4 Large Project Example

If everything seems under control, you're just not going fast enough.

Mario Andretti

We now show how to use the duration estimation formula on the large project presented in section 12.7. We use the same planned and earned value data as was used in the *CEAC* calculation and a sample is shown in Table 13.3.

Table 13.3: The data for the calculation of T_a at time, $t = 15$.

t	PV(t)	EV(t)	$T_e(t)$	$T_a(t)$
11	46.0	25		
12	54.2	31		
13	63.0	37		
14	72.4	43		
15.0	82.4	49.0	11.4	138.5

We wish to estimate the duration at the time, $t = 15$, where the earned value is $EV(15) = 49.0$. To calculate the earned duration, $T_e(15)$, we need to find the time, t_x, where, $EV(15) = PV(t_x)$. We see from Table 13.3 that, $PV(11) = 46.0$ and $PV(12) = 54.2$. Therefore, t_x is roughly in the middle, between 11 and 12.

We can estimate this a little more accurately as follows: Since $EV(15) = 49.0$ and $PV(11) = 46.0$, $T_e(15)$ is 11 plus a fraction and we can calculate the fraction as:

$$\frac{EV(5) - PV(11)}{PV(12) - PV(11)} = \frac{49.0 - 46.0}{54.2 - 46.0} = \frac{3.0}{8.2} = 0.37 \tag{13.15}$$

[21] There is no point in using the decimal, just round up. There is likely to be lots of scatter in the data.

[22] Just like the CEAC equation gives a good estimate for the final cost.

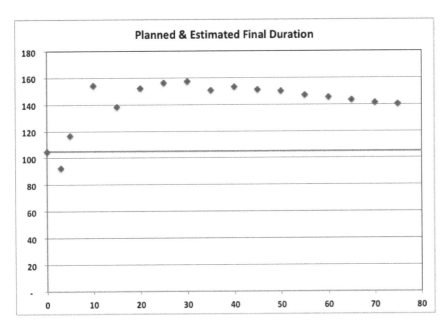

Figure 13.3: A plot of the *Estimated Duration* (points) and the *Planned Duration* (grey line).

Therefore, $T_e(5) = 11.4$. We now use equation 13.13 to estimate the final duration:

$$T_a = \frac{tT_p}{T_e(t)} = \frac{15 \times 105.0}{11.4} = 138. \tag{13.16}$$

At time, $t = 15$, the estimate for the final duration is $T_a = 138$ weeks, as compared to the plan, which is 105 weeks. Our estimate is that we will be 33 weeks late, or $\sim 30\%$ late.

This calculation is repeated every 5 weeks and the results are shown in Figure 13.3.

Duration estimation is inherently less accurate than cost estimation. (The technical issue is summarized in section 13.3.2.) Therefore, one does not have to worry too much about performing the fraction calculation in equation 13.15, one can simply use the integer values of the time.

In the above example, we noted that $EV(15) = 49.0$ falls between $PV(11) = 46.0$ and $PV(12) = 54.2$. If we just use $t = 11$ (without the fraction) and use equation 13.13 to estimate the final duration, we obtain:

$$T_a = \frac{tT_p}{T_e(t)} = \frac{15 \times 105.0}{11} = 143, \tag{13.17}$$

237

which doesn't differ much from the previous estimate of 138 weeks. If we examine the early estimates of the final duration in Figure 13.3, we see a lot of uncertainty around $t = 15$. Some detail is provided in Table 13.4, which shows that the duration estimate fluctuates between 154 and 139, or, about 10%. Therefore, it is not critical to get the fraction exactly correct and an estimate will usually suffice.

Table 13.4: The early estimates of T_a.

Time	Estimate of T_a
10	154
15	139
20	152
25	156

The important result, to the project manager, is that the estimate of the duration is around 150 weeks and this is significantly different from the plan of 105 weeks. The actual duration will turn out to be slightly better, around 140 weeks. It is important to understand that the project manager knows this duration estimate in week 15, which is only about 15% of the way into the project. Therefore, the project manager can begin to explore options for the stakeholders.

13.3 Derivation of the Estimated Duration Equation

Unlike the *CEAC* formula, the duration estimation formula is not obvious. Therefore, to understand its usage, the project manager should know a little about the assumptions involved and how it is derived.

It is straightforward to derive the estimated duration formula for the special case of linear cumulative labor profiles.[23] Linear cumulative cost profiles are where the planned and earned value curves are straight lines. Although a special case, the process is typical and illustrative.

Linear labor profiles occur in a project for which the number of people planned to work on the project is a constant for the life of the project and they work a constant number of hours in each time period. For example, if the staff works 10 units in each time period, the cumulative planned values are, $PV(1) = 10$, $PV(2) = 20$, $PV(3) = 30$, etc. This is shown in Figure 13.4. The project is planned to end in week 10, so the total budget is $BAC = PV(10) = 100$.

The planned end of the project is at time, T_p, where the total cost is the budget,

[23]Students only need to understand the general ideas behind this derivation.

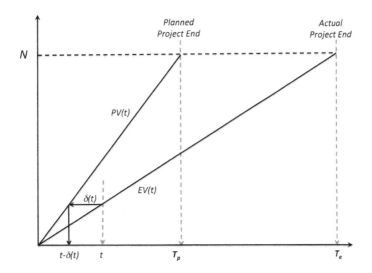

Figure 13.4: Linear cumulative labor profiles. The delay at time, t, is $\delta(t)$ and is denoted by the arrow from $EV(t)$ to $PV(t - \delta(t))$. The earned duration is, $T_e(t) = t - \delta(t)$.

BAC, which we denote as, N. Therefore, the cumulative planned value is given by:

$$PV(t) = N\frac{t}{T_p}. \qquad (13.18)$$

We can easily see this makes sense by substituting a couple of values: For $t = 10$, $PV(2) = 100 \times 2/10 = 20$. At the end of the project, where $t = T_p = 10$, $PV(10) = 100 \times 10/10 = 100$.

During execution, we assume that the project is delayed and that the actual end point of the project is at time, T_a, where, $T_a > T_p$. At the end of a successful project, all of the deliverables have been completed, which means that all of the value that was planned has been earned and the total earned value equals the total planned value. Therefore, $EV(T_a) = PV(T_p)$ and the cumulative earned value is given by:

$$EV(t) = N\frac{t}{T_a}. \qquad (13.19)$$

We can now mathematically define the earned schedule, $T_e(t)$, at time, t, as the time of the intersection of the projection back from the current time in the project,

t, on the earned value curve to the planned value curve. The intersection time is,

$$EV(t) = PV(t - \delta(t)). \tag{13.20}$$

Using the planned and earned values, from 13.18 and 13.19, gives,

$$N\frac{t}{T_a} = N\frac{(t-\delta)}{T_p} \qquad \frac{T_p}{T_a} = \frac{(t-\delta)}{t} = 1 - \frac{\delta}{t}. \tag{13.21}$$

Therefore, the delay in the project at time, t, is,

$$\delta(t) = t\left(1 - \frac{T_p}{T_a}\right). \tag{13.22}$$

The delay, $\delta(t)$, is a function of time, which can be seen in Figure 13.4, where the horizontal distance from $EV(t)$ curve to the $PV(t)$ curve increases over time. The *earned schedule* is defined as:

$$T_e(t) = t - \delta(t) = t\left(\frac{T_p}{T_a}\right). \tag{13.23}$$

This formula contains the quantity, T_a, the estimate of the final duration. By rearranging the equation, we find the formula for the estimate of the final duration:

$$T_a = \frac{tT_p}{T_e(t)}. \tag{13.24}$$

Note that all quantities in equation 13.24 are in time units. In particular, the final duration estimate, T_a, is time units, so we have eliminated the confusion about SV being in currency units.

Knowing the planned duration, T_p, one measures the delay, $\delta(t)$, between the earned value curve and the planned value curve. One then calculates the time of the intersection, which is the *earned duration*, T_e. The estimate of the project's final duration then follows from equation 13.24.

The SPI for Linear Profiles

For project with a constant level of effort, the planned and earned values are given in equations 13.18 and 13.19. Therefore, in this special case, the *SPI* at time, t, is:

$$SPI = \frac{EV(t)}{PV(t)} = \frac{Nt}{T_a}\frac{T_p}{Nt} = \frac{T_p}{T_a}. \tag{13.25}$$

Therefore, for linear cost profiles,

$$T_a = \frac{T_p}{SPI}. \tag{13.26}$$

In this special case, we can calculate the duration form the *SPI* using equation 13.26.[24] However, we can only use equation 13.26 when the *SPI* is constant, which is when the labor rate is constant.

For most projects, the planned and earned value profiles follow S-shaped curves, i.e., they are not linear. Equation 13.26 is only true for projects with linear profiles and using them on a project with an S-shaped profile will give the wrong answer for the duration. This explains why, in general, the *SPI* is only an *indicator* of a delay and does not predict the final duration.

13.3.1   Nonlinear Cost Rate Profiles

Above we derived the duration formula for the case of linear planned and earned value cost profiles. It is important to understand that different duration formulas apply to different cost profiles.

A triangular cost rate profile is often used when the peak spending rate can be estimated reliably, e.g., "duration estimates based on three points with an assumed distribution provide an expected duration." [4] Triangular cost rate profiles result in S-shaped (i.e., non-linear) cumulative cost curves.

Following the above approach, one can determine that, for some triangular profiles, the delay grows linearly with time and the equation for the final project duration, T_a, is identical to the linear case, equation 13.24. However, not all triangular planned and earned curves result in the same duration formula. Therefore, for some projects, using equation 13.24 would be in error.[25]

Another practically important S-shaped cost profile is the Putnam-Norden-Rayleigh (PNR) curve and many studies show that, for large projects, the cumulative earned value data often closely follow the PNR curve. [46, 47, 48, 49] Somewhat remarkably, for projects following the PNR profile, the duration estimation formula is identical to that for the linear case. [39]

That several, quite different, nonlinear profiles give the same duration equation as the linear case reinforces the idea that the duration equation has wide practical value and that the linear formula actually applies to a variety of projects.

For any profile, one can also calculate T_a in terms of the *SPI*, as we did for the linear profile, equation 13.25. However, the SPI-based duration formulas are all different

[24] Equation 13.26 is the equivalent of *CEAC = BAC/ CPI*. It is interesting to ask why the *CEAC* formula works everywhere, but the T_a formula works only for linear profiles. We're still not quite sure why.

[25] For details, see [39].

and, while it is theoretically possible, it is usually not practical to determine the duration from the *SPI*.

13.3.2 Duration Estimation Accuracy

It is not well-known that the accuracy of duration estimation is not a good as that for cost estimation. The theoretical reason is based on the fact that the *delay*, $\delta(t)$, requires a subtraction, which lowers the accuracy of the duration estimate.

As a simple example, suppose you have two quantities whose values are $x = 10$ and $y = 8$, and the errors in x and y are both $\sim 1\%$. If you add them, you get $z = x + y = 18$, and the error in z can be $(0.1 + 0.1)/18$, which is small. But, if you subtract the quantities, you get $z = x - y = 2$, and the error in z can be $0.2/2.0$, which is 10%.

The subtraction operation results in a much larger errors than the other mathematical operations. The *duration* calculation involves a subtraction: the definition of the delay as the difference between the planned and earned value curves. Therefore, the errors in the *CEAC* calculation, which uses multiplication, are much less than the errors in the duration calculation, which uses subtraction.

That the *duration estimate* is much less accurate than the *CEAC* is reflected Figures 12.11 and 13.3, where you can see that the scatter, or uncertainty, in the duration data is much larger than the scatter in the *CEAC* data.

13.3.3 Duration Estimation Summary

We emphasize that there is a sound theoretical basis for project duration estimation as it uses the standard quantities of EVM. Duration estimation uses a duration triad (planned, earned, and actual duration) analogous to the EVM cost triad. The entire theory is completely general and applies to any, even non-linear, cost curves.

It is possible to derive duration estimates from early SPI data. However, the SPI-based duration formulas are not as useful, because, for nonlinear profiles, the duration estimates depend on the parameters of the cost profile and, typically, apply only in the early stages of projects.

While the derivation of the duration formula is complex, the resulting formula is quite straightforward and requires little mathematical skill to use it. Also, since the entire theory was built on standard EVM, it should be familiar and accessible to practitioners.

The duration estimation formula should not be considered as an alternative to *Critical Path* and *Tracking Gantt* techniques. Instead, it offers an additional option for checking duration estimates from other tools. For small projects, schedule control using a Gantt chart is appropriate. However, for larger projects, the potential number of critical paths can grow, making it difficult to determine the duration. In such situations, the duration formula may be an effective, additional option.

While the reader need not remember all of the theoretical details, the theory provides a number of important lessons for a project manager:

- *Duration estimation,* using the T_a formula, is not as accurate as cost estimation, using the *CEAC* formula. The *SPI* is only a constant for a project with a constant level of effort. In general, the *SPI* varies over time and, so, measuring it will tell you little about the final duration estimate.

- Both the earned duration and the schedule delay are functions of time and, so, measuring them at one point does not determine them. We must use the time-dependent formula, equation 13.13, to determine the new duration estimate, T_a.

- The T_a equation is pretty easy to use and, in practice, gives a good estimate of the final duration.[26]

13.3.4 Applications of the Duration Estimation Formula

It is a capital mistake to theorize before one has data.

Sir Arthur Conan Doyle

The analysis of the project's schedule begins by collecting the data for the current period, which consists of what was planned, what was accomplished, and how much it cost. The data are usually presented in dollars, but the calculations are perfectly valid in any set of units.[27] The weekly data are presented in Table 13.5 and the current time is week 10. Note that the time (weeks) is in column B and the last value in column B is the current time, week = 10.

The budget for this project is $1,600 and the planned schedule is $T_p = 20$ weeks. The cumulative data are calculated as follows: The cumulative planned value for week 3 is, $PV(3) = \$87$, which is the sum of the weekly planned values: $\$14 + \$28 + \$45$.[28]

It is useful to plot the data and the cumulative planned and earned values are shown in Figure 13.5. Because the earned value data lags the planned value, we see that the project is delayed and, so, we need to estimate the new schedule.

[26]Just like the CEAC equation gives a good estimate for the final cost.

[27]Students are encouraged to interpret the units in Table 13.5 in creative ways. Our favorite: The number of windows installed.

[28]The data for this project is taken from a famous construction project, see [50].

243

Table 13.5: The project data up to week 10.

		Weekly			Cumulative			
	Week	Planned	Actual	Earned	Planned	Actual	Earned	$t - \delta(t)$
A	B	C	D	E	F	G	H	I
5	0	0	0	0	0	0	0	0
6	1	14	5	5	14	5	5	0
7	2	28	13	13	42	18	18	1
8	3	45	17	14	87	35	32	1
9	4	56	18	18	143	53	50	2
10	5	67	25	18	→ 210	78	68	2
11	6	82	31	22	292	109	90	3
12	7	94	35	24	386	144	114	3
13	8	102	35	30	488	179	144	3
14	9	118	40	32	606	219	176	3
15	10	122	44	34	728	263	← 210	5

We are in week 10, so $t = 10$. The *earned duration* construction for week 10 is shown in Figure 13.5: The line is projected back from $EV(10) = 210$ to the planned value curve and the intersection occurs at $PV(5) = 210$.[29] The time at which the intersection occurs is $t - \delta(t) = 5$. We can now estimate the revised schedule using the *earned duration*, equation 13.13:

$$T_a = \frac{tT_p}{T_e(t)} = \frac{10 \times 20}{5} = 40. \tag{13.27}$$

The estimate of the schedule has grown from $T_p = 20$ to $T_a = 40$ weeks.[30] It turns out that for this real project, the final duration was indeed $T_a = 40$ weeks, confirming the accuracy of the technique.

Once we have the cumulative values, we can calculate the other interesting project quantities, such as *CPI*, *SPI*, *TCPI*, and *CEAC*, see Table 13.6.

We plot the *CPI* and *SPI* in Figure 13.6 and the cost estimate at completion, *CEAC* in Figure 13.7. We also present the estimate of the final schedule, T_a, in Figure 13.8, which shows how it evolves over time. Early on, there is considerable scatter in the estimate, but it settles down and converges to the correct value.

[29] In general, the planned value will not be exactly equal to the earned value. In which case, one selects the week with the nearest value.

The general rule of thumb about the accuracy of the estimate of the final duration is that it is within about 10% of the correct answer about 15%–20% into the project. In this regard, T_e is similar to *CEAC*, both of which have considerable scatter early on, but quickly settle down and converge to their correct final values. The cumulative aspect of the planned and earned value data tends to smooth things out over time

[30] And we know this, already, in week 10.

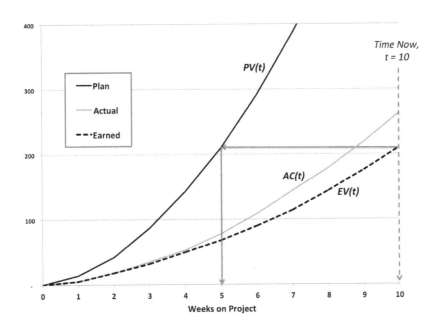

Figure 13.5: A plot of the cumulative planned and earned value data in Table 13.5 showing the *earned duration* construction at time, $t = 10$.

Table 13.6: Project estimates for week 10.

Week	t - δ	T_e	CPI	SPI	BAC	TCPI	EAC
0	0	20	1.00	1.00	1,600	1.00	1,600
1	0	20	1.00	0.36	1,600	1.00	1,600
2	1	40	1.00	0.43	1,600	1.00	1,600
3	1	60	0.91	0.37	1,750	1.00	1,750
4	2	40	0.94	0.35	1,696	1.00	1,696
5	2	50	0.87	0.32	1,835	1.01	1,835
6	3	40	0.83	0.31	1,938	1.01	1,938
7	3	47	0.79	0.30	2,021	1.02	2,021
8	4	40	0.80	0.30	1,989	1.02	1,989
9	4	45	0.80	0.29	1,991	1.03	1,991
10	5	40	0.80	0.29	2,004	1.04	2,004

as more values contribute. Both schedule and cost estimates are available early on in the project and are quite accurate.

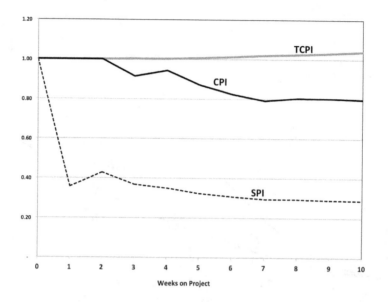

Figure 13.6: The CPI, SPI and TCPI.

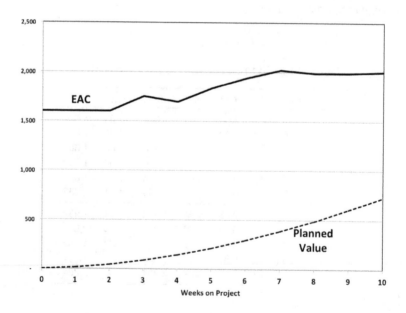

Figure 13.7: The Estimate at Completion (EAC).

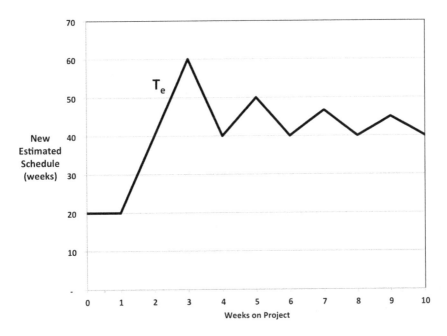

Figure 13.8: The estimated schedule, T_e, over time.

Automating the Excel Calculation of the Delay

The first column (A) in Table 13.5 gives the row number in the spreadsheet. The cumulative PV is in column F and the cumulative EV is column H. Column I gives the values of $t - \delta(t)$. It is slightly tricky to implement this in Excel, but the method is as follows: The Excel formula in column I, labeled $t - \delta$, is (in row 15):

=INDEX($B$5:$B$15,MATCH(H15,$F$5:$F$15))

The MATCH function looks for the row where H15 occurs (*EV=210*) in the PV column, which is specified by F5:F15. Therefore, the MATCH function looks for where the value 210 occurs in the cumulative planned value column (F) and the answer is, row 5. Therefore, the MATCH function returns '5'. The INDEX function then returns the value in the weeks column, defined by B5:B15, for row 5. The result is that this calculation returns '5'.

This process is indicated in Table 13.5 by the arrows. Once the value of $T_e(t) = t - \delta(t)$ is known, we calculate T_a from equation 13.13.

13.4 Writing the Report

We now have all the data necessary to write a report to the stakeholders. There are several ways to do this and, if our students are any indication, there is considerable debate about the best way to do it. Therefore, we will present two approaches and let the reader decide on the style that best fits their taste and situation.[31]

The Short Letter

The idea behind this approach is that your report is probably going to a senior executive who only wants the minimum, essential information. For example, if you are working on a major highway in Boston, your report will probably be sent to the mayor, who only wants a short summary of the key facts.[32]

In this case, write a short letter (about one page) that presents the progress to date, lists the essential data (the cost and schedule overrun), and briefly explains the key issues (why it is late and over budget). Then, one should attach an appendix that presents the data in all its glory.[33] An example is shown in Figure 13.9.

The Long Report

Many people prefer to lay it all out in a continuous narrative. Their rationale is that this allows them to present the situation more carefully, with each topic backed up with the appropriate level of detail and with its own charts and data. In this case, the document is typically of a *formal* report with sections addressing the technical issues; the cost and schedule; risks; and potential solutions.[34]

Comments

Whether you select the short or long form, there are several issues to consider.

- *Should charts go in the letter?*

  We think so.[35] Presenting one really powerful chart with all the data demonstrates competence on the part of the project manager. A chart that we like for this purpose is shown in Figure 13.10. It clearly shows that, even though the project is not very far along, the *CEAC* is well above the budget. Also, the *Earned Duration* method shows a significant schedule delay.

- *Fix it.*

  The customer might regard the letter as a demand for more money and time.[36] Therefore, presenting the data early will mitigate its negative impacts

[31] Even the authors disagree on the best way to do this.

[32] The Mayor will then send it to his staff to check it out.

[33] Charts, data, problems, excuses and mea culpas, which is Latin for "It's the project manager's fault."

[34] In which case, you are going to need an executive summary, which is going to look a lot like the short form.

[35] We also admit that, again, not everyone agrees.

[36] Which it often is.

248

ABC Properties, Inc.
Boston, MA

May 30, 2014
Re: Door Upgrade Project report:

Dear Customer:

Two and a half months ago we embarked on the ambitious project of upgrading all the doors in your building at a cost of $1,000 each. We planned to complete the project within 20 weeks and with a Budget at Completion of $1.6 million.

The strategy was to start upgrading the doors at a rate of 14 per week and then quickly increasing the pace until we reached the apex of 134 doors per week during the winter months. The Appendix contains the data.

Technical Performance

After 10 weeks of work we should have completed 728 doors; however the team only completed a disappointing 200 doors. Inspection confirmed that all doors were installed according to the highest standards. The building occupants liked the new doors and the guards were particularly impressed with the security features.

Cost

Using the concepts of eVM, we present the cost data. To date, we have only spent $263,000, against our plan of $728,000. Therefore, our Cumulative Earned Value is only $200,000 and we are $63,000 over budget (about a 31% overrun). The $CPI = 0.76$, which implies a less than desirable 76% cost efficiency.

The planned Budget at Completion is $1,600,000. However, based on the current data, the new Estimate at Completion is a very concerning $2,105,100.

I'd like to be able to tell you that a mere 5% improvement in our cost efficiency, calculated using the To-Complete Performance Index, TCPI, would get us back on track. However, I also know that the people on your team will remind me that, because our CPI is 0.76, the improvement in efficiency we would actually need is closer to 29%.

Schedule

The indicators confirm that, unfortunately, we have an extremely poor schedule efficiency, $SPI = 0.27$. Even more concerning is that, using the Earned Duration method, I predict the project will take 40 weeks to complete.

So this is the sad state of this affair. We have an issue of cost and an even bigger one of schedule. I suggest that we meet soon to discuss how we might proceed to move forward.

Sincerely,

Michel Laflamme,
Project Manager, ABC Properties

Figure 13.9: Sample short-form letter.

by investigating different approaches for the completion of the project, e.g., reduce the cost by using less expensive doors.[37] There is probably not a lot you can do about the doubling of the schedule.[38]

- *Why wait until week 10?*

  Actually, Figure 13.11 shows the project was in trouble in week 5. While there

[37] Maybe there are backstairs or basement doors that the tenants do not use and that don't need upgrading.

[38] Adding people might reduce it somewhat.

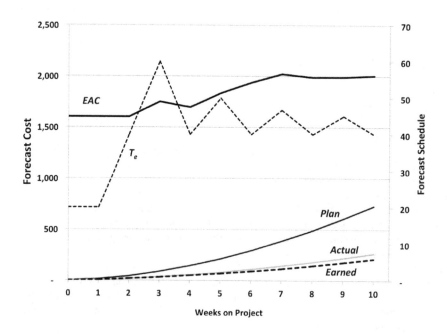

Figure 13.10: The project status at week 10.

is a lot of scatter in the early data, it clearly shows that the schedule might double and that the cost overrun is > 15%. Should we have presented these preliminary conclusions to the customer? Are they sufficiently reliable? [39] On the other hand, the earlier you present the bad news, the more options you have to make adjustments and to solve problems.

- *The Ethical Dilemma*

Finally, is informing the customer at week 5 the correct ethical choice? PMI continually stresses that ethics is an integral part of the profession and has defined a rigorous *Code of Ethics and Professional Conduct*. [7][40] The code says that practitioners will "provide accurate information in a timely manner."

This seems to mandate that the project manager immediately report a delay and overrun. But, is the week 5 data reliable?[41] Are you ethically obligated to report an *indication* of trouble? You might decide to wait for more data, but that introduces a risk: The customer might respond, "You knew in week 5!"

[39]Would it be unnecessarily alarming to present these tentative conclusions?

[40]Also, see Chapter 19.

[41]We actually believe that the week 5 data are pretty clear: The project schedule is in serious trouble. But, we allow that you might disagree.

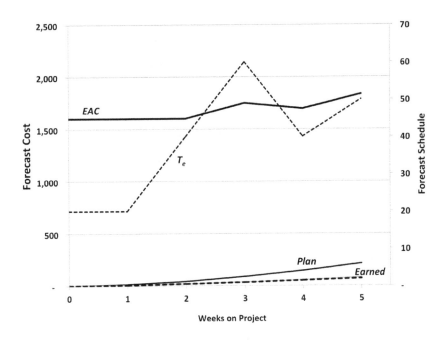

Figure 13.11: The project status at week 5. Should we tell the customer?

13.5 Performance Reports

The project manager is responsible for collecting and disseminating status reports, forecasts, and technical performance status. Two kinds of reports are useful:

1. *A Performance Report:* For the PMA case, an example of a performance report is the *Earned Value Status Report,* which is shown in Figure 13.12.

2. *A Forecast Report:* For the PMA case, the *Forecast Report* is shown in Figure 13.13. The initial budget for the PMA project was $12,500, but the reports show a revised cost estimate of $12,900, with $CPI = 0.97$.

251

EARNED VALUE STATUS REPORT

Project Title: _____ BUPMA   Date Prepared: 4/20/

Budget at Completion (BAC): $ 12,500.00   **Overall Status:** Almost on budget, behind schedule

	Current Reporting Period ($)	Cumulative ($)	Past Period Cum
Planned value (PV)	6,500	10,000	
Earned value (EV)	5,000	8,500	
Actual cost (AC)	5,250	8,750	
Schedule variance (SV)	(1,500)	(1,500)	
Cost variance (CV)	(250)	(250)	
Schedule performance index (SPI)		0.850	
Cost performance index (CPI)		0.971	

Root Cause of Schedule Variance:
(#1) One member of the team was on medical leave.
(#2) Team not on same page on design and implementation issues.

Impact on Deliverables, Milestones, or **Critical Path:**

There is a chance that project deliverables for this week and subsequent weeks will get dela

Figure 13.12: A *Performance Report* showing the status of the PMA project.

Cost performance index (CPI)		0.971		1.000

Root Cause of Schedule Variance:
(#1) One member of the team was on medical leave.
(#2) Team not on same page on design and implementation issues.

Impact on Deliverables, Milestones, or **Critical Path:**

There is a chance that project deliverables for this week and subsequent weeks will get delayed unless the resource is available immediately.

Impact on Budget, Contingency Funds, or Reserve:

No impact on budget   Forecast

Estimates at Completion (EAC):

EAC w/CPI [BAC/CPI]		12,868		1256

Selected EAC, Justification, and Explanation

Figure 13.13: A *Forecast Report* showing the revised forecast for the *CEAC*.

14

QUALITY

**Be a yardstick of quality. Some people aren't used to
an environment where excellence is expected.**

Steve Jobs

In this chapter we focus on the technical concepts, as well as tools and techniques, associated with *Quality*. The goal is to assure the stakeholders that the project meets their needs.[1]

However, according to Garvin, "Quality is an unusually slippery concept, easy to visualize and yet exasperatingly difficult to define." [51] Therefore, we have to discuss many associated philosophical ideas.

Customers will probably have to live with the final project for a long time. Therefore, while delivering the project on time and within budget is important, meeting the customer's needs and expectations is even more important. This might be summarized by saying that the project should meet the customers' quality expectations.

In a project management context, the issue is even more complicated. For example, the project team might define and interpret quality differently from the stakeholders. Since the customer is the ultimate custodian of the final product, the definition of quality must come from the customer, and this must be well understood and communicated throughout the project life cycle.

[1] Easy to say, hard to achieve.

14.1   A Discussion About Quality

The definition of quality is elusive because different people interpret it differently. For example, a banker might define quality of service in terms of the number of transactions completed without error. The advantage of this approach is that, for things like ATM transactions, it can be defined, measured, and improved. On the other hand, the customer might define quality of service as the ability of tellers to solve their problems.

14.1.1   The PMI Definition of Quality

The old definition of quality according to PMI:[2]

> *Quality is the degree to which a set of inherent characteristics fulfills requirements.*

While this is the international standard definition of quality (*ISO 5000*), *meeting requirements* is a complex issue. For example, meeting stakeholder requirements (their wants and needs) is vastly different from meeting performance goals (e.g., speed and throughput).

We can divide customer expectations into two categories: Technical performance goals and quality expectations. Technical goals are the specific and measurable aspects of a project. A well-defined scope makes these requirements clear and meeting them consists of passing a set of user tests. Neglecting the test requirements can lead to contentious debate about whether the requirements have been met.

The customers' quality expectations are likely to be more difficult to define and will encompass a variety of issues. Therefore, in this chapter, we begin with a more philosophical approach.

Also, quality applies to both the product and the management of the project. For example, good quality project management would ensure that the project was delivered within the budget and on schedule, that changes were all approved jointly with the stakeholders, and that the process for managing deliverables was transparent and efficient. All of this might be accomplished with excellent quality, but is of little value if the resulting *product* has low quality.

Process quality does not guarantee product quality, and vice versa.

Another issue is that many of the definitions of quality come from a manufacturing context.[3] Since projects are typically one-time, never-been-done-before creations,

[2]The 6th edition of the PM-BOK does not define quality, it merely says that "quality measures and techniques are specific to the type of deliverables being produced," which is not a very helpful definition.

[3]As does the PMI definition.

254

the applicability of quality concepts from multiple, repeatable, manufacturing processes is highly questionable.

The International Standards Organization (ISO) provides excellent resources on quality standards. The PMBOK approach is claimed to be compatible with a variety of approaches, such as Total Quality Management (TQM), Six Sigma, and Continuous Improvement, as well as approaches from quality theorists such as Deming, Juran, Crosby, and others. However, many of these are oriented to manufacturing, which leaves open the question of how quality applies to projects.

14.1.2 The Evolution of Quality

Before we discuss quality in a project management context, it is useful to cover a brief history of its evolution.

While the idea of quality has been around for a very long time, its formal definition, as a management concept, began in the 18th and 19th centuries as what we would now call, *quality control*.[4] Mass production required interchangeable parts, which in turn, required jigs (to repeatably manufacture parts) and inspection gauges (to ensure the parts were within a specific tolerance).

This also required an inspector and, by the end of the 19th century, the inspector was responsible for the quality of the work. However, quality remained an independent function and not the responsibility of management.

Tools, such as control charts and sampling tables, gradually improved product quality. The Second World War had a major impact on quality, as statisticians played a leading role in defining, implementing, and training several U.S. Government Departments in *statistical quality control*. By the late 1940s, quality control was recognized as an established discipline.

The next step was the emergence of *quality assurance*, as companies began to understand the cost of quality (or its lack) and the impact of defects. Thus, quality emerged from manufacturing departments to become a wider management concern, characterized by the phrase "total quality control."

In February 1962, The Martin Company delivered the first defect free missile to the U.S. Army and it was fully operational less than 24 hours after delivery.[5] This was an extraordinary event and the resulting idea, called "zero defects," changed the perception of quality, because it proved that zero defects was actually possible.

The idea of *zero defects* continued to move the emphasis away from inspection and towards the identification and removal of errors. *Quality assurance* began

[4]In our opinion, Garvin still provides one of the best discussions of the topic. See [51]

[5]Not just the hardware, but the documentation and test setups were also defect free.

255

to encompass philosophical discussions about expectations, motivations, and facilities. All departments, from design to manufacturing, were now involved.

Two trends in the 1980s forced the next evolution in the definition of quality. Japanese products, particularly cars, semiconductors, and electronics, had significantly less defects than their competitive U.S. products. The sales of U.S. goods declined and quality became a strategic issue, which finally attracted the attention of upper management.

Simultaneously, several U.S. Government Agencies began examining the quality of products and issuing recalls, which dramatically increased the costs of defects and affected the company's image. Upper management could no longer ignore quality.

However, the ideas of *quality assurance* were not comprehensive enough to meet the new strategic and competitive requirements of quality. Therefore, new definitions were proposed that focused on the customers' perspective.

- The customer, not the company, is the final arbiter of quality.

- Since the customer defines quality, the concept is now much broader and less precise.

- The customer is likely to define quality relative to other products, rather than by the company's quality control measurements.

An immediate impact was that market research on the competition's quality became a major factor. Also, the focus shifted from the initial purchase price to the customer's perception of the long-term value of the product.

The result was that quality became, not just a technical competency, but a company-wide, strategic goal. Upper management sets the tone and invests in design tools, training, and team building.

As the definition of quality moves towards satisfying the customers' needs, it begins to have relevance to project management.[6]

14.1.3   Views of Quality

There are many different views of quality.

1. *The Transcendental View:*

   This is summarized by, "I can't define it, but I know when I see it." Advertisers employ this view, e.g., Publix, "Where shopping is a pleasure."

[6]But, in our opinion, the study of quality in PM still has a long way to go.

2. *Product-Based View:*

   This is defined by the quantifiable and measurable characteristics of a product, e.g., reliability, which is the mean time between failures. However, it is difficult to objectively measure people's tastes and style.

3. *User-Based View:*

   In this view, quality is an individual matter and products that best satisfy user preferences are those with the highest quality. Consumer preferences vary widely and it is difficult to aggregate preferences into products with wide appeal.

4. *Manufacturing-Based View:*

   Manufacturers tend to focus on conformance to requirements by measuring deviations from standards, which are interpreted as a reduction in quality. Because they are set by the organization, the quality standards are internally focused. This view tends to emphasize reliability and cost.

5. *Value-Based View:*

   Value-based quality is defined in terms of costs and prices. A consumer's purchase decision is based on quality at the acceptable price.[7]

14.1.4 Garvin's Dimensions of Quality

Garvin's eight dimensions of quality are:

1. Performance: The products primary operating characteristics, e.g., speed and mileage for a car.

2. Features: These supplement performance characteristics, e.g., a back-up camera in a car

3. Reliability: The probability of not functioning correctly in a specific period, e.g., the likelihood of needing unscheduled service in the first two years.

4. Conformance: The degree to which the operational characteristics meet the established standards, e.g., meeting the car's legal emission standards.

5. Durability: The measure of products life, e.g., the expected life of a car.

6. Serviceability: The speed and ease of repair, e.g., electronic equipment that quickly diagnoses problems and the availability of parts for repair.

[7] Price is what you pay, value is what you get—Warren Buffet.

257

7. Aesthetics: How the product looks, feels, tastes, and smells, e.g., a car's style and sportiness.

8. Perceived quality: As seen by customer, e.g., the driver's view of the car.

14.1.5 The Software -ilities

Software product quality is sometimes defined in terms of:

Reliability	operates error free
Modifiability	ability to make changes
Understandability	efficiency, speed, and compactness
Usability	ease of learning the system
Testability	ease of testing
Portability	ease of moving to another environment

Other application-specific "-ilities" can be added, e.g., in database applications, the recoverability of the data after a crash.

14.1.6 Grade

Grade is different from quality. ISO defines grade as a category assigned to products or services having the same functional use, but different technical characteristics.

For example, the international grade specifications for sugar range from very high to low. White refined sugar, which has a minimum purity of 99.8%, is considered to be the highest grade. In comparison, crystal sugar has a minimum purity of 99.6%. Brown sugar, which has a purity in the range of 94% to 97%, is classified as lower grade sugar.[8]

However, from a quality perspective all the above three grades of sugar meet the internationally accepted quality standards for human consumption.[9]

14.1.7 Related Concepts

Here is a brief overview of some related concepts.

Total Quality Management

[8]But you might prefer it in your muffins.

[9] Sugar specifications can be found at genesisny.net.

TQM is a quality management philosophy from the noted expert Dr. W. Edwards Deming. It is uses statistical analysis to measure whether a process is in control. More importantly, Dr. Deming introduced the concept that quality should be planned in, not inspected in, and that investing in quality saves money.

Six Sigma

Six Sigma is a methodology also rooted in statistics. The focus of the Six Sigma Quality standard is to reduce process output variation by relentlessly and continuously focusing on processes so as to reduce the defect rate to no more than 3.4 defects per million opportunities. In terms of standard deviation, *six sigma* translates to being 99.99966% defect free.[10]

Continuous Improvement

Continuous Improvement, which is also known by its Japanese name *Kaizen*, is a proactive approach to quality management. It focuses on not being content with things the way they are, but instead seeking continuous process improvement.

Zero Defects

Zero Defects is a quality management philosophy from Philip Crosby. As the name suggests, its basic approach is to do something right the very first time. Investing money up front will minimize the need for rework and reduce expenses down the road associated with fixing defects.

Fitness for Use

Fitness for Use was designed by Joseph Juran and focuses on identifying and meeting the real needs of stakeholders.

Gold Plating

Gold plating is the practice of providing more features than the customer asked for. From a project management perspective, gold plating can result in a project that is risky and expensive.

An example of gold plating is when a programmer implements a digital clock on the website, assuming that it adds value. This could create complexity and additional cost down the road when the product is used in different countries and time zones, or when users want to see the clock in a 24-hour format.

Gold plating might even be unethical if the customer was not informed of the add-on and is later asked to pay for it.

[10]It is worth pointing out that a project is *unique*, so the idea of defects per million does not apply, as there would need to be a million copies of the project.

Mathematical Quality

Mathematically speaking, quality is equal to conformance to requirements plus fitness for use.[11]

14.1.8 QA vs QC

There is a difference between *Quality Assurance, QA,* and *Quality Control, QC.* Since effective QA and QC contribute significantly to the success of a project, it is important that everyone agrees on the meanings of QA and QC, as well as how they will be implemented, because weak and ineffective quality management jeopardize the cost, schedule, and stakeholder satisfaction.[12]

The ISO 9000 standard defines Quality Control as:

> *Quality Control is that part of quality management that focuses on fulfilling quality requirements.*

The ISO 9000 standard defines Quality Assurance as:

> *Quality Assurance is that part of quality management that focuses on providing confidence that the quality requirements will be fulfilled.*

Therefore, the function of QC is to check that the project produces the required internal and external deliverable products. The function of QA is to ensure that the standards, processes, and procedures are appropriate for the project and, also, that they are correctly implemented. We can summarize this as:

- **QA** is about managing the *process.*

- **QC** is about managing the *product.*

14.2 Quality Planning

[11] This says nothing about the quality of the development process.

[12] ISO 9000 family of standards is an excellent resource on quality management.

The quality, not the longevity, of one's life is what is important.

Dr. Martin Luther King, Jr.

The quality plan defines the standards that the project should achieve. The team can either adopt existing, well-defined quality standards, or create new standards by defining quality metrics for the deliverables. A good quality plan guides the project team by identifying procedures for both quality assurance and quality control and provides a means to confirm that quality objectives are being met.

In a software development project, the quality plan might include the use of an existing quality metric, such as measuring code defects per thousand Lines of Code (LOC). The plan could then define the maximum tolerance, or acceptable number of defects, such as: no more than six defects per thousand LOC.

As an example, we present a sample quality management plan for the PMA project, which is shown in Figure 14.1.

14.2.1   Quality Planning Tools and Techniques

The following sections describe the tools and techniques the team uses during Quality Planning to analyze the project's quality.

Quality Metrics

Quality Metrics provide specific measurements of project attributes and are identified in the *Plan Quality* process. Every industry has its own metrics, e.g., many companies have "customer satisfaction" metrics that are tracked over time.

For service-oriented applications, such as call-centers, metrics might include the time to answer the call, the average time to satisfy the customer, and the percent of very satisfied customers. For software products, metrics of interest include code defects per thousand lines, mean time to failure, and mean time to repair.

As an example, for the PMA website project, response time was identified as a key metric. Response times to a user request for information was demanded to be less than 2 seconds for all minor requests, and less than 5 seconds for major database-oriented requests. These are examples of specific, measurable attributes of the web site, and make excellent metrics.[13]

Quality Checklists

Quality is enhanced if *Quality Checklists* are used to ensure that the project team produces all documents and does not miss a process. Well-designed checklists actually simplify the project manager's life. For example, for a small project full-scale plans may not be required. A checklist serves as a reminder that all issues have been covered without writing a long bureaucratic plan.

Organizational process assets will typically include checklists that can be tailored for the current project. Some examples of checklist items are listed below. For

[13]Of course, there is an issue here: Does fast response make the web site friendly? Not necessarily. More metrics would be needed to measure "user friendly,"

261

QUALITY MANAGEMENT PLAN FOR THE PMA PROJECT

A. Overview:

This plan describes the information required to effectively manage PMA project quality from planning through delivery. It defines quality policies, procedures, roles, responsibilities and the authorities involved.

B. Quality Responsibilities and Quality Roles:

    Design and User Interface
        Test User Interface specification – Design Team
    Development Environment
        Unit Testing – Development Team
        Functional testing – Test Team
    Staging Environment
        Testing – Test Team
        Compliance Testing – End User including an Impaired End User
        Performance Testing – Performance Tester
        Execute Training Exercised– Trainers, End Users
    Production
        Production Testing – Test Team

C. Quality Assurance Approach:

Validate: Requirements & functionality of the system; the transition from the requirements specifications to functional & detail designs; and the application is correct and accurate. Adhere to DoJ ADA Compliance Requirements. Customer satisfaction will be measured by industry standard usability practices.

D. Quality Control Approach:

The Test Plan will describe the processes, methods, tools and techniques to be used in performing quality control, specifically supporting the following objectives:

Metrics:	Identify the items that should be targeted for testing.
Types:	Outlines the testing types that will be executed.
Resources:	Identifies the required resources and estimates test efforts.
Deliverables:	Lists the deliverable elements of the test project.

E. Quality Improvement Approach:

Proactively identify approaches to improve processes, and techniques, and provide training to all resources.

F. Tools, Environment and Interfaces:

List tools, tool description, and industry recognized benchmarks.

G. Quality Reporting Plan

The communication matrix will identify all stakeholders, who will be informed continually about all aspects of quality and performance.

Figure 14.1: PMA Quality Management Plan.

each item, the project manager can simply indicate whether the issue has been considered with a 'Yes' or 'No', and a brief comment.

- Are project management activities identified for the project?

- Do we have measurable and prioritized goals for managing the quality of the products?

- Have the following been considered: Functionality, reliability, maintainability, and usability?

- Has the project team received training in project management, quality management, and risk analysis?

Cost-Benefit Analysis

The concept of a quality cost-benefit analysis is similar to a traditional cost-benefit analysis. The team focuses on creating a business scenario for several quality activities and compares the investment in such activities with the perceived benefits, such as higher productivity, less rework, lower-cost, and a better reputation.

Cost of Quality

This is the total cost of quality over the project's life and includes:

- *Cost of Conformance:* This is the money spent to avoid problems and to build a quality product or service. Investing in cost of conformance is money well spent as it reduces failure costs, which includes:[14]

    - *Prevention Costs:* this is an investment in quality through testing and inspection; training of staff; acquisition of automated equipment; investment in time and effort to document processes properly; and creating checklists to communicate the correct way to perform activities.

    - *Appraisal Costs:* These are the costs associated with assessing the quality of the project and include, inspections, testing, and stakeholder product evaluation.

- *Cost of Non-Conformance:* This is the money spent to fix problems that are a result of failures or quality expectations not being met, which includes:

    - *Internal Costs:* The costs identified with scrap or thrown-away pieces, i.e., work judged to be unacceptable and that had to be re-done.

[14]We have already explained that defects found after delivery by the users are the most expensive to fix.

263

– *External Failure Costs:* The costs associated with repairing a project after it was delivered, i.e., warranty repairs, liability costs, and lost business.

Benchmarking

This refers to comparing a project's internal production process with industry standards with the idea that the comparison will result in establishing a viable quality standard for the project at hand.

Design of Experiments (DOE)

This is a statistical method for identifying the factors that influence specific variables of a product or process under development or in production. From a quality planning perspective, it is used to determine the number and type of tests, and their impact on quality. An example given in the PMBOK guide describes automotive designers using DOE to determine which combination of suspension and tires will produce the most comfortable ride at a reasonable cost. [15]

Statistical Sampling

This is the study of a population of interest and involves gathering information from the sample domain and then analyzing it. As a tool, knowledge about various statistical sampling techniques is helpful to a project manager.

For example, many choices may be made during the design phase and selecting the right representative data sample is critical if the project outcome is to produce the right results. A type of statistical sampling that is commonly used is random sampling. An example would be to use a random number generator function to select 20 data points from a population of 1,000.

Flowcharting

This is a graphical depiction of a process flow, see Figure 14.2. It consists of rectangles, which represent processes, and diamonds, which represent decision points. A review of a visual flowchart during quality planning can help identify stumbling points.

---

[15] Another non-project!

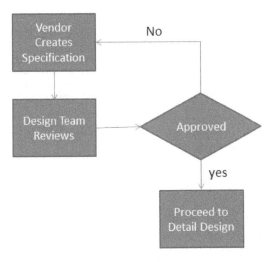

Figure 14.2: A simple flow chart.

14.3 Quality Assurance

Excellence, then, is not an act but a habit.

Will Durant

Quality Assurance (QA) focuses on providing confidence that quality requirements will be fulfilled, that the standards, processes, and procedures are appropriate for the project and, also, that they are correctly implemented. QA is typically conducted through a series of audits and results in good practices to share, deficiencies or defects to be removed, and areas for improvement. QA also results in change requests and updates to the project's documents.

As an example, a QA audit for the PMA case might proceed as follows: The motivation for the audit was that the project manager was concerned about whether quality standards were in place for the website, which might have vulnerabilities to cyber-security threats. Therefore, with the assistance of the QA team, a quality audit was conducted and the results are presented in Table 14.1:

As a consequence of the audit, updates were made to the QA processes and the project management plan. The following improvements were suggested:

265

Table 14.1: PMA Quality Assurance Audit Results

QUALITY ASSURANCE AUDIT		
☐ Project	☐ Project processes	☐ Project documents
☐ Product	☐ Organizational Policies	☐ Quality Management Plan

Software Design: Focus on best practices to ensure that the design specification produces a secure website.

Hosting Environment: Also ensure that the website is secure.

Software Development Life cycle: Introduce software quality assurance steps, including maintenance recommendations.

Personnel: Schedule constraints on programmers will be watched and training will cover proper configuration and security of the software.

Process: A layered system of security will be introduced into the design.

The above example shows that *Quality Assurance* is about the prevention of problems by proactively addressing problems that might occur during the execution phase. The process also provides anxious stakeholders confidence that the final project will be free of defects and of good quality.

Many organizations invest in mechanisms to conduct credible QA and an important aspect is that the team conducting QA is independent of the development organization. Although independent, the QA group works cooperatively with the project team to review deliverables. The key outputs from audits are change requests, project management plan updates, and process asset updates.

14.3.1   QA Tools and Techniques

QA tools and techniques are described in the following sections.

Quality Audits

A quality audit should confirm that the quality processes were implemented correctly and that deliverables met the project's objectives. If a particular benchmark cannot be achieved, a comprehensive review should be undertaken to determine if the initial goals were appropriate and steps should be taken to get the project to the expected level of quality.

Quality audits are formal reviews and should be scheduled for key deliverables and, even randomly, as needed. The internal QA department is involved along with experts from outside, as required. The lessons learned from a quality audit should be documented and both shortcomings and strengths communicated to stakeholders.

Process Analysis

The current processes are analyzed to determine if improvements are needed. For example, a process analysis may reveal an opportunity to reduce waste or save time, in which case the project manager might recommend a new process be implemented. Process analysis may include a root cause analysis.

14.4 Quality Control

Quality Control (QC) focuses on fulfilling requirements of the product by checking that the project produces the required internal and external deliverable products.

14.4.1 QC Tools and Techniques

Several tools play an important role in evaluating the quality of deliverables.

Control Charts

These graphically describe performance data and include upper and lower limits within which a healthy process runs. Such a chart is usually used to reveal if equipment is producing products outside the defined specifications.[16] Control charts can be used, both to establish standards and to monitor output variables.[17]

Figure 14.3 gives an example of a control chart. The goal, or target, which is usually the mean of the process, is the solid line in the middle. In this example, the goal is 10 errors per week and the upper limit is 13 and the lower limit is 7. We see from the chart that one data point is outside the upper control limit and we conclude, therefore, that the *entire process* is out of control. The point outside of the control limits should be investigated.

A process can also be out of control if too many data points are all on the same side of the mean. The "rule of seven" declares that an entire process out of control if seven data points lie on the same side of the mean, even if the points are within the limits, see Figure 14.4.[18] Even though all points are within the control limits, the process is still *out of control.*

[16]Many of the examples of Control Charts are non-projects and routine manufacturing.

[17]We think it is hard to find an example from project management. For example, cost and schedule variances can be tracked against their goals and flags raised if they depart from acceptable upper and lower limits. However, control charts are based on the idea that things are independent, and the *CPI* is a cumulative measure and so correlates the variables. Personally, we don't see how they apply to PM at all!

[18]We have already established that, frequently, all *CPI* values are less than 1.0, which says that the "process is out of control."

267

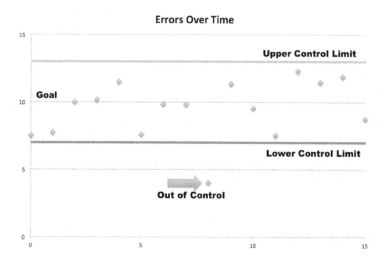

Figure 14.3: A simple control chart with one data point outside the control limits.

Cause and Effect Diagrams

These are also called Ishikawa diagrams, or fishbone diagrams, and are a useful tool for getting to the root cause of a problem. They are used in general problem solving, discovering bottlenecks, and uncovering process issues. In team meetings, an Ishikawa diagram is an excellent communications tool.

The source of a problem is uncovered by asking the 'Why?' question three times. For example, suppose it is observed that pizza delivery is more likely to be late on weekends. The analysis of this problem begins by asking the following question:

- *Why is pizza delivery late on weekends?*

  Assume the response is that there are employee issues, resource issues, and quality issues. Brainstorming continues with a second round of 'Why?'

- *Why are employees inadequate on weekends?*

  The second 'Why?' is trying to uncover possible *causes*. Suppose the causes are: Weekend employees are unhappy and quit frequently. Therefore, adequately trained staff is not available on weekends.

- *Why are weekend employees unhappy?*

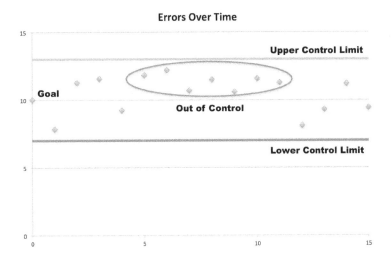

Figure 14.4: The rule of seven. A control chart showing an out of control process: more than seven data points on the same side of the mean.

Brainstorming continues with a third 'Why?' The answers include: Wages are low and benefits non-existent. Also, funding is not available for training and instructors are not available to train the weekend crew.

These issues are documented in an Ishikawa Diagram, see Figure 14.5. The problem (late delivery of pizza on weekends) is shown in the box on the right. The diagonal arrows represent *issues* that are identified, e.g., staffing. The horizontal arrows represent *causes* of the issue. For example, one *cause* of the *resource* issue is, *"Frequently running out of pizza boxes."*

We now have a potential root cause for the problem: Employees are inadequately trained with poor pay. We may even have a solution: If it is not possible to raise wages, then, at least, we should consider providing better training. The Ishikawa diagram in Figure 14.5 shows a detailed analysis of the pizza delivery problem.

Pareto Chart

A small fraction of participants produces a large fraction of the accomplishments. A small fraction of participants also produces a large fraction of the problems.

Augustine's Corollary to Pareto

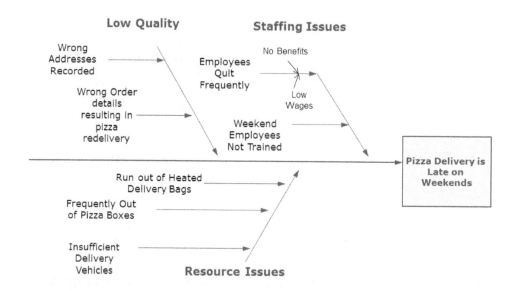

Figure 14.5: *Ishikawa Diagram* for late pizza delivery on weekends.

A Pareto chart is a histogram (bar chart) ordered by frequency of occurrence that shows which issues you should really worry about. The key idea is most of the problems are concentrated in a few issues.[19]

As an example, suppose PMA implemented a new web site to collect data on the number of complaints they received. The website support group analyzed the complaints and assigned them to general categories, such as slow response, poor technical support, broken links, missing features, etc. They sorted the data so that the issues with the most complaints were at the top and the results are shown in Table 14.2.

The first column contains the number of complaints, the second column the cumulative number, and the third column the cumulative percentage. For example, in row 2, there were 55 complaints about slow response, which makes the cumulative total, 66+55 = 121. The total number of complaints was 164, so the cumulative percentage was 121/164 = 74%. The data are plotted in Figure 14.6.

A Pareto chart is useful when there are many issues and you need to concentrate on those that are most significant. The technique is even more useful when followed up with an Ishikawa diagram to address the causes of the problems.

If stakeholders perceive the quality as poor, either of the products or processes,

[19]This is commonly known as the "80-20" rule, because, typically, 80% of the defects are due to 20% of the causes.

Table 14.2: Pareto chart for complaints about the PMA website .

Complaint	Number	Cumulative Count	Cumulative Percent
Broken links	66	66	40%
Slow response	55	121	74%
Poor tech support	18	139	85%
Missing feature	11	150	91%
Confusing	6	156	95%
Poor help	4	160	98%
Site unavailable	2	162	99%
Poor English	2	164	100%
Total	164		

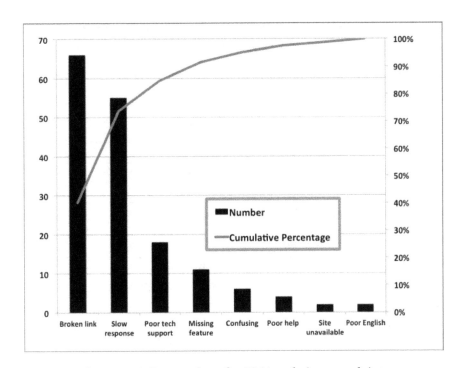

Figure 14.6: Pareto chart for PMA website complaints.

collecting comments and analyzing them in a Pareto chart can help to explain the issues and prioritize the order in which they should be addressed. Fixing the troublesome few may quickly result in a significant improvement in quality.

271

Inspection

This is a technique for examining product quality and goes by names such as reviews, audits, and walks-through. Inspections occur in different formats and at multiple project stages.

14.4.2 Validation and Verification

The purpose of *Verification* is to find defects in documents such as specifications or test cases, but not to fix them. This is accomplished through reviews, meetings, inspections, and walks-through.

The purpose of *Validation* is the testing of the functionality of the product, i.e. does the product meet the customers' requirements.

In the PMA case, the project team conducted *Verification and Validation*. Verification was accomplished by conducting a thorough review of the documentation.

Validation occurred after verification and the result was the *Quality Control Measurements* document, which is shown in Table 14.3.

Table 14.3: PMA Quality Control Measurements.

Planned Result	Actual Result	Variance
Page load 3 seconds.	Average Page Load 10 seconds	7 seconds
Link Navigation 5 seconds.	Average Link Navigation 15 seconds	10 seconds
Root Cause:		Slow response time attributed to the hosting provider.
Planned Response:		Communicate with hosting company. Contingency: Investigate new hosting company immediately.

15

RESOURCES

**Never hire anyone you wouldn't want to run into
in the hallway at three in the morning.**

Tina Fey

This is where the project manager identifies, acquires, and manages the resources needed on the project. There are two types of resources:

- *Personnel Resources:* These consist of the team, who have assigned roles and responsibilities and work to achieve the project goals.[1]

- *Physical Resources:* These consist of equipment materials, facilities, and infrastructure.

Resource management is one of the areas where project management borrows heavily from general management principals. In this chapter we will cover some of the traditional theory about managing resources and wrap up with the tools and techniques that are applicable to projects.

A project manager must possess a wide variety of skills, including leadership, communication, negotiation, influence, and conflict resolution. A project manager must be a mentor and be able to motivate and manage the project team after the

[1] In previous versions of the PMBOK, this was called *Human Resources.*

initial excitement of project kick-off has faded. A project manager also needs strong skills in delegating and follow-up.

15.1 The Resources Plan

The process of organizing and managing the both the physical resources and the project team is described in the *Resources Plan*. The project manager is both a manager and a leader. Management involves keeping the project on track, while leadership is required when trouble arises, or new initiatives are needed.

While the physical resources are important, the critical aspect of the plan is identifying the people with the necessary skills to complete the activities, assigning their roles and responsibilities, and motivating and empowering the team. To assemble the *Resources Plan*, the project manager uses company organization charts and position descriptions to define the positions. To acquire the team requires soft skills, such as networking.

The *Resources Plan* usually contains the staffing plan, which includes timetables for staff acquisition and release, training needs, team building strategies, recognition and rewards, compliance considerations, and safety issues.

For the PMA project, we present a sample *Resources Plan* in Figure 15.1.

15.1.1 Organization Charts

Organization charts are classified as Hierarchical; Matrix; Responsible, Accountable, Consult, Inform (RACI); and Text-Oriented.[2] Most organizations publish organization charts, which are hierarchical and show titles, positions, and reporting relationships. They are easy to understand, see Figure 15.2.

For the PMA project, we present a sample *Organization Chart* in Figure 15.3.

15.1.2 Matrix Charts

These are useful tools that associate a resource name with a work package and project responsibility. One such chart that is frequently used during the planning stages is the Responsible, Accountable, Consult, Inform chart (RACI).

[2]Note: Organization charts should not be confused with organizational structures, which are functional, matrix (weak, balanced, strong), and projectized.

Typically, only one resource is assigned the Responsibility (R) label. The person accountable for the work is given the (A) label. Of course, there might be sharing or delegation involved. Typically, the sponsor is given the Inform (I) label as they need to be kept up-to-date on progress. Staff members who are consulted are designated with the Consult (C) label.

RESOURCES PLAN.

ROLES AND RESPONSIBILITIES

The Project Manager (PM) is responsible for the success of the PMA Website project. The PM must authorize and approve all project expenditures and communicate with the stakeholders. The team members will be responsible for timely execution of the assigned activities and the quality of their work (the activities) should meet established acceptability criteria.

The Design Specialist (DS) is responsible for the design specification & gathering coding requirements.

The Technical Writer (TW) is responsible for training users and the sponsoring IT staff in how to maintain the website. The TW will produce the training manuals, and document configuration changes to the software.

The Database Developer (DD) will implement the backend database connections to the website and will design and build the data tables. The DD must be proficient in PHP and MySQL.

The Business Analyst (BA) is responsible for: Gathering website requirements; building the test cases; and the test plan.

ORGANIZATIONAL STRUCTURE

STAFF ACQUISITION

The project staff will consist entirely of internal resources. No procurement or contracting will be performed. The PM will identify and assign resources in accordance with the organization structure.

STAFF RELEASE

The project staff will be released from the project upon completion and all accounts will be disabled according to information assurance procedures.

TRAINING

Training will be scheduled during the implementation phase and will be documented in the project schedule.

PERFORMANCE REVIEWS

The Project manager will review each team member's assigned work activities at the onset of the project and communicate all expectations of work to be performed. A bonus of 15% of the project cost will be distributed as bonus to recognize team member performance for timely completion of all deliverables within the quality benchmarks.

REGULATION AND POLICY COMPLIANCE

The Department of Justice, American Disabilities Act, will be strictly adhered to. This will require effort in human resources for both development and testing.

Figure 15.1: HR Plan for the PMA case.

An example is shown in Table 15.1. You should avoid giving a person more than one label, as they are either responsible, accountable, consulted, or informed.

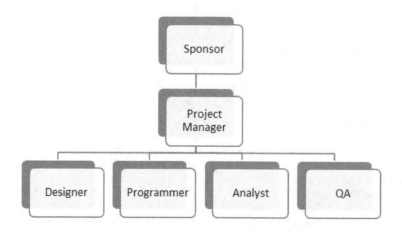

Figure 15.2: A simple organization chart.

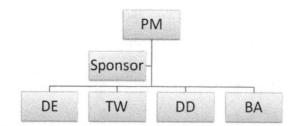

Figure 15.3: The organization chart for the PMA project.

Table 15.1: RACI Chart

Work Package	Analyst	Designer	Programmer	Quality Assurance
Analysis	R	C	C	A
Design	C	R	C	I
Build	C	C	R	I

15.2 Acquiring the Project Team

Talent wins games, but teamwork and intelligence wins championships.

Michael Jordan

One of the first steps in the execution of the project is for the project manager to assemble the team. The project manager develops staff assignments and *resource calendars*, which explain who is assigned to what activity and when. In acquiring the team, the project manager makes sure that it is a balanced and effective mix.

When the project schedule was developed, a resource plan was created to ensure that adequate staff would be available for all required activities. When assigning resources, the project manager also considers previous experience, matches skills with activity requirements, and assesses leadership and communication styles. The personal desires and interests of a team member should not be overlooked.

The key concepts in acquiring a team are:

Pre-Assignment: This refers to the fact that some project team members may be selected in advance.

Negotiation: In a matrix structure, the functional manager controls the resources. The project manager has to influence the functional manager to obtain the best mix of resources.

Acquisition: This is the procurement of resources from outside the project.

Virtual teams: This refers to teams that are not co-located and have very little opportunity for face-to-face contact. Some of the team members could be in another city or, even, another country.

Since distributed project development occurs in many large organizations, the project manager must be able to create an effective pattern of communication and develop a team where the members trust each other.

For example, the PMA project manager consulted the resource plan, which contained information about team skills, an assessment of their capabilities, roles and responsibilities, and their availability. From this information, the PMA project manager developed the project *staffing assignment* form shown in Table 15.2:

Table 15.2: PMA Staffing Assignments

Calendar	Resource	Commitment
Quarter 1, 2012	Project Manager	1 – Full time
Quarter 2, 2012	Business Analyst	2 – Half time
Quarter 3, 2012	Programmer	2 – Half time, 1 – Full time

Like many software scheduling systems, Microsoft Project supports *Resource Calendars*. The above information could be entered into such a tool as soon as the functional managers commit to the staffing assignments.

15.3 Developing the Project Team

> **A person will sometimes devote all his life to the development of one part of his body — the wishbone.**
>
> *Robert Frost*

Once the team is assigned, the job of the project manager is to improve the competency of the various team members and to generate team cohesion.

If the assigned staff does not have the required technical skills, the project manager is responsible for providing training.[3]

For the PMA project, examples for the team directory, operating agreement, and performance assessment are shown in Tables 15.3, 15.4, and 15.5. Each team member should complete all of these forms.

Table 15.3: PMA Team Directory

Name:	Victor King
Role:	Project Manager
Contact Information:	617-555-1212
	vking@somewhere.com
Name:	Mary Contrary
Role:	Systems Analyst
Contact Information:	780-111-1212
	mcontrary@somewhere.com
Name:	Bruce Lee
Role:	Web Programmer
Contact Information:	978-555-1212
	blee@somewhere.com
Name:	Maya Banker
Role:	Cost Analyst
Contact Information:	977-555-1212
	blee@somewhere.com

[3]Did you squirrel away training funds for this eventuality? You didn't assume that all of the staff would be exactly what you needed, did you?

[4]Do not forget that project team members are stakeholders.

The following skills, tools and techniques are used to develop the team:

Soft skills: Project managers that have good soft skills can ensure smooth running of projects by sincere communication with project team members and true empathy. Such skills are vital in negotiation with, and influence of, stakeholders.[4]

Table 15.4: PMA Team Operating Agreement

Purpose:	This team operating agreement provides ground rules to help the team work productively together. Updates to this agreement will be made only after team discussions and obtaining consent from all participants.
Guidelines:	Project team members will report status at each team meeting. Frequency of team meetings and location of meetings. The preferred meeting platform and system for sharing documents, Procedure for managing issues and change requests. Procedure for reviewing action items and updating them. The responsibility of each team member if they miss a meeting.
Communication & Decision Making:	Each team member will be encouraged to bring their area of expertise to the table and communication will be encouraged. All team members will be empowered to make decisions. Also any voting procedures will be covered here to resolve a conflict.

Table 15.5: PMA Team Performance Assessment

Technical Performance:	Rated as *Meets Expectations* or *Needs Improvement*. Example: Programmers: Need Improvement. They do not have experience with WordPress programming and customization.
Interpersonal Skills:	Rated as *Meets Expectations* or *Needs Improvement*. Example: The team members will benefit from some exposure to communication, collaboration, and conflict resolution.
Areas for Development:	*Describe the approach and actions for improvement:* Example: The team will be given half day training in project communication. Programmers will be provided three days' training, either online or at a local company, in WordPress, PHP, and MySQL.

Training: This is essential to ensure that the team members are well prepared to accomplish their tasks, preferably before they start working on them. Scheduling training proactively can mitigate quality risks and reduce costs.

Team-Building Activities: Good team building activities help teams to perform synergistically. Early team building activities may include simple introductions (which help through communicating previous experience and hobbies), clarifying roles and expectations, and describing the management process.

More significant team building may include comprehensive off-site, facilitated, workshops focusing on bonding and integration of diverse personality types.[5]

[5]All of these activities need a line item in the budget.

279

Phases of Working Teams

The project manager must understand the classic stages that teams go through. Dr. Bruce Tuckman published a classic model in 1965, which explains the typical phases that teams go through: [52]

- *Forming:* The team is formed and they look to the project manager for guidance and direction.

- *Storming:* Team members compete for position, as they establish their relations with other team members, and the project manager must intervene proactively, before conflicts get out of hand. The project manager might be challenged at this stage. If a project manager has defined clear roles and responsibilities, the storming stage will be brief.

- *Norming:* Agreement and consensus occurs in the norming phase and the team works well under the direction of a project manager.

- *Performing:* The team is "strategically aware" and motivated, knows what it is doing, and where it is going.[6]

- *Adjourning:* The team breaks up, which occurs during the closing stage.

15.4   Managing the Project Team

> As a coach, I play not my eleven best, but my best eleven.
>
> *Knute Rockne*

Managing the project team consists of tracking each individual team member's performance, providing feedback, and resolving any issues that arise. The project manager should document each team member's performance in an assessment form that includes their strengths, weaknesses, and areas for development. Both the project manager and the team member should add any actions to be taken.

The following tools and techniques can be used when managing project teams:

Observation and Conversation: A simple example of communication with team members is inquiring about their work and the issues they face.

Project Performance Appraisals: Periodic feedback can help team members, especially if constructively given.

[6]The plane is on autopilot and the project manager can relax.

Use of Issue Logs: The project manager should keep a written log of issues with target dates for them to be resolved.

Interpersonal Skills: This involves an appreciation of:

- *Leadership:* Varying leadership styles exist, such as, directing, facilitating, coaching, supporting, autocratic, consultative, and consensus.

- *Influencing skills:* This requires good listening skills, the ability to persuade and articulate points and positions, and building trust.

- *Effective decision-making:* This requires clearly understanding the project goals, having a well-defined process to follow, consideration of risks and opportunities, and the ability to come up with creative solutions.

Conflict Management: Conflicts and frustrations occur in most projects. Conflict is natural in all organizations and often results from different values. The modern theory is that conflict can be positive, as it can create deeper understanding and respect. Two skills that a project manager must develop are:

- *Encouraging functional conflict:* The project manager encourages dissent by asking tough questions, encouraging different points of view, and even asking the team to consider an unthinkable, or even unpopular, alternative.

- *Managing dysfunctional conflict:* This involves working through the natural stages of a conflict: mediate, arbitrate, control, accept, and closure.

The following techniques are methods for resolving conflict:

- *Withdraw:* Avoid or retreat from an actual or potential conflict scenario.

- *Smooth:* This is also called "accommodate," and involves emphasizing areas of agreement, rather than the conflict at hand.

- *Compromise:* This involves concession and conciliation. Neither party involved in the conflict gets what they value the most. This is generally considered to be a *lose-lose* strategy.

- *Force:* One of the parties involved in the conflict imposes their viewpoint at the expense of the others. This is a *win-lose* scenario.

- *Collaborate:* This leads to consensus and commitment and involves consideration of multiple viewpoints.

281

- *Confront:* This is also known as "problem solving." It involves facing the conflict boldly and brainstorming to come up with a *win-win* alternative. This takes more effort than *collaborating* or *compromising*, but is generally considered to be the best approach for resolving conflicts.

If good team building has occurred early on in the project, the project manager can avoid conflicts that are destructive and harmful.

Project managers generally do not have formal, legitimate power. Team members often report to functional managers, so project managers rarely have direct authority over the team and cannot order them around. It is important, therefore, to use soft skills to motivate and lead a project to a successful completion.

A key concern for project managers is to motivate the team and, often, only limited financial resources are available for the task. In such situations, an effective form of power is *expert power*, where the project manager leverages "technical expertise" to drive the project towards success.

We also note that good project managers trust their teams. Poor project managers tend to exhibit "Theory X" behavior — they constantly intervene and micromanage, which results in frustration, dissatisfaction, and drives down productivity.

15.4.1   Recognition and Rewards

Motivation recognizes and promotes desirable behavior and is effective when carried out by the management team and the project manager. Encouraging the required behavior from the team is an important skill for the project manager. Developing teams requires understanding of the following theoretical concepts:

Maslow's Hierarchy of Needs

Dr. Abraham Maslow proposed that a person's needs must be satisfied in the following hierarchy: Physiological, Safety, Social, Self-esteem, and Self-actualization. See Figure 15.4. [53]

The primary motivation for an individual is to satisfy their basic physical needs, such as food, drink, shelter, and warmth. Only when these needs are satisfied can a person begin to deal with the higher-level needs.

The next level deals with safety and applies to needs such as protection, law and order, and stability. Social needs include the desire to belong to a group and involves family, affection, and relationships.

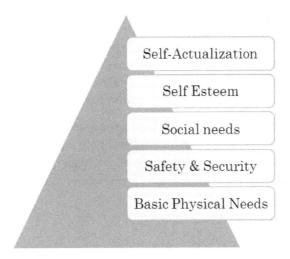

Figure 15.4: Maslow's hierarchy of needs.

The next level in the hierarchy is where individuals are motivated by self-esteem, which includes achievement, status, responsibility, and reputation. Finally, when all of the needs at the lower end of the hierarchy have been fulfilled, a person can begin to deal with self-actualization. Such an individual is motivated by personal growth and fulfillment.

A project manager must realize that team members are usually motivated by personal growth and fulfillment and, so, must take time to identify each member's interests and how to achieve them.

McGregor: Theory X and Theory Y

Douglas McGregor defined two models of worker behavior: Theory X and Theory Y. Theory X managers believe that team members will not perform their duties unless threatened or closely supervised. On the other hand, Theory Y managers believe the team will perform well if given the right motivating environment and appropriate expectations.

Project Managers that practice *Theory Y* behavior are much more likely to succeed in a project environment because, as we learned from Maslow's Hierarchy, project team members tend to be motivated by personal growth and fulfillment.

Herzberg's Theory of Motivation

Herzberg's "motivation-hygiene" theory proposes that certain motivator and hygiene factors affect job satisfaction and dissatisfaction. The *hygiene factors* merely prevent dissatisfaction. Examples are pay, benefits, the conditions of the work environment, and relationships with peers and managers.

The *motivation factors* are those that lead to satisfaction and deal with the substance of the work itself. These include the ability to advance and the opportunity to learn new things. According to Herzberg, pay (a hygiene factor) will not motivate project teams, but new responsibilities (a motivation factor) might.

Expectancy Theory

> **Oft expectation fails, and most oft there where most it promises;**
> **and oft it hits, where hope is coldest; and despair most sits.**
>
> *William Shakespeare*

Expectancy theory deals with how the expectation of a positive outcome can motivate people to perform and drive outcomes. People will behave in certain ways if they think there will be positive rewards for doing so. If a project manager expects the team to succeed, they will. If the project manager believes they will fail, they will not be motivated and just might fail.[7]

15.4.2 Virtual Teams

One of the growing trends is the use of *virtual teams.* The globalization of projects and the availability of world-wide communications has made *virtual teams* feasible. A virtual team is:

> *A virtual team is a group of people with a shared goal who fulfill their role with little or no time spent meeting face-to-face.*

Some advantages of virtual teams are that expertise can be acquired from any geographical area; teams can work different shifts and include people with disabilities; reduced expenses associated with travel and facilities; and staff flexibility, such as working from home. Challenges include feelings of isolation, difficulties in communicating technical details, setting up meetings for disparate time zones, and cultural differences.

[7]We expect our students to succeed.

284

16

COMMUNICATIONS

**It is better to keep your mouth closed and let people think
you are a fool than to open it and remove all doubt.**

Mark Twain.

Projects led by project managers with strong communication skills have a much
better chance of success.[1] *Communications,* in a project context, is about keeping
upper management, stakeholders, and the project team in the loop throughout the
project. In large projects, communications can become a very complex because the
number of communication paths rises rapidly as the number of people increases.[2]

16.1 Planning Communications

There are four main types of communication and, generally, a combination of all
four occurs in projects. The four types of communication are: formal, informal,
written, and verbal and they are used in the following combinations:

Formal Written:	Used to communicate specifications, product requirements and change control.
Formal Verbal:	Used in official presentations such as status reviews.
Informal Verbal:	This includes project team meetings.
Informal Written:	This includes non-legal documents and general notes.

[1] It is often said, especially by Vijay Kanabar, that project management is 80% communications.

[2] One of the most important acts of communication involves identifying and engaging stakeholders, which is covered in Chapter 7, Stakeholders.

Inexperienced project managers often spend too little time planning their project communications. This should be a major concern, as project managers spend a substantial fraction of their time communicating.[3]

The *Communication Management Plan,* which becomes part of the *Project Management Plan,* informs all stakeholders how and in what form communications will be handled on the project.

As an example, a portion of the PMA communications plan is given in Figure 16.1.

Steering Committee

A project steering committee will be created. It includes faculty, the executive sponsor, the team, a member of the IT Infrastructure, and one alumni.

Project steering committee meetings will be held weekly, at 9:00 am on Fridays to allow issues to be raised and addressed without spanning the weekend. The role of the committee will be to make decisions on outstanding items, address issues, and review change requests and resource utilization.

Issues Tracking

Unplanned issues that occur will be collected and tracked by the PM. Any issues that cannot be resolved will be presented to the steering committee. All reported issues will have an owner and a resolution date.

All issues will be captured and tracked in an issues database, managed by the PM, and reviewed during weekly project team meetings. The issues will be assigned a severity based on potential impact to the project.

Figure 16.1: A portion of the *Communications Plan* for the PMA web site

16.2 Identifying Communication Requirements

> **The single biggest problem in communication is the illusion that it has taken place.**
>
> *George Bernard Shaw*

Communication complexity and the number of communication channels increase rapidly as the number of people on the project rises. The number of interactions between n people is $n(n-1)/2$. For example if a project has two stakeholders $n = 2$ and the number of communication channels is $2(2-1)/2 = 1$. If a project has 12 stakeholders there would be 66 communication channels indicating a challenging communication problem if the project manager needs to manage them all.

[3]It is less glamorous and more challenging to identify communication requirements than to analyze risks.

A theoretical communication model is helpful in understanding the communication process. This model, which is shown in Figure 16.2, consists of the following components: Encode and decode; message and feedback; and medium and noise. The *message* refers to the verbal (spoken or written) symbols, as well as nonverbal signs, which also represent information that the sender attempts to convey.

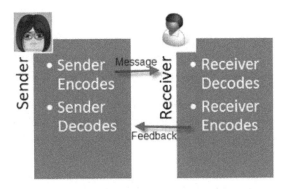

Figure 16.2: The communications model.

The first issue in the above simple model is that unless the sender receives feedback of the message just communicated (e.g., via parroting), the sender cannot be sure that the message was properly received (let alone understood). The model also indicates that both the sender and the receiver have to be good listeners, otherwise the message cannot be decoded properly.

Adding to the complexity of the basic communication model is that many things can interfere with the transmission of the message. We classify such barriers as filters and noise, and list some examples below:

Distance, unfamiliar technology, lack of background information.
Different spoken languages or use of unfamiliar technical jargon.
Physical separation.
Different cultural, educational, or social backgrounds.
Sabotage also hinders communication (hidden agendas, power plays).
A predetermined mind-set, or a self-fulfilling philosophy.
Historical considerations, ("it was always done in the past").

A project manager facing the challenges described above must create a communication plan that clearly specifies the appropriate format, duration and frequency of communications to mitigate the risk of communication failure.

287

16.2.1 Distributing Information

> **Everyone is entitled to his own opinion,**
> **but not to his own facts.**
>
> *Sen. Pat Moynihan.*

Project managers distribute and share information with the team, project sponsors, and stakeholders and this occurs in staff meetings, meetings with individuals, video and audio conferences, and computer chats.

Tools that aid in the distribution of information distribution include electronic communication and conferencing tools, such as e-mail, telephone, and web conferencing, as well as web portals and project management software.

16.2.2 Managing Stakeholder Expectations

Interpersonal skills and management skills fall in this category and examples include building trust, resolving conflict, active listening, and overcoming resistance to change. Examples of management skills include presentation, negotiation, writing, and public speaking.

Project managers can learn from Steven Covey's *Seven Habits of Highly Effective People* to communicate more effectively and manage stakeholder expectations. [54] The steps are pretty self-explanatory and are listed below:

Be proactive.
Begin with the end in mind.
Put first things first.
Think win/win.
Seek first to understand, then to be understood.
Achieve synergy.
Sharpen the saw.

16.2.3 Reporting Performance

> **The speed of communications is wondrous to behold.**
> **It is also true that speed can multiply the distribution**
> **of information that we know to be untrue.**
>
> *Edward R. Murrow*

Tools and techniques for reporting performance include: Variance analysis, forecasting reports, communication methods, and reporting systems.

Variance analysis is a tool for analyzing the difference between what was planned and what actually happened. For example, *EVM* is used to calculate cost and schedule variances. The following steps are performed during a variance analysis:

- Verify the quality of the information to ensure it is complete and credible.

- Determine if the variances are favorable or unfavorable to the outcomes.

- Determine the impacts on project cost, schedule, scope, and quality.

- Note the sources of variation and analyze their trends.

Forecasting methods: Using actual performance data, a project manager should predict the future performance, e.g., the *Cost Estimate At Completion.*

Communication methods: The project manager conducts periodic status review meetings to gather and exchange information about the project progress and performance. The project manager distributes status updates and reports.

Reporting systems: A project management information system (PMIS) can help to capture, store, and distribute information to stakeholders.

For the PM Project, Table 16.1 shows an example of the report of an issue that arose.

Table 16.1: Issues tracking report for the PMA web site.

Project Issue	Severity (H, M, L)	Owner	Resolution Due Date
Need to sign a release form from PMI to allow certain content to be utilized by the site.	H	PM	07/01/2012

16.3 Communications Management Plan

The *Communications Management Plan* describes the communication needs of the project, including audiences, messages, and methods. It also defines the approach to be used for those communications. Typical information includes the sender; the messages to be communicated, and the frequency with which they will be distributed; the audience; and the media, or method, to be used.

A sample communication management plan for the PMA project is illustrated in Table 16.2.

Table 16.2: The PMA *Communication Management Plan.*

Message	Description	Audience	Method	Frequency	Sender
Kickoff Meeting	Introduce team Review goals objectives & processes	Sponsor Project Team Stakeholders Sponsor	Video Conf.	Once	PM
Team Meetings	Review project status	Project Team	Conf. Call	Weekly	PM
Technical Meetings	Status of deliverables	Project Staff	Conf. Call	Weekly, or as required	Project Lead
Monthly Project Status Meetings	Report status of project & technical deliverables	Customer Stakeholders PMO Staff Upper Mgmt.	Face to Face	Monthly	PM

The PMA project manager may tailor the plan by adding communication guidelines and the reasons for the communications, as follows:

- *Kick Off Meeting.* This is an important meeting and the objective is to get to know the stakeholders and communicate the project objectives.

- *Meeting Agenda.* The Agenda will be distributed two days ahead of the meeting, and will specify the presenter for each subject, along with a time limit to prevent meeting overruns. Meeting minutes will be recorded by a team member on a rotating basis, and emailed to all members who attended the meeting within 48 hours.

17

RISKS

Risk?! Risk is our business!

Captain James T. Kirk

Risk Management is the art and science of dealing with risks. This involves identifying the risks that might occur, analyzing their potential impact, and developing a plan to minimize their likelihood of occurrence and their impact if the risk materializes. During execution, the project manager monitors the risks and, if risks materialize, implements the response plan.

Historically, risk management was considered an optional, add-on process, as distinct from activities such as project scheduling or cost estimating, which were always considered to be an essential part of project management.[1] However, the reality is that every project faces risks and, inevitably, some will materialize.

Starting in the mid-1980s project management standards, such as early versions of the PMBOK, formally began to recognize that comprehensive and integrated risk management is fundamental to project success. Today, managing risk is considered an indispensable and integral part of every stage of project management and it must be practiced diligently throughout the life of the project.[2]

Risk management is a proactive attempt to recognize what can go wrong and to plan ahead. Just as in medicine, prevention is better than cure. Here are some questions

[1] For example, Metzger's *Managing a Programming Project* (1996) [55] does not even make reference to the practice of risk management.

[2] Greg Ballesteros, the former CEO of PMI, says "Risk Management is PM for grown-ups."

291

the project manager should ask: What can go wrong? How can we minimize the impact? What can be done in advance? Then, if the risk materializes, what will our response be?

17.1   Definition of Risk

We begin with the definition of a risk:

> *A risk is an uncertain event or condition that, if it occurs, has a positive or negative effect on the project.*

It often comes as a surprise that the definition of a risk includes the idea that a risk can be *positive*. People usually assume that a risk has only negative consequences and that risk management consists of mitigating the impact of the things that can go wrong. However, it is as important to enhance the effects of the positive risks as it is to mitigate the impact of negative risks.[3]

Positive risks are regarded as *opportunities* and negative risks are considered *threats*. Consider the following examples of risks:

1. *The staff may not have the required technical skills.*

   This is a negative risk and the job of the project manager is to develop a strategy either to prevent the risk from occurring (e.g., by changing staff assignments), or mitigating the risk (e.g., by implementing a training plan).

   The staff may turn out to be technically competent, in which case, the risk did not materialize.

2. *The subcontractor might provide the deliverable earlier than planned.*

   This is a positive risk. If the deliverable is on the critical path, this may result in accelerating the schedule. The project manager should work to maximize the positive impact of the subcontractor's early delivery, perhaps by providing extra staff to help with delivery documentation.

Project managers should diligently investigate all risks and apply the correct tactic: Preventing and mitigating negative risks and enhancing positive risks.

It is important to distinguish between the trigger, the event, and the risk. For example, if you are planning an outdoor party, you might identify bad weather as a *risk*. If your weather app predicts an approaching storm, that is a *trigger*. If the

[3]The 6th edition of the PM-BOK redefined positive risks as *opportunities* and negative risks as *threats*, which is more consistent with the conventional view of risk.

292

storm actually materializes, that is the risk *event*. Also, the risk event may not be the disaster, but its signal.

Another key aspect of the above definition of risk is, "if it occurs," which introduces the idea of uncertainty:

- The uncertainty in the likelihood that the risk will occur.

- The uncertainty in the impact of the risk, if it occurs.

- The uncertainty in individual risks, which impact project activities, objectives, costs, and schedules.

- The uncertainty in the overall project risks, which impact the outcomes, stakeholder desires, and customer requirements.[4]

All of these uncertainties must be assessed and their impact estimated. Funds must then be allocated to cover the risks that actually materialize.

17.1.1 Risk Causes and Consequences

Risks have *causes*: For example, people get sick, the customer requests a change to the scope, a construction permit takes longer than anticipated.

Risks also have *consequences*: For example, consequences associated with the above risks are shown in Table 17.1.

Table 17.1: Sources of risk on the kitchen project.

Risk	Consequences
People get sick	Inexperienced, replacement personnel make mistakes. Activities completed late.
Scope changes	The proposed change increases the cost. and delays completion of activities.
Permit delayed	The construction start is delayed.

Notice that a cost increase is a *consequence*, not a risk. Technically, it is incorrect to say there is a *cost risk*. It is also incorrect to speak about a *schedule risk*. Instead, the project manager should explain that there are risk causes that may have schedule consequences, i.e., a delay in the schedule.

There are many potential risks:

- Scope creep.[5]

[4]This was added in the 6th edition of the PMBOK and, while a useful idea, is still somewhat poorly defined.

[5]Can you make this small change for me?

293

- Insufficient or poor resources.

- An expert may be needed simultaneously in two places.

- Pressure to compress the schedule from customers or management.

- Pressure to reduce the cost from customers or management.

- Lack of formal project management processes.

- Uncontrolled changes, which result in confusion.

- Stakeholder friction, which delays approvals.

- Stakeholder interests not satisfactorily addressed.

- Poor communications. Team members might not know what to work on, or how to prioritize their time.

- Customers might not understand the status of the project.

- Stakeholders might not know what is going on.

The above list illustrates an interesting aspect of risks: It is not hard to make a very long list of them. Therefore, the project manager needs a method of prioritizing the risks and determining which ones may require resources to be set aside (personnel, time, and money) in case they materialize.

Examples of risks on a plumbing project are shown in Table 17.2. The consequences are that any one them may contribute to an increase in the cost or cause a delay.

17.1.2 Known Unknowns and Unknown Unknowns

When trying to identify risks, one is always looking into the future, which is an uncertain business. Risks can be classified as follows:

- *Known unknowns*: These are risks that can be *identified*. A good way to identify such risks is by reviewing similar projects. An example from the New Kitchen project is:

We have to install a gas line in the kitchen and, on the last project, the permitting process was delayed by 6 weeks.

Known unknowns are risks that we can "kind of anticipate." According to David Logan, "much of the scientific research .... is based on investigating known unknowns," as we tend to allow for the things we expect.[6]

[6]Even worse, scientists develop a hypothesis to be tested and then, in an ideal situation, perform experiments that are, at-best, designed to test the null hypothesis (and) it is common for the researcher to believe that their result will be within a range of known possibilities. Occasionally, however, the result is completely unexpected—it was an unknown unknown! [56]

294

Table 17.2: Sources of risk on a plumbing project.

Risks in Cost Estimate	Source of Risk
Unforeseen circumstances.	When the plumber opened the cabinet to replace the faucets, he found rusted pipes that had to be replaced.
Use of wrong estimation parameter.	The estimator used the parameter for a new house, instead of the renovation of an old one.
Formula inaccuracy.	The estimation formula is only good to ±20%.
Optimistic estimate.	The PM knew the customer's budget and agreed to do the project for that amount.
Junior plumber assigned.	The estimate assumed an experienced plumber.
The estimate was made by "analogy."	The project turned out not to be "analogous," it was completely different.
It took longer.	Sometimes, this just happens.

- *Unknown unknowns*: These are the events we did not expect, things we had no idea about, as in:

  What?! You can't quit, you're our best programmer!

  Technically, unknown unknowns are the risks that were not identified during planning. NASA space exploration missions provide fascinating examples of things that went wrong that no one could possibly have anticipated. On a more mundane level, it is just not humanly possible to anticipate all risks.[7]

17.1.3 Types of Risk

The understanding of risks is evolving, particularly as it applies to overall project risks. Most of the risks we defined above are *event-based* risks, which means that the event results in a negative project impact.[8] An example of an event-based risk is, an important team member leaves.

There is a growing appreciation for *non-event risks*, which are more loosely defined and tend to impact the overall goals of the project. There are two types:

- *Variability risks:* These reflect uncertainties in the specified characteristics of the project. Variability risks can be associated with the project management, e.g., the activities are consistently taking longer than planned. Variability risks can also be associated with the project's objectives, e.g., the response of a website may be slower than expected.

[7]And if experience is anything to go by, we are not very good at this. Unknown unknowns constantly catch us by surprise.

[8]Event-based risks can also be positive.

295

Variability risks can usually be analyzed with standard quantitative techniques, such as prototyping, simulation, and decision trees.

- *Ambiguity risks:* These reflect uncertainties in the goals and objectives of the project. They are usually associated with imperfect knowledge about the project's objectives, its complexity, and stakeholder desires.

  Ambiguity risks are hard to analyze because they are usually the result of a lack of information. To address technical ambiguities, a prototype can help define the system's performance and give stakeholders information about what the system will eventually look like. When the stakeholders' objectives are uncertain, agile development, with frequent customer interactions, might be more appropriate.

17.2 Steps in Risk Analysis

The general process for analyzing risks is as follows. First, the risk management is planned resulting in a risk management plan.[9]

[9]For small projects, this need only be a brief checklist.

Next, the risks are *identified*, e.g., in a brainstorming session. It is quite easy to make a very long list of the things that can go wrong. Therefore, once you've identified the risks, you need a way to prioritize them and to decide which ones should be actively addressed. This is accomplished by performing a *qualitative* analysis in which risks are classified according to both their likelihood and their impact.

[10]Identified risks (known unknowns) result in contingencies: additional funds and schedule buffers.

It is useful to define an acceptable range of variation for critical project objectives. One can then define acceptable *risk thresholds* that can be monitored for triggers of potential threats.

[11]There is considerable debate over the management reserve. Some organizations require it (e.g., The Federal Highway Administration), while in a competitive situation many companies automatically delete the reserve to lower their bid.

Next, the risks that are both likely to occur and have a significant impact must be analyzed in more detail. This is called a *quantitative* analysis, the goal of which is to estimate *contingency* amounts in case some of the risks occur. Contingencies add costs to the budget and time to the schedule.[10]

Finally, there are allowance for things that just can't be anticipated — the unknown unknowns. The allowance for these unexpected events is called the *management reserve*.[11]

[12]You can't anticipate all eventualities. Plan to bury some funds and schedule some slack time. You never know when you will need them.

The lesson for project managers is serious: Risks will materialize, so plan ahead.[12]

17.3   Planning Risk Management

The *Risk Management Plan* documents the project team's approach to managing uncertainty, threats or opportunities, stakeholder risk tolerance, resources for assisting with risk analysis, identification of risk categories, assigning weights for risk probabilities and their impact, details about risk management funding, and risk audit approaches.

Typically, the plan requires at least preliminary versions of the scope, the cost and schedule, the communications management plan, and a list of the organizational assets. The risk management plan is a key input to the risk register. An appropriate tool for the risk plan is a template with the following key components:

- The scope, objectives, and methods to be used for risk identification, assessment, quantification, and response, as well as for monitoring and control during project execution.

- The roles and responsibilities of the participants in the risk analysis process.

- The risk analysis tools to be used and the identification of helpful templates and other available organizational assets.

- Risk categorization and prioritization, e.g., Do risks impacting cost take priority over schedule?

- The communications approach for risks when distributing status reports, including protocols for elevating risks to sponsors and senior management.

- Stakeholder risk toleration. Stakeholders have varying appetites for different risk classes. Defining thresholds helps to communicate risk exposure.

A *Risk Management Plan* for the PMA website project is shown in Figure 17.1.

Risk Management Plan

Project Title: **PMA Website**   Version: **1.2**   Date: **4-15-2017**

Methods and Approaches:

1. The PMI methodology and best practices will be followed for risk management, including the adoption of identifying, quantifying, identifying responses, and monitoring and controlling risks.

2. The team will use an Agile approach to reduce risk by breaking the project into small modules and iterating, with each iteration each lasting only a week.

3. Escalation of risk to senior management shall occur promptly.

Tools and Techniques:

Risks will be classified in the Risk Breakdown Structure (RBS), which is illustrated in the Risk Categories section below. Techniques used to identify risks will include: Brainstorming, risk auditing, the Delphi technique, interviewing experts, and survey of like projects.

Risk Categories:

From our experience with similar projects, we have identified the following categories of risks:

Category	Risks
Schedule	Tight Schedule, Scope Creep, Poor Estimation
Communication	Communication skills, Previous Experience
Technical	Software quality and browser compatibility risks

Stakeholder Risk Tolerance:

Tolerance: high = 3; medium = 2; low = 1.

Issue	Sponsors	Project Manager	Team Members
Performance	1	0	1
Budget	1	1	1
Schedule	2	0	1

Definitions of Probability:

Fuzzy labels of High (H), Medium (M) and Low (L) will be used. High will imply risks above 80%, Medium will be risks at 40% to 80% and Low will be risks below 40%.

Risk Management Funding: Contingencies and Reserves:

Contingency funding may be requested upon completion of the quantitative risk analysis. If the risk are high, senior management may include a reserve. The quantitative risk analysis may estimate a contingency budget of $10,000 to cover the known unknowns. Unknown unknowns will be covered by a 5% cost reserve and a 6-week schedule reserve.

Frequency and Timing:

Risk Analysis will be conducted every week at the project team meeting.

Figure 17.1: *Risk Management Plan* for the PMA case.

17.4 Identifying Risks

> **Risk comes from not knowing what you're doing.**
>
> *Warren Buffett*

The goal is simply to identify risks and add them to the *Risk Register*. Initially, the *risk register* might simply identify a list of risks, but it evolves to include an assessment of their likelihood and impact, as well as a ranking of their importance.

As with cost estimation, we can identify risks using either a top-down or bottom-up approach. Early in the project life cycle, we capture risks using top-down risk identification. The advantage of the top-down approach is that it is conducted early in the planning process and the team has time to change the scope of the project to mitigate or eliminate risks. This technique is called *Risk Prevention* and mitigating risks early on can make the project significantly less costly.

We recommend the Post-It® approach to risk identification: Provide each member of the project team Post-It notes and ask them to write down all the risks they can come up with. They should be encouraged to briefly document the risk and to add attributes, such as: Risk Category (e.g., Technical, Scope, Communication); and Project Impact (e.g., Cost, Schedule). The risks are then entered into the *Risk Register*, which at this stage may simply appear as:

1. Lack of programming knowledge. Category: Technical.

2. Some team members geographically separated. Category: Communication.

There are many resources available to help identify risks:

- *Historical databases* and *Lessons learned:* These are typically recorded in a debriefing at the end of a project. They identify "What worked?" and "What did not work?" The former is a good source for the under-appreciated *positive risks*, while the latter is a source for threats, or *negative risks*.

  For example, on the PMA project we identified a positive risk called "Expedite purchase of new hardware and software." The team identified this as a way to enhance both the cost and schedule.

- *Checklists:* These provide a useful starting point in risk identification.[13] Typically, a checklist will stimulate the team to come up with useful ideas.

  Checklists have received a huge boost in popularity thanks to a best-selling book entitled *The Checklist Manifesto* by Dr. Atul Gawande.[14] [57]

- *Risk Breakdown Structure (RBS):* The RBS is a tool to classify risks according to their category, e.g., technical, scope, etc. Several RBS templates are available in the public domain and can be used as a starting point.

- *Cause and Effect Diagrams:* These are also called Ishikawa diagrams, or Fishbone diagrams. They provide a useful method of identifying and classifying risks, as well as the responses. This tool is described in Chapter 14, Quality.

---

[13] Of course, anything missing from the checklist is also a risk.

[14] Dr. Gawande is a surgeon at the Brigham and Women's Hospital in Boston, a staff writer for The New Yorker, and a faculty member at Harvard Medical School.

299

PMI introduced a *Practice Standard for Risk Management*, which contains a comprehensive description of risk analysis tools and techniques, their strengths and weaknesses, as well as critical success factors for their effective application. [58] The standard suggests that a useful method of identifying risks is to continually repeat the following mantra:

> Because of **<one or more causes>**, **<risk>** might occur, which would lead to **<one or more effects>**.

The following is a list of risk identification techniques:

- *Risk Breakdown Structure (RBS):* The RBS is a valuable tool for identifying and classifying risks. An example of an RBS is shown in Figure 17.2

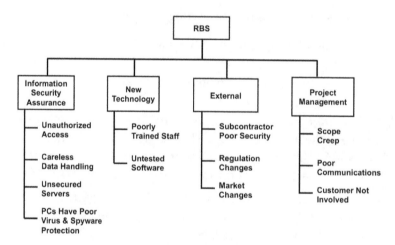

Figure 17.2: A *Risk Breakdown Structure.*

- *Assumptions and Constraints Analysis:* Each assumption and constraint in the project scope statement represents a risk. This can be used as a starting point to identify risks during the planning stage. For example, an assumption might be: The construction permit will be available in 30 days. The associated risk is: Permit schedule delay.

- *Brainstorming:* The project team, and other stakeholders, should be encouraged to generate a list of risks in a facilitated process.

- *Cause-and-effect (Ishikawa) diagrams:* This visual diagram promotes brainstorming, clarifies root causes, and helps develop mitigation strategies.

- *Checklists:* By examining historical data from similar projects, a list of relevant issues can be developed. Project lessons are sometimes available in industry and company databases and are a great source of risk identification.

- *Delphi Technique:* This is similar to brainstorming, but is a structured process that requires formal facilitation and anonymity.

- *Influence Diagrams:* Risks can be inferred from this diagram, which shows the main project entities and decision points, uncertainties and outcomes, and the relationships among them.

- *Interviewing:* This is similar to brainstorming in that expert consultants are interviewed to help identify and understand risks.

- *Historical information:* Organizations with good project management assets often have a repository of lessons learned, which can be an invaluable resource for identifying risks.

- *Questionnaires and Software:* Software that prompts the project team, or stimulates creativity, can help with risk identification.

- *SWOT analysis:* A Strengths, Weaknesses, Opportunities, Threats (SWOT) analysis might be available, since it is often part of the business case. If not, the team can perform a SWOT analysis, focusing on threats and weaknesses.

- *WBS Review:* A comprehensive review of all activities can act as a starting point for brainstorming sources of risks.

Risk Register

The *Risk Identification* process results in the *risk register*, in which each risk has the following attributes: ID, Name, Description, Impact (area and at what stage), Type (positive or negative), Likelihood, and Estimated Severity. During the early stages of risk identification, the *risk register* might simply consist of a worksheet. AS the project evolves and the *risk register* will include more information, such as potential risk responses and the results of qualitative and quantitative analyses.

For the PMA case, Table 17.3 shows an example of a risk register worksheet.

Table 17.3: *Risk Register* for the PMA case (preliminary worksheet).

Risk ID	Risk	Rating (H, M, L)
1	Technical Risk: Lack of WordPress programming knowledge	M
2	Communication Risk: Various stakeholders geographically separated.	H

Risk Register Updates

The risk register is updated as the risk management activities evolve and emerge plans for dealing with the identified risks. These typically include: Prevent/Avoid the risk, Transfer the risk, Mitigate the risk, or Accept the risk, i.e., do nothing for now, just monitor the situation. Once the strategy for dealing with the risks is assigned, the *risk register* is updated.

For the PMA case, Table 17.3 was updated to become Table 17.4.

Table 17.4: *Risk Register* for the PMA case (updated).

Risk ID	Risk	Rating (H, M, L)	Response
1	Technical Risk: Lack of WordPress programming knowledge	M	Training will be provided to mitigate risk.
2	Communication Risk: Various stakeholders geographically separated.	H	Accept risk–we are unable to do anything about this. Mitigate by providing virtual teaming skills

At this point, the risks are simply identified and listed in the *risk register*. No assessment has been conducted as to their likelihood of occurring or their impact.

17.5 Risk Response Strategies

[15]In the 6th Edition of the PMBOK, *risk response strategies* come after qualitative and quantitative analyses. However, risk responses can be performed early on. This is an example of tailoring the PMBOK to your own taste.

The project manager must formulate a strategy for both negative and positive risks.[15]

Risk responses should be conducted at any stage of the risk analysis. For example, changing the scope to eliminate a risk is a classic risk avoidance strategy. In which case, the requirement for both quantitative and qualitative risks analyses is eliminated. Therefore, we present the risk responses before the qualitative and quantitative analyses.

17.5.1 Response Strategies for Negative Risks

Negative risks (threats) can degrade the performance of a project. The negative risk strategies are: avoid, transfer, mitigate, accept, and elevate.

- *Avoid:* If possible, this risk *prevention* strategy should be the first choice.

  A technique for risk avoidance is to change the scope, which changes the project's functionality so that the risk cannot occur. For example, if the kitchen does not have gas, and the installation of a gas stove introduces an unacceptable delay, then propose an electric stove.[16] Another avoidance strategy is to defer risky parts of the specification to a future delivery.

  The advantage of *avoid* is that you do not need any contingency funds or schedule buffers. You have *eliminated* the risk.

- *Mitigate:* In this approach, one attempts to reduce either the likelihood of the event occurring or its impact, or both. This can result in lowering the ranking of the risk from high to medium or, even, to low. In practice, it is unlikely that a risk can be entirely prevented from occurring.

  An example of *mitigation* is as follows: Assume that an information technology project plans to use a new, sophisticated development system, and the organization does not have any previous experience with it. One *mitigation* strategy is to send the inexperienced staff members for training.

  Notice that *mitigation* almost always involves extra cost. In the above case, training funds will be required to mitigate the risk of inexperienced staff.

- *Transfer:* In this strategy, we outsource the risk to a third party. Often, risk *transfer* involves investing in insurance, performance bonds, or warranties.

  An example of risk *transfer* is the hiring an expert consultant to build a difficult piece of the project. The transfer of risk usually involves extra funds.[17]

- *Accept:* In this strategy, we accept the reality that the risk can neither be avoided, mitigated, nor transferred. The project team may decide to take a chance and *accept* the risk. The team recognizes that they will have to deal with this risk if, and when, it occurs. To allow for the risk, the project manager should set aside contingency reserves of time, money and staff.

[16]Of course, the customer may say "No way!" But at that point, she may also be willing to accept the delay.

[17]Do you want to add travel insurance for your trip?

303

An example of *accepting* a risk is: A deliverable is to be supplied by an unreliable subcontractor who holds a monopoly on the technology and there are no alternatives. The only option might be to accept the risk.[18]

- *Escalate:* This is appropriate when the threat could lead to events outside the scope of the project or that would exceed the project manager's authority. Risks are escalated to the Program Office or corporate management.

17.5.2 Response Strategies for Positive Risks

Positive risks (opportunities) can enhance the performance on a project. As there were with negative risks, there are equivalent strategies for dealing with positive risks: Exploit, enhance, share, accept, and escalate. These strategies parallel those for negative risks.

- *Exploit:* Here we leverage our strengths and attempt to take advantage of the risk. For example, the company might have talented programmers and assigning them to critical deliverables may result in early completion at a lower cost.

- *Enhance:* In this strategy, we attempt to increase either the likelihood or the impact of the risk occurring. An example of risk enhancement is as follows: If an activity is finished early freeing up staff, then they can be assigned to activities on the critical path to shorten the schedule.

- *Share:* Here, we enhance the opportunity for project success by teaming with a third party and delegate to them pieces they are better equipped to perform. Large projects usually share risks among several companies, each with their own expertise. For example, Boeing subcontracts the design and development of jet engines to third parties.

- *Accept*: Here we acknowledge that we cannot construct a viable strategy for maximizing the benefits of the positive risk, so we accept the situation.

- *Escalate:* This is appropriate when the threat could lead to events outside the scope of the project or that would exceed the project manager's authority. Risks are escalated to the Program Office or corporate management.

[18]Note that almost all risk strategies involve adding costs and time–the contingencies. You did put those in your budget and schedule, didn't you?

17.5.3 Risk Response

Despite the team's best efforts to mitigate them, some risks will actually occur and, often, in unexpected ways. Therefore, the project manager develops a plan for what to do if any of the risks actually occur. The goal is to reduce the impact of the risk by planning a smart response.

We emphasize that one should not sit around waiting to respond to a risk materializing. The project manager creates a *Contingency Plan*, which defines how the team will react to the risks *before* they materialize. The plan should include responses for both positive and negative risks.

For example, every time you get on a plane the flight attendants mitigate the impact of landing in water by explaining how to put on a life vest. However, if the plane actually lands in the water, i.e., the risk materialized, you need a risk *response* plan. The risk response is:

Get out of the plane!

Risk responses typically fall in the categories shown in Table 17.5:

Table 17.5: Risk response categories.

Risk Response	How
Prevent	Changing the scope of the project.
Mitigate	Reducing the likelihood or impact., Or both!
Transfer	Passing the risk on to a third party.
Accept	Do nothing. Set aside a budget to deal with the risk.
Escalate	Report the risk to the PMO or management.

17.6   Risk Analysis

Given a list of risks in the *Risk Register*, the next step is to analyze them and there are two steps: qualitative and quantitative. The *qualitative analysis* considers all risks and calibrates them in terms of their likelihood of occurring and impact.

The risk data are updated in the risk register by adding both their likelihood and impact, which, at this stage, are usually just in terms of high, medium, and low. Unlikely risks and those with little impact may be placed on a "watch list."

The goal of the *qualitative* analysis is to make visible the risks with the potential to significantly affect project outcomes, either negatively or positively. These significant risks are then further investigated in a *quantitative* analysis, the goal of which is to estimate the required contingencies (cost and schedule).

17.6.1   Risk Audits

A *risk audit* is a tool that is used to monitor and control project risks. For the PMA project, a risk audit it is illustrated in Table 17.6.

Table 17.6: PMA *Risk Audit.*

Audit of Process	Rating	Actions to Improve
Risk Identification and Mitigation	Satisfactory	Risk analysis could be improved by the PMA agenda item at weekly team meetings and communicating to stakeholders

17.6.2   Qualitative Risk Analysis

In a qualitative risk analysis, each risk is analyzed to determine its likelihood of occurring and its impact. Tables 17.7 and 17.8 provide examples of how the likelihood and impact might be defined for a project. Risks are scored on a scale from 1 to 5 in both likelihood and impact, with 5 being 'high.'

Table 17.7: Definition of risk *Likelihood* values.

Rating	Likelihood	Definition
1	Rare	Occurs in exceptional circumstances
2	Unlikely	Could occur at some time
3	Possible	Might occur at some time
4	Likely	Will probably occur in the project
5	Very Likely	Expected to occur in most situations

Table 17.8: Definition of risk *Impact* values.

Rating	Impact	Definition
1	Insignificant	No Damage or Loss No cost or schedule impact
2	Minor	Minor damage or loss Minor cost or schedule impact
3	Moderate	Some damage and/or loss Significant cost or schedule impact
4	Major	Extensive loss and damage Extensive cost and/or schedule impact
5	Catastrophic	Damage to reputation Huge financial loss Unrecoverable cost and/or schedule impact

306

Table 17.9: Definition of *impact* of risks for the PMA case.

Value	Definition	Examples
1	Unacceptable, or Catastrophic Risk:	The system is compromised, and data is visible to hackers.
3	Minor Damage, or Acceptable Risk:	Project completion date slips by a week. Delay in receiving hardware by a week.

Our preferred approach is to use a scale from 1-5, for both the likelihood and the impact.[19] The risks are then plotted on a grid. The advantage of using a 1-5 scale is that it provides useful bands, see Figure 17.3.

The project manager needs to establish agreed-upon definitions for both the likelihood and the impact. Examples help to clarify categories, such as those shown in Table 17.9 for the PMA project.

Table 17.10: The *Risk Analysis* for the PMA web site.

Risk ID	Category	Risk	Impact	Likeli-hood	Mitigation Action
1	Infra-structure	Not set up in time.	3	2	Select highly recommended VAR for servers.
2	Design	PMA Data may be hacked.	5	5	Select developer skilled in tools. Backup: Alternate tools.
3	PM	Aggressive schedule. Schedule fixed, possible delays.	3	5	Accept the risk. Monitor progress closely. Re-assess if slip occurs.
4	Skills	Key resources part time.	4	3	Tool easy to learn. Conduct training sessions.
5	Technology	Fixed price, contract. Added content may need to be purchased.	1	2	Include contingency $2,500 for unforeseen expenses.

Table 17.10 shows an example of a risk analysis for the PMA project, it lists all risks as well as their likelihood and potential impact.

These scores are then used as coordinates on the *Risk Assessment Matrix*, which is

[19]We prefer to use the term *likelihood* rather than probability. Using the term probability tempts people to assign numbers such as 73%, which, at this stage, are meaningless.

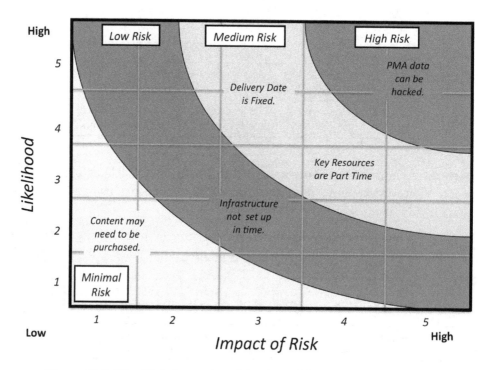

Figure 17.3: The *Risk Assessment Matrix* tool for *Qualitative Analysis*.

a useful visual aid—see Figure 17.3. Likelihood is plotted on the *y-axis* and impact on the *x-axis*. In the *Risk Assessment Matrix*, bands of color help to categorize the risks. The top right-hand corner is red and risks in this area have *high likelihood* of occurring and *high impact* if they occur. Many risks in this area is a sign of trouble. The middle band represents medium risks, while the bottom left corner represents *low likelihood* and *low impact*.

17.6.3 Quantitative Risk Analysis

The risks in the upper right quadrant of the *Risk Assessment Matrix* are classified as candidates for further investigation, which is accomplished using a *quantitative* analysis. When a risk occurs, it affects the cost and the schedule and the goal of the quantitative analysis is to *numerically* estimate its impacts.

Not all identified risks will materialize. Therefore, to fund the risks that actually occur, one assigns contingency funds and time buffers. There should be a contingency for cost (in dollars) and a contingency for schedule (in weeks), which is often called a time buffer.

The goal is to provide a numerical, or quantitative, estimate of the impact of the risks under discussion. The impact is usually measured in dollars, although the same techniques can be used for schedule slippages.

For example, we might be interested in identifying a contingency budget reserve for the risks associated with the Lack of Programming Knowledge on the PMA project. We would perform the quantitative risk analysis calculations as follows:

Risk:	**Probability**	**Impact**
Lack of Programming Knowledge:	50%	$10,000

If the risk occurs, the estimated contingency fund that must be set aside to pay someone to finish the project is:

$$Contingency\ Fund = 0.5 * \$10,000 = \$5,000. \qquad (17.1)$$

17.6.4 Tools for Quantitative Analysis

The following tools can be used to estimate contingency funds and time buffers.

Expected Monetary Value (EMV)

EMV is a technique used to calculate a weighted average, or expected cost, when the outcomes are uncertain.[20] We illustrate the EMV technique with examples:

1. *Rank Order Risks:*

   EMV is can be used to rank order risks. Suppose that all the risks in the risk register are negative. First, we express the risks in monetary form, e.g., *The cost of a one-week delay is $10,000.*

   Next, we assign a probability to each risk, e.g., *The probability of the one week delay is 50%.* Finally, we multiply the monetary impact by the probability to determine the expected value of this event:

   $$Expected\ Value\ of\ Risk = \$10,000 \times 0.50 = \$5,000. \qquad (17.2)$$

   One then rank orders all of the risks by their expected monetary value to reveal which ones are most important and require more attention.

[20]This should not be confused with EVM, Earned Value Management.

2. *Calculate Contingency Amounts:*

The contingency budget is the amount allocated to cover the cost of the risks that actually materialize. (There should be a separate time allowance for the schedule.) The contingency budget can allow for the fact that some risks are positive and some negative, as shown in Table 17.11.

Table 17.11: Calculation of the contingency budget.

Risk Event	Amount at Stake	Probability	Contingency (EMV)
Project will incur cost overrun resulting in financial penalty	-$50,000 (Loss)	0.80	-$40,000
Vendor supplies component early. Early completion of project	+$10,000 (Gain)	0.50	+$5,000
Potential Project Impact			**-$35,000**

Table 17.11 suggests the project manager should set aside around $35,000 to cover the losses associated with identified risks.[21] The probabilities, gains, and losses are all *estimates*. A wise project manager will conduct a sensitivity analysis in which the amounts and probabilities are varied and a range of likely values determined for the contingency funds.

3. *Evaluate Alternative Outcomes:*

When calculating the contingency budget, alternate outcomes for risk events might have to be considered. To show how this is accomplished, we expand the EMV calculation to include several possible events. We then weight the outcomes by their probability of occurrence.

To the above case, we add the idea that the 'reward' can be either high or low. We assess that the probability of the reward being high is 60%, and of being low is 40%. We multiply the Amounts at Stake by the probabilities to obtain the total Potential Project Impact, see Table 17.12.

Decision Tree

The *decision tree* is a tool for evaluating alternative approaches, each with different outcomes, and determining the alternative with the highest payoff.

We illustrate a decision tree with an example from the PMA case. The PMA board proposed a campaign to increase membership and the team thinks the quality of

[21] This does not guarantee that this is the right amount, it is simply the best guess. Both (or neither!) of the risks might occur.

Table 17.12: Calculation of the contingency budget using multiple outcomes.

Outcome	Amount at Stake	Probability	Contingency (EMV)
If reward is High: Demand for new software results in financial penalty	$40,000	60%	-$24,000
If reward is Low: No financial penalty	$10,000	40%	-$4,000
Potential Project Impact			**$20,000**

the web site will be a significant factor in the success of the campaign. Therefore, the team proposed investing in a development tools that would cost around $50,000.

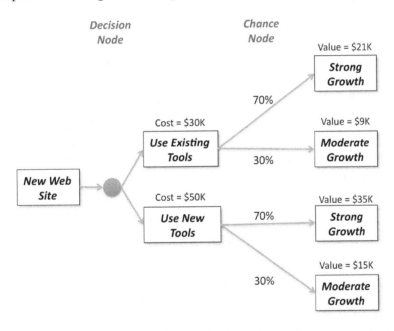

Figure 17.4: A *Decision Tree* analyzing the investment in new web site tools.

Figure 17.4 shows the way in which a decision tree is structured. The decision node, which is represented on the diagram by a small circle, has two options:

1. *Use Existing Tools:* In this option, the investment is $30,000, which is the estimated cost of upgrading the existing tools. This should include staff costs to implement the upgrades, training, and any new hardware.

2. *Use New Tools:* In this option, the investment is $50,000, which is the investment amount for new tools, including staff, training, and hardware.

Next, we allow for multiple outcomes, which is accomplished by assessing and evaluating the potential of the campaign to increase membership. After some analysis, the team proposes that there are two likely outcomes:

1. *Strong Growth with likelihood 70%:* The team believes that the campaign is very likely to succeed, and they propose that there is a 70% chance that the membership growth campaign will be successful.

2. *Moderate Growth with likelihood 30%:* Since nothing is certain, the team admits that there is a 30% chance that the membership campaign will be only moderately successful.

We now calculate the payoff for each outcome. The team estimated that each new member is worth around $1,000 to the organization. Therefore, to determine the payoff, we must estimate the increase in membership for each branch of the tree.

When the team uses the existing tools and the growth is strong, they estimate an increase of 21,000 members. However, when new tools are used, that number should increase to 35,000, as the new tools should reach a wider audience and process potential new members more efficiently. For moderate growth, the corresponding numbers are 9,000 for existing tools, and 15,000 for new tools.

The next step is to determine which is the most effective option. To do this, we calculate the *Expected Monetary Value* of each branch of the tree:

Existing Tools	= -$30,000 + $21,000 x 0.7 + $9,000 x 0.3	= -$12,600.
New Tools	= -$50,000 + $35,000 x 0.7 + $15,000 x 0.3	= -$21,000.

The decision with the highest payoff is for the *Existing Tools* option.[22]

One should ask, "Which data values drive the decision?" The investment amounts are large and negative, while the returns are positive and smaller. Therefore, the decision is driven by the investment and these data should be carefully examined.

Because both options have negative payoff, one may reasonably ask what happens if the team decides to do nothing. That is, what is the impact of conducting the campaign with no upgrade of web tools at all?

In that case, we can add a third decision, *Do Nothing*, with an investment of zero. Further, suppose we estimate that the growth in membership for the two scenarios

[22]It has the smaller negative number.

are *Strong = 2,000* and *Moderate = 1,000.* If we add the *Do Nothing* decision node to the diagram, we will get the following EMV for that branch:

$$Do\ Nothing = -\$0 + \$2,000 \times 0.7 + \$1,000 \times 0.3 = +\$1,700. \qquad (17.3)$$

This option produces a positive payoff and is actually the best option.

This is an example of a sensitivity analysis. After constructing the decision tree, the project manager should present it to a variety of stakeholders. Their feedback will help calibrate the data and evaluate which parameters drive the decision. In this case it was the investment amounts, which drive the decision. Therefore, the natural question to ask was, "What happens if we eliminate the investment?" This led to a third decision option, *Do Nothing*, which turned out to be the best option.[23]

Using Decision Trees

A major problem with decision trees is the so-called, "Myth of Analysis," which covers a variety of issues.

Decision trees can be very useful in the analysis of medical issues because there is often lots of data on the cost of a treatment or drug, along with actual probabilities for patient outcomes, e.g., cure rates, death rates, etc.[24]

- *All options are included.* Not all of the decisions may be included or, even, analyzable. In the first version of the decision tree, we omitted the *Do Nothing* option, and that turned out to be the best approach.

- *All consequences are included.* We can easily add a third outcome: *Weak Growth.* If the economy declines, such an option may be important.

- *The data are valid.* The costs and probabilities are fundamental in assessing the usefulness of the decision. Questions that might be asked in a sensitivity analysis, include: Do small changes in either probabilities or payoff change the decision? If so, the data should be re-assessed.

- *The tree rapidly gets complicated.* It is confusing to analyze multiple decisions with multiple outcomes. A useful approach, then, is to prune obviously bad branches.

- *Belief in impartiality.* A fallacy is that the data, because they are probabilities, are somehow impartially developed. They are not. Analysts bring their biases and preconceptions to the assignment of probabilities and costs.

[23] Only by conducting the sensitivity analysis did we uncover the best option. If we had blindly followed the "best" decision tree outcome, we would have lost a lot of money.

[24] For an interesting discussion of the use of decision trees in medicine, see Farrokh Alemi's web page, *http:// gunston.gmu.edu/ 730/ DecisionTrees.asp.* The page is based on a chapter with the same name in the book *Systems to Support Health Policy Analysis: Theory, Model and Uses.* [59]

- *It is not about the cost.* Making a decision based solely on the estimated future costs is a poor approach.[25]

- *Intermediate decisions.* Sometimes, a branch of the tree may have a decision point built in. For example, when pursuing the option of a new website, there may be an initial investment in a prototype followed by optional add-ons. If the membership growth is going well using just the prototype, the team may decide to purchase additional capabilities.

  Such conditional decisions make the decision tree very complex. The best approach is often to wait until the decision is imminent, at which time one will have better data on the costs and income.

On the other hand, there are definite benefits in the use of decision trees:

- *There is a decision.* The first and most important aspect is that it informs everyone that there is indeed a decision to be made. The tool formalizes the process and allows stakeholders a chance to give input.

- *Open analysis.* The assumptions, data, and decisions are open to everyone.

- *Team discussion.* The process generates an informative discussion. In particular, a sensitivity analysis will strengthen the confidence of the stakeholders that the decision is correct.

17.7   Monitoring and Controlling Risks

This is where risks are tracked and responded to and different risk categories warrant different approaches.

- *High Risk:* These must be continuously monitored. Throughout the project, high risks should be analyzed to determine if there are actions that might reduce the likelihood of occurrence and the impact if it occurs. If possible, risks should be *prevented* from occurring, e.g., change the scope.

- *Medium Risks:* These should be monitored closely and continuous mitigation should attempt to contain their effects, and to ensure that they do not escalate to high impact risks.

- *Low Risks:* These should be routinely monitored at regular meetings to ensure their status remains as 'low.'

[25]In Chapter 3 we learned that the most important critical success factor for new products is a "unique differentiated product." A better question than "What is the lowest cost?" is, "What strategy delivers the most unique product?"

314

17.7.1 Tools for Risk Response

This is where the project manager *responds* to the risks when they materialize. If significant planning has occurred, and a response strategy is in place, this is where the contingency plan is implemented.[26]

There are several tools and techniques to help the project manager to respond to risks, including brainstorming and scenario analysis. In both, participants suggest solutions and analyze their effects.

17.7.2 Tools for Monitoring and Controlling Risks

During execution, the project manager monitors and controls risks. This occurs throughout the life cycle of the project by regularly reassessing and updating the *risk register*. Status meetings and periodic team meetings are an excellent opportunity to review the risks, which should be an agenda item.

Table 17.13: Risk events and some potential responses.

Risk Event	Risk Response
Personnel shortfall	Hire subcontractors. Enhance productivity through training.
Scope unclear	Develop prototype with user input.
Subcontractor not performing adequately	Conduct frequent site visits. Co-locate with team. Invoke performance clauses in contract.

Other tools and techniques that can be used during execution include risk audits, variance and trend analysis, technical performance measurement, and reserve analysis. Table 17.13 lists some potential responses to risks when they occur.

17.7.3 Risk Occurrence Over Time

The PMBOK suggests the probability of risks occurring is initially high and declines over the project's life. We claim that this only applies to the known risks.[27] We are not convinced that the likelihood of occurrence of "unknown unknowns" declines over time, as the following examples from the kitchen project illustrate:

- When the refrigerator arrived, it did not fit in the cabinet opening. The contractor, Mark, immediately measured the opening size, which was correct according to the refrigerator's specification document.

[26] If there is no contingency plan, then the strategy becomes: *Dig Out*.

[27] Probably because the project manager is looking at them and containing them.

315

Mark then measured the refrigerator and found that it was 1.2 inches higher than the specification. Mark was furious and called the refrigerator manufacturer. There was a lot of yelling, which came to a head when the refrigerator manufacturer said, "Standard practice is to allow an extra inch."

"I allowed two inches!" Mark yelled back.

Fortunately, the refrigerator had leveling screws on the bottom and some careful adjustments allowed the refrigerator to *just* fit in the opening. This is an example of a specification error that could have been expensive to fix.[28]

- Hurricane Irene barreled through town and ripped the roof off the finish carpenter's house. Only less skilled carpenters were available and the finish work was delayed. This is an example of a personnel risk.

- The ceiling was scheduled to be insulated with foam. The insulation contractor told us that we could not sleep in the house the night the foam was installed and we planned to stay with friends.

  However, when the insulation contractor showed up, he said that nobody could stay in the house while the foam was being blown in.[29] That happened to be a day when the plumber, painter, and carpenters were all scheduled to work. This is an example of a communication risk.

- Peter, the electrician, suffered an accident that cut his hand rather badly and he was out of commission for a week. His assistant filled in, but could only perform low level electrical work and the project was delayed. This is another example of a personnel risk.

Hurricanes, injuries, and specification errors were all "unknown unknowns," and completely unanticipated. They are all examples of high-impact, low-probability events, and most risk analytical models fail miserably in predicting and allowing for such situations.

17.7.4   Risks, Contingencies and Reserves

Finally, we remind the reader that the results of the risk analysis are amounts (costs and/or schedules) to be included in the *contingency reserves*. Contingency reserves are explicitly assigned to identified risks. On the other hand, *management reserves*, which are allocated to cover unidentified risks, are *not* included in the cost baseline, i.e., reserves are for *unknown unknowns*.

[28] This is also a good example of Mark's planning ahead. When everyone had calmed down, Mark drolly observed, "This is why we add tolerances."

[29] He actually said this at 8:30 am when Eileen not had a chance even to dry her hair. The insulation contractor was less than popular. The project manager was not happy.

18

PROCUREMENT

**I wish to be cremated. One tenth of my ashes shall
be given to my agent, as written in our contract.**

Groucho Marx

Procurement is about contracts and their administration, which is a highly special-ized area.[1] The project manager is not required to know all the legal details, but should possess an understanding of the risks of the various contract types and pay special attention to what is to be delivered by whom.[2]

Procurement Management defines how to buy and sell products and services, which is accomplished through a contract. There are many types of contracts and the project manager selects the type that assigns to the project team both a reasonable risk and the greatest incentive for efficient and cost-effective performance.

We begin with the definition of a contract:[3]

> *A contract is a mutually binding agreement that binds the seller to provide specified products and services and also obligates the buyer to provide monetary or other valuable consideration.*

There are two types of contracts that the project manager must be aware of. The first is the contract for the project itself. That is, the project manager is probably

[1] And a good example of the diverse knowledge required by a project manager.

[2] This is detailed in the State-ment of Work (SOW).

[3] This definition is a simplified version of that found in legal books. Legal definitions add phrases such as, "often in writing." We believe a PM needs practical guidance on contracts and we leave the legal technicalities to the lawyers.

317

working on a contract to deliver the project to the buyer. This contract defines what it is that the project manager must do. In this case, the project manager is the *seller*.

The second type of contract occurs during the execution of the project, when the project manager decides it is necessary to employ a third party to perform some of the work. This is called a subcontract and the project manager is the *buyer*.

The fact that the project manager is both a seller and a buyer means the project manager has to understand all aspects of contracting, its terminology and the different types of contracts. For the rest of this chapter, we will assume that the project manager is the buyer.

For a project, the contract will usually reference the scope document as the definition of what is to be provided. We note here that the scope not only includes the specification (the definition of the project), but also major milestones, schedule constraints, etc. Thus, the scope becomes the fundamental basis of the contract and every statement carries legal implications.

In order to pursue a subcontract, the project manager must have a clear description of the product or service to be delivered. Therefore, the project manager begins the subcontracting process by separating out a well-defined piece of the scope. Next, the project manager creates a Statement of Work (SOW), which is the most important contracting document.

There are other types of contracts that the project manager should be aware of, such as: *Memorandum of Agreement*, which is an informal type of contract agreement;[4] and *Service Level Agreement (SLA)*, which define services the provider will furnish and the performance standards the provider is obligated to meet. Since these are essentially contracts, we will not consider them further.

When developing a subcontract, the project manager must be able to answer the following questions:

What should we procure and how?
When should we procure it?
What type of contract will we use?
What metrics will we use to measure completion and success?
How will we administer the contract?

The work to be completed may not be well specified because the problem is not understood. In that case, the SOW should define the problem to be solved, along with goals, objectives, and success criteria. The document that defines the goals is called a *Statement of Objectives (SOO)*.

[4] The PMBOK defines the plural, *Memoranda of Agreements*, but the singular is more usual.

318

Changes to the contract are often difficult and, even, contentious. Such changes are handled through a *Contract Control System (CCS)*, which defines the process by which a contract's authorized scope may be modified, dispute resolution procedures, and approval levels for authorizing changes. Best practice is to include the contract change procedures in the contract.

18.1 Contract Types

There are three broad categories of contracts:

1. *Fixed Price:* The contractor is awarded a total sum for performing the work, no matter how much time and money it took to deliver the project.[5]

2. *Cost Reimbursable:* All legitimate project costs for performing the work of the project are reimbursed to the contractor. A fee (or profit) may also be added. This is also known as cost-plus contract.[6]

3. *Time and Materials:* The buyer pays a fixed hourly rate for the labor spent working on the project and also reimburses the contractor for all the materials and expenses associated with the project work.

A major trend in modern contracting is towards *performance-based* contracting (PBC), where the project manager defines the desired results or outcomes.[7] When a contract is performance-based, the project manager must carefully define the incentives, the desired performance outcomes, and the criteria for assessing them.

There are two major advantages of performance-based contracts. The first is that the customer (the buyer) is relieved of detailed contract administration and can focus on helping the project team achieve the specified goals. The second is that the project team (the seller) can determine the best technical alternatives and the most cost-effective approach.

Contractors may be awarded *incentives*, or extra fees for completing the project early, or for controlling costs. If the contractor finishes a project at a cost less than specified in the contract, the buyer and seller may split the savings. The opposite of incentives is *penalties*, which are imposed on the seller for poor performance.

Many variations and combinations of the basic three types are possible. The most frequent types of contracts a project manager will encounter are:

- *Firm Fixed Price (FFP) Contract:* The amount to be paid for the project is determined at the time the contract is signed and the contractor bears all the

[5]While the total amount is fixed, it may be paid out over time.

[6]The key word here is *legitimate*. There are strict accounting and government rules and regulations for what is *legitimate*.

[7]This is in contrast to *cost-plus* contracts, where one looks for the *contractor's* best efforts to control the costs.

319

cost risk. It is a very common contract type, because both the buyer and the seller receive relative certainty as far as costs are concerned.

The buyer must be willing to put significant effort into providing a clear, well-defined specification. The seller must be willing to deliver the project for a fixed price. FFP contracts work well when the documentation, especially the scope, is well-defined.

- *Fixed Price Plus Incentive Fee (FPIF) Contract:* This is similar to the FFP contract in that the conditions are determined at the time of signing the contract. However, the buyer is willing to give a bonus to the seller based on some clearly identified superior project performance. Performance criteria may include delivering ahead of the defined schedule or under the defined budget. Penalty clauses may be imposed for late delivery or cost overruns.

- *Costs Plus Fixed Fee (CPFF) Contract:* This provides for the reimbursement of all *allowable costs* plus the award of a fixed fee upon completion. This type of contract is common for projects in which the scope is uncertain, such as research and development efforts and Department of Defense projects.

- *Costs Plus Award Fee (CPAF) Contract:* This is also a cost-plus contract, except that instead of paying a fee, the buyer pays an award based on the buyer's evaluation of the seller's performance. The award amount is earned based on defined criteria, such as completion time, cost effectiveness, quality of work, or technical ingenuity.

  An important issue in a CPAF contract is: Who decides the amount of the award? If the criteria are subjective, the award fee may be determined by an independent external board. The award amount may also be based upon objective performance metrics, e.g., the range of a battery powered car or a web site response time with 1,000 users accessing it simultaneously.

- *Costs Plus Incentive Fee (CPIF) Contract:* This also provides for the reimbursement of contract costs, but the buyer is willing to award a fee if well-defined performance goals are met. For example, if the final cost of the project is less than the budgeted cost, the buyer and seller may share the savings based on a predetermined, contractually documented incentive arrangement.

- *Cost Plus Percentage of Cost (CPPC) Contract:* This provides for the full reimbursement of allowable costs. The seller is also given a fee, which is an agreed percentage of the allowed project cost. The buyer bears all the risk and is used only when there is major uncertainty associated with the project.

The CPPC type of contract is banned in U.S. Federal Contracting and you can understand why.[8] There is no incentive for the contractor to hold down costs because the more they spend, the more money they receive.

CPPC is used only occasionally in the commercial sector. For example, in the pharmaceutical industry, there is so much uncertainty and risk when searching for a new drug that, it is claimed, only the CPPC contract type provides the appropriate motivation for contractors to take on the work.

18.2 Selecting a Contract

> **I'm not going to buy my kids an encyclopedia.**
> **Let them walk to school like I did.**
>
> *Yogi Berra*

When selecting a vendor and awarding a contract, the project manager balances the risks versus the available information.

18.2.1 Fixed Price Contracts

In a *Fixed Price* contract, the seller agrees to pay a fixed amount to the seller. Usually the seller requests a certain percentage at the start (or award) of the contract and progress payments tied to major deliverables. The buyer will usually hold back a certain amount until the job is successfully completed.

Table 18.1 shows the positive and negative incentives of a fixed price contract from both the buyer's and seller's perspectives. For the project manager, a fixed price contract is a good choice when there is an excellent specification.

For large contracts, a third party may be employed to define when the seller's work is satisfactorily complete. This is called a Validation and Verification (V&V) contractor.

Installment payments are often driven by the seller's cash flow. For example, in the New Kitchen contract, Mark requested major payments when he was facing expensive purchases. One such contract condition was: *$3,000 at delivery of blue board*. Since the blue board was a major expense, Mark inserted a provision for a payment at that time.[9]

[8] For example, see an interesting discussion of contracts in the Iraq war at http:// www.dodig.mil/ audit/reports/ fy06/ 06-007.pdf

[9] Notice Mark did not specify a date, but tied the payment to a deliverable. If Mark accelerated the schedule, he would still receive a payment when he needed to pay for the blue board.

321

Table 18.1: The positive and negative aspects of a fixed price contract.

Buyer's Perspective	
Advantages	**Disadvantages**
Predictable, known cost	More costly to prepare
Incentives for lower cost	Requires a good spec & knowledge of needs
	Mistakes in the spec are costly
	Incentive for fast completion at lowest cost
	May require contingency costs
Seller's Perspective	
Advantages	**Disadvantages**
Potentially larger fee	Underestimated costs mean a loss

18.2.2 Cost-Plus Contracts

> **The universe never did make sense;**
> **I suspect it was built on government contract.**
>
> *Robert A. Heinlein*

In a *cost plus* contract, the seller is reimbursed for all allowable costs, which include labor, materials, and travel. The seller must have an audited overhead rate, which determines the rate at which overhead costs are reimbursed. The seller also receives an additional prior-negotiated fee, which is often set as a percentage of the initially specified contract cost.

The major disadvantage with cost plus contracts is that the customer must rely on the project team's best efforts to contain costs. Table 18.2 shows the positive and negative incentives of a cost plus contract.

For example, suppose you negotiate a CPFF contract with a cost of $100,000 and a $6,000 fee (6%). The total contract cost is $106,000. You successfully perform the project and your costs are $90,000. The buyer audits your costs and agrees they are all legitimate. You receive $90,000 for the costs, plus your fixed fee of $6,000. Since the fee was "fixed," your fee rate is actually: $6K/$90K = 6.7%.[10]

On the other hand, suppose you successfully perform the project but your costs are $200,000. You receive $200,000 for the costs, plus your fee of $6,000. You do not lose money, but your boss will probably be unhappy that your fee is only 3% $(6,000/200,000 = 3\%)$.

[10]You need to check the contract carefully to determine if what was "fixed" was the fee in dollars or the percentage.

Table 18.2: The positive and negative aspects of a cost plus contract.

Buyer's Perspective	
Advantages	**Disadvantages**
Maximum Flexibility	Relies on seller's best efforts to contain costs
Minimizes early negotiation costs	No assurances of actual cost
Eases selection of best-qualified rather than lowest bid	
Allows use of same contractor for design and implementation	
Seller's Perspective	
Advantages	**Disadvantages**
Can undertake risky efforts	High costs reduce profitability & fee percent
Can undertake long projects	

18.2.3 Incentive Fee Contract Example

The best way to understand an incentive fee contract is through an example.

The project manager of the PMA website decides to subcontract out the building of the web site and prepares a detailed scope document. A macro estimation formula determines the cost as $10,000. The project manager then assesses the risks and decides that a creative subcontractor might get the job done for less. But the project manager also needs to be able to establish a firm budget not to exceed $13,000.

The project manager therefore selects a CPIF contract with a 70%/30% sharing of the savings. The project manager also proposes that a profit of 10% should be a sufficient incentive for sellers to take on this small job. The contract summary is shown below.

Target Price:	$11,000
Target Cost:	$10,000
Target Fee (or Profit):	$1,000
Contract Ceiling:	$13,000
Profit / Loss Sharing:	Seller Share: 30%
	Buyer Share: 70%

We now explore what happens in the several scenarios:

Case 1: Under Run

The subcontractor completes the contract at a cost of $8,000, i.e., less than the originally budgeted cost of $10,000. The fee, or profit, calculation is:

Seller Cost:	$8,000
Cost Savings:	$2,000
Profit / Loss Sharing:	Seller Share: 30% of $2,000 = $600
	Buyer Share: 70% of $2,000 = $1,400
Seller Profit:	$1,000 + $600 = $1,600
Contract Price:	$8,000 + $1,400 = $9,400

We note that incentive fee contract calculations are based on the costs, since these are always auditable and verifiable. In this case, the seller made an additional profit of $600, while the buyer's total cost is $9,400. Notice that the seller receives the agreed fee ($1,000) as well as a share of the cost savings, which was $600.

The customer (the buyer) should be pleased, as the contract was completed for $9,400, which was less than the estimate of $10,000. The project manager should also be happy because, while they completed the project under budget, they received an increased profit ($600 more than the plan of $1,000).

Case 2: Over Run

The subcontractor completes the contract at a cost of $11,000, i.e., more than the originally budgeted cost of $10,000. The fee, or profit, calculation is as follows:

Seller Cost:	$11,000
Cost Savings:	-$1,000
Profit / Loss Sharing:	
	Seller Share: 30% of -$1,000 = -$300
	Buyer Share: 70% of -$1,000 = -$700
Seller Profit:	$1,000 - $300 = $700
Contract Price:	$11,000 + $700 = $11,700

In this case, the seller made a slightly smaller profit of $700. The buyer's total cost is $11,700, which consists of the costs ($11,000) plus the reduced profit.

Case 3: Exceeding the Ceiling

The seller's cost is $15,000. The buyer informs the seller that the contract ceiling is $13,000 and so the buyer receives only $13,000. The seller has lost $2,000 on the contract and these costs will have to be paid by the seller's company.

Case 4: Low Risk

If the project were not very risky, then the percentage share of the profit might be adjusted. For a low risk project, the buyer might adjust the share to a 30%/70%

ratio, so that the contractor gets less in the case of an overrun. Using a 30%/70% split, Case 2 becomes:

Seller Cost:	$11,000
Cost Savings:	-$1,000
Profit / Loss Sharing:	
	Seller Share: 70% of -$1,000 = -$700
	Buyer Share: 30% of -$1,000 = -$300
Seller Profit:	$1,000 - $700 = $300
Contract Price:	$11,000 + $300 = $11,300

The seller's profit is reduced significantly.

18.2.4 The Scope and Contract Types

There is direct relationship between the quality of the project scope, its specification, and the type of contract that should be employed. The specification defines what is to be produced and when it is well defined, the buyer is in a position to request a fixed price contract. If the specification is incomplete, or its development is technically risky, the buyer should move towards a cost plus contract.

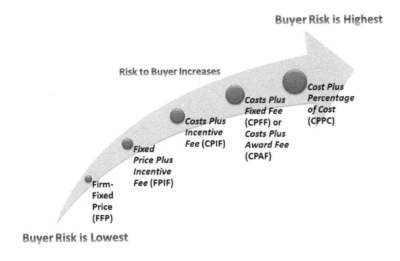

Figure 18.1: Buyer risk versus contract type.

The buyer risk versus contract type is shown in Figure 18.1. Buyer risk is lowest for fixed price contracts, because the cost is known in advance. The buyer risk

Figure 18.2: Seller risk versus contract type.

increases for cost plus contracts because the seller's costs are not known and may increase as the specification is refined.

The seller's risks are shown in Figure 18.2. Sellers have more risk on a fixed price contract because they must specify their bid in advance, with only the scope document to go on. Seller risk is lower for a cost-plus contract, because they will be reimbursed for all contract costs.

18.2.5 Statement of Work

The major effort in preparing a contract is the writing of the Statement of Work (SOW). It defines the tasks to be completed and who is to perform them; the milestones and deliverables; reporting procedures; and the payment schedule, from which the project manager computes the cash flow needs.

Table 18.3 shows an example of a Statement of Work for the PMA contract.

If the PMA case study did not have any procurement, all the project work would be done with internal resources. This is an example where the item could be checked off with no further work required.

Table 18.3: Statement of Work for the PMA contract.

Statement of Work for the PMA Project

Project Manager: Dr. Vijay Kanabar
Project Start Date: March 10th, 2010
Projected Finish Date: April 25th, 2010

Project Objectives:

The PMA web site is a social network site dedicated to all BU students interested in project management, including alumni. The primary stakeholders are students interested in becoming certified as PMPs, as well as those wishing to maintain their certification status. The website provides a channel for PMPs to earn PDU's to maintain their certification. Other stakeholders include any students interested in PM who will benefit from the website.

It is conceivable that a non-BU audience interested in the field of project management will access the site. Therefore, the website will have resources that anyone can use, such as templates, links to project management websites and links to interesting research.

Only the following personal information will be captured and maintained: First name, last name, email address. The email address will act as proof of a current or past BU association. MailChimp will be used to store all student names and email addresses, because it comes with a built-in database. Students with data in the system will be considered to be *registered*.

The web site will have a designated *Director*, who will email to registered students: the newsletter and special information such as job postings and internships. Students will be requested to link to resources such as Facebook, Wordpress, and Linkedin. Jobs and internships will also be posted.

While we are not dictating functionality, Social Networking site features that will be useful to members are: A News and Announcements Section; User Blogs and Forums; a Reading Room (document repository); an Event Calendar; BU TV PM related videos; Resource Links – split into two PM and IT PM categories; a link to the Project Management in Practice Conference website; Job tips and opportunities; PMP Certification links and resources; PM templates and papers; and an "Ask the Expert" feature, for users to post questions about their projects and receive advice from other PMA members.

Budget Information:

Hosting investment has already been made for this site to the tune of $200 per year. The majority of costs for this project will be internal labor. An initial estimate provides a total of 40 hours per week per team. Other proposed budget items will be considered.

18.3   Closing Contracts

> **Acceptance of what has happened is the first step to overcoming the consequences of any misfortune.**
>
> *William James*

To close a contract, the customer must formally accept the project deliverables.[11]

[11] Usually, the deliverables were previously validated by the *Quality Control* group.

327

Activities at this stage consist of:

- *Formal Acceptance of the Project.* The project manager must obtain final acceptance of the project.

- *Post Implementation Activities.* These include soliciting and documenting the lessons learned, releasing all project resources, archiving project materials, and conducting post-project reviews.

- *Closing Out Contracts.* If a seller was involved, the final procurement details must be completed.

Projects come to an end when they have completed their deliverables and satisfied their stakeholders.[12] Sometimes projects are suspended or killed for business reasons, or for failure of the team to perform adequately. Whether successful or not, the project manager must complete the project closure activities.

Before closing the project, the project manager should be able to answer the following questions:

- *Organizational Issues.* Who will be involved in the project closure? When and where will project closure be conducted?

- *Project Evaluation.* How did the project perform against its stated objectives? How did the cost and schedule compare against the plan?

- *Lessons.* What lessons were learned? What could have been done differently?

A team meeting at this stage will be a good learning experience for everyone. Typically this meeting might involve asking questions such as:

- How well did we plan the project?

- How well did we execute the project?

- How well did we monitor and control the project?

- How well did we communicate internally and externally?

- How would you rate your satisfaction working on this project?

- How can we improve on the above aspects?

---

[12]Hopefully, successfully!

Closing the project is referred to as, *administrative closure*, which is the name given to the collection and archiving of project reports and documents; creating project archives; and the capturing of lessons learned from the project.

The completion of the project results in a final product, service or result, and the outcome is described in the formal sign-off document. This is usually known as *Formal Acceptance*, and includes documenting the stakeholder comments that emerge during the acceptance process.

An important result from closing a project are lessons learned, which should be transferred to the organizational knowledge base for use by future project managers. Another useful document the project manager may decide to write is the *Transition Plan*, which guides the sponsors in the future use the product. This will also help the transition the project into its operational role.

A final face-to-face meeting with the sponsor is desirable and is where the final product and transition plan are discussed. This helps to create a positive lasting experience for the stakeholder.[13]

An issue with this phase of the project is that the team members are very busy and, most likely, are released to work elsewhere. Therefore, lessons learned from a project are frequently not captured. To resolve this problem, organizations should commit to continual improvements by budgeting time for the process of lessons learned and disseminating them.

The project manager may be responsible for some post-project activities, such as working with company managers to re-assign personnel. Also, the project manager may write an honest performance assessment for each team member for consideration by the company's managers. The project manager should discuss such appraisals personally with each team member.

Another suggested post project activity is to follow up with the customer after the product has been in use for a while. As well as generating goodwill, it can help determine if the strategic business reasons for undertaking the project actually materialized.[14]

18.3.1 Lessons Learned

The project manager should create a *Closeout Report*, which includes an executive summary of the project and highlights of the scope. The report should also document the project management processes, commenting on any significant schedule, cost, quality, and communication issues. The lessons learned should also be recorded here. Finally, the *Closeout Report* should be widely disseminated so that people in the organization can benefit from the accumulated wisdom.

[13]The last impression is the best impression.

[14]A good project manager would celebrate success and reward participants with a party.

329

A sample *closeout report* document containing lessons learned from the PMA project is illustrated in Figure 18.3.

Closeout Report containing lessons learned from the PMA project

Project Name: PMA Date Prepared: 5/9/11 Project Manager: V. Kanabar

Summary:

The PMA project was a successful project: It fully met its objectives. The scope and sponsor requirements were fully implemented and accepted. Product quality was verified and validated and the project stayed within the planned schedule and cost baselines.

The sponsors communicated during acceptance they were happy with the deliverables. The team members communicated that the project was a great learning experience for all. They attribute this in part to the excellent collegiality and communications among team members. They also observed that team members were willing to pick up slack for each other, especially when one of the team members was on medical leave of absence.

Lessons learned:

1. The project was well-planned and the team executed it very well.

2. The project team's focus on cost estimation and risk management paid off. Since the estimates were on target, the project schedule stayed on track. Since a comprehensive risk response plan was created, issues and risks were mitigated satisfactorily.

3. Very few technical risks materialized, which appeared due to good risk management.

4. We communicated with the sponsor about the project scope and requirements early on. This was very important for the final success of the project.

5. We created a code of conduct for the team, which dictated how communications should take place and how conflicts were to be resolved. This helped avoid conflicts.

6. We conducted team-building exercises early on. Since some team members were working virtually, it was very important to investigate and implement virtual team-building techniques. Personality issues were resolved early on according to the code of conduct.

7. We were honest about problems, and so we resolved many early before they became difficult issues.

8. We completed project deliverables in a timely manner and engaged stakeholders on a regular basis. This involved final updates to all documentation, and migration of the new website to the production server for live use.

Figure 18.3: Project Closeout Report and Lessons Learned

CHAPTER

19

ETHICS

Relativity applies to physics, not ethics

Albert Einstein

Ethics plays an important role in project management. The Project Management Institute (PMI) continually stresses that ethics is an integral part of the project management profession and has defined a rigorous *Code of Ethics and Professional Conduct*, which we will refer to as the *code*. [7]

PMI has emphasized their position by including questions about ethics in the PMP exam. In addition, PMPs are continually held accountable to the *code*.

The *code* defines the rules for the professional practice of project management. More important from a practical perspective is that it communicates to stakeholders the values and standards that project management professionals will bring to their work. Values that the PMI community defined as most important were responsibility, respect, fairness, and honesty. [60]

Some of the more interesting aspects of the *code*, at least to us, are:

- We do what we say we will do.[1]

- When we make errors, we own up promptly, accept responsibility and make amends.

[1] Since we are both PMPs, the word, "we" applies to us.

331

- We listen to others' points of view.

- We negotiate in good faith.

- We provide accurate information in a timely manner.[2]

- We disclose conflicts of interest of stakeholders.

- We report unethical or illegal conduct.[3]

In a 2010 PMI Member survey, awareness of the *code* rose to 83% and virtually everyone found it useful in helping to resolve ethical issues. Ethics is not just a theoretical concept. The practical implications are illustrated by the fact that 'loss of trust' was cited as a major reason motivating workers to seek new jobs.

19.1   An Example of an Ethical Issue

You are the project manager holding a team staff meeting. In last week's meeting, the Technical Director (TD) reported that his design group had run into technical difficulties, which had resulted in a delay of a deliverable. You assigned the Assistant Project Manager (APM) the task of determining the impact on the cost and schedule.

In this week's staff meeting, the TD said that the design issues were now resolved. The APM reported that the because of the delays, the new $CPI = 0.93$. The APM projected a small, but significant, overrun in both the budget and the schedule.

In a staff meeting, the following conversation took place between the TD and the APM:

TD: The technical issues are resolved and we will be able to get back on track. I don't foresee this as a problem.

APM: The issue was an error in the spec. The $CPI = 0.93$, which reflects the true productivity. We should not assume that was the only spec error. We should inform the customer.

TD: It is way too early to go to the customer. We have fixed the only error.

APM: We owe it to the customer to explain the situation.

TD: We don't want to bother the customer yet. It will work out.

As the project manager, what do you do?[4]

First, let's discuss some of the surrounding issues:

[2]Emphasizing, once again, the political overtones of the cost and schedule.

[3]The real challenge is not just to behave ethically yourself, but to report unethical conduct. What do you do if your good friend is behaving unethically?

[4]*Beware. This is not an easy question.*

- *Legal vs. Ethical:* We should immediately remove any legal issues. Nobody in this meeting is suggesting that the team should deliberately hide data, pad estimates, or engage in dubious behavior. If that were to happen, the approach of the project manager is clear: Call the police.

- *Difficult vs. Ethical:* Not all difficult decisions involve ethical issues. For example, a really difficult decision that project managers often face is to lay someone off (perhaps their task is complete and there is no more work). This would indeed be difficult for anyone, but if there is no money to hire someone, it is inevitable. Although difficult, we would not consider this an ethical dilemma.[5]

- *Competence:* We assume that all of the actors are well qualified and that their conclusions are based on reasonable data and informed opinion.

- *Integrity:* All actors are behaving well and genuinely believe in their respective positions.

Project management is complicated and invariably involves many gray areas of judgment and interpretation. For example, let's examine the claim of the TD that he can make up the cost and schedule. Consider the following alternatives:

1. The TD is deliberately falsifying his estimate.

2. The TD has made an error in his estimate.

3. The TD is exaggerating his estimate due to optimism.

4. The TD believes that he can complete the project within his estimate.

We suggest the first three interpretations of the TD's behavior are: illegal (#1), incompetent (#2), and dumb (#3). The fourth is legitimate but creates an ethical dilemma. How does the project manager proceed? At this point, some terminology is required. First, we define an ethical dilemma as:

> *An ethical dilemma is one in which it is difficult to decide on the right outcome.*

An ethical dilemma is usually a complex situation that involves a choice. Often however, the issue is not resolved by the selection of *any* of the alternatives. A

[5]We often say that laying off good people is the hardest thing we've ever had to do.

further complication is that your ethics are your own *personal* standards of right and wrong.[6]

It's not just about opinions and personal differences and here's at least one reason why: There are two approaches to ethical decisions that philosophers use in handling ethical dilemmas:[7]

1. *Deontology:*

   Deontology is from the Greek "deon" meaning duty and "logos" meaning logic. Deontology is therefore the study of ethics based on *duty*. You do it because you think it is "right." The basic duties are usually considered to be:

Fidelity	Keeping promises
Reparation	Righting the wrongs you've done
Justice	Distributing goods equitably
Beneficence	Improving the lot of others
Self-Improvement	Improving one's own intelligence and virtue
Gratitude	Exhibiting when appropriate
Non-injury	Avoiding injury to others

2. *Teleology:*

   Teleology is from the Greek "telos" meaning end and "logos" meaning logic. Teleology is therefore the study of ethics based on *the end result*. This is often summarized as "The end justifies the means." You evaluate whether the decision is a good one by examining the consequences or outcomes. Correct actions produce the most good, while wrong actions do not contribute to the general good. Outcomes are usually classified as:

Egoism	Focusing on self-interest goals and asking if the action benefits oneself.
Utilitarianism	Operating in the public interest rather than for personal benefit.
Altruism	Maximizing the benefits of some, even at the expense of oneself.

[6]And, of course, quite different from everyone else's.

[7]Our intent is not to debate philosophy, but to provide practical guidance.

Altruism is generally regarded as the highest moral virtue. Notice that deontology and teleology are alternative views and that neither is right nor wrong. They are different approaches to an issue.

A project manager must be able to recognize and understand these different world-views in order to understand conflicts within the team. If two people are arguing from two different sets of ideals, it is often difficult for them to compromise—they both think they are right.[8]

19.2 More Ethical Examples

A student was explaining to the class that his company had not reported their earnings correctly. He was carefully explaining the rationale for dealing with the failure by updating the latest reports and explaining the legal and political issues.

Suddenly, another student yelled, "That's just wrong!"

Everyone immediately took sides and chaos ensued. This is a classic example of an ethical issue.

The students were approaching the problem from two different ethical points of view. The first student was going through the *teleological* argument: Justifying company actions by the idea that it would be OK in the end. Meanwhile, the second student reacted from the *deontological* viewpoint: It was offending their morals.

This is a good example of the dilemma faced by a project manager. The project manager (in this case the instructor) needs to understand that the two students have completely different world views and it is unlikely they will agree. Proposing a compromise is unlikely to work in this situation.

In our experience, progress can only be made when everyone understands the difference between deontology and teleology and that there are two legitimate, but different, points of view.[9] Notice that we are not presenting an easy fix. All we can say is that when people understand the different ethical approaches, they can begin to work on the practical issue: Shall we tell the customer?

Here's an approach that produces interesting discussions and helps to resolve the issue: The deontological camp tends to take a righteous stand and refuse to compromise. Therefore, pick a member of the other—the teleological—camp and try to modify the issue gradually until they reach the point of saying, "That would be wrong." At that point they have reached a deontological truth and often begin to understand the other point of view.

Then, take the opposite approach: Move the deontologists until they are in the teleology camp. Once the camps begin to understand each other, the project manager can get back to discussing the cost and schedule.

[8]And they both will be right.

[9]The next time someone asks you what you learned in your project management class, you can say, "I learned the difference between deontology and teleology."

Here's another example from a classroom discussion. Students were asked to list things they thought were of personal importance. Nestor said:[10]

"I always call my mother on Sundays."

How do we classify this? Deontology or teleology? I asked Nestor why he did that and he quietly said, "It's the right thing to do." He clearly regarded it as his *duty* to call his Mom on Sundays. Nestor was practicing deontology.

Suppose you tried to convince Nestor to go out and get some Pizza and that he really doesn't need to call his Mom this week. You might suggest that his Mom won't mind if he misses a week and that his Mom will understand that he's busy.

In fact, when I tried this in class, Nestor just sighed, looked down, and politely shook his head. "I have to," he said. When someone is motivated by duty they will resist attempts to make them change their behavior, especially if you are using an *end-justifies-the-means* argument.

Here's another example: Julie said:

"I always do my homework."

I asked Julie, "Why?" She said, "I want to get a good grade." Julie was not doing her homework because she thought it was her duty to do so, she was doing it because of the end result—a good grade. Julie was practicing teleology.

It is important to realize that the same action can result from different ethical perspectives. Two different students said:

"I am always good to my classmates."

When asked, "Why?" one student said, "It is the right thing to do." (Deontology) The other student said, "Because they will be good to me in return." (Teleology) Here we have two students with the same action, but motivated by completely different ethical perspectives.

19.2.1 TD vs. PM Revisited

We now have the vocabulary to discuss the debate between the APM and the TD. Table 19.1 provides a summary of the ethical positions on whether to inform the customer about a possible schedule slip.

Both actors are approaching the issue from a sound ethical position. The project manager must recognize when team members believe that they are operating ethically, because an attempt at compromise might be viewed as an attack on their integrity. It might be impossible for the project manager to resolve this issue.[11]

[10] I want to thank Nestor Taffor, an undergraduate at Boston University, for allowing me to use his real name. His presentation was so moving that it stuck with me (RW).

[11] This is one of the few times when we freely admit that we do not have an answer. All the project manager can do is to make everyone aware of the issues and the ethical choices. People will have great difficulty compromising on these types of issues.

Table 19.1: An *Ethical* Summary of the TD and APM positions.

Role	Argument	Ethical Position
TD	I don't expect any more issues. We will get back on track	The outcome justifies the position —teleology
APM	We owe it to the customer to explain the situation.	It is our duty —deontology

19.2.2 Ethical Situations Test

Look at Table 19.2 and try to decide whether the issue in the left-hand column is an ethical dilemma or not.

Hint: When analyzing the issues, you need to pay careful attention to the words and think about them. Don't rush in.

We emphasize that in Table 19.2, we are giving our *opinion*. It is guidance and there may be situations where you disagree.[12]

Answering questions on ethics, more than any other topic, involves a very careful inspection of the precise words used and an understanding of terminology. Complicating the situation is the fact that the audience may come from different cultural perspectives.[13]

Ethical issues require a subtle and patient approach on the part of the project manager, as emotions can run high on questions of integrity. A calm, unemotional presentation usually works best.

19.2.3 Sleeping at Night

As a final comment, we note that making the right ethical decision is a personal issue. At some point in your career, you will be confronted with a very difficult choice, such as:[14]

- Should you quit a good job and risk your family's well-being because you are uncomfortable with management?

- Should you tell what you know and risk censure or, even, being fired?

The only advice we can offer is that you are the one who has to sleep at night. Only you can make this decision. Only you will know whether you sleep peacefully.

[12]As always, you can disagree, but you have to back up your claim.

[13]PMI is often accused of imposing U.S. ethics on the world, a criticism with which we sympathize.

[14]Beware. Fate has a way of constructing the exact situation guaranteed to give you the most discomfort.

337

Table 19.2: Ethical Issues Test.

Issue	Ethical Dilemma?
Padding a cost estimate because you know the customer can afford it.	Not really–this is basically lying. You have a responsibility to make money. The key word here is "padding," implying a deliberate act, hence lying.
Report an environmental violation by your own company.	Yes. A classic ethical dilemma. You have a conflict: 1) Company loyalty, which may even be protected by legal non-disclosure agreements. 2) A desire to do the right and honorable thing.
You discover confidential information in the copier. Do you report it?	This is not an ethical dilemma. The right thing to do is to report it. It may be your own salary review (tricky), but using the information is wrong.
Approving sub-standard work to shorten the schedule.	No. This is a difficult decision, but not an ethical dilemma. Do not approve the work. Take the cost and schedule hit.
Changing the schedule due to pressure from your boss.	This is an ethical dilemma that depends on circumstances. You and your boss disagreed, but she insisted you report her version to the client—a genuine ethical dilemma. If your boss pressures you, then the path is clear: Tell the truth.
Assuring customers the project is on track when you suspect it's not	Trick Question. We deliberately added the word "suspect." The answer depends on why you *suspect* the project is late. A "gut feeling" you do not have to report. If it is based on earned value, you should report it.
Falsifying the schedule data.	No. This is not an ethical dilemma. It is just plain unethical and, maybe, even illegal.
You listen to your team about the schedule and report the optimistic case to your boss.	Yes. This is an ethical dilemma. If you lie, then it's not an ethical dilemma. If there is genuine disagreement among the team and you believe you can accelerate the schedule (for valid reasons), it might be OK to report the optimistic version.
Firing a problem employee.	This may be an ethical dilemma, depending on the "problem." If he is simply annoying, it is wrong to fire him and the right path is to work with him. If he disrupts the team, it might be best to remove him.
An employee tests positive for an illegal drug. Do you fire them?	Not an ethical dilemma. Nasty perhaps, but not ethical. The company policy should be clear on this. Unless you discover the test results accidentally, then you have ethical issues.
Accelerating progress by ignoring standards.	Not an ethical dilemma. Probably illegal.

Part III

Agile Project Management

20

THE AGILE FRAMEWORK

You can't be agile when you're knee-deep in mud.

Martin Fowler

Agile Project Management is a hot topic.[1]

Agile software development is changing the perception of how one should develop software. However, how to transfer the agile approach to projects in other industries is very much an open question.

In this chapter, we will describe the rationale for agile development and its evolution. We will then describe the agile process as it applies to software development, where it is a successful method. Along the way we will discuss the issues that arise when the agile process is applied in other industries.[2]

20.1 Why Agile?

Agile development models are evolutionary in nature and the product's requirements evolve as the system is developed. There is flexibility in the development of components, as well as their cost and schedule. The model is particularly appropriate when the product's requirements are vague or in doubt.

[1] In fact, agile is rapidly becoming the rage.

[2] The reader should be aware that, while we don't dispute the agile framework's practical successes, many of the claims have a questionable academic foundation.

341

There are several variations of the agile development approach but they all share the following characteristics:

- The development process, the product, the cost, and the schedule all evolve.

- Proactive development of test cases and user scenarios ahead of time to analyze and test both the current and future iterations of the product.

- Periodic delivery and installation of product versions in the operational environment to ensure timely and increasingly effective functionality.

- Continuous evolution based on user input.

20.2   The Software Development Life Cycle

The software development life cycle consists of:

1. *Definition phase:* During this phase the customer's problems are defined and the requirements elicited. The team conducts systems analyses and develops the project plan. The deliverable is the specification, which contains the user requirements, and a test plan to measure compliance.

2. *Design phase:* The software and business analysts design an acceptable solution for the customer. The deliverable is the design document. Also, the project manager finalizes the baseline cost and schedule.

3. *Construction phase:* The software is coded, and unit testing may occur here.

4. *Testing phase:* The product or service is tested against the specification.

5. *Acceptance phase:* The customer analyzes the acceptance test results and, if satisfactory, signs the acceptance agreement. Customer training may occur during this phase. The operation phase begins after customer acceptance.

The software development cycle is made up of four phases, but, depending on the size of the project, there may be additional phases or sub-phases. Each phase and sub-phase must have clear objectives, as well as achievable milestones and deliverables–see Table 20.1.

Table 20.1: Software life cycle: Major deliverables and milestones.

Phase	Deliverables	Milestone
Definition	Project Plan, Specification Acceptance criteria	Customer acceptance of plans & the specification
Design	Design Document Detail Design	Customer acceptance of design 40% complete point
Construction	The project	Successful Validation & Verification
Acceptance	Acceptance Test Results	Customer acceptance of project Contractual Close Out

20.2.1 The Old Way: Waterfall

Historically, the *Waterfall* development cycle was the most widely used method for software development and is regarded as the classical approach. The waterfall approach is characterized by sequential steps. Once a step has been completed, it is not visited again. In this respect it is rather like a waterfall in that the water only trickles downward.

The characteristic aspect of the waterfall method is that the requirements are developed up-front and frozen. Then the software is designed, built, and tested. The drawback is that the final software arrives long after the requirements were developed and, often, user needs have evolved and the system may be obsolete.

It is widely acknowledged that the key strength of the waterfall is its strong managerial control over the process and, in particular, the schedule and costs.[3]

20.2.2 Evolutionary

To address the limitations of the waterfall model, researchers and practitioners introduced alternate methods, which we classify as *evolutionary*. One such model is rapid prototyping or rapid application development (RAD).[4] Widespread agreement on what this approach actually entails is difficult to achieve, however it typically involves:

- *Throwaway prototypes.* These are developed to clarify the user requirements and to test design approaches. The prototype is discarded and one subsequently moves to a more structured approach (perhaps even waterfall).

- *Built-upon development.* Development is iterative, designed to clarify user requirements and analyze the system design, continually delivering incremental improvements, and gradually refining the product.

[3] Since the requirements are nailed down, scope creep is minimized, and the cost should be relatively stable. Unless, of course, the problem is poorly defined, in which case, all bets are off.

[4] The approach was pioneered by Barry Boehm in his *Spiral Model* [61].

343

- *Gathering requirements.* Focus groups are used to define requirements.

- *Reusing software components.* Previously tested components are used to enhance productivity and reduce errors.

- *Iterating the software design.* This ensures the system continues to meet performance requirements, even as the system loads and user base increase.

- *Deferring major improvements and enhancements to the next version.* Builders resist the urge to implement changes in the current iteration.

- *Less formality throughout the software development life cycle.* The focus is on the products and whether they satisfy the customer.[5]

- *Continuously evaluating the outcome with users.* To keep them happy.

20.3   Choosing a Development Model

We present some considerations for selecting between the waterfall, evolutionary, and agile processes. The selection should be based on the characteristics of the project's requirements, the project team, and the commitment and availability of the stakeholders. Table 20.2 is a guide.[6]

One of the genuine criticisms of the traditional phased approach to project management is that it rests on two key assumptions that have directly influenced the discipline: [64]

- That project goals and targets are clear and given from above.

- That the means of reaching those targets are identifiable and can be planned.

For example, the PMBOK tends to focus on deviations from a well-defined plan and assumes that uncertainty elimination and control are feasible. These assumptions are rarely true in ambitious, novel projects, in log-term strategic initiatives, and when the goals and technology are emergent. This deficiency in project management motivates the agile approach that embraces uncertainty as a source of opportunities. This is summarized in Table 20.3.[7]

[5]This appears to imply that formality is burdensome. We prefer to emphasize that the focus is on satisfying the customers by providing real products, rather than on attempting to define every detail in a document.

[6]We have adapted the attributes from earlier research conducted by Mo Mahmood. [62] Table 20.2 was adapted from Richard Fairley's *Managing and Leading Software Projects*. [63] Note that Fairley has a more liberal interpretation of the waterfall as he included incremental builds.

[7]Adapted from Lendle and Loch. [64]

Table 20.2: Considerations for selecting either waterfall, evolutionary, or agile.

Considerations Based On	Project Attribute	Preferred Model
Stakeholders	Flexibility in approach needed	Agile
	Evolution of User Requirements	Evolutionary or Agile
	Extensive User involvement	Evolutionary or Agile
	Strict PM Control Required	Waterfall
	Flexibility in Development	Evolutionary or Agile
	Completion on schedule	Waterfall
Requirements	Well known, easily defined	Waterfall or Agile
	Defined during development	Waterfall
	Likely to change often	Evolutionary or Agile
	Demonstrations needed to develop the requirements	Evolutionary or Agile
	Proof of concept needed to determine feasibility	Evolutionary
Team	New to the problem domain	Evolutionary
	New to the technology domain	Evolutionary
	Might be reassigned	Waterfall or Evolutionary
Users	Limited availability	Waterfall or Evolutionary
	New to requirements definition	Evolutionary
	Want to be involved	Evolutionary or Agile
Risk	New area for organization	Evolutionary
	Involves system integration	Waterfall
	Involves Enhancements	Any
	Funding Is Unstable	Evolutionary or Agile
	Schedule Is Constrained	Waterfall or Agile

20.3.1 When Not to Use Agile

While the agile framework has had considerable success in software development, there are project types where it may not be appropriate. The fundamental property of the agile method is the incremental development of product requirements in the backlog. Therefore, when the requirements cannot be incrementally developed, agile methods may not be applicable. This suggests that projects with the following characteristics may not be suitable for agile development:

1. *Immutable Requirements:*

   Some projects have requirements that cannot be negotiated and that must be met or the system will be compromised. These include:

Table 20.3: Traditional vs. Novel Projects.

	Traditional	**Novel**
Requirements	Defined and given from above.	Vision and direction exists, but details unknown & emergent.
Activities	Can be articulated & derived from experience.	Partially emergent.
Capabilities	Existing or identified.	Don't exist or not understood.
Uncertainty	Variation from plans. Anticipated, measurable risks in known variables.	Unforeseeable uncertainties. Unanticipated effects. New variables & actions.
Relevant Domains	Known markets & customer reactions, performance drivers, & environmental parameters.	New markets, unknown reactions. New system performance drivers. Unknown technology. Complex, unforeseeable interactions. New geographies. Unforeseeable regulatory challenges. New stakeholders, emergent demands.

- *Military Systems:* These are characterized by specific, defined attributes that must be met. For example, a plane may be specified to fly at Mach 2.2 so as to be faster than any other plane. There is no compromise on this requirement because flying at Mach 2.0 is unacceptable.

  An agile development process might not prioritize the speed and might result is a plane that does not satisfy its primary mission, which would be unacceptable.

- *Medical Systems:* Like military systems, medical these have defined requirements that must be met. A blood pressure monitor must measure to a defined accuracy or it is worthless.

- *Pharmaceutical Products:* These are constrained by strict regulations, especially if human subjects are involved.

- *Banking and Financial Systems:* These are also constrained by highly technical regulations.

2. *Defined Process Order:*

   For some projects, the implementation can only be performed in a specific order. These include:

   - *Bridges:* You cannot build the roadway first, you have to start with the towers, then string the cables, and, only then, can you hang the roadway.

You can only process the backlog in a specific order.

- *Buildings:* You cannot build the roof before you have laid the foundation and the erected the walls. Even though the #1 priority may be your office on the third floor, you still have to build the lower floors first.

20.4 The Agile Framework

> **The Agile Manifesto: A license for avoiding documentation and not having a plan.**
>
> *Yuriy Zubarev*

The agile framework has its roots in *The Agile Manifesto*, which has a well-defined philosophy that values:

Individuals and interactions	over	processes and tools
Working software	over	comprehensive documentation
Customer collaboration	over	contract negotiation
Responding to change	over	following a plan

The Agile Manifesto contains 12 philosophical aspirations:[8]

1 Customer satisfaction by rapid delivery and integration of useful software.
2 Welcoming changing users' requirements, even late in the development.
3 Working software is delivered in weeks rather than months.
4 Working software is the principal measure of progress.
5 Sustainable development–maintaining a constant pace.
6 Daily cooperation between business people, users and developers.
7 Face-to-face conversation is strongly preferred.
8 Projects are built around motivated individuals, who should be trusted.
9 Continuous attention to technical excellence and good design.
10 Simplicity is the key in everything.
11 Self-organizing teams.
12 Regular adaptation to changing circumstances.

20.4.1 Scrum

Scrum is the most popular framework for agile developments and is based on the principles laid out in the agile manifesto. The name *scrum* is borrowed from the game of rugby and the game's spirit is inherent in the methodology.[9]

[8] *The Agile Manifesto* consists of 12 philosophical statements, which were first described in the *Manifesto for Agile Software Development* by Beck, Kent; et al. in 2001. [65]

[9] It was first described by Peter DeGrace, Leslie Stahl, and Leslie Hulet in *Wicked problems, righteous solutions.* [66]

347

The rugby scrum metaphor helps us visualize what happens in the scrum model: A small team, determined to deliver a product or service, is grouped together (interlocked) to work (push) towards a goal. In rugby there are planned "set" scrums and spontaneous "loose" scrums. The project is "set" by the *Scrum Master* who ensures that scrum practices are understood and followed. The *Scrum Master* also encourages the team to be self-directed, spontaneous, and creative, in analogy with the "loose" scrum.

The claim for *scrum* is that it is focused on delivering the highest business value in the shortest amount of time. The business sets the priorities and teams self-organize to decide the best way to deliver the highest-priority features. Progress is made in an iterative and incremental fashion via fixed-length production cycles called *sprints* of one week to one month. At the end of each sprint, the product is usable[10] and the business can decide to release it as-is or continue enhancing it.

There are two key roles: The *Product Owner* and The *Scrum Master*.

- The *Product Owner* is an active and contributing player throughout, proposing the features to be implemented from the *Product Backlog* at the start of each sprint, reviewing the functionality at the end of each sprint and, in between, constantly tuning the backlog and prioritizing features to provide the most value.

- The *Scrum Master's* role is to coach and motivate the project team, to resolve issues, and to enhance the realization of the goals of each sprint. Therefore, the *Scrum Master's* role is often considered similar to that of a project manager.[11]

The agile scrum framework is based on the following ideas:

- The customer is the *Product Owner*. The *Scrum Master* coaches the team and facilitates the development. The software engineers are the team.

- Development iterations are called *sprints*, which are fixed in duration.

- The product features to be implemented in a sprint are determined during the sprint planning meeting and the output products are called the *increment*.

- Brief 15 minute, stand-up meetings are held each day to review the previous day's work and to plan the current day's work. These are called *daily scrums*.

[10]At least in theory.

[11]Beware, there is considerable debate over the idea that the Scrum Master's role is like that of a PM.

348

- The team is self-organizing and decides what they will accomplish in the sprint.[12]

- Daily meetings allow the *Scrum Master* to determine the productivity rate (and refine estimates and schedules) and to manage risks.

- A sprint ends with a *sprint review*, which assesses the product, and a *sprint retrospective*, which assesses the process. Suggestions for improvements in future sprints are proposed.

In the agile scrum methodology, development occurs in *sprints*, which are fixed in length and anywhere from 15 to 30 days. Each sprint delivers a working piece of the product and the system is developed incrementally. The agile scrum methodology works as follows:

1. At the start of the agile project, the *Product Owner* defines the current requirements and creates the *Product Backlog*. It is important for the sponsor to prioritize the list of features so as to deliver maximum value.

2. From the *Product Backlog*, the scrum team creates a *sprint* by defining the features it can complete in the first sprint iteration.

3. The team is then left on its own to work during the *sprint*. No outside interference or influence is allowed from any source, including the *Product Owner*, to impact the team's performance during the sprint.

4. The team meets for a *Daily Scrum*, which is a short stand-up meeting where each member of the team gives a brief report and discusses what was accomplished yesterday, what is to be accomplished today, and any obstacles that may have come up.

5. *Sprint Review:* At the end of the sprint, everyone gets together with the *Product Owner* to evaluate the *product*. If the *Product Owner* accepts the product, a new sprint begins with a list of prioritized tasks to be implemented from the backlog.

6. *Sprint Retrospective:* At the end of the sprint, everyone gets together with the *Scrum Master* to evaluate the *process*.[13] Changes to the process may be suggested and implemented.

7. The above process continues, with a series of sprints, until there are no more items to implement in the *Product Backlog*.[14]

---

[12]This is challenging for traditional project managers.

[13]Notice that the sprint review covers the product and the sprint retrospective covers the process.

[14]Or, as is usually the case, the money runs out.

349

20.5   The Agile Team

The members of the agile team were briefly introduced above. Here we provide more detail on the various roles in the agile framework.

Product Owner

The *Product Owner* manages the backlog to ensure that it continues to meet the strategic needs of the business. This involves:

- Adjusting and prioritizing the backlog to keep the project on track.

- Deciding which features will be included in each sprint.

- Answering the team's questions about the product's requirements.

- Ensuring that the team stays on track, i.e., building the right strategic product.

The *Product Owner* understands the product requirements, but they don't always understand the details of implementation. The person with the implementation knowledge is the *Scrum Master* to whom the *Product Owner* may look to for help in determining sprint content and the estimation process. Another important role is deciding if the product meets its acceptance criteria.

When the team has questions, the *Product Owner* helps to clarify the requirements. Partaking in the estimation process gives the *Product Owner* insight into the level of effort for each work sprint, which then feeds back into an improved assessment of the item's relative priority.

Scrum Master

A *Scrum Master* acts as the coach and the facilitator to the *Product Owner* and the team. The *Scrum Master* also makes sure that the agile process is followed to maximize the benefits.

The *Scrum Master* coaches the *Product Owner* in how to achieve the goals and how to adapt and prioritize the backlog. The *Scrum Master* is also the link between the Product Owner and the team. The *Scrum Master* helps the team in solving problems, which in the agile vocabulary, is referred to as *removing blockers*. If necessary, the *Scrum Master* acquires external resources to remove the *blockers*.

The *Scrum Master* monitors the sprints, helps to improve the team's productivity, and facilitates the sprint planning meeting, daily scrums, and other meetings.

An important responsibility of the *Scrum Master* is to shield the team from outside pressures. Along with the *Product Owner*, the *Scrum Master* interfaces with the stakeholders to communicate the current product content and project progress. The *Scrum Master* can enhance communications by organizing reviews and soliciting feedback from stakeholders.

Development Team

The team is tasked with developing the product, which requires understanding the product, accurately estimating resources, and building the product. The *Scrum Master* helps through coaching and facilitation, but the team is responsible for managing itself.

Agile teams tend to be cross-functional and assembled from people with a variety of competencies and domain knowledge so that they do not depend on help from outside the team. If external help is required, it is the responsibility of the *Scrum Master* to acquire the necessary resources.

Agile teams are encouraged to develop solutions collectively using a technique called, "swarming." With swarming, all team members collectively work on a task to finish it before moving ahead and working on the next task. This is an excellent trait that enhances teamwork.

Lead Developer

A *Lead Developer* may be assigned when there is a need for specific skills and knowledge. As the most experienced team member, the *Lead Developer* helps analyze options and develops technical solutions. The *Lead Developer* focuses on implementing the technical requirements, which is different from facilitation and coaching role of the *Scrum Master's*.

20.6 Agile Planning

Planning agile projects is very similar to planning traditional projects. It is important to establish a clear vision for the product, a legitimate business case, and realistic cost and schedule estimates. This work establishes that the project is strategically important and viable and motivates the formal approval of the project.[15]

Therefore, the planning documents required for an agile development are very similar to those of traditional projects. Sometimes, however, the agile framework uses slightly different names.

[15]As does the Charter in traditional projects.

- *Business Case:* This establishes the reason for the project's existence and demonstrates why it is *essential* to the company's business goals.

- *Product Vision:* A document that clearly defines what the product will do and answers questions such as: Who are the customers? Does it provide value?

- *Financial Analysis:* The financial justification for the project's existence.

- *Release Plan:* The timetable for product releases and a roadmap of milestones and content deliveries.

20.7 User Stories

Agile projects have their own vocabulary for describing the product's requirements. *User Stories* express the desired business value using natural language statements that should be understandable by both business and technical people.

User stories shift the focus from eliciting and writing down detailed requirements to informal discussions about what the users actually want. User stories are usually maintained in note form and refer to conversations about the users' goals. They are often written on index cards so that they can be used in the estimation process. In the agile philosophy, discussions with users are considered more important than what's written on the card.

A useful way to develop a *User Story* is in the form of a template, whose structure is shown in Table 20.4.

Table 20.4: User Story Template.

As a	<User Role>
I want to	<Goal>
So that I can	<Benefit>

As an example, consider the user story for a student who wants to search for relevant courses:

Story 1: Student Course Search
 As a student I want to be able to search for courses being offered so that I can select them for the upcoming semester.

User stories should include *acceptance criteria*, which explain how the feature will be tested and form the foundation of the product's acceptance testing by stakeholders at the end of a sprint. *Acceptance criteria* consist of logical statements, such as:

When [x] happens, [y] should happen.

In the example we used above where a student wants to search for relevant courses, the *acceptance criteria* might be:

When a student has selected a course, but has not yet saved it to the result's page, the course should be stored for later retrieval.

Even items such as bugs can become user stories in the product backlog. For example, a user might state that a feature is not working as proposed. This issue could be documented as a bug by the development team and also written up as a user story. If a new feature is needed to resolve the bug, the new requirement can also be written up as a user story.

20.7.1   The Product Backlog

An essential aspect of the agile framework is the document known as *Product Backlog*. This consists of a list of user stories, which are features and technical tasks to be addressed by the team.

Whenever a new feature of the product is uncovered or imagined, it is added to the backlog. Each feature is assessed and its relevance to the project established. The backlog is the single authoritative source for all work associated with the project.

The backlog is maintained by the *Product Owner* who updates it dutifully and continuously. If an item on the backlog list is no longer relevant to the project's goals, it can be removed. The product backlog can be maintained in a spreadsheet or, more professionally, using tools such as *Jira*.

20.8   Estimating Agile Projects

Agile teams are no different from traditional project teams in that they need to be able to provide cost and schedule estimates for work to be performed. However, as is often the case with the agile framework, a different approach to estimation has evolved and is, even, considered by some to be the *agile method of cost estimation.*

One of the improvements that has arisen from the agile estimation process is that it explicitly includes the entire team. The product owner, the scrum master, and the development teamwork together to estimate the cost of the project. The problem is, of course, that in an agile development the requirements are undefined and the team does not know how much time it will take or how much it will cost.

20.8.1 Relative Estimation

We remind the reader that traditional project estimation is performed on WBS activities, which are estimated individually in absolute units (hours or dollars). In contrast, agile estimation is performed using what is called *relative estimation*. In relative estimation, tasks or user stories are not estimated individually in absolute units, but by comparison with other tasks.

Because estimation is regarded as an inaccurate process, especially when the requirements are not well understood, the goal is not to estimate the effort required to develop a story in hours or dollars. Rather, the goal is to estimate the *relative* effort for a user story and, it turns out, that is both quick and reliable.

Relative estimation attempts to avoid some of the pitfalls associated with traditional estimating, such as seeking unwarranted precision and confusing the estimate with a commitment.

A common claim in the agile community is that people are better at relative than absolute estimation.[16] Such studies have given rise to the claim that "people are better at relative than absolute estimation." Unfortunately, the formal, verifiable evidence for that claim is still rather poor. This doesn't mean that relative estimation isn't better, just that it's not *proven* to be better.

However, what does seem to be true is that software sizing using the paired-comparisons method is especially well suited to agile development where the system knowledge available to project team members is uncertain.

The process is effective in practice because the first few sprints are calibrated in terms of story points. Then, the remaining sprints are re-estimated based on this calibration.[17] As the team learns how many story points they can complete in a sprint, their estimates of the number of story points they will complete in future sprints becomes more accurate.[18]

Relative estimation provides a cooperative approach for teams to estimate quickly the effort required without getting bogged down in the intricacies of cost estimation. Also, people seem to be much more comfortable estimating the *relative* sizes of tasks, i.e., determining whether a specific task requires more or less effort than another specific task.

Agile estimation is a team effort and should include the *Product Owner*, who represents the content; the *Scrum Master*, who facilitates the meeting; and the team. Everyone participates in the estimation, which brings in diverse perspectives.

It is useful to identify a *control* story, i.e., one that everyone understands and is confident about their estimate. As future stories are estimated and completed, they

---

[16] A typical example is Miranda's *Improving Subjective Estimates Using Paired Comparison*, which presents data suggesting that paired comparisons lead to more accurate judgments than ad hoc estimates. Miranda states, "The paired comparisons method offers a more accurate and precise alternative to "guesstimating." [67]

[17] In our view, this is precisely the same as Earned Value Management. EVM determines actual productivity versus the plan.

[18] Just like EV estimates based on the CPI.

can be compared against the *control*.

20.8.2 Story Points

Agile estimation begins with a list of *user stories* that populate the backlog. The size of a user story is measured in story points and the definition is:

> A story point is a relative unit of measure of the effort required to implement the story.

A *user story* is a particular business requirement and it may be difficult to estimate the effort required to implement the story. However, it is easy to estimate if a particular story takes more effort than another story, in which case it should be assigned more story points. The story point measure explicitly includes the complexities and risks.

Story Points are designed to make agile estimation easier by using relative estimation rather than absolute estimation, i.e., it is not in hours or dollars. In fact, story points are estimated without a commitment to either a cost or a schedule. When estimating in hours, there is an implied commitment, but estimating in story points explicitly avoids any commitment. You are not assigning a particular number of hours to the story, you are just assigning a relative size.

Story points will become calibrated in terms of actual hours and dollars after the first few sprints when the productivity of the team will be known. The team can then compute its average *velocity* as the number of story points completed per sprint. Once the velocity is known, the team can develop more accurate estimates of their productivity and more reliable assignment of story points to sprints.

20.8.3 Steve Bockman's Team Estimation

One popular estimation method is referred to as Bockman's game. The purpose of the game, however, is serious: to come to a consensus about the relative effort required for each story.[19] The process consists of two steps:

1. Order the stories by the increasing amount of effort, or work, required.

2. Assign scores, which are called *story points*.

[19]There are many interesting games available to teach this process.

20.8.4 Order the Stories

Everyone is included in the estimation, including the *Product Owner*, who is the expert on the product content and can answer questions. Each person brings his or her own perspective and experience, which is in concert with the entire agile philosophy.[20] Since insight from multiple experts is obtained, the process is similar to the Delphi Technique.

The first step in ordering the stories is to make a card for each one that briefly describes the story.[21] Next, the development effort of each story is estimated, not in an absolute sense, but relative to the other stories, as follows:

1. Place all the story cards in a single pile on a table.

2. The first team member places the top card in the middle of the table and provides a brief description of the story.

3. The next team member takes a card from the story pile and places it either to the left or the right of the first card, i.e., *relative* to the first story card. The team member may provide a very brief comment. If the team member thinks that the story requires less work than the first story, it is placed to the left and, if it requires more work, it is placed to the right.

   If the team member considers the story to be about the *same* amount of effort, the card is placed below the first card.

4. The next team member can either:

   - Take the top card from story pile and place it relative to the other cards.
   - Move a card. The team member changes the order of effort for the stories on the table.
   - Pass, the team member has nothing to contribute at this time.

5. The steps are repeated until no more cards remain in the story pile.

6. With all of the story cards placed in relative order of estimated work required, the team can continue to take turns, refining the order. At this stage, a brief explanation might be appropriate.[22]

The team has now ordered their stories left to right, from smallest to largest effort required. The team has reached a consensus that the story on the far left will require the least effort and the story on the far right will require the most effort.

[20] For an excellent, brief, description of this process, see *The Elements of Scrum*, by Chris Sims & Hillary Johnson. [68]

[21] 3x5 cards are perfect for this.

[22] Also, an explanation might avoid two people just moving the same cards back and forth.

What is remarkable is that the team usually reaches a consensus fairly quickly on the ordering of the effort required by the stories. Team members should minimize presentation of opinions; they should be encouraged to ask questions, but only to solicit clarifications.

Example of Ordering Stories

The following example shows how this might play out.[23] Suppose we are assigned the task of estimating the effort required to cook five meals:

1. Spaghetti & Meatballs [S].

2. Peanut Butter & Jelly Sandwich [P].

3. Beef Wellington [B].

4. Swordfish & Vegetables [W].

5. Fish & Chips [F].

We don't know how much effort is required, but we can begin the relative estimation process as follows. We make five cards, one for each meal (and representing user stories). We have three team members, Alice, Bob, and Carol. Alice goes first, takes the first card, [S], and places it in the center of the table.

Bob takes the next card, [P], and says that PB&J requires a lot less effort than Spaghetti & Meatballs [S]. Therefore, he places the [P] card to the left of the [S] card.

Carol takes the next card, [B], and remarks that Beef Wellington is a very complex and time-consuming recipe. She places the [B] card to the right of the [S] card. Note that Carol does not attempt to estimate how much effort is involved in making Beef Wellington, only that it takes more effort than Spaghetti & Meatballs. At this point the table looks like Figure 20.1.

Figure 20.1: The first three story cards in the meal estimation game.

Alice takes the next card, [W], and says that Swordfish requires more effort than Spaghetti, but less than Beef Wellington. She places the [W] card to the right of the [S] card. Bob takes the next card, [F], and remarks that the effort for Fish & Chips is

[23]A more detailed example is in Chapter 22, where we cover the SAMPL App.

357

similar to Swordfish and places the [F] card under the [W] card. A consensus has been reached on the *relative* cooking efforts and the table looks like Figure 20.2.

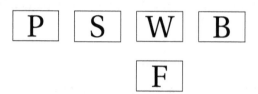

Figure 20.2: The completed story cards in the meal estimation game.

20.8.5 Assign Story Points

After the ordering, the next step is to assign story points and the *Scrum Master* produces a deck of cards with Fibonacci numbers on them.[24]

1. The first team member considers the leftmost story, which, by definition is the story with the least amount of effort. The team member places the card with the '1' next to that story.

2. The next team member selects the card labeled '2' and places it on the table at about the place where a story is considered to be about *twice* as much work as the story with the '1' next to it.

3. Team members continue placing Fibonacci cards above the stories where they believe there is a significant change in the size of the stories.

4. A team member can also change the position of a size, e.g., move the size card with a '5' to the right or the left.

5. A team member might also replace a size card with another one, e.g., replace the '8' with a '13,' suggesting that the team member thinks the story is about 50% more work, but, not about three times as much, which would require the '21' card.[25]

6. When all team members are comfortable with the result, the estimation process is concluded.

[24] The Fibonacci number $F(n)$ is the sum of the two previous numbers, i.e., $F(n) = F(n-1) + F(n-2)$. We start with the first two numbers as $F(1) = 1$ and $F(2) = 1$, so that $F(3) = F(1) + F(2) = 2$ and $F(4) = F(3) + F(2) = 2 + 1 = 3$. The Fibonacci sequence is 1, 1, 2, 3, 5, 8, 13, 21, 34, 55, 89, 144.

[25] Team members can only select values from the Fibonacci sequence.

The reason for using the Fibonacci sequence is that it spreads out the estimates and discourages false precision. After all, these are estimates. The more complex a task is, the more room for error exists when estimating, which is why the Fibonacci sequence (1, 2, 3, 5, 8, 13, 21) is used.

When assigning scores, the team member should explicitly acknowledge the complexity of the story, as well as the risks and uncertainties. For example, if after asking questions, the team is still unclear about what is required, that uncertainty should be reflected in the score.

Example of Assigning Scores to User Stories

We now continue the above example by adding story points. The *Scrum Master* produced a deck of cards with the Fibonacci numbers on them.

Alice took the first card with a '1' on it and placed it above the first story, [P]. Bob thought about the relative size of the next story and decided that Spaghetti was about three times as much effort as PB&J and placed a '3' above the [S].

Carol was next and her assignment was to place a story point value above the [W][F] pile. She thought that both meals involved significantly more effort than Spaghetti, so she was required to pick another card. Carol's choice was to pick either '5' or '8.' Carol decided that Swordfish and Fish & Chips were both around twice as much effort, but not three times as much. Therefore, she selected the '5' and placed the card above the [W][F] pile.

If Carol had estimated that the effort to prepare Swordfish and Fish & Chips were both about the same as Spaghetti, she would have just moved the '3' card to indicate that all three meals required about the same effort.

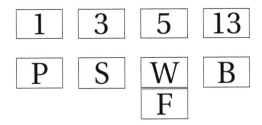

Figure 20.3: Fibonacci scores for the story cards in the meal estimation game.

Finally, Alice had to select a story point value to place above the Beef Wellington pile. Alice said that she had prepared it once and it was very complicated and took much more effort than the [W][F] pile. Her choices were either '8' or '13.' Alice remembered that Beef Wellington took her several days of preparation and, therefore, she selected the '13.' The table now resembled Figure 20.3.

Other Sizing Methods

T-Shirt Sizing is an approach that is less granular than the Fibonacci numbers. The process is the same, except that the effort is estimated using T-shirt sizes, i.e., XXS, XS, S, M, L, XL, XXL, and XXL.

Another sizing game is *Planning Poker*, which is a fun way to learn agile sizing and estimating. Planning Poker uses a deck of cards, one for each player (team member). The team takes turns in displaying a card that represents an estimate for a particular task. Like Bockman's game, it focuses on relative sizing.[26]

20.9   Agile Cost Tracking

It might be disconcerting to a customer to realize that the agile estimation process has not produced a cost estimate. Story points simply represent a measure or relative effort and do not indicate how much the job will cost or how long it will take. Despite the fact that the story points represent effort, they are not (yet) related to hours, dollars, or duration.

What is necessary, therefore, is to determine how many story points a team can complete in a sprint, which is known as the *velocity*. Once the team has completed the first few sprints, a velocity metric can be computed. The team can use their established velocity as a guide for how much work they can comfortably accept in each sprint. The *Product Owner* can use the team's velocity to estimate how much of the product backlog can be completed by certain dates.[27]

After a few sprints, the team can revisit their story point scores to reinforce their understanding of what an '8' or a '3' means. For example, a velocity of 20 story points per sprint means that a team completes 20 story points during a single sprint. This information can be summarized in a burndown chart.

20.10   The Project Manager's Role in Agile

In the above sections, you may have noticed that we did not include the role of a project manager (PM) and you might be wondering how a project manager might fit into an agile development. Is a project manager needed at all?

This is an interesting question and one about which there is considerable debate. Agile purists tend to suggest that the role of the project manager is unnecessary and should be eliminated.

Our view is more nuanced. We believe that in an agile development many of the project manager's functions still exist, but are distributed among the Product

[26]For more information, see http: // www. planningpoker. com.

[27]Jeff Sutherland, the co-author of the Scrum Guide takes a rather extreme view of story points: [69] "Story points are faster, better, and cheaper than hours and the highest performing teams completely abandon any hourly estimation as they view it as waste that just slows them down."

Owner, the Scrum Master, and even to the team. This brings up several interesting questions. How do the necessary project management skills get embedded in an agile organization? Can a PM perform any of the agile team's roles?

Below, we discuss these issues. However, to be effective in any of the roles a PM will need a thorough understanding the agile vocabulary, the methodology, and the team's roles. But, even that is not enough, a traditional project manager will need to embrace flexibility and support the empowered team that is such a characteristic feature of the agile framework.[28]

20.10.1 PM as Agile Planner

Planning agile projects is similar to planning traditional projects and many of the same priorities and issues apply. Everyone wants to know, what the system will do, how much it will cost, and when it will be completed.

Such questions are answered in the vision, the business case, and the cost and schedule estimates. These are all necessary before the project can be approved for development and funds allocated.[29] These topics fall in the category of a fairly traditional Project Management Plan and a PM can play a significant role in creating the required documents and developing accurate estimates.

The major difference in planning an agile project is that a detailed scope is replaced with a prioritized backlog, which is continuously updated. This requires constant stakeholder engagement, another key PM skill.

Agile planning does have some differences from traditional developments, e.g., user story development, backlog prioritization, and sprint planning. Although, we point out that eliciting requirements, stakeholder engagement, and project planning are all PM skills that are particularly relevant to those tasks.

20.10.2 PM as Product Owner

The *Product Owner* (PO) is responsible for the product, which sounds superficially like the role of the PM. However, traditional project management usually involves rigid change control, which is entirely against the agile philosophy. An agile PO must deal with continuous change, even when the changes are significant and redirect the project.

On the other hand, a traditional PM is used to managing change and, if flexible, should be comfortable with the more open PO role.

An interesting question is, Who does the PO work for? Suppose your company hires a contractor to develop a new software system. As the keeper of the backlog, the PO's

[28] Personally, we believe that these characteristics are not special to the agile framework, but are essential skills of a modern PM.

[29] Relevant PMO questions might also be asked, e.g., Is the product unique? Is it a strategic necessity?

role is significant and time-consuming. In order to ensure that the system actually does what the company wants, the PO role may require a significant investment of time.

20.10.3   PM as Product Expert

A PM can also play the role of a product expert, or business analyst, someone who is familiar with the art and science of requirements elicitation and documentation, and who can communicate the requirements to the stakeholders.

In some agile projects the role business analyst is missing altogether. The logic in that case is that requirements are highly dynamic and business analysis occurs on the fly. This works well when the project's requirements are dominated uncertain user needs that can be captured in the user stories and the backlog.

However, on-the-fly requirements development does not work well when there are highly specific performance requirements imposed from outside, e.g., legal, tax, banking, and accounting regulations, environmental regulations, security constraints, and health-care regulations. In that case, it is wise to employ an expert for the development of the requirements. A PM can play a key role in this context as stakeholder engagement and requirements elicitation are key PM skills.

20.10.4   PM as Scrum Master

A PM can play the role of Scrum Master.[30] Indeed, the current PMBOK guidelines and Agile Practice guide from PMI both recognize the idea that PM skills significantly overlap with those of the Scrum Master.

A major aspect of the Scrum Master's role is "impediment remover," which a traditional PM should be good at. After all, one role of a PM is to get the team the resources they need.

Agile proponents often characterize a PM as a decision maker responsible for meeting project objectives and that the role of the *Scrum Master* is different, being more of a facilitation role. This, however, is an old-fashioned view of the PM as good PMs act like facilitators.

There is a personal spectrum for both PMs and Scrum Masters and a wide variety of agile projects with varying levels of discipline. Rather than say that PMs won't make good Scrum Masters, we prefer to say that you should match the person and their skills to the job.

[30]Although this view is often controversial. Agile protagonists often assume project management equals waterfall and, therefore, that PM skills do not translate well to agile. We view this as an outdated view of PM.

20.10.5 PM as Program Manager

Another role that a conventional PM can play is the role of a "Program Manager" for agile projects. An *Agile program* is a group of related agile projects that benefit from being coordinated. An experienced PM would be well-suited to play this role.

20.10.6 PM as Cost and Schedule Estimator

Typically, a scrum team takes on the role of managing the cost and schedule, which involves several related kills: estimating their actual progress (the velocity), calculating the variance from the plan, and re-estimating sprint content.

The velocity and variance calculations are shown in section 22.4 and these are classic project management skills and a project manager can educate the team in these techniques. Especially for larger projects, the velocity can form the foundation of accurate predictions of how much content will be completed in future sprints. This will help stakeholders to decide on the backlog priorities.

Once a velocity has been determined for the first few sprints, the development team and the product manager can refine the planned schedules and estimates. In such activities, experienced project managers can be of value to product owners.

20.10.7 Characteristics of an Agile PM

Here is a useful summary of the characteristics of a PM and how they might play out in agile developments:[31]

> If you're a manager who gets your hands dirty and dives into the details with the team, then the role of *Scrum Master* is likely to be a good fit. The *Scrum Master's* job is to help the team plan, to get roadblocks out of their way, and to facilitate their delivery of the software.
>
> On the other hand, if you prefer to analyze what your company needs and are willing to spend the time to communicate it to the team, you are assuming the role of the *Product Owner*.[32]
>
> If you are a Project Manager who prefers to play a more conventional supervisory role, you typically won't end up on an agile team. However, you can still have an important role as an agile champion who promotes agile values and pushes teams to adopt agile practices.

[31] This is according to Greene and Stellman. [70]

[32] The job of the *Product Owner* is to manage the backlog and to answer the team's questions.

363

20.11   Agile and the PMBOK

The PMBOK handles agile project management by including notes in each knowledge area that relate to agile principles. Most of the discussion is fairly generic.

For example, the scope discussion says that "Agile methods spend less time trying to define and agree on scope and more time establishing the process for its ongoing discovery and refinement." This seems, to us, typical of the PMBOK, in that it does not give the reader any advice on how to deal with changing requirements and actually proposes that time be spent on *process* development.

Some comments on the PMBOK notes about agile follow:

- *Integration:* Noting that agile approaches promote engagement, the PMBOK recommends that a collaborative environment is built so that the team has the ability to respond to changes. It doesn't say how.

- *Schedule:* "Adaptive approaches use short cycles ... and rapid feedback" Fairly generic advice.

- *Quality:* Agile methods ... "aim to uncover inconsistencies and quality issues earlier ... when the costs of change are lower." Fairly generic advice.

- *Communications:* Agile methods need to communicate ... "details more frequently and quickly. This motivates streamlining access to information, frequent checkpoints, and co-locating team members." Useful advice.

- *Risks:* "Environments with high degrees of uncertainty incur more risk. This places more emphasis on risk management in agile developments. However, the methods of risk management remain the same." A constructive suggestion in the PMBOK would provide guidance on techniques for conducting a risk analysis appropriate to changing requirements.

- *Stakeholders:* "To accelerate the sharing of information, agile methods promote aggressive transparency (by) inviting stakeholders to meetings, posting project documents in public spaces, and surfacing issues as quickly as possible." Adaptive environments require active engagement of stakeholders.

21

AGILE SPRINTS

Service to others is the rent you pay for your room here on earth.

Muhammad Ali

The heart of the agile framework is the *sprint*. The agile philosophy insists that, for each sprint, the team should deliver a specific piece of the backlog, called an *increment*.

21.1 Agile Start Activities

For agile projects, just as for traditional projects, there is significant work to be completed before the first sprint can begin.

Activities before the first sprint are sometimes referred to as *Sprint Zero* by practitioners, but this is not an official term in the scrum guidelines. In fact, the founders of Scrum discourage the use of this term.[1] A central tenet of the scrum methodology is that each sprint is supposed to deliver value to the organization and sprint zero doesn't do that.[2] Therefore, we will simply refer to them as *Agile Start* activities.

The goals of the *Agile Start* activities are to ensure that the project has a valid reason for existing, i.e., a business case, vision, and financial justification. Next, the product requirements should be confirmed, which is referred to as populating the

[1] From a conversation with Dr. Sutherland, the Scrum co-founder, with author Vijay Kanabar on 5/25/2018.

[2] Some scrum advocates insist that each sprint deliver working code. We prefer that the sprint deliver value, rather than insist on working code.

backlog. The logistics must be in place, i.e., the agile methodology, the software development environment, and the hardware. Finally, the team must be identified and available.

The next step is to develop a roadmap for the work to be performed in sprints. The *Sprint Backlog* contains the list of features to be implemented and these should be assigned to sprints based on the anticipated velocity and the estimation process. Finally, the contents of the first sprint, called *Sprint #1*, are assigned.

Agile Start activities are most easily described in terms of a checklist of questions to be addressed during an *Agile Start* meeting:

- Do we have a business case, vision, and sound financial analysis with defined benefits for the agile project?[3]

- Do we have a preliminary product backlog and a preliminary release plan with milestones?

- Do we have a commitment for the required *scrum* resources and to organize a team?

- Do we have the logistics for project execution?

- Do we have a defined plan for the software architecture?

- Are coding practices and standards in place?[4]

- Do we have access to coding tools for the hosting platform?

- Do we have a testing strategy using knowledgeable end-users?

- Do we have adequate knowledge of project risks, quality assurance and control, procurement, and other associated processes and procedures?

- Is the project team ready for continuous communication and interaction with users, a major requirement of agile developments?

- Even though it appears trivial, do we have the rooms available for planning meetings, discussing charts and boards, and demonstrating the product?[5]

[3] For example, does the project fit strategically within the organization?

[4] Be sure that the standards apply to the actual development, e.g., mobile or web development, or mandated laws and standards for visually impaired users.

[5] From our experience, this is often a key challenge with agile projects.

366

21.2 Sprints

The agile process consists of a series of the *sprints*. Each Sprint has a goal and a flexible plan for achieving the work. The sprint goal is a specific product *increment* and an important condition is that, during a sprint, no changes are made to the goal. Neither should there be a compromise on quality so that the goal is maintained. However, changes are encouraged and, as more is learned, the requirements may be clarified and re-negotiated with the *Product Owner*.

According to the Scrum Guide, the definition of a sprint is: [69]

> *A sprint is a time-box of one month or less during which a "Done," usable, and potentially releasable product increment is created.*

Sprints have a consistent duration throughout the project and a new sprint starts immediately after the conclusion of the previous sprint. Sprints are never longer than one month and are frequently two-weeks.

Sprints consist of:

- Sprint Planning

- The first sprint

- Daily Scrums

- The sprint backlog

- The development work

- The Sprint Review

- The Sprint Retrospective.

21.3 Sprint Planning

Each sprint begins with a *Sprint Planning Meeting* where the work to be performed is planned collaboratively by the entire team. The scrum method recommends holding a *Sprint Planning Meeting* on the first day of the sprint and daily scrum meetings each day thereafter.

The main functions of sprint planning meeting are to decide what can be delivered in the sprint and how that work will be accomplished. During this meeting, the team sets the goals to be achieved and prioritizes which backlog items are to be worked on. Particularly in the early sprints, it is important to stress that these are *goals* and that the team's estimate of their velocity is likely to be unreliable.

Like all events in the agile framework, the *Sprint Planning Meeting* is time-boxed. For a two-week sprint, it is suggested that no more than four hours be allocated for the sprint planning meeting. If the sprint is one week in duration, the sprint planning meeting may be two hours or less. For more complex projects using month-long sprints, the planning meeting may require as long as eight hours.

The *Scrum Master* schedules the meeting and ensures that the team understands its purposes. The team develops a plan for the work to be delivered. Work is selected from the *Product Backlog* and assigned to the *Sprint Backlog*.[6] The only characteristic of a sprint is its time-box, not the work planned.

21.4   The First Sprint

Sprint #1 starts immediately upon conclusion of the Sprint Planning Meeting. Once that the preparatory work has been completed, the team is ready to start on the first sprint. The first sprint will be a baseline and set the tone for the project. It is also an opportunity for the team to engage in the philosophy of agile development.

Barnaby Golden, the agile coach and scrum master, warns against doing too much in the first sprint and, yet, he still encourages delivering a small amount of business value. [71] Golden recommends the following important goals for the first sprint:

- Start understanding the backlog story details early to prepare the team for sprint two.

- Establish what constitutes "done" for each story and a testing approach, especially the acceptance criteria, test frameworks, etc.

- Try and get some business value out of the first sprint, which will start engaging the stakeholders.

The first sprint begins with a sprint planning meeting where the team picks the user stories for the first sprint. For example, a useful first sprint might be to design and prototype the user interface so that the users can immediately provide feedback and direction.

[6]It is important to remember that the sprint backlog is not a commitment, it is a forecast.

Golden recommends that the team should focus mainly on a story that will get the infrastructure up and running and that will put the agile processes in place. It should also provide a demonstration at the end of the sprint that shows value. Golden also recommends that everything should be kept as simple as possible for the first sprint, which should set the stage for good practices going forward.

The story point estimates for the first sprint are likely to be inaccurate because the team will not have data on their velocity or an understanding of what they can accomplish on the project.

Throughout the sprint, the team participates in the daily scrum meetings where they note any obstacles that are preventing them from completing their tasks. The *Scrum Master* will work with the team to remove those obstacles. At the end of the sprint, the team holds a sprint review meeting, product demonstrations that should include stakeholders, and the sprint retrospective.

21.5 Daily Scrums

The team meets daily in the *Daily Scrum* to discuss progress and any issues that have arisen. Each daily scrum discusses which items from the backlog are going to be worked on that day. The team can plan, or re-plan, work.

According to the Scrum Guide, the *Daily Scrum* is a stand-up event that is time-boxed at 15 minutes. The team reviews the scrum board and updates the *Do, Doing, Done* list for all tasks. A new category called "Deferred" can be added for stories that are postponed to a future sprint

The three questions used as starting point for the meetings are: What did you do yesterday? What do you plan to do today? What impediments appear to be disrupting the daily progress? The development team participates in the *Daily Scrum* along with the Scrum Master, whose job it is to remove impediments.

21.6 The Sprint Work

Each Sprint is given a goal to keep the team focused. The sprint goal is created in the *Sprint Planning Meeting* and is an objective that can be met by implementing pieces of the *Product Backlog*.

The goal guides the team on why it is building the backlog item, which should deliver specific coherent functionality. However, there is flexibility within the Sprint. If the work turns out to be different than the team expected, they collaborate with the *Product Owner* to re-negotiate the scope of backlog item.

The team works to understand the goals of the sprint and to forecast the story points that will be developed during the sprint. The *Product Owner* discusses the objective that the sprint should achieve and the *Product Backlog* items that will achieve the sprint goal. The team selects the number of items from the *Product Backlog* for the sprint because only the team can realistically assess what it can accomplish during the sprint.

Next the team identifies the sprint stories that are goals for the sprint and referred to as the *sprint backlog*. The sprint backlog is a goal and not a commitment. For example, the sprint backlog stories for a sprint to define a user interface might be:

- Create a mock-up of the primary pages.

- Design a preliminary database and retrieve sample data for the mock-up.

- Create sample buttons and menus.

- Create sample detail pages showing the types of data to be displayed.

The team has no idea what their actual velocity will be at the outset of the sprint. However, based on their performance during the few sprints, a reasonable velocity estimate will emerge that will allow them to forecast the number of stories they can complete in future sprints.

21.7   The Sprint Backlog

The *Sprint Backlog* is different from the *Product Backlog*. The *Sprint Backlog* consists of items selected for the Sprint, plus a plan for delivering the product *increment*. It is important to note that the *Sprint Backlog* is a *forecast* by the team about what functionality they expect to be able to deliver in the next *increment*.[7]

The *Sprint Backlog* highlights the work that the team has identified as necessary to meet the sprint goal. To ensure continuous improvement, it should include at least one high priority process improvement identified in the previous *Sprint Retrospective*. The *Sprint Backlog* is reviewed in the *Daily Scrum*.

The team may modify the *Sprint Backlog* throughout the sprint as they learn more about the work and the sprint goal. If new work is required, the team adds it to the *Sprint Backlog*. As work is completed, the estimated remaining work is updated. When elements are deemed unnecessary, they are removed.

[7]In scrum language, this is called the "Done" *increment*.

370

Only the team can change the *Sprint Backlog* during a Sprint. It is a highly visible, real-time picture of the work that the team plans to accomplish during the Sprint, and it belongs solely to the team. [69]

21.8 The Sprint Review

The *Sprint Review* is an informal meeting held at the end of the sprint. This is a time-boxed event of no more than 4 hours for a one-month Sprint and smaller for shorter sprints. The team analyzes and discusses the work that was completed during that sprint. As the user stories were completed, direct feedback is given to the *Product Owner*, who adjusts the *Product Backlog* and updates priorities.

21.9 Sprint Retrospectives

The goal of the *Sprint Retrospective* is for the team to assess itself and create a plan for improvement.[8] The team discusses what worked well, what did not work well, and what could be improved. This meeting is time-boxed at three hours for a one-month sprint and less for shorter sprints.

21.10 Sprint Velocity

We conclude this chapter with a discussion of sprint *velocity* using an example.

The Cheese Company needs a new software system and they have written down the key features that they want. They looked around and found the Modern Agile Company (MAC) that specializes in developing agile software for clients.

After several weeks of tense negotiations, MAC agreed to build Cheese's new system. Cheese agreed to assign one of its business analysts as a *Product Owner* (PO), who would work on the project with MAC. The PO analyzed the features of the new system and provided MAC with a list of 48 prioritized user stories.

During the negotiations, MAC analyzed the user stories provided by the PO and proposed to build the system for $400,000 in six months.[9] MAC also proposed to complete the system in six one-month sprints, each delivering eight user stories.

The contract was signed and MAC started work. At the end of the first sprint, they reported that they had successfully completed all eight assigned user stories.[10]

At the end of the second sprint, MAC reported that they had completed six more user stories out of the planned eight. Two user stories were more complex than anticipated and two were lower priority and the team decided to drop them from

[8]The sprint review examines the product, while the retrospective examines the process.

[9]These are similar to the characteristics of a typical project for a very successful agile software development company in New England. [72]

[10]This is not unusual for the first sprint, everyone wants things to start well. Also, the first sprint is often the one that is best understood.

371

the sprint. However, Cheese was quite satisfied with the progress as they could begin to see their new system emerging and completely understood about the two user stories that turned out to be more complex than they realized.

At the end of month 2, MAC had planned to deliver 16 user stories and actually completed 14. Therefore, their average velocity was 7 user stories per sprint, 14/16 = 88%.

At this point, we can analyze the situation as follows:

1. *Classic Project Management:* A MAC project manager might analyze the situation using classic project management concepts:

   - *Fixed Price Contract:* MAC is performing at 88% efficiency (14 out of 16 stories delivered), which means they are projecting an overrun of $57,000. They can either absorb this loss,[11] ask for more funds based on the poor specification of the user stories,[12] or hope they can make it up.[13]

   - *Cost Plus or Incentive Contract:* MAC will propose to charge Cheese for the extra costs and accept a lower profit margin.

2. *Agile Project Management:* At this point, we like to quote a colleague of ours, Chad McCallister, who points out that:

   - Between 40% and 60% of the errors in a system are requirements errors, i.e., in the user stories,

   - Anywhere from 25% and 40% of the budget is consumed by fixing requirements errors, i.e., fixing the user stories, and

   - 58% of the original features change.

   This tells us is that user stories are inherently unreliable and provides a persuasive motivation for adopting the agile framework.

[11]Assuming they built some reserve funds into the contract.

[12]Classic PM negotiation tactic when there is a poor spec.

[13]Rarely happens.

Let's now complete the scenario. MAC and Cheese continue working with the understanding that MAC has not completed the desired work and is unlikely to complete all the user stories. At the end of six months, MAC actually completed six sprints and delivered 45 user stories. Of these, 10 were not part of the original backlog list, but Cheese agreed that they were critical. Cheese agreed to eliminate another 10 as low priority items.

Both companies regarded the project as a success:

- Cheese ended up with a new system that is even better than they had originally conceived. Management was pleased because the system came in at the allocated budget. Cheese's users were happy because the new system worked well. The engineers responsible for the requirements remained quiet about the fact that their specification was poor; the users were happy.

- MAC boasted that they delivered the project on time and on budget. They have another satisfied client.

We can view the project from a contractual perspective as *Design to Cost*. Cheese allocated $400,000 for the project and MAC delivered everything they could for that amount of money. While this makes sense, few people would be comfortable writing a contract based on trusting a contractor to do their best. One way to look at the agile framework is that is formalizes the *Design to Cost* approach in a way that makes people comfortable.

21.10.1 Sprint Velocity = CPI

The sprint velocity is actually the CPI in disguise. Earned Value Management (EVM) calculations can be performed in any set of units and, for agile projects, the units are *user stories*. Let's analyze the Cheese project according to EVM.

The Cheese project had a Budget at Completion (BAC) of $400K and planned to complete 48 deliverables (user stories). The project plan was to complete 8 deliverables per month (8 user stories per sprint). The planned value of each deliverable was $PV\$400K/48 = \$8.3K$.

At the end of month 2 (sprint #2), MAC completed 14 deliverables and had, therefore, earned $EV(2) = 14 \times \$8.3K = \$116.7K$.

The actual cost was two month's work and 2/6 of the budget, $AC(2) = \$400K \times 2/6 = \$133.3K$.

Therefore, at month 2, $CPI(2) = EV(2)/AC(2) = \$116.7K/\$133.3K = 0.87$. This is precisely the velocity calculated above, where it was simply stated as 7 user stories per sprint.

We can learn from this *EVM* calculation. The agile framework simplifies *EVM* calculations to the point where people may actually use them, which is significant progress. Also, recognizing that the *sprint velocity* is a legitimate *EVM* concept means that its accuracy is validated because it inherits all the established *EVM* research.

22

THE SAMPL APP

Experience is the name everyone gives to their mistakes.

Oscar Wilde

In this chapter we follow the development of the Student Academic Mobile Planning App (SAMPL). The project is developed according to the agile framework in a series of *sprints*. We introduce the agile team and follow the scrum framework with sprints, daily scrums, sprint reviews, and sprint retrospectives. We give examples of the agile products, including the backlog, and user stories. Finally, we track costs using the sprint velocity and present a burndown chart.

22.1 SAMPL Agile Start Activities

We begin with *Agile Start* activities, which are the activities conducted before development begins, i.e. before the first sprint. The SAMPL app requires significant up-front planning to establish the viability of the project: vision, business case, and preliminary cost and schedule estimates.

22.1.1 SAMPL Vision

The need for the SAMPL app arose because College faculty and staff reported that they were frequently answering simple student questions about class schedules and course details, such as instructor information, syllabus, and textbooks. These questions occur at the beginning of each semester when they are busiest.

The requested information already exists, but it is scattered among the web site, databases, and documents and is difficult to access. Therefore, the College proposed the development of a mobile app that would allow students to seek the information for themselves, anywhere, and at any time.

Because modern students use their hand-held devices for virtually all of their day-to-day activities, the app should be developed for mobile devices. A mobile app would reduce faculty and staff load at the most critical time of the semester. It would also reduce anxiety for students who would be able to find the course information and make informed decisions about courses.

The College's Marketing Department thought the app would be useful to prospective students, who also request information about courses relevant to their field of interest. The current information is difficult to search and, therefore, the ability easily find information is an important feature.

The vision is for the app to allow students to:

Search for classes they might be interested in.
List classes they need to take to complete a degree program.
List electives and optional classes they can fit in their schedule.
List class schedules for relevant courses in an upcoming semester.
View course outlines and reading lists for identified courses.
View course details, such as schedule, room, instructor, syllabus, etc.

A template approach for the SAMPL vision is shown in Table 22.1:[1]

Data integrity and security are important issues because there are many government regulations and legal requirements that apply to student data. The College is also bound by stringent disability regulations. While no financial data will be stored, the storage of student requires multiple security layers.

Students should be able to select courses that they are interested in and save them in a results page. Selected courses should link to detailed course information: catalog description, instructor, textbooks, assignments, learning outcomes, and the detailed syllabus. Students should be able to add, edit, and delete saved information. The College may wish to adapt the above requirements as the app structure emerges. Further, the precise look and feel of the app is unclear.

[1] Templates are an efficient way to get started as they often exist for previous projects.

The app will be made available to students at no cost and must eventually work on both Apple iOS and Android devices. Initially, the goal is to support iOS devices

Table 22.1: The SAMPL Vision.

Topic	Content
Product Name:	The SAMPL App
Target Audiences:	Enrolled students, prospective students Faculty and College administrators
Needs:	The product creates value by giving students the ability to select and save a list of courses for purposes of registration in an upcoming semester.
Competitive Alternative:	Unlike the current system the app will provide anytime, anywhere, mobile access to course information.
Business Goal:	The financial justification is that the app will free up faculty and administrator time; enhance the productivity of staff responding to course and schedule questions; and mitigate risks of missed opportunities to register students.

only and Android devices will be supported in future releases. The app will require a review and acceptance by the app stores.

22.1.2 SAMPL Business Case

The College conducted a survey of faculty and staff to estimate the time spent answering simple student questions about courses. From that data, the College estimated the cost of wasted staff time and missed opportunities in registering potential future students at $250,000. Therefore, the College decided to allocate $125,000 to address this problem by creating a mobile application that would allow both potential and current students to query a database containing course information.

As well as the above tangible (financial) benefits, the College administration believes that the app will have intangible benefits:

- The app will increase the visibility of courses and programs that the College offers to students, providing them additional value.

- The convenience of a mobile app brings with it "anytime anywhere" capabilities, giving students access outside normal office hours.

- Since student data, such as email addresses, are being captured, it may be possible to market courses and programs to students directly.

- Apps provide a technologically modern look that builds brand recognition and helps the College to stand out from the competition.

- The app may provide accurate usage statistics and data on student behavior for further analysis.

22.1.3   SAMPL Release Plan

The SAMPL app consists two distinct modules:

1. Search Courses: Students will be able to query the course database with keywords or phrases to find courses of interest to them.

2. Course Information Display: The app will present detailed information about courses.

The first step in the release plan is to select an implementation method and the team considered both the waterfall and agile methodologies. The team analyzed the key characteristics of the SAMPL app and, while the general goals are clear, the detailed requirements are not well understood and may well change during development. Also, there are several user communities with diverse interests.

Additionally, the project is associated with an aggressive schedule and tight deadlines, a high degree of complexity associated with student data privacy and security issues, considerable novelty, and communication risks associated with the diverse stakeholders, i.e., several student audiences, faculty, and College staff.

Given these characteristics, it was proposed that an *agile* development be undertaken. The scrum-based approach is well suited for web and mobile development projects. Therefore, it was decided that the project would be developed using the Scrum Framework. The team has experience with two-week sprints and so is comfortable proposing that time-box for the SAMPL project.

The team proposed a timetable for releasing the product, which is known as the *release plan*, which is shown in Table 22.2. The highest priority is the iOS app and, within that, the search courses feature. The display of course information is slightly less important. It is estimated that development of the app will take six months.

Table 22.2: The SAMPL Plan.

Milestone	Activity
1/1/2019	Development Start
6/30/2019	iOS Product Release
8/30/2019	Android Release

Module	Contents
Search Courses (Module #1)	Allows user to: Search for courses Create course list Edit course list.
List Courses Information (Module #2)	Allows user to: Display course information: Schedule, instructor, Syllabus, reading.

22.1.4 SAMPL Scrum Team

The next step was to acquire a team with the required skills:

- *Product Owner (PO): Jane*

  The PO's role is to represent stakeholder interests and Jane has the necessary knowledge because she works in the Student Services Department, where she spends considerable time working with students on their schedules. Jane will work with the development team, students, and staff to translate their expectations into user stories. Jane's responsibility will be to develop and maintain the backlog, to prioritize its items, to answer developers' questions, and to determining whether the delivered items are satisfactory.

- *Scrum Master (SM): Rumen*

  Rumen has previous experience on projects that used the scrum framework. His roles are to ensure that the scrum framework is understood and followed, to be good servant-leader for the development team, to remove impediments, and to assist the team in the creation of a valuable mobile app.

- *Scrum Development Team: Ashley, Harry, Vinay, and Julia*

  The scrum team consists of four members, who have a range of skills. Ashley and Harry were selected to perform the app development because they are experienced in mobile app design, development, and testing.

Ashley will also be the lead user interface (UI) designer because she previously designed app UIs. The vision prioritizes the user experience and an early prototype of the UI is planned to obtain feedback.

Vinay was selected as the database designer. Vinay is an expert in database design and knows how to design tables, queries, and app data interfaces.

Julia has expertise in apps and information security.

This cross-functional team possesses all the key competencies and domain knowledge required to develop the SAMPL app.[2] When issues arise, the team should be capable of collectively resolving the issues by "swarming,"[3] which is an excellent approach to problem solving that demonstrates and promotes teamwork.

22.1.5 User Stories

The SAMPL *user stories* express the desired business values:[4]

S1 Story 1: Student Search

As a student, I want to be able to search for courses being offered at the college so that I can select them for the upcoming semester.

S2 Story 2: Staff Search

As a staff member, I want to be able to search for courses being offered at the College to help a student develop a schedule for the upcoming semester.

S3 Story 3: Prospective Student Inquiry

As a prospective student investigating the courses available at the College, I want to be able to inquire about courses being offered at the college so that I can see if I am interested in them.

S4 Story 4: Save Searches

As a student, I want to be able to save selected courses in my app so that I can view them later.

S5 Story 5: Edit Saved Searches

As a student, I want to edit the saved courses so that I have a useful list.

S6 Story 6: Course Details

As a student, I want to be able to see the details of a course that I selected: schedule, instructor, syllabus, readings, and assignments.

[2]Such cross-functional teams are an important aspect of agile developments.

[3]*Swarming* is an activity where all team members collectively work on a task to finish it before moving ahead and working on the next task.

[4]These are in template format.

380

S7 Story 7: Data Protection

As a student, I want my personal information to be protected.

User stories have *acceptance criteria*[5] and an example of an acceptance criteria for user story [S5] is:

When the user adds a course, but has not yet saved it to the results page,
the course title should be stored and be accessible later.

The Product Backlog became the single authoritative source for all work on the SAMPL project. As the sprints proceeded it was planned that bugs to be addressed would also be expressed as stories and maintained in the product backlog.

22.1.6 SAMPL Estimation

The *Scrum Master* began by inviting everyone to the estimation meeting where the *Product Owner* reviewed the user stories to ensure that the development team understood them. The team refined the stories and produced the list in Table 22.3.

Table 22.3: The SAMPL user stories.

Story ID	Story Description
I	User Interface
DBP	Preliminary Database Design
M1P	Preliminary Module #1
M2P	Preliminary Module #2
DBF	Final Database
M1F	Final Module #1
M2F	Final Module #2
S	Security Layer
T	System Test
U	User Acceptance
H	Application Hardening

Next, the team began placing the user stories in relative order of effort. Ashley went first, briefly discussed the first story, the user interface [I], and placed the card in the center of the table. Harry went next and drew the [M1P] card (Preliminary Module #1). He judged this would require more effort than user interface, so he placed the card to the right of the [I] card.

[5]See section 20.7

Julia drew the [DBP] card, the preliminary database design. She thought the database design was complex and Vinay, the database expert, agreed as data existed in many places and there was a lot of text searching. Julia placed the [DBP] card to the right of the [M1P] card.

Vinay drew the [S] card, the security layer, which he thought would take less effort than the database, but more than the Preliminary Module #1 [M1P]. Therefore, he placed the [S] between the [M1P] and [DBP] cards. The team continued taking cards and placing them until they reached a consensus on the relative efforts, which is shown in Figure 22.1.

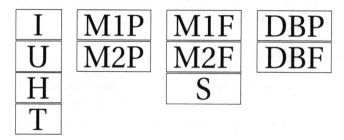

Figure 22.1: The SAMPL app stories ordered by effort.

The next step was to assign story points. Harry placed the '1' card above the [I] [U] [H] [T] column. Vinay studied the [I] [M1P] [M2P] column and thought that those tasks required significantly more effort than those in the first column. His choices were either a '2' or a '3' card and he decided that the '3' was appropriate.

Julia was next and reviewed the [M1F] [M2F] [S] column and noted that the final modules and the security story were significantly more complex than the [I] column and would require more work. However, she said that she not sure whether a new authentication program needed to be designed or whether the app could be using College security protocols. The Scrum Master, Rumen, made a quick phone call to IT Department, who said that the app could piggyback on existing authentication. Therefore, Julia decided that that her estimate was a '5.' She would have selected an '8' if a new security protocol had to be designed.

Vinay said that he still thought the database design was even harder than the security and he assigned an '8,' the next available Fibonacci number. The meeting concluded with a consensus, which is shown in Figure 22.2.

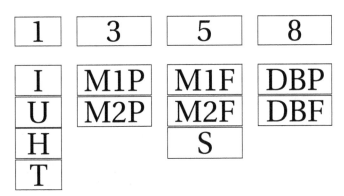

Figure 22.2: The SAMPL app stories ordered by effort and with story points.

22.1.7 SAMPL Agile Start Checklist

Table 22.4 presents the checklist of activities for the *Scrum Start [S]* phase of the SAMPL project. The team determined that all items on the Scrum Start checklist had been addressed. Therefore, with the *Agile Start* activities complete, the team was ready to start the first sprint.

Table 22.4: The SAMPL Scrum Start Checklist.

Topic	Action
Business case, vision, financial analysis & defined benefits	Yes. See 22.1.3.
Product backlog and release plan with milestones?	Yes. See 22.1.3.
Commitment for Scrum resources and Scrum team?	Yes. Dean has authorized development.
Logistics?	Environment is installed: software development, security, ISP hosting.
Software architecture plan?	No. To be developed in Sprints #1 and #2.
Coding practices and standards?	Yes. College IT standards apply.
Development fits within College? midrule Tools and technology	Yes. IT Department signed off. Yes. IT Department standards.
Mandated laws and standards for visually impaired users.	Yes. College disability standards enforced.
Testing strategy	Yes. Dean has committed staff resources.
Knowledge of project risks, QA & QC other PM procedures?	Yes. Rumen is an Agile and PM expert.
User communication & interaction	Yes. Student volunteers will be recruited.
Rooms meetings & product demonstrations	Yes. College has many classrooms.
Sound financial analysis	Yes. See section 20.8

22.2 SAMPL Sprint #1

Sometimes it pays to stay in bed on Monday, rather than spending the rest of the week debugging Monday's code.

Dan Salomon

We remind the reader that each sprint includes sprint planning, daily scrums, execution of the work of the sprint, a sprint review, and a sprint retrospective.

22.2.1 Sprint #1 Planning

The goal of the first sprint was to design the user interface, which is a key requirement, as it should provide a clear visual representation of what the final product would look like. Also, at the end of the sprint, the team should receive feedback from all stakeholders about the user interface. The first step is the *Sprint Planning Meeting*, which Rumen called on the first day of the sprint.

SAMPL First Sprint Planning Meeting

The team focused on identifying the most important user stories and proposed the following *Sprint Backlog* items as their forecast for sprint #1:

Create a mock-up of the search courses page.
Create a mock-up of retrieval of selected course schedules for a semester.
Create a simple search routine that displays the search results.
Create a mock-up of a screen with a selected course.
Create a mock-up of the save process for the selected courses.
Create a mock-up of the editing page where students can modify
    the list of selected courses.
Create a mock-up of detailed course data items.

The team has no idea what their actual velocity would be at the outset. However, they made assumptions about the velocity they might achieve in the first sprint, but with the clear understanding that this could be inaccurate. Based on their performance in the first few sprints, a reliable velocity should become available and estimates for later sprints should become more reliable.

Additional backlog items were discussed during the sprint planning meeting and comments were documented so that the information would be available if the items were included in subsequent sprints:

Query Courses: High priority, early prototype required.
Add Courses: Low priority as new courses are rarely added.
Color Code Courses: Good idea, but unclear what should be colored.
Create Calendar: Low priority, deferred. Other tools exist for this.
Menu Changes: Build in flexibility because requirements uncertain.
Remove course assignments as not relevant to course selection.

At the end of the sprint planning meeting, the team had created a sprint backlog and estimated its relative effort using story points. The SM ensured that all team members were comfortable with the sprint backlog and that they did not plan too many items.

22.2.2 SAMPL Sprint #1 Daily Scrum

It was impossible to get a conversation going, everybody was talking too much.

Yogi Berra

The daily scrum was scheduled by the Scrum Master and the team discussed issues that had arisen and which items from the sprint backlog were going to be worked on that day. The three questions used as the starting point for the daily scrums were: What did you do yesterday? What do you plan to do today? What impediments appear to be disrupting the daily progress? As the Scrum Master, Jane was actively involved as it was her job to remove impediments.

Day #4 of the first sprint, yielded the following discussions:

Ashley: I will create the wire-frame for the search courses page.
Vinay: I am going to create a mock-up of the data for Search Courses.
Julia: I will investigate the student privacy issues that impact the app.
Harry: I have an issue: The mock-up I built yesterday keeps hanging up and there may be an issue with the button tool.

The Scrum team self-organized and decided to discuss what to do about the button tool issue. They considered changing to a more reliable software system. Jane (SM) took the assignment of investigating whether alternative software tools were available and what the extra cost might be.

As the team discussed each task, they updated the Scrum board with its tasks and completion dates. See Table 22.5. Table 22.5 is an example of an *information radiator*, which communicates project progress to everyone. This chart was kept in plain sight so that the project team and other stakeholders were aware of the project status, as well as the assignments.

Table 22.5: The SAMPL Team Task Board.

ID	Do	Doing	Done
1	Wire-frame search courses	Form design	
2	Mock-up search form	Form design	
3	Investigate student privacy	Student data protection	
4	Investigate button tool	Alternative tools	

The SAMPL team decided to keep the *Task Board* simple and used a spreadsheet available on the College network. They did not have to create any extra protocols as everyone was already familiar with the access procedures. Jane made sure that the team understood what constituted "Done" and discussed the acceptance criteria for each story.[6]

22.2.3 Sprint #1 Review

An informal meeting was held at the end of sprint #1 to analyze the user interface, mock-ups, and wire-frames and to review the views of students and staff who were represented by Jane (PO), who coordinated the feedback and updated the product backlog. They also analyzed the work that was completed against the plan.

At an early daily scrum, the team recognized that not all of the proposed features could be completed. Therefore, it was decided not to continue with the calendar feature because that type of functionality is available in other tools and it adds little value to the SAMPL app.

The team also decided that assignments data, which was planned for the detailed course data page, were not always available in the College databases. Students also confirmed that it was a low priority when searching for courses and, so, the team created a separate user story for that and assigned it a very low priority.

Key conclusions by the team about Sprint #1 were documented as follows.

- Sprint #1 consisted of the development of the user interface, which was critical in establishing the features required and the usability of the system. Review of the interface by the PO allowed the team to gain direct feedback on the initial layout and to build the feedback into future sprints.

- The design of the user interface for the major screens was completed.

- The PO reported that many users thought the screens to be too complex with too many activities on each screen. It was decided to increase the number of screens and to reduce the number of items on a screen.

- No adjustments were made to content and no new features were added.

- Most of the activities planned for sprint #1 were completed in the two-week time-box with the assigned team.

22.2.4 Sprint #1 Retrospective

The Scrum Team discussed among themselves the work in the sprint #1 and created a plan for improvement.[7] This meeting was time-boxed at 2 hours and the following questions were discussed:

[6] "Done" is the recommended terminology in the agile framework for completed activities.

[7] While the sprint review examines the *product*, the sprint retrospective examines the *process* for what worked and what did not work.

What do you think went well?

The team managed to successfully complete the sprint backlog so the velocity estimation seems reasonable. Using the Scrum Master to remove impediments worked for less complex issues. The product owner was pleased with the availability of the stakeholders and their willingness to review the mock-up.

What would you like to change?

A key issue was that work was completed, but collaboration could have been better. Therefore, communication and collaboration issues needed to be addressed.

How should we implement suggested changes?

To improve communications, the team designed a spreadsheet that implemented the functionality of a Trello Board, which documents tasks as they are completed. They also installed an integrated GitHub and parallel Slack channel.

22.3 Examples of Sprint Activities

22.3.1 Sprint #2 Review

Sprint #2 consisted of building a preliminary database. This was a technically sophisticated sprint and had little impact on the requirements. The designer used the screens from Sprint #1 to construct normalized data tables.

At the end of sprint #2, approximately 75% the proposed data items were designed and the data tables populated. Key data items required for course searches and presentation of detailed course information were available. However, many of the remaining data items were either not readily accessible, incomplete, or missing.

The database designer discussed the issues with the PO, the SM, and the team. Obtaining the missing data would delay the product but, since most of the items were only required for low priority features, the team decide to create user stories for them and add them to the backlog. Future sprints could implement them if the data became available.

22.3.2 Sprint #2 Retrospective

The work required for sprint #2 was significantly underestimated. There was far more data than the team anticipated, and it was distributed in many places. Also, much of the data is in text form, which required sophisticated search algorithms. Therefore, the data base design took much longer than anticipated. The team adjusted the value of its velocity on future database work.

The definition of "Done" was not clear to all team members for certain tasks. While the software was completed, the software did not always meet the requirements of the PO. They decided to request that the PO develop clearer acceptance tests to determine when a task is considered done.

22.3.3 Sprint #6 Issue

The SAMPL Product Backlog listed not just user stories, but also bugs to be addressed by the team. During sprint #6, Build Module #1, a bug arose and was documented in a new user story:

S8 Story 8: Edit Course button freezes.
   1.   Go to 'Edit Results' page, the edit course list appears.
   2.   Select any course.
   3.   Click 'Edit' button, nothing seems to happen.

22.3.4 Sprint #11 Review

As the project ended, the product owner, the scrum master, and the development team reflected on the completed app. Overall the PO was very satisfied. Students who tested the app were be able to select courses, save them to a results page, edit the list as desired, and access detailed course information. The team concluded that the SAMPL app had passed all significant tests and could be released.

The team also reviewed the remaining backlog, which contained low priority features, a list of required fixes, and deferred items. The team noted that the calendar feature was not implemented and the menu option was removed. The calendar feature did not impact the functionality of the app and was added to the backlog as a proposed future feature. There were a few minor issues, but they did not affect the overall performance of the app.

22.3.5 Sprint #11 Retrospective

As the project ended, the team held a last retrospective and concluded that the suggestions from the first sprint's retrospective improved communication between and resulted in more successful later sprints. The team also concluded that the communication and collaboration that occurred in the daily scrums generated excitement and encouraged further teamwork.

The SM and PO noted that the students' initial response to the SAMPL app was positive and administrators thought it appeared to be saving them time. The PO and SM praised the development team for their efforts. The SM noted that team was empowered and self-organizing and choose how best to accomplish each task without too much outside help.

22.4 SAMPL Cost and Schedule Tracking

There are at least two ways to measure the progress of an agile project: using hours and using story points. In both cases, one measures the plan versus the actual. For the SAMPL project, Table 22.6 presents the data.

Table 22.6: The SAMPL Team Hours Planned.

ID	Sprint	Hours		Story Points	
		Plan	Actual	Plan	Actual
1	User Interface	120	130	8	6
2	Prelim DB	210	240	21	18
3	Prelim Mod #1	120	140	8	6
4	Prelimin Mod #2	120	150	8	6
5	Final DB	220	200	8	6
6	Final Mod #1	150			
7	Final Mod #2	150			
8	Security Layer	140			
9	System Test	70			
10	User Acceptance	90			
11	User Req. Changes	80			

We analyze the status of the SAMPL project after the completion of sprint #5. The velocity is simply the story points completed per sprint.[8] The planned and actual story point data are listed Table 22.6 and plotted in Figure 22.3. The black velocity bars are shorter than the gray planned velocity bars, which means that we have not delivered as many story points as was planned.

We can also present the consumption of hours, which is called a *burn-down chart*. We begin with the total planned hours: 1,470 and, after each sprint, subtract the hours consumed.[9] See Table 22.7 and Figure 22.5.

The actual burn-down line for hours (solid) is below the planned line (dashed), which shows we are using more hours than planned. The burn-down chart using story points is shown in Figure 22.4 and the actual burn-down line (solid) is above the planned line (dashed), so we are not completing as many as planned.

The interpretation of these charts depends on context. Not completing as many story points as planned may not be an issue if the stakeholders are satisfied with

[8]You don't get credit for story points until the story is completed, which is exactly the same as in EVM.

[9]For both planned and actual.

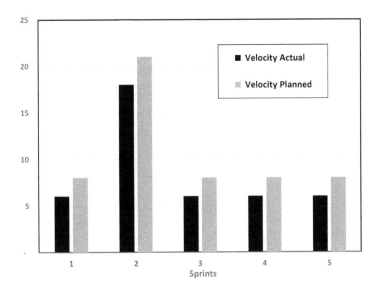

Figure 22.3: Planned and actual sprint velocity after sprint #5.

Table 22.7: The planned and actual hours in burn-down format.

Sprint	Planned Hours	Actual Hours
0	1470	1470
1	1350	1340
2	1140	1100
3	1020	960
4	900	810
5	680	
6	530	
7	380	
8	240	
9	170	
10	80	
11	0	

the app. We eliminated some low priority stories, which may not be a problem either. The burn-down in hours shows we are using more hours than planned and, if this continues, we will run over budget. We can of course, eliminate some stories and only consume the planned hours.

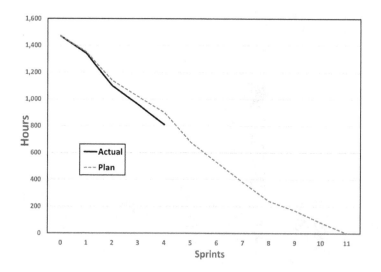

Figure 22.4: Burndown chart in hours after sprint #5.

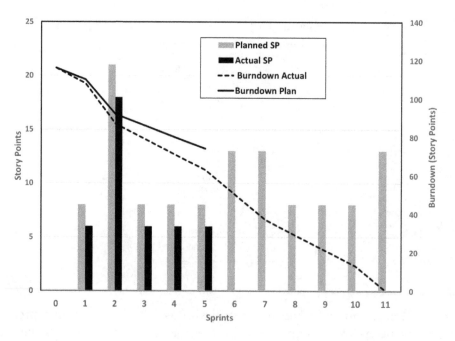

Figure 22.5: Burndown chart in story points after sprint #5.

Part IV

Sample Projects

23

A NEW KITCHEN

You're not using that project management stuff on me, are you?

Eileen Warburton

In this chapter we follow a project through all its phases and give examples of the essential project management deliverables, tools, and techniques.

23.1 Why?

Like many projects in our house, it started with a book: *The Not So Big House*, by Sarah Susanka.[1] [73] Sarah is a brilliant architect, who suggests that most people do not need a bigger house, they need to examine the way they live and how they use their existing space. The key idea is that many houses have dead spaces and rethinking their use can lead to innovative redesign. That proved to be true.

We began discussing a new kitchen project, except that at this stage, it was not yet a project. It would take a year to get to preliminary planning.[2]

Figure 23.1 shows a plan of the house before construction. The kitchen had old units and appliances and Eileen had been campaigning for a while to redo it. We never used the fireplace room, which was dark and looked over the street. The living room looked over the garden and was a much nicer room in all respects. Eileen's key realization was that the fireplace room was dead space and could go.[3]

[1] This is a simplified account of the design and construction of Roger's new kitchen. The conceptual and design work was done by his wife, Eileen. We took the opportunity to record what was happening as an example of a project. The new kitchen project seemed to go through all the typical project management issues.

[2] Projects do not spring fully formed from nothing. They begin with an idea, which is explored and worked on until it begins to look like a project.

[3] This plan did not exist back then, it is used here to explain the problem.

Figure 23.1: Conceptual plan. The dotted lines show the proposed new position of the kitchen and closet walls. The arrow indicates the goal of creating a sight line from the front door through to the garden.

Another key idea emerged when we admitted that the garage was really a *1.8 car garage* and it was never going to hold two cars. The chimney was awkwardly placed and Eileen proposed to expand the kitchen into the garage to create a pantry and into the fireplace room to generate more space. We needed an architect.[4]

23.2 The Pre-K Project

A mistake that people often make is that they assume they have one project when they really have two. In this case, there are actually two projects. The first project is the *Pre-K* project, the goal of which is to *define* the kitchen project by analyzing architectural options, developing the scope, and estimating the cost and schedule.[5]

Often, when a project is proposed, people start writing down what they want and quickly realize that there are many approaches, conflicting goals, and lots of missing information, especially about the cost and schedule. At this point, you need a project to define the project.

[4]In project management language these discussions constitute the *business case,* which includes the justification for the project as well as the goals.

[5]The *Pre-K* project satisfies the definition of a project, as it is unique and has specific objectives.

396

23.2.1 Requirements Analysis

We knew that we did not yet have a project. We did not know enough to define the project. We needed to develop the requirements: What did we want? We needed to answer the following questions: Is a new kitchen design possible? Can the chimney be eliminated? Will the new garage space reasonably hold one car? Also, we needed a rough cost estimate.[6]

Therefore, in late September we selected an architect, Scott, who had redesigned several rooms in a friend's house and we liked what we saw. Thus began the pre-kitchen project, which we refer to here as *Pre-K*. The goal of *Pre-K* was to specify the kitchen project.[7] We invited Scott to look around and discuss the project. We liked him immediately. Scott did not freak out at the over-stuffed bookcases everywhere. He also indicated that he "liked the challenge." Scott sent us a contract and we signed it.[8]

We then had a requirements session where we discussed everything we thought we might want, the idea being that Scott should design everything. We could eliminate things later if the cost was too high (which of course, it was). However, it would be much harder to add to the design later.

We ran into our first problems: Scott explained that he did not do cost estimates or schedules and neither was he good at designing kitchens. We would need to hire a kitchen designer to do that. This required a new plan: Scott would produce a preliminary design, which we would discuss and evaluate. Then we would put the kitchen project out to bid to three contractors. After we had selected the contractor, all of us together would produce a complete specification for the job.[9]

The immediate impact was that the *Pre-K* project had just become much longer. Scott's design would take 4-6 weeks and the bidding process would take another month. That put us into December. Nothing much happens in December, so a realistic date for contractor selection was the following January. The next steps were that we would all meet and revise the plans and we would get the loan.

Therefore, by October, we realized that the kitchen project would not start before next March. Scott went ahead and produced the preliminary design, Figure 23.2. While we made some major changes, we were thrilled.[10] Scott had several new ideas, which we thought were excellent, but the "lav" in the middle of the kitchen had to go. However, Scott's proposal to move the front door to get a clear line of sight all the way to the rear windows was an excellent idea.

[6] Requirements analysis requires preliminary design work because the purpose of the requirements phase is to produce a *feasible* project.

The project must be both technically and financially feasible: the design must resolve all (or most) of the issues; and the cost must be affordable. You cannot simply list a series of wants and desires, the resulting project will almost certainly be unaffordable.

[7] You have to iterate. In fancy project management language, the project is progressively elaborated. You produce a rough design and estimate the cost and schedule. You modify the design (usually to reduce the cost) and try again.

[8] The architect is a key player and one of the goals of contract negotiations is to feel comfortable with the people you will be dealing with.

[9] I would get to referee a bidding cycle. Cool.

[10] Our fantasy of a new upper-floor bedroom was quickly eliminated by the cost.

397

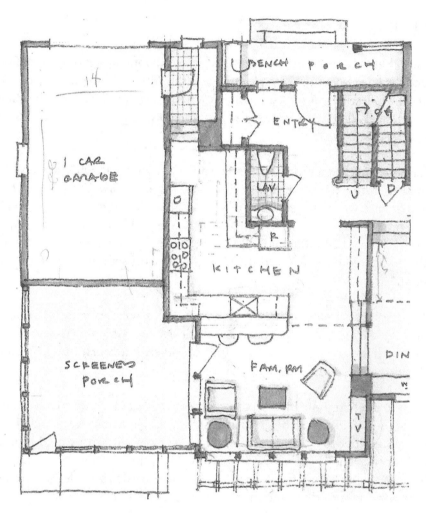

Figure 23.2: The preliminary design for the new kitchen, which was used for the bidding cycle. The lav in the middle of the kitchen had to go.

[11] The bidding process is not just about cost, it is also about evaluating potential bidders. Can you work with them? In the case of the up-state guy, the answer was a comfortable, 'No'.

[12] It was interesting from a project management perspective, it was a classic macro estimate: He simply measured the square footage of the job and multiplied by $200 per square foot.

23.2.2 The Bidding Cycle

We invited three contractors to bid. Scott recommended someone from up-state and we contacted two locals that we knew. The up-state guy was the first to visit and a week later delivered an outrageously expensive bid. We eliminated him.[11] His bid was simply a one-page statement of the cost and not very useful for our purposes.[12]

The two local contractors walked through the house, discussed the project, and examined the plans. Both were pleasant, eager for the work, and had creative suggestions. Joe had done a large addition for a friend of ours and was well thought of around town. Mark had done some work for us before and his finish work is excellent. We knew him to be is smart, courteous, a great planner, and, most significantly, he always told the truth. We thought it was going to be a tough decision and felt bad that we would have to choose.

Two weeks after the walk through, Mark produced a 10-page bid, carefully laid out with multiple options. Each piece was clearly explained and estimated. Mark also suggested several cost saving measures and proposed a kitchen designer he had used in the past for the detailed kitchen layout. It was a well thought out bid.

Joe did not get back to us and, when we called him again, he said he was working on it. A week later, we had still not heard from Joe and, with the holidays approaching, we decided to go with Mark. We called Mark, he came over and we congratulated him. We also felt good about the whole process.[13]

The next step was the production of a detailed design, which would involve the architect, the contractor, and us. Scott estimated that it would take a couple of months. From Scott's design, Mark would produce a detailed cost estimate, to be followed by the bank financing activity, which would take 4-6 weeks.

23.3 The New Kitchen Project

We now had all the elements for a project: The detail design provided the scope; Mark had produced a rough cost estimate, which was within our budget; and the schedule was realistic.

23.4 The Charter

The charter is the first step in the project, as it grants authority to the project manager to spend money and assign resources.[14] The Charter for the new kitchen project is shown in Figure 23.3.

[13] One of the key ideas of the bidding cycle is that you end up comfortable with the contractor you have selected. It is not just about the cost.

[14] Before a project can formally begin, a *Charter* must be created and a project manager assigned. This is the *preferred* order, but few projects follow it.

399

The Charter for the New Kitchen Project.

1. Increase the kitchen size by moving the garage wall and the fireplace room wall.

2. Create a walk-in pantry.

3. Create a one-car garage.

4. Re-purpose little used spaces.

5. Create lines of sight from the front door through the kitchen.

6. New doors and windows to let in more light as appropriate.

7. Investigate more efficient utilities.

8. Cost: Budget $60,000 plus appliances.

9. Schedule: Begin indoor work around March 1st. Outdoor work as weather permits. Work essentially complete within 6 months to comply with city permit restrictions.

Figure 23.3: *Charter* for the New Kitchen project.

23.5 The Scope

> **Few things are harder to put up with than the annoyance of a good example.**
>
> *Mark Twain*

Figure 23.2 showed a part of the preliminary design for the kitchen. It shows a new screened in porch, which was eliminated as too expensive during cost estimation.[15] The detailed design, which is shown in Figure 23.5, is part of the detailed specification of the project.[16] There was little scope creep, the project was merely refined.

23.5.1 Deliverables

- The Scope. This actually consisted of three separate deliverables: The Concept Design, the Preliminary Design, and the Detailed Design.

- Cost Estimate. A multi-page spreadsheet of the estimated costs.

- Cabinets.[17] The cabinets turned out to have the longest delivery time, so determined the critical path, i.e., the schedule.

---

[15] This is a good example of a *Technical Requirement:* The existing deck was sound, but not within the new code, which required that any small change would require an entirely new deck.

[16] Here we see an example of the scope being refined—progressive elaboration.

[17] These turned out to be a big deal.

400

Scope for New Kitchen Project

Objective:
To renovate a kitchen within 6 months at cost of $60,000.

Justification:
Old cabinets and small work space.
Unused spaces of little value.

Deliverables:
Conceptual Design and the Detailed Design.
Sheet rock (Partial Payment required).
New Cabinets.

Milestones:
Demolition Complete	Estimated March 31st.
Gas line installed	Estimated April 15th.
Cabinet Delivery	Estimated July 1st.

Specification:
See Figure 23.2 and associated discussion.

Cost Estimate:
See spreadsheet of estimated costs, $63,000.

Risks:
Cabinet Delivery: Schedule Risk.

Limits and Exclusions:
Contractor responsible for all construction permits.

Constraints:
Schedule: Work substantially complete for guests arriving September 1st.

Assumptions:
Contractor responsible for all subcontractors and their costs.
Painting not included in the bid.

Technical Requirements:
Architect responsible for all safety and loading requirements.
All construction to be consistent with local regulations and codes: carpentry, plumbing, electrical, safety, environmental, etc.

Customer Reviews:
Monthly meetings with Joan Smith (PM) and John Smith (Sponsor).

Figure 23.4: *Scope Statement* for the New Kitchen project.

23.5.2 Milestones

Demolition Complete.	Estimated March 31st.
Gas line installed.	Estimated April 15th.
Cabinet Delivery.	Estimated July 1st.

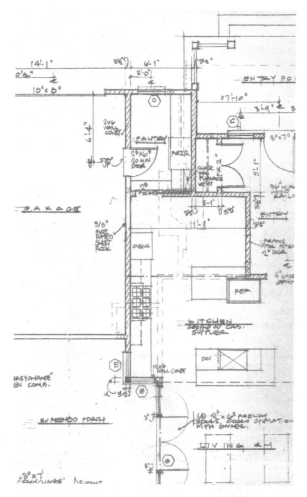

Figure 23.5: The detailed design—the specification—shows the new entry room closet, pantry, and kitchen island.

23.6 WBS

Figure 23.6 presents the high level WBS in graphical form, which suitable for managing the project. The low level WBS is given in outline form in Figure 23.7 and is more suitable for managing the project details and estimating the costs.

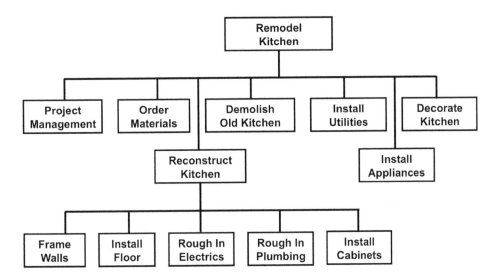

Figure 23.6: The graphical form of the WBS for the New Kitchen Project.

```
0    Kitchen
  1.    Plan Project
      1.1        Obtain Loan
      1.2        Obtain Permit
      1.3        Detailed Architectural Plan
      1.4        Detailed Cost Estimate
  2.    Order Everything
      2.1        Select & Order Cabinets
      2.2        Select & Appliances
  3.    Demolish Old Kitchen
  4.    Manage Utilities
      4.1        Install Rough Plumbing
      4.2        Install Rough Electrics
      4.3        Install Appliances
            4.3.1        Install Gas Range
            4.3.2        Install Refrigerator
            4.3.3        Install Appliances
                  4.3.3.1        Install Dishwasher
                  4.3.3.2        Install Garbage Disposal
      4.4        Finalize Utilities
            4.4.1        Install Lights
            4.4.2        Install Refrigerator
            4.4.3        Install Electric Appliances
  5.    Do Carpentry
      5.1        Install Floor
      5.2        Install Frame Walls
      5.3        Install Blueboard
      5.4        Install Under Floor Heating
  6.    Decorate Kitchen
      6.1        Plaster Walls
      6.2        Paint Walls
      6.3        Install Floor
      6.4        Install Counter Tops
```

Figure 23.7: WBS in outline format for the New Kitchen Project.

23.7 Cost Estimate

The cost estimate in Table 23.1 showed we were already overrunning.[18]

Table 23.1: The cost estimate for the New Kitchen Project

Code	Item	Cost
1.0	Plan Project	
1.1	Obtain Loan	
1.2	Obtain Permit	$3,000
1.3	Architectural Plan	$5,000
1.4	Cost Estimate	$35,000
2.0	Order Everything	
2.1	Select & Order Cabinets	$10,000
2.2	Select & Order Appliances	$7,500
3.	Demolish Old Kitchen	
4.	Manage Utilities	
4.1	Install Rough Plumbing	
4.2	Install Rough Electrics	
4.3	Install Appliances	
4.4	Finalize Utilities	
5.	Carpentry	
6.	Decorate Kitchen	
6.3	Install Floor	$1,500
6.4	Install Counter Tops	$1,000
	Total Cost	**$63,000**

23.8 The Network Diagram

The first step in the creation of the network diagram is the development of the Table of Activity Times and Predecessors, which is shown in Table 23.2. The most important aspect of the table is the estimated activity times. The predecessors are the first pass in the design of the schedule and will change as the schedule evolves.

From Table 23.2, we developed the network diagram using Microsoft Project®and the resulting Gantt chart is shown in Figure 23.8. In Figure 23.9, the Gantt chart for the end of the project is blown up to show the interaction of the activities. Microsoft Project can also output a network diagram and an example is shown in Figure 23.10.

[18]The budget was $60,000.

Table 23.2: Time estimates for the activities in the New Kitchen Project

Code	Item	Predecessors	Time (days)
1.0	Plan Project	None	
1.1	Obtain Loan	None	30
1.2	Obtain Permit	1.3	30
1.3	Architectural Plan	None	30
1.4	Cost Estimate	1.3	14
1.5	Project Approval	1.1, 1.2, 1.3, 1.4	0
2.0	Order Everything		
2.1	Select & Order Cabinets	5.2	60
2.2	Select & Order Appliances	1.5	10
2.3	Select & Order Counter	1.5	60
3.	Demolish Old Kitchen	1.5	10
4.	Manage Utilities		
4.1	Install Rough Plumbing	3.0	5
4.2	Install Rough Electrics	3.0	3
4.3	Install Cabinets	4.1, 4.2	4
4.4	Install Appliances	5.1, 6.1	2
4.4.1	Install Gas Range	5.1, 6.1	1
4.4.2	Install Refrigerator	5.1, 6.1	1
4.4.3	Install Appliances		
4.4.3.1	Install Dishwasher	5.1, 6.1	1
4.4.3.2	Install Garbage Disposal	5.1, 6.1	1
4.4.4	Appliances Complete	4.3, 4.4	0
5.0	Do Carpentry		
5.1	Install Floor		3
5.2	Install Frame Walls	3.0	10
5.3	Install Blueboard	5.2, 4.1, 4.2	5
5.4	Install Under Floor Heating	5.2, 4.1, 4.2	2
6.0	Decorate Kitchen		
6.1	Plaster Walls	4.1, 4.2	2
6.2	Paint Walls	6.1, 4.4.4	4
6.3	Install Floor	5.3	2
6.4	Install Counter Tops	4.3	2

[19]This is perfectly normal and acceptable.

[20]We are using the word *task* here because *Project* uses it. Normally, we prefer to stick to the PMBOK terminology and use *activity*.

23.8.1 Designing the Schedule

The list of tasks in the network diagram in Figure 23.11 is different from the activities in Table 23.2. Once you get into the network, you will quickly find yourself moving tasks around to clarify the schedule.[19]

A good example is the movement of the install tasks.[20] Initially, we placed them

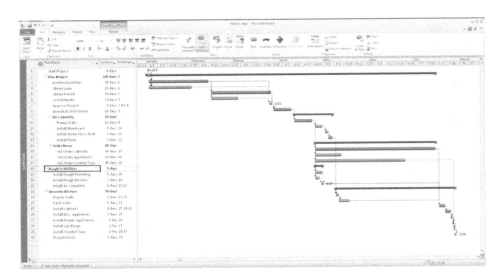

Figure 23.8: The Microsoft Project Gantt chart for the New Kitchen Project.

in the same order as they occurred in the WBS. Once we started working on the schedule, it became clear that installation of the appliances came at the end of the project, after most of the *Decorate* tasks and made the install tasks sub-tasks of *Decorate Kitchen.*

Moving the install tasks produced a Gantt chart that was easier to read and to manage.[21] This is typical of the analysis that occurs as the project planning proceeds. Microsoft Project can produce a WBS automatically and this is shown in Figure 23.11.[22] However, because we moved the tasks around, this WBS is different from the previous version. We have two different WBS.

The WBS structure was ruined when the tasks were moved around to get a better network diagram. However, our opinion is that the original WBS is still the right one to use. Why? The original WBS was *designed* to help manage the project.[23] When we designed the original WBS, we grouped activities, so they could be managed coherently.[24]

From the WBS, we estimated the costs for all plumbing activities, which made things easier for the plumber because all plumbing-related activities were in one place. Also, the actual costs will be collected in one place, which makes it easier to check them against the planned costs.[25]

When we moved the tasks in the network diagram, *Project* re-numbered them, which was acceptable, as it made the *network diagram* clearer and easier to manage.

[21] If you don't move tasks around, the arrows begin to look like spaghetti and you can't figure out what is going on.

[22] Right click on the column header, select *Add Column*, go to the bottom of the list that pops up, and select *WBS*.

[23] Remember, we kept insisting that the construction of the WBS is a *creative* process and that a well-designed WBS is essential to a well-managed project.

[24] For example, we collected all of the plumbing activities together so we could manage them effectively, i.e., everything to do with plumbing went into one box.

[25] If we had scattered the plumbing tasks throughout the WBS, it would be easy to miss something.

407

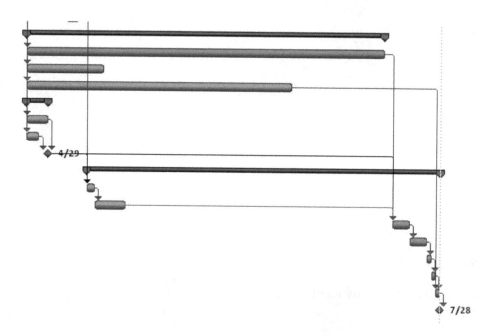

Figure 23.9: The Gantt chart for the end of the New Kitchen Project.

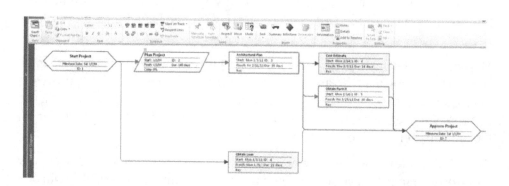

Figure 23.10: The network diagram for the start of the New Kitchen Project.

[26]Which is why we refer to the *Project WBS* as the "lazy person's WBS."

[27]In our opinion, the WBS produced by *Microsoft Project* is not a real WBS, it is merely a task numbering scheme for managing the schedule.

However, the resulting WBS produced automatically from *Project* destroyed our carefully designed WBS.[26] So which WBS do we use? The well-designed version, of course.[27]

		Task Name	Duration	Prede	WBS
1		Start Project	0 days		1
2		⊟ Plan Project	140 days	1	2
3		Architectural Plan	30 days	1	2.1
4		Obtain Loan	21 days	1	2.2
5		Obtain Permit	30 days	3	2.3
6		Cost Estimate	14 days	3	2.4
7		Approve Project	0 days	3,4,5,6	2.5
8		Demolish Old Kitchen	10 days	7	2.6
9		⊟ Do Carpentry	20 days		2.7
10		Frame Walls	10 days	8	2.7.1
11		Install Blueboard	5 days	10	2.7.2
12		Install Under Floor Heat	2 days	11	2.7.3
13		Install Floor	3 days	12	2.7.4
14		⊟ Order Items	60 days		2.8
15		Sel/Order Cabinets	60 days	10	2.8.1
16		Sel/Order Appliances	14 days	10	2.8.2
17		Sel/Order Counter Tops	45 days	10	2.8.3
18		⊟ Rough in Utilities	5 days		3
19		Install Rough Plumbing	5 days	10	3.1
20		Install Rough Electrics	3 days	10	3.2
21		Rough In Complete	0 days	19,20	3.3
22		⊟ Decorate Kitchen	59 days		4
23		Plaster Walls	2 days	13,21	4.1
24		Paint Walls	5 days	23	4.2
25		Install Cabinets	4 days	15,24,21	4.3
26		Install Elec. Appliances	2 days	25	4.4
27		Install Plumb. Appliances	1 day	26	4.5
28		Install Gas Range	1 day	27	4.6
29		Install Counter Tops	1 day	28,17	4.7
30		Project Finish	0 days	29	4.8

Figure 23.11: The WBS output from *Microsoft Project* for the New Kitchen Project.

23.9 Risks

Known unknowns were the risks identified during the planning stage:

- *Cabinet Schedule Risk:* The longest activities on the critical path were the delivery and installation of the cabinets: 12 weeks.[28] The cabinets could not be ordered until the kitchen studs were in place, because only then were the exact measurements available. The mitigation strategy was to get the kitchen studs up as soon as possible so the kitchen designer could finalize the measurements and order the cabinets.[29]

- *Counter Top Schedule Risk:* We selected counter tops that were not in pro-

[28]The longest critical path items should always be analyzed carefully.

[29]After the studs were up, the contractor worked on other tasks while waiting for the cabinets.

409

duction and there were no samples in the store. The mitigation strategy was to pick an alternate counter top design that was readily available.[30]

Unknown unknowns were the risks that actually occurred.[31]

- During construction there was nowhere to store the good china.[32] We hired a moving company to pack the china store it, which added $100 per month.

- Mark applied for a gas permit from the city, which took four weeks. Only *after* the city gas permit was granted would the gas company schedule the installation of the gas line, which took another three weeks. As a result, the installation of the new gas boiler was delayed three weeks.

The Week Things Really Went Awry

One week, frustrations boiled over when the following occurred:

1. On Monday morning the electrician called to say he had badly cut his hand and sent over his assistant. Eileen had planned to select sconces and the junior assistant was not up to the task.

2. Over the weekend, the finish carpenter's roof was damaged in a storm, so he was at home fixing his roof. The substitute carpenter was not a skilled, finish carpenter and could not handle the week's activities.

3. The kitchen appliances were delivered on Tuesday and the refrigerator did not fit in its opening. Mark called the appliance store, who condescendingly said, "You should have left an extra inch." Mark yelled back, "I left two inches!" The refrigerator specification was incorrect.[33] Fortunately, the refrigerator was nudged into place using leveling screws.

4. The insulation contractor showed up wearing a chemical protection suit and demanded that everyone leave the house: contractor, plumbers, and electricians.[34] Eileen was unhappy. she was working on a writing deadline.[35]

Positive Risks

Risks can be positive, as well as negative, and a good example of a positive risk was the new gas boiler. During planning, the plumber examined the heating system and discovered an old and inefficient boiler. He proposed that we could save on heating bills by installing a new, efficient gas boiler. After analyzing the purchase and installation cost vs. the ongoing monthly savings, we decided to purchase a new gas boiler.[36] This was a positive risk that we attempted to *enhance*.

[30] This risk would actually materialize, the company did not make samples available and, rather than wait two months, we selected another design.

[31] And that we had no idea about.

[32] Breakage would be catastrophic.

[33] Remember, spec errors are the most expensive if they are not caught until implementation. This is a good example.

[34] When I explained this to Vijay, he said, "Oh Cool. Communication risk. Be sure to put it in the book.

[35] For the first time in 20 years, Eileen wrote a theater essay on a yellow pad with a pen, sitting in her car.

[36] Project management in action: Examine the proposed change for cost and schedule impacts before deciding.

23.10 Acceptance

The last few weeks of the construction involved a lot of negotiation about the remaining activities to be completed. Mark's original contract included a final payment upon completion of $8,000. We held back part of that payment until he had completed the "punch list."

This was not confrontational. Mark had his own punch list that he was working on. He also understood that when he finished our list, we would be happy and he would get paid. We also understood that complaining at this stage would only annoy Mark and delay things even further.

Some of the items on our list were clearly *add-ons* and would increase the cost. But the entire process went smoothly, because we were in constant communication about what was to be done. The process dragged out several weeks because Mark had started another job and showed up intermittently, but he always told us what was happening.

24

THE PICNIC CASE

If the rain spoils our picnic, but saves a farmer's crop,
who are we to say it shouldn't rain?

Tom Barrett

In this chapter we present the Picnic Case project, but we cover it in a different format from the New Kitchen Project. We present the Picnic case using a complete set of templates for the graduation party picnic project.

This chapter follows the order in the 6th Edition of the PMBOK. To help you quickly find a particular template, Table 24.1 summarizes where the Initiation and Planning templates are to be found in this chapter. Table 24.2 summarizes where the Executing, Monitoring and Controlling, and Closing templates are to be found.

24.1 The Picnic Project

Some graduating students who have studied project management decided to hold a picnic at the end of the academic year. The student council was tasked with listing the requirements for the picnic and they selected a *Classic American* theme: hamburgers, hot dogs, and beer. The party is to be an informal, evening picnic with the goal of facilitating the socialization among the students. Entertainment will be provided by a DJ who will play music selected by the students.

Table 24.1: Summary Guide to the Initiation and Planning Templates.

Section	Process	Table or Figure	Page
20.2	**Initiating Process Group**		
.1.	Project Charter	24.3	416
.2.	Identify Stakeholders	24.4	417
.3.	Stakeholder Register & Engagement	24.5	418
20.3	**Planning Process Group**		
.1.	Project Management Plan	24.6	420
.2.	Collect Requirements	24.7	421
.3.	Project Scope Statement	24.8	422
.4.	Work Breakdown Structure (WBS)	24.1	424
.5.	Define Activities	24.10	423
.6.	Milestone List		
.7.	Estimate Activities & Resources	24.11	425
.8.	Estimate Activity Durations	24.12	425
	Risks		
.9.	Risk Register	24.13	426
.10.	Risk Contingency Plan	24.14	426
	Quality		
.11.	Quality Roles & Responsibilities	24.16	428
.12.	Define Quality	24.17	428
.13.	Measure Quality	24.18	429
.14.	Assure Quality	24.19	430
.15.	Control Quality	24.20	430
.16.	Quality Management Plan	24.15	427
.17.	Human Resources Plan	24.21	431
.18.	Team	24.22	432
.19.	Stakeholders	24.23	432
.20.	Communication Management Plan	24.24	433
.22.	Analogous Cost Estimation Template	24.25	434
.23.	Parametric Cost Estimation Template	24.26	434
.24.	Three Point Cost Estimation Template	24.27	434
.25.	Bottom-Up (WBS) Estimation Template		434

Table 24.2: Summary Guide to the Executing, Monitoring & Controlling, and Closing Templates.

Section	Process	Table or Figure	Page
20.4	**Executing Process Group**		
.1.	Acquire & Develop Project Team	24.29	436
.2.	Manage Project Team	24.30	437
.3.	Distribute Information	24.32	438
.4.	Manage Stakeholder Expectations	24.33	438
20.5	**Monitoring & Controlling Process Group**		
.1.	Update Project Schedule	24.2	441
.2.	Cost and Schedule Variance Analysis	24.35	442
.3.	Change Control	24.37	444
.4.	Quality Control Measurements	24.38	445
.5.	Update Risk Register	24.39	445
.6.	Administer Procurements		445
20.6	**Closing Process Group**	24.40	446

24.2 Initiating Process Group

24.2.1 Project Charter Template

The Project Charter Template is shown in Table 24.3.

24.2.2 Identify Stakeholders Template

The Identify Stakeholders Template is shown in Table 24.4.

24.2.3 Stakeholders Register & Engagement Strategy Template

The Stakeholders Register & Engagement Strategy Template is shown in Table 24.5.

How Did We Rank the Stakeholders?

We determined the rank of the stakeholders as follows. We identified who had substantial interest in the outcome and who had substantial power to help the project manager achieve the project's goals. See chapter 7, Stakeholders.

1. *High Power and High Interest in Project Outcome.* Only one stakeholder fits this group: Dr. Rebecca Johnson, who is the Dean and the project sponsor.

Table 24.3: The Charter Template.

Project Title:	Picnic Project
Organization:	The University
Start Date:	January 10, 2015
End Date:	May 15, 2015
Project Champion:	Student Council
Description:	It is an annual tradition for the graduating class to celebrate the earning of their degrees and the Student Council plans to organize a unique graduation party for the Class of 2015.
Justification:	1) It is a school custom with benefits for the college and students. 2) The party builds lasting positive memories. The event encourages students to stay involved as alumni and builds solidarity in the class. 3) It is a reward for the students' hard work over the past four years and an opportunity for faculty and staff to appreciate this.
High Level Requirements:	A four to five hour party with food and entertainment. It will be organized on campus by the student council.
Success Criteria & Approvals:	1) High levels of participation and sign-up. (Participation thresholds approval: Student Council President) 2) Party runs smoothly. (Approval: Project Manager) 3) Follow-up survey, two days after completion of project, determines levels of satisfaction with the party. (Approval: Student council president & Project Manager)
Stakeholder List:	Executive stakeholder: Dean of students. Stakeholders: Student council president, Student class representative.
Budget: Sponsor:	$5,000. Dean of Students
Milestones:	Fundraising Complete: February 15th, 2015. Venue Selected and Approved: March 15th, 2015 Detailed Organization Plan for Logistics: April 15th, 2015 Preparation Complete: May 1st, 2015
PM: Responsibility: Authority:	Sandy Nestle. Sandy will report to Student Council President and Dean of Students during planning. Upon conclusion, PM to report project success. PM has the authority to charge students for participation; and to obtain additional funding from sponsors.
Signatures:	PM, Sandy Nestle; Dean of Students; Council President.

Table 24.4: The Identify Stakeholders Template.

Stakeholder	Interest
Dr. Rebecca Johnson	Dean of Students. Project Sponsor
James Burke	Student Council President. Project Sponsor
Jane Bedford	Head of Campus Security and Emergency Medical Services Liaison
Maria Sanchez	Director of On-Campus Catering Company
Dr. Kip Becker	Faculty member and Chair of Department
Neil Das	Student Representative. Possible project champion
Xin Li	Manager of Logistics for Venue
Julia Feinstein	IT Manager of resources for the project
DJ	Vendor who will provide entertainment

2. *High Power but Low Interest in Project Outcome* and *Low Power but High Interest in Project Outcome*: Several stakeholders fall in this group.

3. *Low Power and Low Interest in Project Outcome*: We classified Julia Feinstein in this group, as the Information Technology department is typically busy with several mission critical projects around graduation and will have low interest in the student party project. However, the project team would like to obtain some free web-based resources for the project, such as advertising.

Assessing Stakeholder Engagement

The project manager must engage all the stakeholders properly and at the correct project stage. For instance, Officer Bedford, who is head of campus security, must be engaged twice: Once at the start of the project to inform her department about the event and to determine if there would be any issues with the venue or the nature of the party; and a second time the day before the party so that she, or her staff, can be on hand during the party to check to see if there are any security issues.

The stakeholder assessment matrix is a plot that defines where the team wants the level of engagement to be for each stakeholder. This ranges from a stakeholder being unaware to a stakeholder being very supportive and, even, leading. In the case of Officer Jane Bedford, the PM has assessed the level of engagement as *Neutral*. In which case, no further engagement action needs to be taken in increasing her support for the project.

417

Table 24.5: Stakeholder Register & Engagement Strategy Template.

Stakeholder	Rank (Hi, Med, Lo)	Role	Goal
Dr. R. Johnson	High Power, High Interest	Approving Student Council's plans and signing off on them.	Guiding the student council's decisions for effective planning, anticipating obstacles, and correcting flaws in plans.
Xin Li	High Interest, Medium Power	Logistics of the venue	Making sure venue is available, sound system is working, & tech stuff is without glitches
Dr. Kip Becker	Medium Power, Medium Interest	Chair of the largest department	Participating in the event. Motivating his staff and faculty to participate in the party.
James Burke	Medium Power, High Interest	Sponsoring & funding project	Approves the scope.
Maria Sanchez	Medium Power, Medium Interest	Providing the hors d'oeuvres & refreshments	Providing good food, taking into consideration allergies, special dietary needs, etc.
Officer Jane Bedford	Medium Power, Medium Interest	Securing the safety of the event	Making sure traffic is re-routed and providing student EMTs on scene for medical emergencies.
Neil Das	Medium Power, High Interest	Communicates with students and project organizers	Acts as a project champion. Identifies requirements for project and communicates the scope to the project manager.
Julia Feinstein	Low Power, Low Interest	Provides IT support	Project requires website, *MS Project*, and email tools. Julia has these resources.

Now, however, let us review the case of the stakeholder, Dr. Kip Becker, who is the chair of the largest department with a large number of graduating students who will attend. From previous experience with college student parties, the PM has assessed that Dr. Becker's interest in the party project is *Neutral*.

Even though Dr. Becker has tentatively agreed to participate in the student graduation party, it is a good idea to engage him more closely for several reasons:

- Visibility of senior faculty is good for the image of the department and communicates commitment.

- Students typically like to take pictures with faculty and staff around the time of graduation.

- Dr. Becker is in a position to influence other faculty and staff to attend, which will help to make it successful.

- As someone who has attended many of these functions, his experience is invaluable.

The Project Manager should increase communications with Dr. Becker and convert him to *Supportive* or *Leading*. This can be accomplished by making him aware of the benefits to the department of a successful picnic, regularly reporting to him on the progress, and making him aware of any issues that arise. As an experienced department chair, Dr. Becker should have good ideas to contribute.

24.3 Planning Process Group

24.3.1 Project Management Plan Template

The Project Management Plan formally communicates the details of the project plans to all stakeholders, such as the project sponsor, company senior management, customers and the project team. The Project Management Plan Template is shown in Table 24.6. Like most plans, it is not a standalone document, it usually has links to other planning documents, which is the standard technique for avoiding duplication of information.

Scope Comments

The scope references several related documents. These are included *by reference*, which means that the content of the scope is considered to include explicitly all of requirements, conditions and goals in the referenced documents. It is as if they were actually included.[1]

It is important that scope information not be repeated, see the example in the Scope Chapter, section 8.6.2. Once the party has been planned, the core student group will receive training and guidance in the execution of the party.

24.3.2 Collect Requirements Template

The Collect Requirements Template is shown in Table 24.7.

24.3.3 Scope Statement Template

The Scope Template is shown in Table 24.8.

[1] Except, if they were included you would have duplicate information.

Table 24.6: Project Management Plan Template.

	Project: Graduation Party Picnic Project
1.	**Executive summary of project charter**, see section 24.1. Insert relevant excerpts from the charter here. Document any relevant additions to the charter.
2.	**Scope Management** See Scope Statement. See Requirements Document: Table 24.7.
3.	**WBS and Schedule** See WBS and *MS Project* Schedule Reports.
4.	**Milestones** (Preliminary: Estimated Time-frame) Fundraising Complete: February 15th, 2015 Preparation for Party Completed: Mary 15th , 2015 Completed Plan for party logistics: April 15th, 2015 Preparation for Party Completed: May 15th, 2015 Post Party Survey: May 17th, 2015
5.	**Subsidiary Plans** The following plans are included *by reference*: Schedule Management Plan Cost Management Plan Quality Management Plan Human Resource Management Plan Communications Management Plan Risk Management Plan
6.	Deployment Plan

24.3.4   The Priority Matrix Template

Table 24.9 shows the *Priority Matrix* for the picnic project. This is created during scope development, and its purpose is to establish the relative priorities between scope, cost, and schedule.

24.3.5   WBS Template

The WBS Template is shown in Figure 24.1.

24.3.6   Define Activities

The Define Activity Resources Template is shown in Table 24.10.

Table 24.7: Requirements Document (Specification) Template.

Category	Requirement	Stakeholder	Acceptance Criteria
Funding	Preliminary Funding	Dean of Students Student Council President	Sign off on the preliminary cost estimate.
Funding	Additional Funding	Students	Class representative signs-off on amount students will pay to attend.
Food	Hors d'oeuvres Dessert	Maria Sanchez Student body	To save money & make menu interesting this is planned as a "pot luck" event.
Food	Dinner	Maria Sanchez	Official contract signed off by *Completed Plan* milestone date.
Entertain-ment	Music selection Music system	DJ Student body	DJ Party Rentals Submits a signed contract.
Entertain ment	Volleyball Frisbee	Neil Das, Student body	Organized by students. Submits to PM detailed arrangements & costs.
Planning	Schedule & Budget	Sponsor & Student champion	Final Party details are formally approved by sponsors and student representatives & published on the website.
Party	Organization Committee	Student leaders assigned in charge of various activities.	A dry run meeting takes place with full participation of student activity leaders.
Party	Clean up	Student Clean up crew	No evidence of party on scene.
Satisfaction	Post-Party Survey	Sponsors will approve questions	Results of electronic survey will be provided to sponsors.

Table 24.8: Scope Statement Template.

Project: Graduation Party Picnic
Project Objective
Organize a party for graduating students on May 15th 2015 within a budget of $5000.
Deliverables
Cost Estimate
Party Plans and Logistics
Contract from Food Services for dinner
Entertainment contract for music
Party Invitations mailed formally
Post Party Survey (May 17th, 2015)
Milestones
Fundraising (February 15th)
Get a venue (March 15th, 2015)
Contract from Food Services for dinner being served (March 30th, 2015)
Entertainment contract for Music (April 5th, 2015)
Preparation for Party Completed. (May 7th, 2015)
Party completed (May 15th, 2015)
Post Party Survey (May 17th, 2015)
Techncial Requirements
DJ must be willing to accommodate a play list from students and play the "school's sports anthem song."
Catering must provide sample meals to volunteer group before final food contract is signed.
All dietary restrictions must be accommodated.
Assumptions
Student council and Dean of Students will provide some funding.
Additional funding will come from students participating in the event.
BU will provide party venue at no cost.
Limits and Exclusions
Entertainment: DJ is responsible for the audio equipment, special lighting, etc.
Food Services will provide plates, cutlery, napkins, etc.
The venue has time restriction which must be complied with.
Review of Final Deliverables
Customer and Sponsor:
Formal sign off Dr. Rebecca Johnson and James Burke.

Table 24.9: The *Priority Matrix* for the Graduation Party Picnic.

	Scope	Schedule	Cost
Constrain (Must Have)		No sacrifice on date	
Enhance (Nice to have)	Small details can be eliminated		
Accept			Some cost overrun ok

Table 24.10: Define Activities Template.

Activities

Prepare proposal for party and budget
Identify potential locations
Obtain Permission for Venue
Inform Security, Custodians
Identify Food Vendor
Select Menu
Identify music vendor (DJ)
Negotiate vendor contracts
Create Party Event Committee
Create invitations
Email invitations
Make guest list
Dry run the day before
Close all contracts
Document lessons learned
Send out survey
Identify key PM processes and complete documentation

24.3.7 Milestone List Template

Milestones occur in several sources. For example, high level project milestones are often introduced in the charter or business case, where they define strategic schedule constraints. For complex projects, more detailed milestones may also be provided, such as the end of each phase. In the picnic project, the milestones were listed in the scope. It is important to try to keep a single list of milestones so that when they change, only one document is updated. Tools such as *Microsoft Project* can print milestone reports.

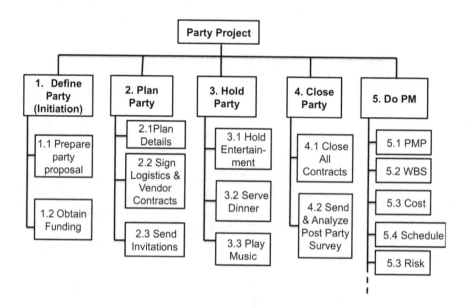

Figure 24.1: The WBS template

24.3.8   Estimate Activities & Resources Template

The Estimate Activities and Resources Template is shown in Table 24.11.

24.3.9   Estimate Activity Durations Template

The Estimate Activity Durations Template is shown in Table 24.12.

24.3.10   Risk Register Template

The Risk Register Template is shown in Table 24.13, where the first risk is that of under-age students consuming alcohol. The goal for this risk is "prevention," a much stronger category than "mitigation."

In risk prevention the goal is to move the risk completely outside the project scope. Banning alcohol consumption would do this. However, the students have selected an American theme, which includes beer, so this is not an option. Therefore, the

Table 24.11: Estimate Activities & Resources Template.

Activity	Resources		Quantity
	Type	Detail	
Create Requirements	Labor	Business Analyst	1
Estimate Funding	Labor	Cost Estimator	1
Website Development	Labor	IT specialist	1
& Invitations	Tools	Hardware & SW	1
Project Management (Including procurement)	Labor	Project Manager	1
Planning (All activities)	Labor	Student Leaders	4
Travel (Cost of identifying Food, Catering, DJ	Material	Actual travel costs	$500
Sports equipment	Material	Volleyballs, Nets, Frisbees	1
Sports Coordinator	Labor	Student	1

Table 24.12: Estimate Activity Durations Template.

Activity	Duration (days)
Create Requirements & Specifications	2
Estimate Party Funding	5
Website Development & Invitations	1
Project Management (All tasks)	8
Planning (All activities)	14
Sports Coordinator	3

risk prevention strategy is to check two IDs, which should make it difficult for underage students to consume alcohol. A student may have a fake ID, in which case a single ID check may not prevent the risk, and so would fall more in the mitigation category.

24.3.11 Risk Contingency Plan Template

The Risk Contingency Plan Template is shown in Table 24.14.

24.3.12 Quality Management Plan Template

Here, the project manager describes the roles and responsibilities of the project team, quality attributes and metrics, and the plans for quality assurance and quality control.

There are several ways to construct the Quality Management Plan (QMP). If the previous quality templates have already been developed, then the QMP need only

Table 24.13: Risk Register Template: Quantification and Risk Response Strategy.

Risk	Rating Before Risk Response H, M, L	Response Prevent, Mitigate Transfer or Accept
Alcohol consumption by under-aged attendees could cause legal liabilities	H	Prevent: Two IDs will be checked by security.
Rain will disrupt the party	M	Mitigate: Rent a backup tent to shelter the attendees
Dessert was planned as Pot-Luck. This might result in allergy, food poisoning, quality issues.	M	Transfer: Obtain Dessert from a reliable party
Sun burn, heat, insect bites, etc.	L	Accept: Develop contingency plan: Identify EMTs & post hospital numbers.
Good Risks	**Rating**	**Response** Exploit, Share, Accept
Advertise vendors on the back of the invitation card	H	Exploit. This is a good risk. It will result in a 5% pricing discount from the vendors.

Table 24.14: Risk Contingency Plan.

Risk	Rating After Risk Response H, M, L	Contingency Steps should the risk materialize
Alcohol consumption by under-aged attendees could cause legal liabilities	None	This risk was eliminated by risk analysis and response.
Rain will disrupt the party	None	The party committee will guide members into the sheltered tent area.
Dessert was planned as Pot-Luck. This might result in allergy, food poisoning, quality issues.	None	This item was outsourced to a reliable food vendor who provided desserts with clear labeling of ingredients.
Sun burn, heat, insect bites, etc.	None	Low $100 has been assigned to obtain medications from the local drug store. If serious complications arise, EMTs will be called and dial 911.

426

Table 24.15: Quality Management Plan Template.

Project: Graduation Party Picnic	
1.	**Overview:** Three metrics were identified for the project team to measure party quality: participation, engagement, and safety. Quality of food and music is tied to the engagement metric.
2.	**Quality Responsibilities and Quality Roles:** For each of the above drivers a dedicated team leader will be allocated.
3.	**Quality Assurance Approach:** Throughout the project QA will conducted. Audits of participation in the party by students and faculty will take place at key milestones.
4.	**Quality Control Approach:** Review of metrics at key milestones. On day of party, random communication with 10% participants will be conducted by the project manager or leader appointed by her.
5.	**Quality Improvement Approach:** Nothing is off limits. Walking tour of baseball park, which is nearby, and other minor tweaks to project scope will be considered to increase party attendance. On the day of the party, contingency plans will be made to increase party engagement.
6.	**Tools, Environment and Interfaces:** Website analytics, survey responses (survey monkey) will be used. Spreadsheets will be used for budgeting. Website will be used to communicate with participants.
7.	**Quality Reporting Plan:** Weekly team meetings will be used to obtain quality data.

reference the existing sub-components.[2] For a small project, the QMP can simply incorporate the sections directly. The Quality Management Plan Template is shown in Table 24.15.

24.3.13 Quality Roles and Responsibilities Template

The first step in the quality process is to identify quality roles and responsibilities, which include mentoring and coaching, auditing work products, auditing processes, and participating in quality assurance and quality control reviews. The Quality Roles and Responsibilities Template is shown in Table 24.16.

24.3.14 Define Quality Template

Here, the project manager:

[2]Again avoiding duplication of information.

427

Table 24.16: Quality Roles and Responsibilities Template.

Role	Responsibility
Project Manager	Obtain funding; manage budget and schedule. Ultimately responsible for project quality.
Sponsors	Provide funding. Additional funding will be raised from students who participate in the party or by other means.
Entertainment coordinator	Responsible for planning and coordination of sports and music.
Food & Refreshments	Responsible for coordinating the team in charge of this important activity, selecting the best vendors and ensuring timely delivery of food and refreshments.
Party Team coordinator	Responsible for planning and managing the hired & volunteer work force at the party.

Table 24.17: Define Quality Template.

Quality Goal/Attribute/Standard	Person or Entity Responsible
Participation	Project Manager
Safety	Entertainment Coordinator
Engagement on Event Day	Party Team coordinator

- Identifies the project's quality standards and expectations for customers, the parent organization, and government or industry observers.

- Defines customer and project goals, quality standards, and critical success factors

- Defines quality standards and continuous quality improvement and process innovation strategy, e.g., how team will undergo quality control training.

- Defines how organizational quality standards, such as ISO 9000 if applicable, and company policies and procedures will be used.

- Defines project management quality goals, e.g., meeting budget goals and delivering products on schedule.

The Define Quality Template is shown in Table 24.17.

Table 24.18: Measure Quality Template.

Metric	Definition
Participation	Percent of students who agree to attend the party.
Engagement	Percent of students who stay through the duration of the party.
Safety	Number of accidents and incidents playing sports at the party.

24.3.15 Measure Quality Template

The most important metrics measure product performance, project status and the acceptance criteria for deliverables. Along with identifying the metrics, the project manager defines the methods of data collection, the timeframe for conducting the measurements, and reports the results.

Examples are shown in the Measure Project Quality Template, which is shown in Table 24.18. For the party, the most important critical success factor is participation and engagement, so the RSVPs will be measured weekly by the techie and reported to the project manager.

24.3.16 Assure Quality Template

The project manager describes how the team will know if the project is achieving the established quality goals. If project quality is not acceptable, then there should be contingency plans to improve project quality. The Assure Quality Template is shown in Table 24.19.

24.3.17 Control Quality Template

Here, the project manager defines the quality tools that will be used to measure project quality and level of conformance to defined quality standards and metrics. Also, the project manager identifies those responsible for monitoring and improving project processes. The Control Quality Template is shown in Table 24.20.

24.3.18 Human Resources Plan Template

The Human Resources Plan Template is shown in Table 24.21.

24.3.19 Core Team Template

The Core Team Template is shown in Table 24.22.

Table 24.19: Assure Quality Template.

Metric	Definition
Participation	Participation is the biggest quality driver prior to the party. At each milestone, we will gather data about participation and interest. If participation is low, the party date, venue, or activities will be revised.
Engagement	Engagement is the big driver on the day of the party, and it includes quality of food and music. The project manager will gather party satisfaction and engagement data from random participants as the party is unfolding. If there are concerns, the committee will react in a timely manner. For example, if food is not satisfactory or sufficient in quantity, additional pizza will be ordered and served. Pictures taken by various participants will be shown at the party so that participants can enjoy the memories created by fellow classmates. Contingency plans will be made ahead of time for this.

Table 24.20: Control Quality Template.

Item	Action	Responsibility
Attendance	Weekly participation numbers will be monitored	Project Manager
Food	Food will be sampled before the event at the vendor for quality and taste. Preferences will be obtained ahead of time from participants (Chinese, Vegan, etc). On the day of the event, if possible, quality will tested on upon delivery.	Food and Refreshments Coordinator
Entertainment	Music quality/selection will be monitored. Playlists will be submitted ahead of time by participants. Quality of audio and music selection will be monitored by assessing participation on the dance floor.	Entertainment Coordinator
Engagement	Project Manager will randomly talk with participants about the party and gather intelligence.	Project Manager

Table 24.21: Human Resources Plan Template.

Project: Graduation Party Picnic

1. **Roles & Responsibilities:**

   - Project Manager (PM) is responsible for the success of the Party project. The PM must approve all project expenditures and communicate with the stakeholders. The team members will be responsible for timely execution of the assigned activities and the quality the work activities should meet established acceptability criteria.

   - Business Analyst (BA) is responsible for gathering requirements for the party project.

   - Student Leaders (SL) are responsbile for coordinating the various activities like entertainment, means, invitations, website and music.

   - Student Champion (SC) will communicate with students and get buy in on the party specifications.

2. **Organizational Structure:**
   All the above identified roles report the PM. The PM works with the Sponsors.

3. **Staff Acquisition:**
   The project staff will consist entirely of internal resources. There will be procurement or contracting of two functions: food, and music.

4. **Staff Release:**
   The project staff will be fully released from the project two days after the party.

5. **Training:**
   Dry run will be scheduled during the implementation phase and will be documented in the project schedule.

6. **Performance Reviews:**
   The PM will review each team member's assigned work activities at the onset of the project. Throughout the project the PM will communicate all expectations of work to be performed to the team.

7. **Regulations and Policy Compliance:**
   All BU Policies and Procedures for hiring and treatment of staff will be followed.

Table 24.22: Core Team Template.

Name	Title	Address	Email	Phone
Dr. R. Johnson	Dean of Students Project Sponsor	755 Comm Ave Room 217	rj@bu.edu	x3-3999
James Burke	Student Council President Project Sponsor	Dunce Hall Room 777	jb@bu.edu	999-3999
Jane Bedford	Head, Campus Security EMS Liaison	201 Comm Ave	bed@bu.edu	x3-4999 x3-4999
Maria Sanchez	Director, On-Campus Catering	117 Bedford St.	sz@bu.edu	x3-5999

Table 24.23: Stakeholders Template.

Stakeholder	Role	Goal
Dr. R. Johnson	Approving of the Student Council's plans and signing off on them	Guiding the student council's decisions for more effective planning and anticipating obstacles as well as correcting flaws
Dr. Kip Becker	Participating in the event.	Motivating his staff and faculty to participate in the party.
James Burke	Sponsoring and funding the project.	Approves the scope of the project.
Officer Bedford	Securing the event	Making sure traffic is rerouted, and providing student EMTs on scene for medical emergencies.

24.3.20 Stakeholders Template

The Stakeholders Template is shown in Table 24.23.

24.3.21 Communications Management Plan Template

The Communications Management Plan Template is shown in Table 24.24.

Table 24.24: Communications Management Plan Template.

Message	Description What is it about?	Audience Who is invited	Method Of comm- unication?	Frequency When & how?	Sender Who?
Kick-off Meeting	Stakeholders & Project Team discuss goals	Entire team Sponsors Stakeholders			
a) Announce- ment			Email & Phone	Once	PM
b) Minutes	Action Items		Email & Phone	Once	PM
Requirements Meeting	Identifying Party needs	Project Team Sponsors	Email & Phone	Once Once	Business Analyst
PM Meetings PM Meetings	Review Progress. Review deliverables. Update documents.	Team	Email	Every Friday at Noon	PM
Milestone Meetings	Team addresses progress on , entertainment, meals, etc.	Project Team Sponsors	Email	Each Milestone	PM
Dry Run	Meeting on site to go through all aspects of party.	Student Leaders	Email	Once	Project Champion
Completion Meeting	Administrative Closure.	Project Team	Email	Once	PM

24.3.22 Cost Estimation Templates

To estimate the cost of the picnic party, we use four methods of cost estimation: analogous, parametric, three point and bottom-up (from the WBS). All methods can be used early in the project. Even the scope statement will require a rough cost or effort estimate. Using more than one method is desirable because they check each other.

Analogous Cost Estimation Template

The project manager uses previous similar projects as a benchmark for the analogous estimate. Using experience, the project manager applies a multiplier to a previous project.

For example, suppose last year's graduation party was a formal reception and cost $10,000. The project manager could use a multiplier of 0.50 to estimate the cost

Table 24.25: Analogous Cost Estimation Template.

Previous Similar Project	Previous Project Effort / Cost	Multiplier	Current Estimate
The project manager managed a party graduation event last year. The party was formal and at a restaurant.	$10,000 party	0.5	$5,000

Table 24.26: Parametric Cost Estimation Template.

Unit of Measure Cost per student	Project Size Number of Students	Parametric Estimate
Column 1	Column 2	Column 1 * Column 2
$45	100	$45*100 = $4,500

Table 24.27: Three Cost Estimation Template.

WBS Item	Pessimistic, p (Highest) 1% Probability	Likely, l Estimate	Optimistic, o (Lowest) 1% Probability	Expected Cost $C = (p + 4*l + o)/6$
Total Cost	$7,000	$5,000	$4,000	$5,170

of this year's picnic, which is informal and a lot less complex. The Analogous Cost Estimation Template is shown in Table 24.25.

Parametric Cost Estimation Template

The Dean of Students provided the cost estimate, which is shown in the Parametric Cost Estimation Template, Table 24.26.

Three Point Cost Estimation Template

The Three Point Method, also called the PERT method, is described in detail in the chapter on cost, Chapter 10. The Three Point Cost Estimation Template is shown in Table 24.27.

24.3.23 Bottom-Up (WBS) Cost Estimation Template

In the bottom-up method you would typically add up the effort associated with all the work packages in the WBS. This estimate can be performed when the WBS has been created. For the picnic, we developed a detailed bottom-up estimate from the WBS, which can be found in the *Microsoft Project* Tutorial chapter.

Table 24.28: Detailed Activity Cost Estimate.

Activity Cost Estimate				
WBS ID	**Start Date**		**End Date**	
12.1.6	3/15/2014		4/20/2014	
	Description: Select Food Vendors			
Total Cost	**$275**			
Labor	Personnel Project Leader	Cost per hour $25	Hours 2	Total $50
Materials	Type Food Samples	Cost per unit $10	Quantity $7.50	Total $75
Costs	Item Taxi to Vendors	Description Three vendors will be visited to check the menu and sample the food.		Total $150

Note: All of the estimates are in the range $4,000 to $5,000, which is within the budget established by the sponsor.

Detailed Activity Cost Template

Estimating costs requires consideration of expenses other than human labor. The categories of expenses are:

Human	Hourly Rate	Analyst, programmer
Materials	Cost per unit	Party tent, chair
Cost	Varies per unit	Travel expense, taxi

Table 24.28 shows an example of a detailed cost estimate for an individual activity. The costs for all activities would be rolled up to constitute the bottom-up WBS cost estimate.

24.4 Executing Process Group

The executing process group contains the processes required to implement the project. The key activities conducted here are Acquiring and Developing the Project Team, Managing the Project Team, Distributing Information, and Managing Stakeholder Expectations.

Table 24.29: Staffing Assignments for the picnic project.

Date	Role	Resource	Commitment
2/10/2015	Student Leader	Jason Smith	1, Full time
2/10/2015	Business Analyst	Lisa Smith John Jones	2 Analysts, Half time
2/10/2015	Techie	Jay Bacaram Margaret Dell	2 Analysts, Half time

24.4.1   Acquire & Develop Project Team

When the project was scheduled, a project resource plan was created to ensure that student leaders and volunteers would be available to perform the required tasks. During the execution phase, the project manager must ensure that the identified resources are actually available.

An important issue that tends to arise is that some of the staff might need training. The techie position is critical and an effort was made to hire a contractor who was very knowledgeable in all aspects of the web development task: email marketing, analytics, creating a website, and using *Microsoft Project*.

The PM consults the resource plan, which lists the required staff, and conducts a skills assessment. The PM then acquires the appropriate staff, assigns them to tasks such as entertainment leader and food services leader, and clarifies their responsibilities. A project staffing assignment form can be completed, such as the one shown in Table 24.29.

24.4.2   Manage Project Team

Once the project manager has acquired the team, the important ongoing task is to help the individual members of the team to improve. This can be accomplished by having each member of the team conduct a self-assessment. The project manager asks each team member to comment on their own individual performance, as well as their perspective on how the team is functioning. The project manager can then review these comments and suggest ways that the team member might improve.

The sample template shown in Table 24.30 can be used to improve the competency of the individual team members, to assess team performance, and to encourage team cohesion.

A review of the self-assessments can be integrated into the project manager's own observations. Individual extremes can be smoothed out and an honest assessment

Table 24.30: Self-Assessment of team members.

Self Assessments:
Name of the Team Member:
Individual Assessment: Provide honest comments on: Attendance, communication, ability to listen, accepting responsibility, exceeding expectations, solving problems, making sure that team members can understand the solution you are working on, and whether you are completing work on schedule.

Team Assessment:
Comment on whether your team is:
    Feeling Empowered.
    Functioning in a collective manner or are some team members
       working independently.
    Spirit of Cooperation.
    Conflict Resolution and ability to handle differences of opinion.
    Balancing the workload evenly amongst all.
    Communication as a team.
    Driven to deliver on schedule.
    Motivated.

Table 24.31: The PM's assessment of an individual team member.

Name of the Team Member: Jason Smith **Assessment Date:** 3/12/2015
Comments: You have not missed any meetings. That is outstanding dedication to the project. Your communication ability is outstanding; an essential skill for a lead. You have accepted several responsibilities that have abruptly come along. Great at solving problems and ensuring your team understands your approach. Exceptional performance!

can be developed. The overall assessment of the individual team members should be communicated promptly at a private meeting. See Table 24.31. The assessment of the team as a whole should be communicated at a staff meeting.

If it appears that the team is not functioning well, the project manager will need to establish well-defined procedures and identify clear expectations for the team as a whole. Further, the project manager should explain the consequences of failing to follow procedures and of not meeting established goals.

24.4.3 Distribute Information

The communication plan identifies all of the major deliverables, as well as *how they are to be distributed* to team members and stakeholders. Since the team is using

Table 24.32: The "Who does what, when?" report.

Resource Name	Task	Date
Techie	Create Website for Party	2/26/2015
Techie	Create custom invitations	3/31/2015

Table 24.33: The Stakeholder Issues Log for the picnic project.

Stakeholder Issues Log
Change Request: Picnic Party date change Date: 3/30/2015
PM Plan Updates: The entire plan needs to be updated and contract modifications need to be approved and signed by all stakeholders and vendors.
Project Document Updates: Update MS Project documentation and other templates.
Comments: Need to talk with all three stakeholders immediately!
Resolution Date: 4/5/2013

Microsoft Project, one way to accomplish the distribution is to give password access to the various stakeholders.

Project contains several built-in reports that can be developed and distributed, and one that is popular is, "Who does what, when?" That report shows the weekly assignments and it can be distributed to all team members. An example of the "Who does what, when?" report is shown in Table 24.32.

24.4.4   Manage Stakeholder Expectations

This requires the project manager to work with all stakeholders to meet or exceed their expectations, and to handle issues as they arise. In the case of the party project, the project manager must communicate with stakeholders about issues stemming from cost over-runs and the change of the date of the party. Stakeholders will be extremely disappointed if the date changed is not immediately communicated to them.

After communication with stakeholders, the project manager should complete an issue log, such as the one shown in Table 24.33.

24.5 Monitoring and Controlling Process Group

Monitoring and controlling the project consists of verifying deliverables; determining cost and schedule variances; responding to threats and opportunities; managing changes and using the change control procedures; and controlling procurement.

Monitoring is always approached at a particular point in time. At any point, there are completed tasks, tasks in process and pending tasks (not started). The actual status of tasks must be compared to what the plan says should be happening at that time. Also, the project manager must keep the project plan up to date.

A specific amount of funds have been spent from the budget, usually in the form of invoices received. The actual expenditures must be compared to the planned expenditures.

Therefore, we will assume that the picnic project has started and we have completed the "Planning Complete" milestone, which was due on April 30th, 2015. Email invitations were sent out and RSVPs have started coming back. A substantial amount of the planning is complete and contracts for food and entertainment have been agreed to and signed, so they will be hard to change.

At this time, the project manager observes that several schedule changes have occurred:

- The task "Obtain Funding" took two more days than planned.

- "Select Menu" took three more days than planned.

- "Identify Food Vendor" completed eight days earlier than planned.

- "Identity Music Vendor (DJ)" took six more days than planned.

- "Vendor Contracts" finished two days earlier than planned.

Also, there were variations associated with the costs. As it turned out, Food Services and Entertainment was more expensive than projected because it was the time of many convocations in the city when food services are in demand. Several hundred events take place in the in the month of May as many thousands of students graduate from local colleges. The caterer also wanted a large deposit of money up front.

The date was constrained because BU students tend to leave the city after graduation, so there was no flexibility in moving the picnic date. Also food quality could not be sacrificed, as the objective was to have a memorable event.

439

At this point the project manager should consult the priority matrix in the scope. We assume that Table 24.34 is the priority matrix for the picnic project. It says that the most important factor is the schedule (before graduation). After holding to the schedule, the project manager must attempt to enhance the performance (food and entertainment). Finally, of least importance is the cost.[3]

Table 24.34: The *Priority Matrix* for the picnic project.

	Scope	Schedule	Cost
Constrain		■	
Enhance	■		
Accept			■

The date is constrained by graduation and food quality cannot be sacrificed, so the project manager must accept the cost overrun. The stakeholders may not like the idea, but this is what was established when the requirements were developed and documented in the priority matrix, which is in the scope.

The following sections detail the typical sorts of analyses that might be conducted by the project manager.

24.5.1 Update Project Schedule

We use *Microsoft Project 2013* throughout this case study.[4] The project manager updated the picnic party schedule:

- The project manager first set the baseline (see *Project* Tutorial).

- The project manager set the Status Update date to Thu 4/30/2015 (the current date) and updated all tasks as complete. The command is: Project → Status Date.

- The tasks were updated to 100% complete by clicking the Update Project icon. These steps are illustrated in Figure 24.2.

[3]Which does not mean that it is not important, only less so than the schedule and scope.

Since the duration and effort of some tasks were different from the baseline, the project manager updated them individually using the command: Task → Mark on Track, and the selected Update Task.

[4]For more details on *Microsoft Project*, see the tutorial in Chapter 26.

We illustrate how to enter that the vendor contract negotiation completed ahead of schedule by 2 days in Figure 24.3. The task duration was 2 days instead of the planned duration of 4 days.

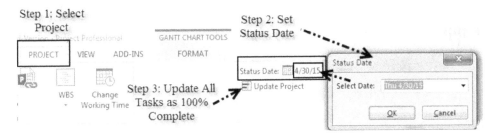

Figure 24.2: Updating the project tasks rapidly to the status date.

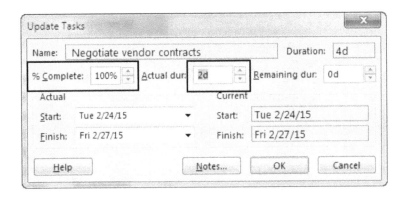

Figure 24.3: Individually updating tasks with a change in duration (variance).

24.5.2 Cost and Schedule Variance Analysis

The project manager uses variance analysis reports, and the scheduling software's cost and schedule reports, to obtain a snapshot of the project status.[5] Figure 24.4 shows a cost variance analysis report. The Actual Cost is higher than expected, due to the reasons explained earlier; however, the project is on schedule.[6]

Next, the project manager analyzed the work remaining, which is shown in Figure 24.5. The majority of the remaining work is assigned to event day coordinators, the student leaders and the volunteer team. Only the student leaders are paid, so that is the only task on which there is an opportunity to reduce costs in the near future.

The percent Work Complete stands at 67%; the Remaining Work is 164 hours; and the Actual Work Completed is 327 hours.

The project manager has two options to deal with the cost overrun: Raise more

[5] Earned Value calculations can be done more easily, and in more detail, using a spreadsheet. However, *Project* can provide a quick snapshot of the status, which can be valuable.

[6] Remember, the Earned Value calculation uses cumulative costs.

441

Figure 24.4: Cost variance analysis.

funds (perhaps from sponsors) or spend less on the remaining tasks. The costs associated with the remaining activities are primarily the payments to student leaders and event day coordinators. The project manager decided to explore the possibility of saving money on staff by studying the cost data in the resource sheet, which is shown in Table 24.35.

Table 24.35: The Resource Cost Sheet for the picnic project.

Name	Actual Work (hours)	Actual Cost	Standard Rate /hour
PM	41.87	$1,046.67	$25.00
Volunteer Team	85.33	$0.00	$0.00
Student Leaders	117.78	$1,766.67	$15.00
Publicity Coordinator	19.00	$285.00	$15.00
Picnic Event Day Coordinators	0.00	$0.00	$0.00
Dean of Students	5.60	$0.00	$0.00
Student Council President	5.60	$0.00	$0.00
Faculty Chairman	0.00	$0.00	$0.00
Techie	52.33	$1,046.67	$20.00
Dumpster	0.00	$0.00	$50.00
PM @ 5%	0.00	$0.00	$0.00

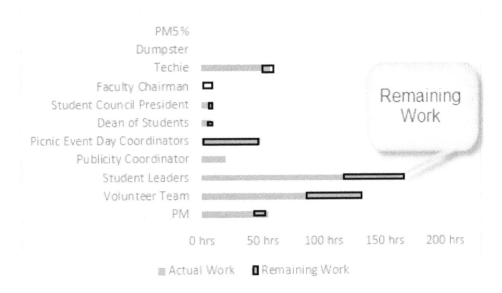

Figure 24.5: Remaining work on the picnic project.

Examining the resource cost sheet shows that the project manager has several options: First, voluntary student leaders might be hired to manage the project. Second, student leaders could be asked to work some hours as volunteers. Finally, the techie, who was hired as a consultant, might be replaced with someone from the IT department to take over the IT tasks for less money. Any decision needs to be made quickly before the costs are spent. The project manager documented the overrun by completing the template shown in Table 24.36.

Table 24.36: Variance Analysis and Work Performance Results.

Project Title:	**Picnic Project**	Prepared:	**5/20/2015**
Planned Result	Actual Result for Schedule	Variance	
$2,948	$4,145	$1,197	
Root Causes:			
#1	Catering expensive		
#2	Techie & leaders organizing the event were expensive.		
Response:			
#1	Consider Volunteers		
#2	Substitute IT staff for techie		

24.5.3   Change Control

If a change is proposed, it should first be analyzed to determine the impact on the scope, cost and schedule. The project manager can perform a variance analysis to estimate how significant the impact of the change will be. The change is submitted to the Change Control Board (CCB), and if approved, the project manager creates a new baseline and updates all project documentation.

An example of a Proposed Change Form is shown in Table 24.37.

Table 24.37: Proposed Change Form for the picnic project.

Project Title:	**Picnic Project**	Prepared:	**5/20/2015**
Person Requesting:	Project Manager	Change ID:	1001

Category of Change:			
☐ Scope	☐ Quality	☐ Requirements	
☐ Cost	☐ Schedule	☐ Documents	

Detailed Description of Proposed Change: Invest in a dinner to invite student volunteers. Seeking $300 for the dinner meeting.

Justification for Proposed Change: Project budget is slipping and we will benefit from more volunteers.

Impacts of Change: Scope: Description: N/A	☐ Increase	☐ Decrease	☐ Modify
Quality: Description: N/A	☐ Increase	☐ Decrease	☐ Modify
Requirements: Description: N/A	☐ Increase	☐ Decrease	☐ Modify
Cost: Description: N/A	☐ Increase	☐ Decrease	☐ Modify
Schedule	☐ Increase	☐ Decrease	☐ Modify

Description: At the dinner meeting we will motivate the volunteers to join the project, bring them up to speed, and explain their roles and responsibilities.

Justification: If the volunteer pool increases, costs will go down.

Disposition:	☐ Approve	☐ Defer	☐ Reject

Change Control Board Signatures:			
Name	Role	Signature	Date
Dr. Rebecca Johnson	Dean of Students		4/1/2015
James Burke	Student Council President		4/1/2015

24.5.4 Quality Control Measurements

Table 24.38 shows quality control measurements for the picnic project. The most important critical success factor was the percentage of students returning RSVPs and this was constantly measured and discussed at staff meetings.

Table 24.38: Quality Control measurements for the picnic project.

Planned Result	Actual Result	Variance
RSVPs by milestone date:		
50% RSVPs	10% RSVPs	40% students not signed up.
Root Cause:		
Many students are leaving upon graduation. Also they want to be with their parents & family who are visiting from far away.		
Planned Response:		
Communicate venue planning to see if an earlier date is available immediately after final exams.		

24.5.5 Update Risk Register

Table 24.39 shows the updates to the risk register. The "traffic light" indicator summarizes the status of each risk. Red: serious risk and needs to be dealt with immediately; Orange: risk carefully monitored; Green: risk not a concern.

Table 24.39: Risk Register Updates.

Risk ID	Risk	Response	Resource Responsible for Mitigation	Current Status Traffic Light
1	New Risk: Low RSVPs	Party date cannot be after convocation	Student Leader	Red
2	New Risk: Resource Costs high	Try to get volunteers for PM tasks	Student Leader	Orange

24.5.6 Administer Procurements

The project manager paid close attention to the food and entertainment vendors to ensure that they met their formal deliverables and performed according to the contract. Contract information and deliverables were documented in the Records Management System.

The contract required the DJ to inspect the lights and power sources. The project manager audited the DJ's activities to ensure that these inspections took place. When the project manager was unavailable, a student volunteer was assigned. The project manager fulfilled the Dumpster contract by paying the deposit up front.

When the student volunteers audited the menu, they discovered the vendor had made changes that eliminated the vegetarian and vegan food. The project manager called the food vendor and pointed out that these items had been contractually specified. The vendor agreed to add the vegetarian and vegan food.

It was proposed to move the picnic to before graduation, which required updates to the contracts. The Change Control System (CCS) was used to make formal changes and, after discussion, the CCS Board approved the date change and the project manager re-negotiated the vendors contracts.

24.6   Closing Process Group

A major goal of the closing phase is to document lessons learned, which is more effective if they are collected as the project proceeds. Therefore, at the regularly scheduled staff meetings, the picnic project manager monitored the project's lessons and filled out the lessons learned template in Table 24.40,

Table 24.40: Lessons learned from the picnic project.

Phase	What Worked?	What Did not Work?	Lessons for Next Project
Initiation	Good meeting with two key sponsors.	Failed to connect with faculty stakeholder early on.	Build proactively on stakeholder communication.
Planning	Good project planning by team.	Did not communicate well with students about menu preferences.	Early on, email all students asking for menu preferences.
Planning		Did not communicate well with leadership about party date	Early on, discuss party date with student leaders.
Monitoring & Control	Schedule Tracking.	Cost Overrun.	Techie expense was high. Should have planned more options.

Part V

Knowledge Areas, Process Groups, and Processes

25

KNOWLEDGE AREAS, PROCESS GROUPS, AND PROCESSES

> When one has finished building one's house, one suddenly realizes
> that in the process one has learned something that one really
> needed to know in the worst way —before one began!
>
> *Friedrich Nietzsche*

The major components of project management are: Phases, Process Groups, Processes, and Knowledge Areas. In this chapter, we briefly describe these components and the interactions between them.

Each process produces deliverables. The expertise in the knowledge area is the skills, tools and techniques that a project manager needs to produce the deliverables. Therefore, the knowledge areas focus on the technical aspects of actually producing the deliverables. Processes are associated with both *knowledge areas* and *process groups*, and their relationships are shown in Table 25.1.

25.1   The Process Groups

If you want to build a ship, don't drum up people together to collect wood, but rather teach them to long for the endless immensity of the sea.

Antoine de Saint-Exupery

The PMBOK does not define the process group, it merely says that the processes are combined into five process groups. For our purposes, a process group is a logical grouping of the project management processes.

The process groups are inter-dependent and are performed in the same sequence on each project. Many of these dependencies are intuitive; for example, you cannot rank risks in order of importance unless you have identified them first.[1]

There are five process groups:

1. *Initiating Process Group*

   The purpose of this process group is to charter the project and to identify the stakeholders. The *initiating* process authorizes a new project, the start of a phase of a multi-phase project, or the re-start of a halted project. This is also where a project is divided into phases and large projects into sub-projects.[2] There are only two processes in this group: *Develop Project Charter* and *Identify Stakeholders*.

2. *Planning Process Group*

   The *planning* process group is the largest group and is the heart and soul of project planning. This process group defines the action plan, or roadmap, for the entire project. The processes in this group include defining and refining the scope, developing the project management plan, and identifying and scheduling all project activities. Many planning processes interact and, often, can be worked on concurrently. For example, *quality planning, risk management planning*, and *human resource planning* can all be done concurrently. Changes to a project are inevitable and the planning processes allow for revisiting and re-planning one or more processes.

3. *Executing Process Group*

   This is where the work on the project actually occurs and, therefore, the *executing* process group dominates the work and the expenditure of funds. The key project management activities include acquiring and developing

[1] There are still some fuzzy areas, however. The PM-BOK specifies that resources (people and materials) be identified before the activity durations are estimated. While desirable, we frequently have to estimate costs without having a list of people available.

[2] Note: A significant portion of *initiating* is often accomplished outside the project, e.g., a project may be created and authorized by the company or the program office, often as part of the portfolio management process.

the project team, generally coordinating people and resources, and getting the work completed on schedule and within budget. As work proceeds and the project is refined, other aspects of the project manager's job include distributing information, managing stakeholder expectations, and managing quality.[3]

4. *Monitoring and Controlling Process Group*

   In this group the project manager tracks, reviews, and regulates the performance. The project manager identifies required changes, monitors and controls the cost, schedule, and risks, and manages any variances to the plan.

5. *Closing Process Group*

   The *closing* processes are those performed to formally terminate all activities of a project.[4] The most important activity is to obtain acceptance of the project by customers, sponsors, or stakeholders. These processes may also be used to close a canceled project.

25.2 Processes

To live means to finesse the processes to which one is subjugated.

Bertolt Brecht

The PMBOK has changed significantly with each new edition. In the 5th edition, *Stakeholder Management* became an entirely new knowledge area, while in the 4th edition, *Integration Management* changed drastically.[5] The PMBOK defines a process as follows:

> *A process is a set of interrelated actions and activities performed to achieve a pre-specified product, result, or service. Each process is characterized by its inputs, the tools and techniques that can be applied, and the resulting outputs.*

For example, *Develop Project Charter* is a process. It is member of the *Initiating* process group and the *Integration Management* knowledge area. More informally, a process is a project management step that helps you complete your project successfully. Processes fall into one of two major categories:

- *Project management processes:* These are selected, tailored, and followed to ensure a smooth and effective flow of work throughout the life of the project.

[3] Note that we are concerned here with managing the project, not doing the project. The project manager does not actually do the work.

[4] Or phase of a multi-phase project.

[5] The continuing changes to *Integration* suggest that PMI still hasn't quite figured out this knowledge area.

451

- *Product oriented processes:* These make up the product life cycle and vary by application domain, i.e., construction, information technology, defense, pharmaceutical, entertainment, etc.

Processes have inputs, tools and techniques, and outputs. As an example, we will focus on the process named *Identify Risks.* Before the project team can begin to identify the risks that may arise, they must have access to key information and data, which are the *inputs.* The inputs to *Identify Risks* consist of examples of risks from historical projects and templates for their development. Risks may also exist as outputs from previous work on the current project. For example, risks might have been identified in the *Define Scope* process.

Formally, the *Identify Risks* process requires the following inputs: Risk Management Plan, Project Management Plan, Cost and Schedule Management Plans, Scope Baseline, Organizational Process Assets, and Enterprise Environmental Factors.

The project team analyzes all of the above information and creates a *Risk Register,* which is the output for this process, and consists of a list of risks that the team thinks might occur during the execution of the project.

Since developing and assessing the impact of risks is a creative process, the team uses a variety of tools and techniques to assist in the analysis. These might include interviewing stakeholders who might have experience on similar projects, brainstorming, and Delphi techniques. Historical checklists from previous projects also help to identify risks and create the risk register.

25.3 The Knowledge Areas

> **If a man empties his purse into his head no one can take it away from him.**
> **An investment in knowledge always pays the best interest.**
>
> *Benjamin Franklin*

The PMBOK defines knowledge as understanding a process, practice, or technique, or how to use a tool. Each *Knowledge Area* is an identified skill of project management, defined by its knowledge requirements and described in terms of its processes, practices, inputs, outputs, tools, and techniques.

[6]In the PMBOK, all of the *Knowledge Area* titles have the word, *Project* in front of them, e.g., *Project Integration Management,* which seems redundant.

The *Knowledge Areas* are:[6]

1. Integration Management

2. Scope Management

3. Schedule Management

4. Cost Management

5. Quality Management

6. Resource Management

7. Communications Management

8. Risk Management

9. Procurement Management

10. Stakeholder Management

The relations between *Knowledge Areas*, *Process Groups*, and the individual *Processes* are shown in Tables 25.1 and 25.2.

In the PMBOK, the Knowledge Areas are numbered starting with *4. Project Integration Management*. This is so that the first process can be numbered, *4.1 Develop Project Charter* and it can be found in section *4.1* in Chapter 4 of the PMBOK.

Table 25.1: The relation between Project Management *Process Groups, Knowledge Areas* and *Processes*. Page 1 of 2.

Knowledge Areas	Process Groups				
	Initiating	Planning	Executing	Monitoring and Controlling	Closing
Project Integration Management	Develop Project Charter	Develop Project Management Plan	Direct and Manage Project Work	Monitor and Control Project Work	Close Project or Phase
			Manage Project Knowledge	Perform Integrated Change Control	
Project Scope Management		Plan Scope Management		Validate Scope	
		Collect Requirements		Control Scope	
		Define Scope			
		Create WBS			
Project Schedule Management		Plan Schedule Management		Control Schedule	
		Define Activities			
		Sequence Activities			
		Estimate Activity Durations			
		Develop Schedule			
Project Cost Management		Plan Cost Management		Control Costs	
		Estimate Costs			
		Determine Budget			

Table 25.2: The relation between Project Management *Process Groups, Knowledge Areas* and *Processes*. Page 2 of 2.

Knowledge Areas	Process Groups				
	Initiating	Planning	Executing	Monitoring and Controlling	Closing
Project Quality Management		Plan Quality Management	Manage Quality	Control Quality	
Project Resource Management		Plan Resource Management	Acquire Resources	Control Resources	
		Estimate Activity Resources	Develop Team		
			Manage Team		
Project Communications Management		Plan Communications Management	Manage Communications	Monitor Communications	
Project Risk Management		Plan Risk Management	Implement Risk Responses	Monitor Risks	
		Identify Risks			
		Perform Qualitative Risk Analysis			
		Perform Quantitative Risk Analysis			
		Plan Risk Responses			
Project Procurement Management		Plan Procurement Management	Conduct Procurements	Control Procurements	
Project Stakeholder Management	Identify Stakeholders	Plan Stakeholder Management	Manage Stakeholder Engagement	Monitor Stakeholder Engagement	

25.4 Notes on the PMBOK 6th Edition

The first thing to understand about the 6th edition is that it actually consists of two documents:

1. *The 6th Edition:* This is the updated (6th) edition of the PMBOK.

2. *The Standard for Project Management:* This is a new international standard for project management approved by the American National Standards Institute (ANSI): ANSI/PMI 99-001-2017.

The document includes the ANSI standard, which, like all standards, is open and freely available.[7] Since there are now two documents, it is worth quoting the ANSI standard on how the documents differ.

- The ANSI standard "serves as the foundation and framework" for the 6th edition of the PMBOK.

- The PMBOK "expands on the standard by providing more in-depth description of the context, environment and influences on project management. The PMBOK also "provides project management processes inputs and outputs, identifies tools and techniques, and discusses key concepts and emerging trends associated with each Knowledge Area."

The PMBOK describes the knowledge within the project management profession and is not a methodology, but a foundation upon which methodologies can be built. The PMBOK also explicitly references other documents and standards, such as PMI's *Code of Ethics and Professional Conduct.* [7]

The significant changes in the PMBOK 6th edition are:

- There is a new chapter on project manager's role, which includes PMI's Talent Triangle.[8]

- The number of processes changed, e.g., *Close Procurements* was eliminated from the *Closing* process group and *Close Project or Phase* was added to the *Integration* process group. *Manage Project Knowledge* was added to the *Integration* process group.

- The names of processes were changed, e.g., several processes names were changed from "control" to "monitor," e.g., *Communications, Risks,* and *Stakeholder Engagement* were all changed from *Control* to *Monitor. Perform Quality Assurance* was changed to *Manage Quality.*

[7] The interesting question will now be, If everything is in the ANSI standard, why do we need the PMBOK?

[8] This was covered in Chapter 2.

456

- The *Time Management* knowledge area was renamed *Schedule Management* and the process *Estimate Activity Resources* was moved to *Resource Management*.

- New deliverables were added, e.g., the *Project Benefits Management Plan*, which describes how the project benefits will be delivered.

- *Agile Project Management:* Each process now contains a section on how it is affected by, and can be adapted for, agile project management.

- The *Human Resources* Knowledge Area has been renamed Resources.

- Several types of project structures were added: Organic, Virtual, Hybrid, and PMO.

- There is a new section on the project manager's skills: *Technical Skills, Leadership Skills, and Strategic and Business Skills.*

There are some interesting paragraphs, at least to us:

- The PMBOK still insists on using non-scientific, totally non-standard notations in equations. The PMBOK uses multiple letter combinations for variables, e.g., the PERT equations use tM for the most likely value, tO for the optimistic value, etc. This is confusing.[9]

- *5.2 Collect Requirements:* "The PMBOK does not specifically address product requirements since those are industry specific." Not much help there.

- *6 On Demand Scheduling:* This is totally oriented to manufacturing, non-project, systems.

- *6.6.2 Burn Down Chart:* This is in the schedule section, not the cost section.

---

[9]And also leads to ugly equations.

Part VI

Microsoft Project® Tutorial

26

MICROSOFT PROJECT TUTORIAL

*Software is like entropy. It is difficult to grasp, weighs nothing,
and obeys the second law of thermodynamics;
i.e. it always increases.*

Norman Ralph Augustine

In this chapter, we present a tutorial in the use of *Microsoft Project®*. We implement
the Graduation Picnic Project described in Chapter 24. [1]

26.1   Start Project

Open *Microsoft Project 2013*. To do that, click the "Start" button on the task bar,
click "Programs" and then "Microsoft Office Project 2013." You will see the Main
Project Window—see Figure 26.1.

On the Main Project Window, you will see various templates and on the left side of
the screen you have the opportunity to open recent projects. On the right side of
the screen are icons. Select "Blank Project" and you will see The Main Task Window
(Figure 26.1).

The "Quick Access Toolbar" is at the very top and is a place for you to add short
cuts to your frequently used functions. For example, you will see an icon for File

[1] In this chapter, we follow
the *Microsoft Project* notation,
which uses the term *task*.
Previously, we have followed
standard project management
vocabulary by using the term
activity.

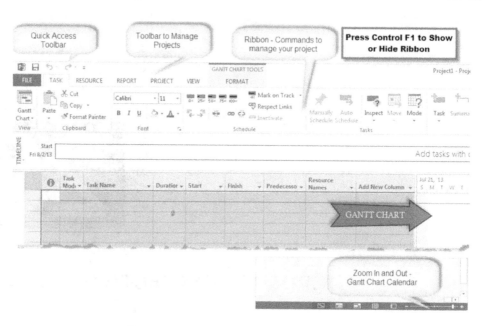

Figure 26.1: The *Project* Main Window.

Save.[2] Two other icons, there by default, are arrows for "Redo" and "Undo." These have short cuts of Control-Z and Control-W and give you a chance to cancel any changes you made or to reapply them. These are very useful options.[3]

You should also see the "Toolbar" with menus such as "Task," "Resource" and "View." When you click on a menu option, you will see additional menus. For example, the "Scroll to Task" icon is in the "Task" menu. This is a useful feature that is frequently asked for by students: It scrolls the Gantt time scale and shows the bar for the task you select. The Report menu option is new in *Project 2013*.

If you want more room on your screen, you can collapse the Ribbon. To do that, right mouse click anywhere and select the "Collapse Ribbon" option. Or you can use the "Control F1" command. To see the Ribbon again, hover over the menu bar at the top and uncheck "Collapse Ribbon." The Ribbon automatically adjusts itself based on the width of your window.

26.2 Change Project Settings

Before you get going with *Project*, there are two settings you may want to change:

---

[2] Frequent saving is even more important in *Project* than in other programs.

[3] Don't be afraid to click on buttons and make changes while you are learning—you can usually undo any ghastly mistakes. But not always.

1. *Setting up Project Options*: Click on "File" and then select "Options." Here, you can change the calendar date format, the currency, the project start and end dates, the number of work hours per day or per week, the week's start day, the language, and more exotic options such as the cloud storage location. You may want to change the default storage location to your own computer, instead of "Microsoft Skydrive."

2. *Auto Schedule vs. Manual Schedule*: The most important option that you should change is to "Auto Schedule."

Before you start entering data into *Project*, you should change the default setting of the scheduling engine to *Auto Schedule*.[4] When a new task is inserted, say with duration of two days, the project finish date is updated automatically by two days.[5]

The other option is *Manual Schedule*, which can be viewed as "do-it-yourself scheduling." When you insert new tasks, they will not impact the schedule, you have to manually insert task start and end dates. Manually scheduled tasks have unique indicators and the task bar indicates how the task is scheduled.

Especially for beginners, it is much easier to understand *Project* when tasks are automatically scheduled. Therefore, we strongly recommend changing the default to *Auto Schedule* as shown in Figure 26.2.

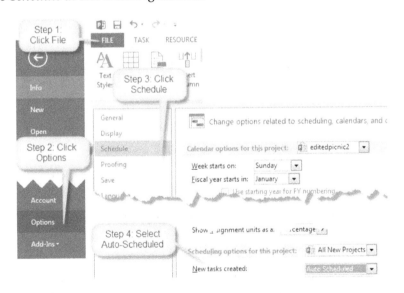

Figure 26.2: Changing the Default Scheduling Setting.

[4] In earlier versions of *Project*, the scheduling engine defaulted to scheduling project dates automatically.

[5] Also, dependent tasks dates are adjusted appropriately with new start and finish dates.

463

26.3 Enter Project Information

You are now ready to start entering your project data. One of the first things to do is to select a name for your project and save it with an appropriate file name, e.g., "Picnic Project-1."[6] Next, you set the start date and your scheduling preference: either forward from the "Start Date" or backward from the "Finish Date."[7]

To set the project start date, click the "Project" menu option in the Ribbon. Then select the "Project Information" option (see Figure 26.3). In this chapter we will indicate such commands by: Select Project → Project Information.

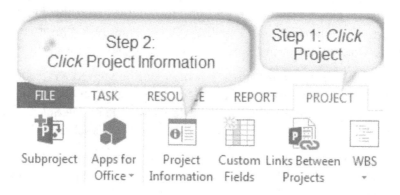

Figure 26.3: Setting the project Start Date.

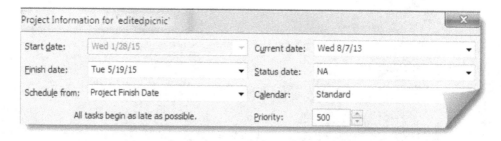

Figure 26.4: Scheduling from the project Finish Date.

[6]We encourage you to use lots of version numbers as you progress (-1, -2, etc.) so as not to lose your work.

[7]For beginners, we recommend selecting forward from the "Start Date."

Notice that the default project start date is the current date. We changed it to January 1, 2015, which is when we wish to start working on the project.

You have the option to schedule your project forward from the "Start Date" or backward from the "Finish Date. In our example, we have a specific end date in mind: The picnic is to be held before graduation in the middle of May. Therefore, we entered the project "Finish Date" as 5/19/15, as shown in Figure 26.4. We also selected "Schedule from: Project Finish Date."

26.4 Enter the Tasks

Before entering tasks, you must already have developed a work breakdown structure (WBS). Since we already have a WBS for the picnic from the project plan templates (Chapter 24), we will use that and proceed to enter the key tasks into the default Gantt View window.

As illustrated in Figure 26.1, the main project window consists of the Gantt chart calendar and a spreadsheet-like entry table. A split bar separates the entry table on the left from the Gantt chart form on the right. You can move this bar to make more or less room for the Gantt chart.

Use the entry table to enter the Picnic Project task information shown in Table 26.1 by simply typing the names of the tasks into the box. You can also import your tasks from Excel or copy and paste them from just about any other source document. Click on the "Task" menu option in the ribbon and enter the tasks shown in Table 26.1.

The information in Table 26.1 is interpreted as follows: In the first column, *Project* has assigned the unique ID = 12 to the task named "Negotiate vendor contracts." The second column contains the "Duration" of Task 12, which is estimated at 4 days. The third column contains the predecessors and Task #12 has two of them: Tasks #10 and #11.[8] Tasks with duration of zero are milestones and have no predecessors, e.g., "Charter & Funding Complete."

We have also entered a summary task for the entire project, called "Party Project," which is the top level of the WBS tree. In addition, we have included activity tasks that will be designated as lower level subtasks. Later, we will show how to indent these lower-level tasks and create subtasks, so that the structure will be more understandable.

[8]Remember, this means that Task #12 cannot start until both #10 and #11 are complete.

465

Table 26.1: Tasks, their ID, durations and predecessors.

Task ID	Task Name	Duration (days)	Predecessors (ID from col 1)
3	Prepare proposal for party and budget	5	
4	Obtain Funding for party	5	3
	Charter & Funding Complete	0	
6	Identify potential locations	5	4
7	Obtain Permission for Venue	2	6
8	Inform Security & confirm venue	1	7
	Venue Obtained	0	
9	Identify Food Vendor	30	8
10	Select Menu for the Party	3.75	9
11	Identify music vendor (DJ)	1	8
12	Negotiate vendor contracts	4	11, 10
13	Create Party Event Committee	1	9
14	Create invitations	1	13
15	Email invitations	2	14
	Party Planning Completed	0	
16	Dry Run for the Picnic 1	1	15
18	Manage the Party	1	16
	Party Completed	0	
33	Close all Contracts	1	29
34	Send out survey	1	29
24	Identify key PM processes & IS Needs	20	
25	Complete & Maintain PM templates	60	24
26	Implement & Maintain Project IS	30	24
21	Document lessons learned	0.5	26, 34

26.5 Creating Summary Tasks and Subtasks

A summary task is made up of two or more lower level tasks, which are called subtasks. To create subtasks:

1. Select the tasks you want to designate as lower level or subtasks.

2. Create the subtasks by clicking on the "Indent" button, identified by the arrow key icon ($\rightarrow$), which indents the tasks and designates them as subtasks.

An indented task becomes a subtask of the task above it, which is now the parent task. Figure 26.5 shows the "Indent" button. The "Indent" button was used to create the summary tasks and subtasks, which are illustrated in Figure 26.6.

Once you have created summary tasks you can collapse the subtasks by clicking on the small triangle that appears to the left of the "Party Project" and "Define

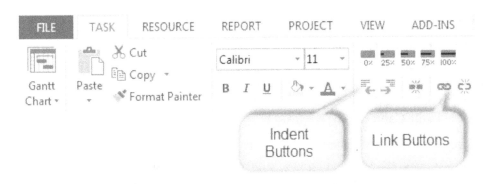

Figure 26.5: Indent and Link Task Menu Buttons.

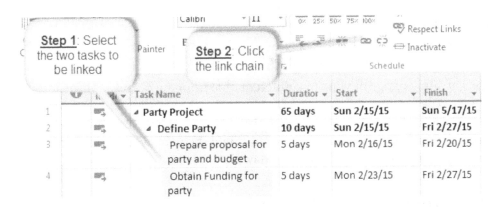

Figure 26.6: Linking Tasks.

Party" tasks. This gives you a summary view of your project by including only the high-level tasks. If you click the triangle again, you will see the subtasks. The small triangles are shown in Figure 26.6. Click the "Outdent" icon (the left arrow), which is next to the "Indent" icon, to move a task back to the level of the task above it; now they are no longer subtasks.

26.6 Link Tasks

The next step is to add network dependencies by using the "Link" button, which is shown in Figure 26.6. When you link a task to other tasks, you answer the question "For this task, which predecessor tasks must be completed before it can start?" There are two steps to linking tasks and we show them in Figure 26.6.

Consider the task, "Obtain funding for the party." Before it can start, the predecessor task "Prepare Proposal for party and budget" must be completed.[9] To link tasks, select (i.e., highlight) the predecessor and then select the successor task so that they are both highlighted. Next, click on the "Link" button. A link arrow will be created in the Gantt chart.

It is very important to select the tasks in the correct order—select predecessor and then successor, i.e., select "Prepare Proposal for party and budget" and *then* select "Obtain funding for the party." If you select them in the wrong order, the tasks will be linked incorrectly. Upon completing the link steps, study the project start and finish dates and you will notice that they have updated appropriately.

If you make a mistake, you can unlink tasks by clicking the "Unlink" icon, which is to the right of the "Link" icon, see Figure 26.5. Or, you can double click on the "Task Information" and a dialog box opens; click the "Predecessors" tab where you can enter the dependency information for the task.

You can also change the link to a different type from the default: Finish-to-Start (FS). You can change the link type by adding the abbreviation for a start-to-start (SS), finish-to-finish (FF), or start-to-finish (SF).[10] Once you have linked all of the tasks, you have your first project plan. It should show that you could successfully finish the party project by the 17th of May.[11]

26.7 Displaying the WBS ID

It is easier to read and understand the task hierarchy if you introduce a column called "WBS," as shown in Figure 26.7. When you insert the WBS column, it automatically creates an outline number for each task based on where the task appears in the hierarchy. We illustrate the three steps required to insert the WBS column in Figure 26.7. Here, we see that the "Create Invitations" task has a WBS ID of 1.2.9.

[9]We remind the reader of that this is the definition of the network arrow, and the finish-to-start constraint.

[10]We highly recommend against this. Stick with the standard finish-to-start (FS) task type.

[11]In agreement with the proposed plan.

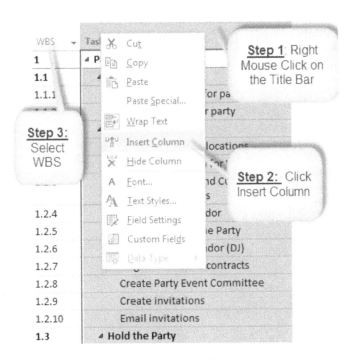

Figure 26.7: Inserting a WBS Column.

26.8   Assign Durations

You assign a duration to a task by simply typing a number in the duration column. Figure 26.8 shows the durations of the tasks, as well as indented subtasks.[12] When you enter a task, *Project* automatically assigns it a duration of one day, followed by a question mark. To change the duration, type a number in the duration column. Durations are measured in units (days, weeks, etc.), which are shown in Table 26.2.

The duration consists of both a number and an appropriate duration units symbol.

Table 26.2: The units, and their symbols, for task durations in *Project*.

Unit Symbol	Unit
d	days (default)
w	weeks
m	minutes
h	hours
mo, or mon	months

[12]Remember, at this point, these are still estimates.

Task Name	Duration	Start	Finish
- Party Project	80 days	Wed 1/28/15	Tue 5/19/15
- Define Party	23 days	Wed 1/28/15	Sat 2/28/15
Prepare proposal for party and budget	5 days	Wed 1/28/15	Tue 2/3/15
Obtain Funding for party	5 days	Wed 2/4/15	Tue 2/10/15
Charter & Funding Complete	0 days	Sat 2/28/15	Sat 2/28/15
- Plan Party	45 days	Wed 2/11/15	Wed 4/15/1!
Identify potential locations	5 days	Wed 2/11/15	Tue 2/17/15
Obtain Permission for Venue	2 days	Wed 2/18/15	Thu 2/19/15
Venue Obtained	0 days	Sun 3/15/15	Sun 3/15/15
Inform Security, and Custodians & formalize	1 day	Fri 2/20/15	Fri 2/20/15
Identify Food Vendor	30 days	Mon 2/23/15	Fri 4/3/15
Select Menu for the Party	3.75 days	Mon 4/6/15	Thu 4/9/15
Identify music vendor (DJ)	1 day	Mon 2/23/15	Mon 2/23/15
Negotiate vendor contracts	4 days	Tue 2/24/15	Fri 2/27/15
Create Party Event Committee	1 day	Mon 4/6/15	Mon 4/6/15
Create invitations	1 day	Tue 4/7/15	Tue 4/7/15
Email invitations	2 days	Wed 4/8/15	Thu 4/9/15
Party Planning Completed	0 days	Wed 4/15/15	Wed 4/15/15
- Hold the Party	2 days	Wed 5/13/15	Fri 5/15/15
Dry Run for the Picnic	1 day	Wed 5/13/15	Wed 5/13/1!
Manage the Party	1 day	Thu 5/14/15	Thu 5/14/15
Party Completed	0 days	Fri 5/15/15	Fri 5/15/15
- Close Party	3 days	Fri 5/15/15	Tue 5/19/15
Close all Contracts	1 day	Tue 5/19/15	Tue 5/19/15
Send out survey	1 day	Fri 5/15/15	Fri 5/15/15
- Project Management	80 days	Wed 1/28/15	Tue 5/19/15
Identify key PM processes & Project Information System Needs	20 days	Wed 1/28/15	Tue 2/24/15

Figure 26.8: Duration estimates for the picnic project for tasks and subtasks. Milestones have duration zero.

When you type a number into the duration column, the units are automatically assigned in days. If you are unsure of the duration estimate, and want to review it again later, enter a question mark after it. Do not enter durations for summary tasks as these are automatically calculated based on the subtasks.[13]

[13]In fact, *Project* will not allow you to enter or change the duration of a summary task.

Table 26.3: The milestones for the picnic project.

Task Name	Date
Charter & Funding Complete	Sat 2/28/15
Venue Obtained	Sun 3/15/15
Party Completed	Sun 5/17/15
Project Complete	Sun 5/17/15

26.8.1 Inserting Milestones

In the task ribbon you will see the milestone icon. To create a milestone, click the icon and enter a task name such as, "Charter & Funding Complete." Another way to create a milestone is to select a task and just enter its duration as *zero* days. The task symbol changes from a bar on the Gantt chart to the symbol for a milestone, which is a triangle. The milestones for the picnic project are shown in Table 26.3.

In *Project*, milestones are actually tasks, they just have a zero duration. However, because they are tasks, they can be linked to other tasks. Therefore, there are different ways to implement milestones:

- You can link an important milestone to the tasks that precede it. That way, if any of the tasks are delayed, the milestone moves to the time of the completion of the last linked task.

- You can insert the milestone date directly, so that its date is fixed and it does not move. If tasks get delayed, they might extend beyond the milestone, indicating trouble. However, since the milestone is not linked to the delayed tasks, you may miss the fact that the milestone is actually late.

You can also use multiple milestones assigned to a single event. That way, you get the best of both options: One milestone linked to its predecessor tasks, which will be the best estimate of when the milestone will occur, and a static milestone, which will not move, for the planned date (from the scope).

We recommend that you enter the milestones for important events as "manually" scheduled tasks with a hard date. After you have entered all your tasks and fine-tuned your schedule, link the milestone to the predecessors. Otherwise, your milestone will keep moving as you tweak your schedule.

Note: If you want a milestone with finite (i.e., non-zero) duration, you can use the task properties box. After entering the task duration, just double click the task, and click on the "Advanced" tab of the "Task Information" dialog box. Click the "Mark Task as Milestone" check box and click OK.[14]

[14]We do not recommend using a milestone with a finite duration. The formal definition of a milestone says that it is an *event*, which, by definition, has zero duration.

471

It is important to continually analyze the network as it develops. For example, after we inserted milestones from the project scope statement, we noticed an issue: The 2/15 milestone appears to be after its planned date, see Figure 26.9. Either we have to start the project earlier or we must move the milestone later.

Figure 26.9: Milestones in the Picnic Project.

26.9 Showing and Hiding Summary Tasks

If you want to hide the summary tasks, you can uncheck the option "Summary Tasks" in the Format menu on the ribbon. You will only see tasks that are low level, i.e., usually work packages. To show the summary tasks again check the "Summary Tasks" again as illustrated in Figure 26.10

If you checked the option called "Project Summary Task," you will see that a root-level summary task was inserted with the WBS ID of 0. In our project, we created a summary task and we hard-coded the root WBS with an ID = 1.0.

If you have many tasks, say more than 40 tasks or a page full, do not create a root WBS for the project. Let *Project* create the root summary task and provide the summary view of the project whenever you need it.

Figure 26.10: Showing and Hiding Summary Tasks.

26.10 Resources

Projects use resources, such as people, materials, and even cash, such as money for travel and training. You can define resources and assign them to tasks. *Project* then allows you to produce reports that specify the total resource requirements, their cost, and even to balance and level their consumption.

All resources are defined with the "Resource" menu option in the ribbon. Here you can add people, create a resource pool, and manage and level the workload. The following menu options are used to manage resources:

1. *Resource Menu:* This is used to define the resources, i.e., to name them and to assign their costs.

2. *Task Menu:* This is used to assign particular resources to individual tasks.

3. *View Menu.* This is used to view the resource usage over time.

Before entering resource data into *Project*, you should have a clear picture of the costs of each resource. Here is a brief summary of resource costs:[15]

- *Direct Costs*: Direct costs are those billed directly to the project, and include labor for team members as well as material, supplies and equipment used wholly by the project. Direct costs also include travel to perform specific project work and procurement costs associated with subcontracts.

- *Overhead Costs*: These are costs not directly associated with a specific task but are required to run the organization. Overhead costs include occupancy

[15]We remind the reader that labor and overhead costs are all defined in section 10.12.

473

Table 26.4: Resource sheet for the picnic project.

Name	Type	Material	Std. Rate	Cost/Use
Project Manager	Work		$30.00/hr	$0.00
Volunteer Team	Work		$0.00/hr	$0.00
Student Leader	Work		$20.00/hr	$0.00
Publicity Coordinator	Work		$20.00/hr	$0.00
Event Day Coordinator	Work		$20.00/hr	$0.00
Dean of Students	Work		$0.00/hr	$0.00
Student Council President	Work		$0.00/hr	$0.00
Faculty Chairman	Work		$0.00/hr	$0.00
Techie	Work		$20.00/hr	$0.00
Dumpster	Work		$50.00/hr	$100.00
Food Services	Cost			
Music DJ Cost	Cost			
Printing Cost	Cost			
Taxi Cost	Cost			
Container for Trash	Material	Can	$50.00	$0.00
Tables	Material	Table	$50.00	$0.00
Chairs	Material	Chairs	$10.00	$0.00
Tent	Material	Tent	$0.00	$500.00

costs, e.g., mortgage or rent, utilities, supplies, etc. In the picnic project case study, a storage room will also be used to store party supplies, computers and more. This room is not dedicated to the picnic project.

- *General and Administrative (G&A) Costs*: These include company expenses, such as payroll, information technology, legal, and accounting.

We will assume, as is usual, that direct labor costs include overhead and G&A, since that is typically what is presented to the customer.[16]

26.10.1 The Resource Sheet

Resource data is entered on the "Resource Sheet." When you entered the tasks into the Gantt view, you started identifying the resources for your project. Most of them were probably of type "Work," i.e., labor. There are other resource types, such as the costs associated with the procurement of goods and services, e.g., Music and Food. You can click on View → Resource Sheet to see the resources defined for the party project, which are shown in Table 26.4.

We now discuss the resource types:

[16]If you told the customer that the project manager costs $30 per hour, then that is the number to use in *Project*. The fact that the project manager only takes home $10 per hour is irrelevant.

1. *Work Resources*: Resource costs for labor, such as the project manager and other project team members, can make up the majority of a project's costs. The proposed labor rate for the project manager is $30 per hour and $20 per hour for the other student coordinators. Later, you will assign these student coordinators to the appropriate tasks, i.e., the ones they will perform.

   In our picnic project, in order to cut down on labor expenses, we are using unpaid student volunteers. Also, the Dean and the Department Chair are assigned zero cost, since their management oversight is considered part of their normal job assignment.

   Project uses an hourly rate to calculate the cost of an assignment to produce a cost report. For example: If the project manager works 5 hours on the "Prepare proposal for party and budget" task, the cost is calculated as:

$$Cost = \$30 \times 5 = \$150. \tag{26.1}$$

   You can also use non-labor resources, e.g., in our party we plan to use a "Dumpster" for all the trash that has a charge of $100 per use, and an additional $50 per-hour rental cost. The dumpster cost estimate is:

$$\$50 \times 6 \ hours + \$100 \ charge = \$300 + \$100 = \$400. \tag{26.2}$$

   Note that *Project* automatically prorates costs over time. You can, however, change this default setting so that you pay for the resource either at the start or at the end of the task. For example, the Dumpster provider may ask for the entire rental fee up front.

2. *Material Resources*: Many resources are classified as "Material." You do not assign material resources over time, as we did with work resources. Instead, material resources are assigned by quantity.

   For example, chairs, tables and the tent are all assigned as material resources for the picnic project. We simply enter a cost per unit as shown in Table 26.5. Therefore, if your party uses three tables, the cost estimate is:

$$Table \ Cost = 3 \times \$50 = \$150. \tag{26.3}$$

3. *Cost Resources*: Cost resources are used when a resource is not associated with an hourly rate or quantity. Cost resources are assigned directly to tasks— not on the resource sheet. This also allows you to change the costs each time

Table 26.5: Material resources for the picnic project.

Resource Material	Cost/Use
Container for Trash	$50.00
Tables	$50.00
Chairs	$10.00

the resource is used. Consider, for example, a taxi, which might be used for visits to the DJ, the Catering Company, and to pick up food. Depending upon the distance traveled, the taxi cost will vary, and different amounts will be assigned to different tasks.

26.11   Assigning Resources to Tasks

Once you have completed the resource sheet, the next step is to assign resources to the tasks. Go to the Gantt View and select the "Resources" column of the task for which you want to assign resources. You will see a drop-down box showing the resources. Select a resource. Put a check mark next to the resource, and you are done, see Figure 26.11.

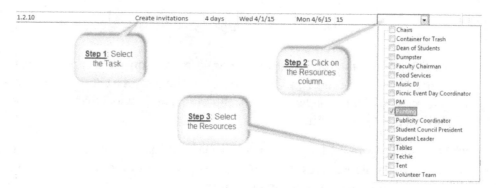

Figure 26.11: Assigning Resources to Tasks.

If you look at the Gantt chart you will now see the assignments (i.e., the names) of the resources to the tasks in the bar chart, see Figure 26.12.

The above process only allocates a quantity of one resource. To assign more resources, double click on the task, select the resources column, and change the quantity. For example, if we need three tables for the party, we double click on the task, select the resources column, and change the quantity to '3,' see Figure 26.13.

476

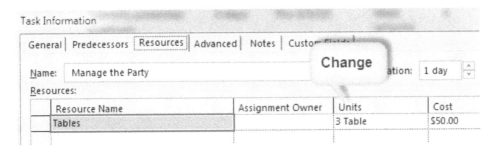

Figure 26.12: Resources Displayed in Gantt View.

Figure 26.13: Changing the Quantity of Resources.

26.12 Changing Assigned Resources

You can change the resource name. For example, we started with a generic resource name, i.e., "Student Leader." Once we have assigned the leader, we can use his or her real name. You can also replace a resource with another one. Reasons to replace a resource are that someone is no longer available or that they are over allocated.

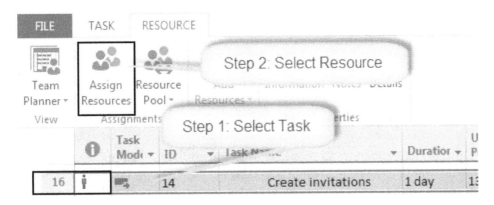

Figure 26.14: Changing the Over-Allocated Resource.

477

To replace a resource, highlight the task and then use the command: Resource →
Assign Resources. Select the appropriate resource. See Figure 26.14.

One of the valuable options is the ability to query *Project* for resources with time
available. Figure 26.15 shows how to search for an alternate resource that has two
hours available to replace the Student Leader, who is over-worked.

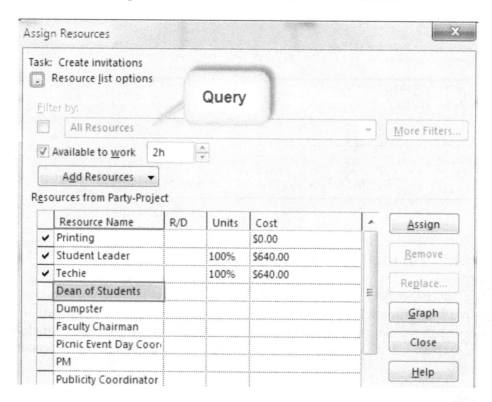

Figure 26.15: Query for Available Resources.

26.13   Project Calendars

A project calendar defines the working time, the non-working time, holidays, vacations and more. There is a standard calendar that comes with *Project* and it defines
the typical work schedule: Monday to Friday, eight hours per day.[17] Calendars are
used when a particular resource is only available for a specific time interval. For
example, the Techie may only be available for picnic project web site work during
the month of April.

[17]The standard calendar
is more than adequate for
simple projects.

478

If you wish, you can change the standard calendar and create a new one. For example, you may want to consider the fact that on the picnic project the students are busy with schoolwork during the day time. In that case, you can assign the working time as being from 7 PM to 11 PM. Also, since the students are truly dedicated to the picnic project, you can even make it a seven days-a-week schedule.

There are various types of calendars in *Project*. They include the Standard Calendar (comes with the default install); the Base Calendar (defines new working hours and working days); the Resource Calendar (can be created for each resource, with variations from the base calendar to accommodate things like annual vacations); and the Task Calendar (used, for example, for board room meetings) and is similar to the Resource Calendar.[18]

26.14 The Work Column

So far, we have not explained the Work column, as we have done all our scheduling using durations in days. For example, the estimate for the very first work package, called "Prepare Proposal for Party & Budget," is 5 days. There is only one person, the project manager, who is allocated to perform this task. Since the project manager is working full time over this 5-day period (8 hours per day), the task will consume 40 hours of work.

The project manager may have an "Assistant Project Manager" to help with the preparation of the proposal. With two people on the task, its duration could be reduced to 2.5 days. However, the task's work, or effort, will remain at 40 hours.

26.14.1 Units

In the above examples, we assumed that the resources work full time on a task. Therefore, they are considered as 100% resource units. If a resource were assigned to work only half time on a task (50%), the work would be only 20 hours per week instead of 40. Resources are assigned in what *Project* calls "units." A half time resource assignment will appear on the Gantt chart as: **Project Manager [50%]**, which is a half unit.

Suppose a task is estimated to take 10 days and the project manager assigned to the task has a rate of $30 per hour. The default is a full-time resource (100%), so that the cost is 10 days × 8 hours × $30 = $2,400.

If the task were smaller, then the project manager might only need to work half time, and so the cost of the task would be at a 50% work rate: 10 days × 8 hours

[18]We do not cover the details of the calendars in this tutorial. However, you will find more information about changing the calendars in *Project Help*. Click F1.

479

× \$30 ×50% = \$1,200. For a larger task with two full-time people assigned, then the cost doubles to \$4,800.

The mathematical relationship between duration and Work is:

$$Duration = \frac{Work}{Unit}.$$

(26.4)

This can be switched around to calculate Work as: Work = Duration × Unit. Also, *Project* can calculate the resource units if the duration and work are available: Unit = Work / Duration. For example, the project manager takes 40 hours to finalize the project plan. The duration is two weeks (80 hours). Therefore,

$$units = \frac{40 \; work\text{-}hours}{80 \; hours} = 0.5.$$

(26.5)

This 0.5 unit is 50%, which means that the project manager works half-time on the task "Finalize the Project Plan" over a period of two weeks. We have an example of this for the "Project Management" activity. The project manager works only 10% of the time on the tasks listed there, such as: "Identify key PM processes & Project Information System Needs," and "Complete & Maintain PM templates."

When we talk about work (also called effort) we do not include holidays or non-working days, such as weekends. However, you can use the term "Elapsed Time" if you want to refer to calendar time, which is the span of time associated with the actual elapsed duration of a task. For example, a week of work is 5 days, but a week of elapsed time is 7 days.

26.15   Fine Tuning the Schedule

We are almost done with our first cut at the project plan for the picnic project. At this stage, it is a good idea to take a step back and analyze the schedule. This might include the following activities:

1. Align Milestones with the Project Plan: Study the planned milestone dates and see how well they align with the proposed schedule.

2. Change the Gantt Chart Timescale.

3. Investigate Resource Conflict: Study over allocated resources.

4. Study the Critical Path: Provide resources to the critical path if needed to compress the schedule.

5. Examine Costs: See if they fall within the budget proposed by the sponsor.

6. Identify Bottom up Risks: While we have looked at system level risks, we now have the opportunity to identify risks at the task level and mitigate them. For example, risks on critical path tasks may delay the schedule.

7. Create a Baseline.

26.15.1 Aligning Milestones with Project Plan

We have identified several milestones, which are tasks with zero duration. Our first goal is to see how well these milestones compare with the planned milestone dates, which we promised to our sponsors in the charter and scope statement. The milestones in the scope statement are presented below:

Fundraising Complete:	February 15th, 2015
Preparation for Party Completed:	May 15th, 2015
Completed Plan for party logistics:	April 15th, 2015
Preparation for Party Completed:	May 15th, 2015
Post Party Survey:	May 17th, 2015

We can now compare this to the output from *Project*, which seems to fit in pretty well so far, see Table 26.6. A key indicator is that the planning should be completed a month before the party. Fundraising has slipped by 15 days, but since the sponsors provide a large amount of the party funding, this is not a risk.

Table 26.6: Milestones output from *Project*.

Task Name	Milestone Date
Charter & Funding Completed	Sat 2/28/15
Venue Obtained	Sun 3/15/15
Party Planning Completed	Wed 4/15/15
Party Completed	Sun 5/17/15

26.15.2 Displaying Milestones with Filters

It is easy to display the milestones in your project. You can filter and sort dates before viewing and printing them. Filtering also allows you to see just the tasks you want. In our milestone table shown above we have taken the following steps: 1) In the ribbon click: View → Filter and select "Milestones" from the drop down box, see Figure 26.16; and 2) Click: Form → Uncheck Summary Tasks.

481

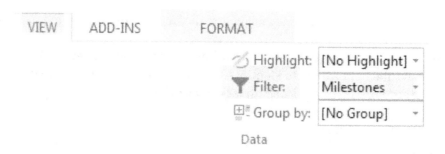

Figure 26.16: Project Filters.

26.15.3 Changing the Gantt Chart Timescale

Changing the Gantt chart timescale is very helpful when studying the project schedule. You can adjust the timescale to show the schedule on smaller or greater time unit scales, from minutes to years. This gives you an opportunity to compress your project onto one or two pages and to get a birds-eye view of the bar chart. There are three tiers of timescales and you have to ability to format each of them.

Figure 26.17: Formatting the Gantt Chart Timescale.

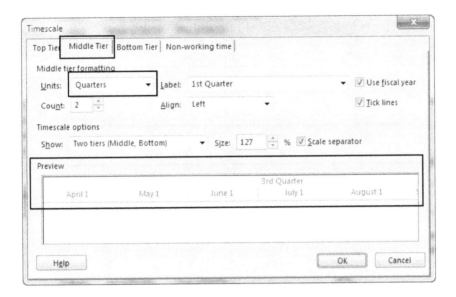

Figure 26.18: The three tiers of the Gantt Chart Timescales.

In Figure 26.17 you see the key steps required to change the timescale. The command is: View → Timescale. There are three tiers you can format: top, middle and bottom. For example, in Figure 26.18, we formatted the middle tier to show quarter years (i.e., three months) as the time-scale. This middle tier will appear above the bottom tier, which is in months. A preview of what the three tiers will look like is shown at the bottom of Figure 26.18.

In this context, the scroll-to-task function is useful. The command is: Tasks → Scroll to Task (or Control-Shift-F5). This will center your view on the task you are interested in. You can also use the zoom button, at the bottom right corner, to get a detailed view of your project bar chart.

Finally, you can right mouse click anywhere in the Gantt chart and change the display options of the bar styles. For example, you can show and hide critical tasks, slack, late tasks, baseline, and slippage.

26.15.4 Investigate Resource Conflicts

A resource is over-scheduled when a person is expected to work more than the allocated eight hours per day. In that case, we have a resource conflict. Analysis revealed that the project manager was assigned to several activities in parallel, and the total utilization exceeded 100%, or more than 8 hours per day. *Project* flags these resource conflicts for you, see Figure 26.19. Therefore, we added Student Leaders to some tasks, which removed the conflict.

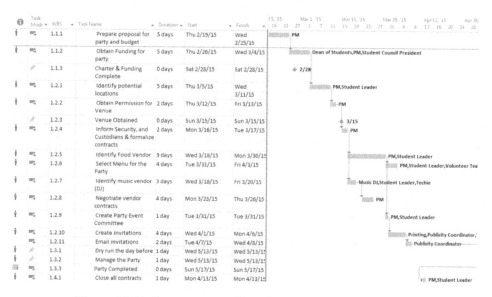

Figure 26.19: Resource Conflicts flagged in the Gantt View.

Project provides a tool that uses "resource leveling" to resolve resource conflicts. The command is: Resource → Level Resources from the Project ribbon. The dialog box that appears gives you several options to resolve resource conflicts. Over-used resources are spread out, so that, invariably, resource leveling will increase the project duration.[19]

Another approach to resolving a resource conflict is simply to add resources. In this case, the conflict was obvious: We only had one resource—the coordinator—for several key tasks, see Figure 26.20. We added the following resources:

1. Five members who will play a key role in the Volunteer Team. These are unpaid volunteers.

2. Student leaders: In the project plan we had budgeted leaders for various aspects of the project such as Music, Food, and Entertainment. These were paid positions.

3. Picnic Day Event coordinators: These are additional volunteers who will help the leaders.

[19] In real projects, we strongly recommend against using *Project* to do automatic resource leveling. It often destroys the look of the network and results in a mess. Also, the results are difficult to understand, which means the PM loses control. We suggest the project manager add and subtract resources by hand to get the desired result.

484

	Indicators	Resource Name	Type	Mater Label	Max Units
1	◈	PM	Work		100%
2	◈	Volunteer Team	Work		100%
3	◈	Student Leader	Work		100%
4		Publicity Coordinator	Work		100%
5	◈	Picnic Event Day Coordinator	Work		100%
6		Dean of Students	Work		100%
7		Student Council President	Work		100%
8		Faculty Chairman	Work		100%
9		Techie	Work		100%
10		Food Services	Cost		
11		...usic...	Co...		

Figure 26.20: Over allocated Resources as they appear in the Resources Sheet.

After adding resources (units), and re-balancing the project manager's workload, we have no flags and a reasonable resource listing, see Figure 26.21. Recall that the 500% you see in the figure refers to five units or five resources.

26.15.5 Study the Critical Path

The critical path is the sequence of tasks that are critical to the timely completion of the project. Several techniques allow you to see just the tasks that are on the critical path. The simplest approach is to use filters: In the ribbon, click: View → Filter, and then select Critical. You will see the critical path tasks. Alternatively, click: View → Highlight, and then select Critical.

Our project schedule is quite comfortable and so we don't need to add additional resources to the critical path tasks to shorten it. However, once the project starts, the project manager should carefully manage tasks on the critical path.

Resource Name ▼	Type ▼	Materi Label ▼	Max Units ▼
PM	Work		100%
Volunteer Team	Work		500%
Student Leaders	Work		500%
Publicity Coordinator	Work		100%
Picnic Event Day Coordinators	Work		500%
Dean of Students	Work		100%
Student Council President	Work		100%
Faculty Chairman	Work		100%
Techie	Work		100%
Food Services	Cost		
Music DJ	Cost		
Printing	Cost		

Figure 26.21: Balanced Resource Listing.

26.15.6 Examine Costs

While we have a good grip of the project schedule and its duration, we have not looked at the estimated costs to see if they are in line with the project sponsors' expectations, i.e., the budget.

Assuming the costs for resources have been entered correctly, it is easy to view the overall project cost and determine if it is within budget. Our favorite approach is to simply insert a new column called "Cost."

Table 26.7 shows the new Gantt View with the addition of the Cost column. The Picnic Party Project has a total budget of $4,773. This is well within the amount allocated to plan and hold the party. Therefore, we do not need to tweak the project costs anymore.

Table 26.7 displays five summary tasks: Define Party, Plan Party, Hold the Party, Close Party and Project Management. It also shows the sub-totals for various subtasks. We expanded "Hold the Party" to reveal three subtasks.

Table 26.7: Picnic project cost report.

Task Name	Work (hrs)	Cost	Duration (days)	Start	Finish
Party Project	374	$4,773	80	1/28/15	Tue 5/19/15
Define Party	16	$200	23	1/28/15	Sat 2/28/15
Plan Party	179	$2,467	45	2/11/15	Tue 4/14/15
Hold the Party	126	$1,090	23	4/15/15	Sun 5/17/15
Dry run for the Party	6	$30	1	4/15/15	Wed 4/15/15
Manage the Party	120	$1,060 0	1	5/15/15	Fri 5/15/15
Party Completed	0	$0	0	5/17/15	Sun 5/17/15
Close Party	12	$280	2	5/18/15	Tue 5/19/15
Project Management	40	$736	80	1/28/15	Tue 5/19/15
Charter & Funding Cmplt					Sat 2/28/15
Venue Obtained					Sun 3/15/15
Party Planning Complete					Wed 4/15/15
Party Completed					Sun 5/17/15

The top-level summary task provides comprehensive statistics about the entire project: The total effort is 373 hours, the duration is 80 days, the project start date is January 28th, the party is executed on May 15th, and the entire project is fully wrapped up by May 19th. The total cost is $4,773.

26.15.7 Identify Bottom up Risks

While creating a project plan we identified risks and developed plans for mitigating them. For example, we set aside funds for a tent in case a drenching rainstorm was forecast. Now we have to the opportunity to identify additional risks by reviewing the *Project* version of the plan.

From our experience, we recommend flagging risks associated with "Email Invitations." Such tasks should be analyzed, especially if they are on the critical path or involve dependencies external to the project, e.g., a student might not receive the invitations as it might end up in the Spam folder. To mitigate this risk, the project manager might decide to mail invitations out via regular mail as well.

The project manager should also examine the tasks that are on the critical path to determine if they are considered high risk. For example, a problem in "Venue Selection" might cause a delay in the schedule.

26.15.8 Baseline the Project

Now that the project plan has been analyzed and we are happy with it, we can set a baseline using the command: Project → Set Baseline, and selecting "Entire Project."

Creating a baseline is a very important activity, and you should communicate the baselined project schedule and budget to the stakeholders. This should be done formally, as the baseline represents a commitment between the project manager and the sponsor to the estimated project cost and schedule.

Prior to the execution phase of the project, you can delete a baseline at any time. If you update the schedule, you can create a fresh baseline. With the establishment of the baseline, the planning phase of the project is complete and you are ready to enter the execution phase.

26.16   Tracking Project Progress

This section explains how to track the progress of your project as it evolves. First, we will show you how to update the project schedule and, then, we will show you some reports. *Project* uses three terms:

1. *Baseline*: The planned dates developed prior to project start.

2. *Actual*: Completed and partially completed tasks as of a given date.

3. *Schedule*: Tasks that have not yet started as of a given date.

Project data such should be updated regularly.[20] *Project* recalculates and reschedules your entire project as you enter task completion data.

26.16.1   Updating the Schedule

Progress is measured by entering completion data for tasks. We can enter actual start and finish dates for a task, or we can enter progress information as percent complete. The best approach is to have each team member report actual work completed, and then also to estimate the percent complete of tasks still in progress. We will look at several approaches to updating project progress.

Quick Approach: Right mouse click on the task and indicate it as 100% complete. Alternatively, you can right mouse click on the bar graph on the right side inside the Gantt Chart and select 0%, 25%, 50% or 100% complete. See Figure 26.22.

Update using the Ribbon: In the ribbon, select the command "Task" and then select one of the choices you see there: 0%, 25%, 50% or 100% complete.

Update Tasks Window: In the ribbon you can activate the Update Tasks window by entering the command: Task → Mark on Track, and select "Update Tasks." You will

---

[20]Usually, at the end of each week.

488

Figure 26.22: Updating Project Progress Data.

see a window where you can you can enter percent complete, along with the Actual Duration and Remaining Duration. Alternatively, you can simply enter the Actual Finish date and the percent complete. See Figure 26.23.

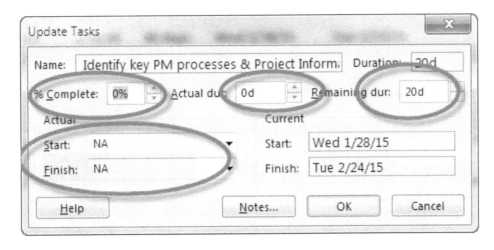

Figure 26.23: Alternate Approaches to Updating Progress.

26.17 Comparing Actual Progress against the Baseline

We set a baseline before the picnic project started and we can now monitor how well we are progressing by using filters and the Tracking Gantt Chart view.

In order to see values for task variance, we set the actual duration for the task "Obtain Funding for Party" to 10 days–double the baseline value of 5 days. We also entered it as 100% completed. See Figure 26.24.

Next, from the ribbon, select View → Table → Work. Next select View → Filter and select "Completed Tasks." We do not want to see summary tasks, and so select Format → (Uncheck) Summary Tasks. You should see the "Actual vs. Baseline" report, which is shown in Table 26.8:

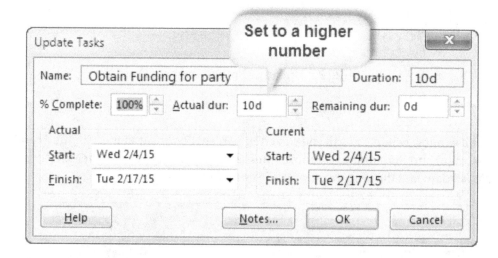

Figure 26.24: Updating a task with variance.

Table 26.8: Actual vs. Baseline report.

Task	Work (hrs)	Baseline (hrs)	Variance (hrs)	Actual (hrs)	Remaining (hrs)	Percent Complete
Prepare proposal & budget	4	4	0	4	0	100%
Obtain Funding	24	12	12	24	0	100%

We note the following points: Work refers to the effort put in and is a combination of values found in the Actual plus Remaining columns. Variance is the difference between the values found in the Work and the Baseline columns. In the second task, this is 24 - 12 = 12.

Project provides several visual reports, such as the one shown in Figure 26.25, which displays a summary overview of cost overruns by resource. This report can be obtained by simply clicking the following commands in the ribbon: Report → Cost → Cost Overruns.

26.17.1 Tracking Gantt Chart

The Tracking Gantt Chart provides graphical representation of Actual vs. Baseline for the entire project. In the ribbon, select the following commands: View →

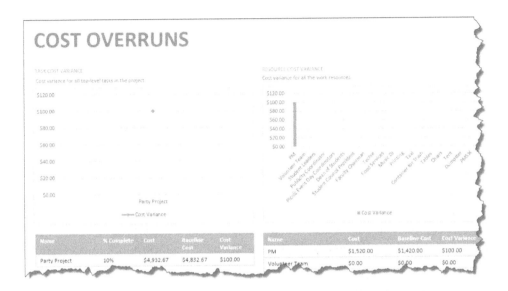

Figure 26.25: Cost Overrun: An example of a Visual Report.

Tracking Gantt. This icon is usually in the same location as the Gantt Chart icon. If you do not see it, click "More Views" and then select "Tracking Gantt." The Tracking Gantt Chart provides a nice bar chart that shows when tasks are either slipping or ahead of schedule.

26.18   Printing Reports

Project contains an extensive set of predefined reports and dashboards under the "Report" menu option in the ribbon. An example was shown in Figure 26.25. Any view or screen that you work with can be printed.

To print a report Click File → Print → Print.

However, you must do some work to generate a report that is clear and engaging. First format the view:

- Pick the view you want.

- Change the view so it shows only the data you want to display. Hide subtasks to show only top-level tasks. Sort tasks or dates to highlight specific information. Hide columns temporarily so they do not appear in the printout.

- Click File → Print.

- Under Settings, choose how much of the project to print. You can print the whole thing or pick date and page ranges.

- Set other printing options, like the number of copies, page orientation, and paper size.

- Add a header, footer, or legend.

You can also simply do a "Screen Print" of your screen. This keystroke copies the contents of your screen to memory, and you can then simply paste it into Word or Excel. There, you can crop, shape and magnify the relevant parts of the screen. This allows you to build a comprehensive report highlighting important project features, such as the critical path. The report can also be printed.

Finally, don't forget that instead of printing, you might want to save the project report as a PDF file.

27

QUOTATIONS

Quotes are slippery things and, like any currency, they get passed around. We've made every attempt here to give credit where credit is due and to respect the rights of everyone quoted, but for some quoted remarks it hasn't been possible to identify the original use, or even to confirm the author with certainty.

In an interview with Tasha Robinson, Steven Wright[1] described the widespread mis-attribution of quotes, commenting, "Someone showed me a site and half of what it said I wrote, I didn't write. Recently, I saw one and I didn't write any of it." Wright also expressed the distress this can cause for an author: "I wish it was just my material and people could like it or not like it. Just as long as it was really mine."

Our goal is to honor the contributions and rights of all the authors quoted. If you have concerns about the accuracy of an attribution or the appropriateness of use, please contact the authors.

[1] Wright, S. (2003, Jan 29) Interview by T. Robinson. Retrieved from http:// www.avclub.com/ articles/ steven-wright, 13796/.

BIBLIOGRAPHY

[1] Lewis. (2006). Carroll. *Alice in Wonderland*. Project Gutenberg, Urbana, Illinois, USA., 2006.

[2] Paul McDonald. It's time for management version 2.0: Six forces redefining the future of modern management. *Futures*, 43:797–808, 2011.

[3] S. Leybourne, R. D. H. Warburton, and V. Kanabar. Is project management the new management 2.0? In *Proceedings of the PMI Research and Education Conference*, Limerick, Ireland, July 2012. Project Management Institute.

[4] Project Management Institute. *A Guide to the Project Management Body of Knowledge*. Project Management Institute, Newtown Square, PA, USA, 6th edition, 2017.

[5] Project Management Institute. *A Guide to the Project Management Body of Knowledge*. Project Management Institute, 5th edition, 2013.

[6] V. Kanabar and R. D. H. Warburton. *MBA Fundamentals: Project Management*. Kaplan Publishing, New York, NY., 1st edition, 2008.

[7] Project Management Institute. Code of ethics and professional conduct. Technical report, Project Management Institute, Newtown Square, PA, 2018.

[8] K. Jugdev and R. Muller. A retrospective look at our evolving understanding of project success. *Project Management Journal*, 36(4):19–31, 2005.

[9] The Standish Group. The CHAOS report. Web page: www. projectsmart. co. uk/ docs/ chaos-report.pdf, 1995.

[10] L. Eveleens and C. Verhoef. The rise and fall of the chaos report figures. *IEEE Software*, 27(1):30–36, January/February 2010.

[11] Oracle. Oracle agile product lifecycle management pharmaceuticals. Web page: http:// www.oracle.com/ us/ products/ applications/ agile/ index.html, Oct 2011.

[12] Microsoft. Home construction project plan. Web page: http://office.microsoft.com/en-us/templates, June 2014.

[13] Project Management Institute. Project Management Curriculum and Resources, Volume I. Newtown Square, PA. USA., 2015.

[14] Project Management Institute. Talent triangle. Technical report, Project Management Institute, 2018.

[15] Erik Larson and Clifford Gray. *Project Management: The Managerial Process*. McGraw-Hill Irwin, NY, NY, 5th edition, 2011.

[16] James Wilson and Michelle Harrison. The necessity of driving to Abilene. *Organization Development Journal*, 19(2):99–109, 2001.

[17] Project Management Institute. *The Standard for Program Management*. Project Management Institute, Newtown Square, PA, fourth edition, 2017.

[18] Kevin Korterud. A different mindset: From project to program manager. from the voices on project management blog. Technical report, ProjectManagement.com, 2018.

[19] Robert G. Cooper. *Winning at New Products: Accelerating the process from idea to launch*. Perseus Publishing, Cambridge, MA, 3rd edition, 2001.

[20] Ivan Petit and Brian Hobbs. *Project Portfolios in Dynamic Environments: Organizing for Uncertainty*. Project Management Institute, Newtown Square, PA, USA, 2012.

[21] Jack Meredith and Samuel Mantel Jr. *Project Management: A Managerial Approach*. John Wiley & Sons, Hoboken, NJ, 8th edition, 2012.

[22] Richard C. Emanuel. Do Certain Personality Types Have a Particular Communication Style? *International Journal of Social Science and Humanities*, 2(1):4–10, 2013.

[23] Frederick P. Morgeson, Michael A. Campion, Robert L. Dipboye, John R. Hollenbeck, Kevin Murphy, and Neal Schmitt. Are we getting fooled again? coming to terms with limitations in the use of personality tests for personnel selection. *Personnel Psychology*, 60(4F):1029–1049, 2007.

[24] Wendell Williams. Dissecting the DISC. Technical report, ERE, December 2008.

[25] Stephen Leybourne. Project Management and high-value superyacht projects: An improvisational and temporal perspective. *Project Management Journal*, 41(1):17–27, 2010.

[26] T. DeMarco. *Software State-of-the-Art: Selected Papers*. Dorset House Publishing, New York, NY, 1990.

[27] R.S. Pressman. *Software engineering: A practitioner's approach*. McGraw Hill: Higher Education. McGraw-Hill, 2005.

[28] Frank Sietzen Jr. Spacelift Washington: International space transportation association faltering: The Myth of $10,000 per pound. *Space Ref.*, March 2001.

[29] Barry Watts. The military use of space: A diagnostic assessment. Technical report, Center for Strategic and Budgetary Assessments (CSBA), Washington, DC, February 2001.

[30] Project Management Institute. *Practice Standard for Project Estimating*. Project Management Institute, Newtown Square, PA, 2011.

[31] V. Kanabar and R.D.H. Warburton. Leveraging the new practice standard for project estimating. In *PMI World Congress, Dallas*, October, 2011. PMI.

[32] Merriam Webster. *Dictionary*. Merriam Webster, 2018.

[33] B. Boehm. *Software Engineering Economics*. Prentice-Hall., Englewood-Cliffs, NJ, 2001.

[34] Jr. Frederick P. Brooks. *The Mythical Man-Month*. Addison-Wesley., 1995.

[35] David S. Christensen and Scott Heise. Cost Performance Index Stability. *National Contract Management Journal*, 25(Spring):7–15, 1993.

[36] David S. Christensen, Richard C. Antolini, and John W. McKinney. A review of estimate at completion research. *Journal of Cost Analysis*, 25(Spring):41–62, 1995.

[37] Roger D. H. Warburton. A time-dependent earned value model for software projects. *International Journal of Project Management*, 20:1082–1090, 2011.

[38] EunHong Kim. *A Study on the Effective Implementation of Earned Value Management Methodology*. PhD thesis, The George Washington University, 2000.

[39] Roger D. H. Warburton and Denis F. Cioffi. Estimating a project's earned and final duration. *International Journal of Project Management*, 34(8):1493–1504, 2016.

[40] Quentin W. Fleming and Joel M. Koppleman. *Earned Value Project Management*. Project Management Institute, Newtown Square, PA, 3rd edition, 2005.

[41] Q. W. Fleming and J. M. Koppelman. The two most useful earned value metrics: the CPI and the TCPI. *PM World Today*, XI(VI), June 2009.

[42] F. T. Anbari. Earned value project management method and extension. *Project Management Journal*, 34(4):12, 2003.

[43] Elizabeth Kubler-Ross. *On Death and Dying*. Scribner, New York, NY, reprint edition, 1997.

[44] W. H. Lipke. Schedule is different. *The Measurable News*, pages 31–34, Summer 2003.

[45] Stephen Book. Earned Schedule and its possible unreliability as an indicator. *The Measurable News*, pages 24–30, Spring 2006.

[46] R. D. H. Warburton. Managing and predicting the costs of real-time software. *IEEE Transactions on Software Engineering*, SE-9(5):562–569, 1983.

[47] V. R. Basili and J. Beane. Can the Parr curve help with manpower distribution and resource estimation problems? *The Journal of Systems and Software*, 2:59–69, 1981.

[48] David Lee. Norden-Raleigh analysis: A useful tool for EVM in development projects. *The Measurable News*, March:21–24, 2002.

[49] Mark A. Gallagher and David A. Lee. Final-cost estimates for research and development programs conditioned on realized costs. *Military Operations Research*, 2, 2:51–65, 1996.

[50] W. Allen. A pragmatic approach to using resource loading. production and learning curves on construction projects. *Canadian Journal of Civil Engineering*, 21:939–953, 1994.

[51] David A. Garvin. *Managing Quality: The Strategic and Competitive Edge.* The Free Press, New York, NY., 1988.

[52] B. W. Tuckman and M. A. C. Jensen. Stages of small-group development revisited. *Group and Organization Studies*, 2(4):419, 1977.

[53] A. Maslow. A theory of human motivation. *Psychological Review*, 50(4):370–396, 1943.

[54] S. R. Covey. *The 7 Habits of Highly Effective People.* Free Press, 1st edition, 1990.

[55] P. W. Metzger and J. Boddie. *Managing A Programming Project: Processes and People.* Prentice Hall, 3rd edition, 1996.

[56] David Logan. Known knowns, known unknowns, unknown unknowns and the propagation of scientific enquiry. *Journal of Experimental Botany*, 60(3):712–714, 2009.

[57] A. Gawande. *The Checklist Manifesto: How to Get Things Right.* Metropolitan Books, 1st edition, 2009.

[58] PMI. *Practice Standard for Risk Management.* Project Management Institute, Newtown Square, PA. USA., 2011.

[59] D. H. Gustafson, W. L. Cats-Baril, and F. Alemi. *Systems to Support Health Policy Analysis: Theory, Model and Uses.* Health Administration Press, Ann Arbor, Michigan, 1992.

[60] Louis Mercken. Ethics has proven a useful tool for the project management profession. *PMI Today*, page 3, December 2011.

[61] Barry Boehm. A spiral model of software development and enhancement. *ACM SIGSOFT Software Engineering Notes*, 11(4):14–24, August 1986.

[62] Mo A. Mahmood. A comparative investigation of system development methods. *MIS Quarterly*, 11(3), 1987.

[63] R. E. Fairley. *Managing and Leading Software Projects.* Wiley, IEEE Computer Society, 1st edition, 2009.

[64] Sylvain Lenfle and Christoph Loch. Lost roots: How project management came to emphasize control over flexibility and novelty. *California Management Review*, 53(1):32–55, 2010.

[65] Kent Beck, Mike Beedle, Arie van Bennekum, Alistair Cockburn, Ward Cunningham, Martin Fowler, James Grenning, Jim Highsmith, Andrew Hunt, Ron Jeffries, Jon Kern, Brian Marick, Robert C. Martin, Steve Mellor, Ken Schwaber, Jeff Sutherland, and Dave Thomas. Manifesto for Agile Software Development. Technical report, Agile Alliance, 2018.

[66] P. DeGrace and L. H. Stahl. *Wicked problems, Righteous solutions: A Catalog of Modern Engineering Paradigms.* Prentice Hall, 1990.

[67] Eduardo Miranda. Improving subjective estimates using paired comparisons. *IEEE Software*, pages 87–91, January/February 2001.

[68] Chris Sims and Hillary Louise Johnson. *The Elements of Scrum.* Dymaxicon, Foster City, CA. USA., 2011.

[69] Ken Schwaber and Jeff Sutherland. The scrum guide. the definitive guide to scrum: The rules of the game. Technical report, Scrum Guides, November 2017.

[70] A. Stellman and J. Greene. *The Agile Principles*. O'Reilly, 2018.

[71] Barnaby Golden. Your first agile sprint: A survival guide. Technical report, TechBeacon, 2018.

[72] Diana Getman. The Agile PMO: How the Traditional Project Management Office fits into the Agile Landscape. Presentation to the Ocean State PMI Chapter, April 2018.

[73] S. Susanka and K. Oblensky. *The not so big house: A blueprint for the way we live*. The Taunton Press, Newtown, CT, 2nd edition, 2008.

[74] Lars Madsen. *Various chapter styles for the memoir class*. MemoirChapStyles.pdf, 2009.

[75] Peter Wilson and Lars Madsen. *The Memoir Class for Configurable Typesetting: User Guide*. The Herries Press, Normandy Park, WA, 8th edition, August 2009.

INDEX

Colophon

This book is set in Computer Modern Roman, 11-point size using the LaTeX typesetting system created by Leslie Lamport. The layout follows the *memoir* class with Lars Madsen's chapter styles. [74] Acknowledgments go to Peter Wilson for creating the memoir class and to Lars Madsen for maintaining it. [75] And of course, none of this would be possible without Donald Knuth who wrote the original TeX. The bibliography was produced in BibDesk. LaTeX produced the final POSTSCRIPT file that was sent to the printer.

CPSIA information can be obtained
at www.ICGtesting.com
Printed in the USA
BVHW050458240920
589464BV00008B/646